Street law

Practical law for South Africans

Street law

Practical law for South Africans

THIRD EDITION

By
David McQuoid-Mason
(General Editor)

with **Lindi Coetzee, Lloyd Lotz, Malebakeng Forere and Rowena Bernard**

Illustrated by
Andy Mason
with **Jeff Rankin, Grant Cresswell, Luke Molver and Themba Siwela**

JUTA

First edition 1990
Second edition 2004
Third edition 2015

Production Coordinator: Deidre du Preez
Editor: Robyn Evans
Cover design: Drag and Drop
Proofreading: Sarah Johnston & Leila Samodien
Indexer & Glossator: Daphne Burger
Design and layout: Nicole de Swardt – Fly Creative

A special thank you to *Proudly South African* for the use of their logo

ISBN: 978 0 70218 555 7

Printed by

Preface to Third Edition

In 1973 I established one of the first university legal-aid clinics in South Africa. Subsequently I had been considering introducing a programme of public legal education which would enable members of the public to enforce their legal rights and avoid conflicts with the law. In 1984, during a visitor's programme sponsored by the United States Information Service (USIS), I met Ed O'Brien of Georgetown University Law Faculty, Washington DC, a co-founder of the American street-law programme. I invited him to South Africa in 1985 and his trip was paid for by USIS. It was an inauspicious time as President PW Botha declared a state of emergency while Ed O'Brien was in the country conducting non-racial street-law workshops with me. He and I brainstormed a curriculum with a multi-racial group of high school teachers and pupils and then persuaded the president of the Association of Law Societies, Graham Cox, to provide financial backing for a pilot street-law programme for South Africa - the first such programme outside of the United States.

In 1986 a pilot street-law programme under Mandla Mchunu was set up at the University of Natal (Durban) to operate in five schools - according to the apartheid context: two African and two white schools and one Indian school. The programme was a success and soon expanded to 16 other universities with financial assistance from the Attorneys Fidelity Fund. The Fund continued to sponsor the programme until South Africa's transition towards democracy in the early 1990s, when funding ceased. I produced a series of five user-friendly cartoon-illustrated books for school children together with accompanying teacher's manuals. Initially I acted as national coordinator of the programme and was responsible for training the street-law coordinators at the different universities. Mandla Mchunu was subsequently appointed as the national street-law director at the Centre for Socio-Legal Studies (CSLS), University of Natal, which had been established in 1987.

After the release of Nelson Mandela in 1990, the South African street-law programme decided to introduce South Africans to the Universal Declaration of Human Rights. With assistance from an American civic education school teacher, Eleanor Greene, and field-testing by the 16 street-law coordinators, Ed O'Brien and I produced a workbook, together with an instructor's manual, in the South African street-law format, entitled *Human Rights for All*. I was the general editor and coordinator of the project which was done in partnership with Lawyers for Human Rights (of which I was Durban chairperson at the time) and Street Law Inc (then known as the National Institute for Citizen Education under the Law (NICEL)). An American version of the book was subsequently published in 1996.

In 1992, with assistance from the United States Agency for International Development (USAID) the CSLS in partnership with NICEL decided that it was necessary to introduce South Africans to the principles of democracy in preparation for the country's first democratic elections. The local street-law team met with the 26 NGOs involved in voter education in KwaZulu-Natal and we agreed to work together to produce a workbook on democracy. The NGO contribution was to help design the curriculum for the programme and to field- test the materials in their constituencies. Over a period of a year the CSLS coordinated the process and I was general editor of the book that was produced, together with an instructor's manual, entitled *Democracy for All*. There was consultation with, and field-testing by, the 26 NGOs and 16 street-law coordinators throughout the process. I worked as a writer and editor with a writing team consisting of two Americans (Ed O'Brien and Mary Curd Larkin of NICEL) and two South Africans (Mandla Mchunu of CSLS and Karthy Govender of the University of Natal). One spin-off from the book was the development by Chuck Scott and the CSLS of the *Democracy Challenge Game* which requires players to identify and define 13 different signposts of democracy using interactive techniques in a board game involving quizzes and debates. The game was field-tested in over 500 high schools in South Africa and has been translated into Swahili. It has also been adapted to embrace the Convention of the Rights of the Child in Nigeria.

In 1997 I began assisting the Ford Foundation, the Open Society Institute and Street Law Inc to develop street-law programmes and materials and provide workshop training in Eastern and Central Europe, Central Asia and the former Soviet Union. The countries involved in the project were Albania, Belarus, Croatia, the Czech Republic, Estonia, Hungary, Kazakhstan, Kyrgyzstan, Latvia, Macedonia, Moldova, Mongolia, Romania, Russia, Slovakia, Ukraine and Uzbekistan. The programme was aimed at assisting the countries to develop cadres of school teachers, law students and law teachers who could teach and develop indigenous curricula and materials on street-law, human rights and democracy for inclusion in the formal school curriculum. My experience in dealing with the transition from apartheid to democracy in South Africa resonated strongly with the countries that were undergoing the transition from communism and dictatorship to democracy. By the end of 2001 street-law, human rights and democracy materials had been published by Belarus, Croatia, the Czech Republic, Estonia, Kazakhstan, Kyrgyzstan, Latvia, Macedonia, Moldova, Mongolia, Russia, Slovakia, Ukraine and Uzbekistan. In addition *Human Rights for All* and *Democracy for All* were translated into Croatian, Mongolian and Russian. *Democracy for All* was also translated into French for use by Civitas International.

The street-law books, *Human Rights for All* and *Democracy for All* have also been used in street-law, human rights and democracy workshops in Egypt, Haiti, Lesotho, Zimbabwe, Zambia, Namibia, Mozambique, Tanzania, Uganda, Ghana, Nigeria, Morocco, Ethiopia, India and Bangladesh. In addition they have been used in British Commonwealth Secretariat human rights workshops in Tanzania, Lesotho, Uganda, Mozambique and in the annual African Human Rights Education camps in different parts of Africa. Street-law programmes in one form or another exist in Kenya, Uganda, Nigeria and Ghana.

The support given to the initial founding of the South African street-law programme by the Attorneys Fidelity Fund, and the subsequent funding of the South African *Democracy for All* street-law programme for the decade since 1992, primarily by the USAID, has paid handsome dividends. In 2003 Street Law South Africa (incorporated as an association in terms of s 21) was established. Street Law South Africa is in the process of applying to the POSLEC SETA (Police, Private Security, Legal, Correctional Services and Justice Sector Education and Training Authority) as a service provider to use the training materials produced in this *Street Law South Africa: Learner's Manual and the Educator's Manual*. It also intends to apply to the South African Qualifications Authority (SAQA) for approval of a street-law unit standard. These steps are being taken to ensure that Street Law South Africa becomes more self-sustaining and less dependant on donor funding.

The South African street-law programme has produced a valuable tool for the teaching of law, human rights and democracy to civil society, particularly school children, university students, school teachers, prison officials and police officers, as well as community groups. Aspects of it have been successfully replicated in a number of developing countries ranging from Africa, Asia and the Caribbean to Eastern and Central Europe, Central Asia and the former Soviet Union, as well as the United States itself.

David McQuoid-Mason
President, Commonwealth Legal Education Association
James Scott Wylie Professor of Law
University of KwaZulu-Natal
Durban

June 2015

Acknowledgements

Acknowledgements for the first edition of *Street Law* were due to the Association of Law Societies (ALS) and the Attorneys Notaries and Conveyancers Fidelity Guarantee Fund for financing the first street law projects; Graham Cox for enlisting the support of the ALS and the Attorneys Fidelity Fund and overseeing the project; Edward O'Brien, co-director of the National Institute for Citizen Education in the Law (NICEL), Washington DC, for introducing the concept to South Africa (with David McQuoid-Mason) and acting as a consulting editor; the pioneering American textbook *Street Law: A Course in Practical Law* 3 ed (1986), published by West Publishing Co, and NICEL, on which the South African *Street Law* books were based; and the Legal Resources Centre's *Advice Office Training Manual* (1986) for aspects of South African public interest law. Thanks were also due to the 1985 University of Natal legal-aid students who assisted in preparing an early *Street Law* draft; the 1986 legal-aid students for helping to field-test the materials in the pilot schools project; Mandla Mchunu for running the 1986 pilot project; Alan Rycroft for supervising the pilot project; and Anne Kroon of the Careers Information Centre for assisting in setting up the pilot project.

Acknowledgements for the second edition of *Street Law South Africa: Practical Law for South Africans* were due to the European Foundation for Human Rights which funded the project; the United States Agency for International Development (USAID) which provided funds for many years to keep the running after funding was no longer available from the ALS (now the Law Society of South Africa) and Attorneys Fidelity Fund; to Murray Wesson for assisting with the updating of some of the materials; and to the enthusiastic law students in the different parts of the country who over the past 18 years have provided, and continue to provide, the life-blood of the street-law programme. Last, but not least, acknowledgements are due to Isabelle de Grandpré who has admirably handled the difficult task of coordinating the publication of the second edition; Jess Nicholson who has done the layout for the new edition; and to Suloshini Pather of Juta who has unstintingly and enthusiastically supported the project.

Acknowledgements for this third edition of *Street Law South Africa: Practical Law for South Africans* are due to my co-authors Lindi Coetzee, Lloyd Lotz, Malebakeng Forere and Rowena Bernard; Melanie Reddy of the National Street Law Office for administrative support; Nicole de Swardt of *Fly Creative* for the lay out; Marlinee Chetty and Deidre du Preez of Juta & Company (Pty) Ltd for their help and encouragement to produce the third edition and Seanokeng Makgala of *Proudly South African* for the permission to use their logo.

David McQuoid-Mason
General Editor

CONTENTS

General introduction to Street law in South Africa

PART ONE

Introduction to South African law and the legal system

PART TWO

Criminal law and child justice

PART THREE

Consumer law

PART FOUR

Family law

PART FIVE

Socio-economic rights

PART SIX

Employment law

CONTENTS

General introduction to Street law in South Africa

General introduction to Street law in South Africa

A. Introduction to Street law

Street law recognises that the law affects people in their daily lives and it is therefore necessary for everyone to understand the law. 'Street law' refers to the fact that the programme is designed for the average person in the street. Learners will be shown how the law, including the Constitution, affects people's lives 'on the street'.

The thesis of Street law is that since the law affects ordinary people in their daily lives, they are entitled to practical legal information that can help in making day-to-day decisions: How can they prevent legal problems from happening? What do they need to know if legal problems arise? What are their rights? The programme seeks further to develop appreciation for the rule of law. In the United States, it has also been a factor in reducing the incidence of juvenile delinquency.

Information on the United States Street law programme can be obtained from Street law Incorporated, 1010 Wayne Avenue, Suite 870, Silver Spring, MD 20910, USA (tel: 091 301 589 1130; fax: 091 301 589 1131; website: www.streetlaw.org).

Information on the South African Street law programme can be obtained from Street Law South Africa, (Centre for Socio-Legal Studies), University of KwaZulu-Natal, Durban, 4041 (tel: 031 260 1210; fax: 086 590 5683; website: www.streetlaw.org.za). The *curriculum* addresses the practical legal issues facing South Africans, based on some of the principles and techniques used in the American Street Law books (see, for instance, Lee P Arbetman & Edward L O'Brien *Street Law: A Course in Practical Law* 7 ed (2005) (McGraw Hill – Glencoe).

The sections in this *Manual* dealing with the elements of a good Street law lesson and Street law lesson plans are adapted from David McQuoid-Mason & Robin Palmer *African Law Clinicians Manual* (2013) (Open Society Justice Initiative).

This programme has as its stated goals:
1. To provide a practical understanding of law and the legal system which will be of use to learners in their everyday lives.
2. To improve understanding of the fundamental principles and values underlying a democracy, and the laws and the legal system of South Africa.
3. To promote awareness of current issues and controversies relating to law and the legal system.
4. To encourage effective citizen participation in South Africa.
5. To bring about a greater sense of justice, tolerance and fairness.
6. To develop a willingness and an ability to resolve disputes through informal and, where necessary, formal resolution mechanisms.
7. To improve basic skills including critical thinking and reasoning, communication, observation, and problem solving.
8. To provide an opportunity to consider and clarify attitudes towards the role that law, lawyers, law enforcement offers, and the legal system play in South African society.
9. To provide an opportunity for exposure to the vocational opportunities which exist within the legal system.

B. Content and organisation of the Street law text

The street law programme is designed to be taught to learners by law students and educators who have no background in law. Two texts have been written: a *Learner's Manual* (3 ed 2015), and an *Educator's Manual*, each of which is divided into six parts. The *Educator's Manual* sets out how the lessons in the *learner's text* can be conducted and the solutions to the problems.

The *Learner's Manual* and *Educator's Manual* each cover the following topics:

Part 1. Introduction to South African law and the legal system
Part 2. Criminal law and juvenile justice
Part 3. Consumer law
Part 4. Family law
Part 5. Socio-economic rights
Part 6. Employment law.

Each part begins with a brief introduction that outlines its general theme and content. Following the introduction, the parts are divided into chapters and sections. Each of these sections represents a major topic for classroom study.

Substantive legal information, practical advice, and competency-building activities are provided in each part. In addition, the text includes numerous interactive teaching methods designed to promote active learning and classroom involvement. A list of references is given at the end of each part.

C. Organisation of the Educator's Manual

The *Educator's Manual* has been prepared to assist educators in teaching Street law. Street law educators do not need to be lawyers, but some background knowledge and information is useful to clarify the many questions raised by learners.

This *Manual* provides answers to all the problems in the *Learner's Manual*. It also provides additional information, classroom activities, suggested community resources and supplementary materials to the text.

This introductory chapter gives a short description of Street law, outlines the goals of the curriculum, explains the content and organisation of the *Learner's Manual*, describes the organisation of the *Educator's Manual* and provides information on the various teaching methods of law-related curricula which can be used in the classroom.

The layout of the *Educator's Manual* corresponds with the chapter and section headings of the *Learner's Manual*. Most of the chapters include the following features: (1) specific outcomes and assessment criteria; (2) answers to problems and additional text which expands on the material in the learner book; and (3) a list of references for further reading.

D. Elements of a good Street law lesson
1. Outcomes: knowledge, skills and values

Outcomes are what the learners should have learned by the end of the lesson. When developing a lesson plan educators should bear in mind that the ideal lesson should include knowledge, skills and values.

Knowledge outcomes refer to what the learners will *know* by the end of the lesson about the relevant substantive or procedural law principles, skills or values being taught (eg 'At the end of the lesson students will be able to explain . . .').

Skills outcomes refer to what the learners will be able to *do* by the end of the lesson (eg 'At the end of this lesson students will be able to conduct . . .').

Values outcomes refer to what the learners will *appreciate* by the end of the lesson (eg 'At the end of this lesson students will appreciate the importance of . . .').

The outcomes regarding knowledge, skills and values should be explained to the learners at the beginning of each lesson so they know what to expect. The inclusion of the outcomes in the educator's lesson plans ensures that the educator has the necessary guidelines regarding what he or she is trying to achieve in the lesson. The outcomes also enable the instructor to check whether or not he or she has achieved the objective of the lesson.

2. Elements of a good Street law lesson

Street law educators do not rely on the traditional lecture approach to teaching because it is the least effective method of imparting knowledge to students.

In order to use interactive teaching methods it is necessary to consider the elements of an effective lesson and what should be included in a lesson plan that uses interactive strategies.

As has been pointed out, an effective lesson is not merely a lecture. An effective lesson goes beyond using the lecture technique in order to stimulate cognitive learning by law students. It is recommended that for an effective lesson the following elements should be included:
1. The substance of the actual topic (eg law, human rights, legal ethics, procedure or practice);
2. The policy considerations affecting the topic (eg why the law was introduced, how it works in practice, etc);
3. Conflicting values – a lesson will be more lively and motivating if students are exposed to different, competing values (eg the need for the police to combat crime weighed against the right of accused persons to a fair trial);
4. An interactive teaching strategy; and
5. When possible, practical advice – students need to know what can be done in practice about relevant aspects of the law.

E. Street law lesson plans

1. Outline of a detailed Street law lesson plan

Unlike in the case of lectures, where time management is relatively easy, interactive learning methods require very careful time management.

Although this *Manual* includes abbreviated lesson plans, the following outline for lesson plans involving interactive learning methods can be used for more detailed Street law lesson plans:
Step 1: Set out the topic of the lesson.
Step 2: Set out the outcomes for the lesson – state what students will be able to do at the end of the lesson in respect of knowledge, skills and values.

Step 3: Set out the content of the lesson in respect of the areas that have to be covered regarding knowledge, skills and values (ie what has to be taught in respect of each).

Step 4: Set out the interactive strategies that will be used together with their time frames in respect of each outcome, eg:

    4.1 Focuser: Brainstorm (5 minutes).

    4.2 Divide students into small groups and allocate questions (5 minutes).

    4.3 Small group discussions of questions (10 minutes).

    4.4 Report back from small groups (20 minutes).

    4.5 General discussion and checking questions (10 minutes)

    Total: 50 minutes

Step 5: Set out the resources needed for the lesson (eg case study handouts, flip chart, overhead projector, PowerPoint projector, etc).

Step 6: Make a list of questions for the concluding session to check that the outcomes for the lesson have been achieved.

2. Example of a more detailed lesson plan

The following is an example of a case study and a more detailed Street law lesson plan for how to conduct the lesson in para 2.11.1.3 Problem 1 in the *Learner's Manual* and para 2.11.1 of this *Manual*.

Problem 1: Mr Msomi is stopped and questioned by the police

A man in plain clothes stops Mr Msomi while he is walking down the street with a box full of second-hand clothes that had been given to him by his employer. The man says he is a policeman and asks Mr Msomi to give him his full name and address. He also asks Mr Msomi where he obtained the clothes. Unless the policeman identifies himself Mr Msomi refuses to give his name and address. The policeman gets angry with Mr Msomi and takes him to the police station for questioning.

1. Role-play the incident between the policeman and Mr Msomi in the street, and at the police station.
2. Is Mr Msomi required by law to answer any questions? Why might he decide to answer questions? Give reasons for your answer.
3. If you were Mr Msomi, what would you have done?
4. Should people have the right to refuse to answer questions by the police? Give reasons for your answer. If people have the right to keep quiet, should the police tell them about it? Give reasons for your answer.

Lesson plan: Mr Msomi is stopped and questioned by the police

1. Topic: The powers of the police to question people
2. Outcomes: At the end of this lesson you will be able to:

    2.1 Explain the powers of the police to question a person.

    2.2 Explain what people should do if stopped and questioned by the police.

    2.3 Appreciate what to do if you are stopped and questioned by the police.

3. Procedure:

    3.1 Focuser: Ask students who of them has been stopped by the police and questioned (5 minutes).

    3.2 Ask learners to prepare for the role-play of Mr Msomi being stopped by the police and being questioned (5 minutes).

3.3 Conduct the role-play (5 minutes).

3.4 Debrief the role-play (10 minutes).

3.5 Divide learners into small groups of not more than 5 each (2 minutes).

3.6 Allocate one of questions 2–4 to each group for discussion (8 minutes).

3.6 Report back (10 minutes).

3.7 General discussion and checking questions (10 minutes).

Total time: 60 minutes

4. Resources: Hand out copies of Mr Msomi scenario from *Learner's Manual*.

5. Checking questions: Question and answer on the powers of the police to question people, eg:

5.1 What are the powers of the police to question people?

5.2 What are the rights of people who are questioned by the police?

5.3 What should you do if you are stopped and questioned by the police?

F. Rationale for interactive teaching methods

Studies such as those that underpin the 'Learning Pyramid' have conclusively demonstrated that interactive learning is the most effective way for people to learn. The origins of the Learning Pyramid are somewhat controversial and there is confusion about who the original author was (see http://lowery.tamu.edu/Teaming/Morgan1/sld023.htm and http://thepeakperformancecenter. com/educational-learning/learning/principles-of-learning/learning-pyramid/. However, it is a useful method of illustrating the importance of interactive teaching and learning methods. The Learning Pyramid indicates that the rate of memory retention increases as more learner-centred interactive teaching methods are used. For example, if lectures are used learners remember 5%. If learners read for themselves they remember 10%. If audio-visual methods are used (eg an overhead projector or PowerPoint) learners remember 20%. If learners see a demonstration they will remember 30%. If they discuss issues in small groups they will remember 50%. If they see a demonstration and then practise what they have seen by doing, they will remember 75%. And, finally, if the learners teach others or immediately use the information they have been given they will remember 90%.

G. Interactive teaching methods

There are many teaching methods and techniques that can be effectively used in practical law courses. The interactive learning and teaching methods mentioned below are just some examples of what can be done to ensure that students and other participants participate in an active learning process. There are many other methods that can be used. Law teachers are encouraged to be as creative as possible in their attempts actively to involve students in the learning process.

The following section briefly outlines some of the most common interactive teaching methods.

1. Brainstorming

Brainstorming is a means of encouraging a free flow of ideas from students. It is an important learning technique because it encourages students to generate creative ideas without fear of criticism.

During brainstorming the law teacher invites students to think of as many different ideas as they can, and records all the suggestions on a black board or flip chart even if some of them might appear to be wrong. If the answers seem to indicate that the question is not clear, it should be rephrased. Law teachers should postpone any criticisms of the suggestions made until all the ideas have been written down. Thereafter, the suggestions may be criticised and, if necessary, ranked in order of priority.

2. Ranking exercises

Ranking exercises involve making choices between competing alternatives. The law teacher can either use a brainstormed list developed by the students or give the students a list of items to rank, for example, 5 to 10 different items. Students should then be required to rank the items from eg 1 to 5, or 1 to 10, with 1 being the most important and 5 or 10 the least. Students can be asked to: (a) justify their ranking, (b) listen to people who disagree, and (c) re-evaluate their ranking in the light of the views of the other participants. For example, students may be asked to rank certain crimes from the most serious to the least serious.

A variation of ranking is to ask students to place themselves on a continuum based on their feelings about some statement or concept. For example, students may be asked to indicate their feelings on the death penalty by standing in a line and placing themselves on a scale from 'strong approval' of the death penalty at one end and 'strong disapproval' at the other. Students should then have an opportunity to justify their ranking, to listen to students who disagree with their viewpoints, and to re-evaluate their position based on the discussions they have heard. They could indicate this by moving their position on the line. (See eg problem 1 in para 2.1.1 in *Learner's Manual*).

3. Small group discussions

Small group discussions should be carefully planned with clear guidelines regarding the procedure to be followed and the time allocated. The groups should usually not exceed five people to ensure that everyone has a chance to speak. The groups should be numbered off by the law teacher (eg 1 to 5), or formed by taking every five people in a row or group and designating them as teams for group discussions.

The groups should be given instructions concerning their task – including how long they will have to discuss a topic or prepare for a debate or role-play and how the group should be run (eg elect a chairperson, and a rapporteur who will report back to all the other students).

Groups should be told to conduct their proceedings in such a way as to ensure that stronger students do not dominate and everyone has a fair opportunity to express themselves. A simple way of achieving this is to use 'token talk' whereby group facilitators give each participant five matches or other tokens and require the participants to surrender their token each time they speak. Any person who speaks on five occasions will have no tokens left and can no longer speak.

4. Case studies

Case studies are usually conducted by dividing students into three large groups of lawyers for plaintiffs or defendants (or prosecutors and accused persons) and judges, and then further sub-dividing the large groups into small groups to consider suitable arguments or solutions. Individuals from each group can be selected to present arguments or to give judgments on behalf of the group. A variation might be for one group or set of groups to argue for one side, another group or set of groups to argue for the other side, and a third group or set of groups to give a decision or judgement on the arguments.

When requiring students to discuss case studies an eight-step procedure can be used:
Step 1: Select the case study.

Step 2: Get the students to review the facts (ensure that they understand them – in plenary).

Step 3: Get the students to identify the legal issues involved (identify the legal questions to be answered – in plenary).

Step 4: Allocate the case study to the students (in small groups).

Step 5: Get the students to discuss the relevant law and prepare arguments or judgments (in small groups).

Step 6: Get the students to present their arguments (arguments on behalf of the plaintiff and defendant should be presented within the allocated time – in plenary or in small groups).

Step 7: Get the students to whom the arguments were presented to make a decision (eg students allocated the role of judges or the students as a whole – in plenary or in small groups).

Step 8: Conduct a general discussion and summarise (in plenary).

Case studies are often based on real incidents or cases, and at the end, after the students have made their decisions, the law teacher can tell them what happened in the real case. Case studies help to develop logical and critical thinking as well as decision-making.

5. Role-plays

In role-plays students draw on their own experience to act out a particular situation (eg a police officer arresting somebody). Students use their imagination to flesh out the role-play. Role-plays can be used to illustrate a legal situation.

The law teacher should use the following seven steps when conducting role-plays:

Step 1: Explain the role-play to the students (describe the scenario).

Step 2: Brief the students who volunteer (or are selected) to do the role-play.

Step 3: Brief the other students to act as observers (give them instructions on what to look out for).

Step 4: Get the students to act out the role-play (this can be done by one group in front of all the students or in small groups consisting of role-players and observers).

Step 5: Ask the observer students to state what they saw happen in the role-play.

Step 6: Ask all the students to discuss the legal, social or other implications of the role-play and to make a decision on what should be done to resolve the conflict in the role-play (this can be done using small groups).

Step 7: Conduct a general discussion and summarise.

A variation of Step 6 would be to ask the students to act out a conclusion to what happened during the role-play.

Although the law teacher sets the scene, he or she should accept what the students do. A role-play often reveals information about the students' experiences as a story in itself.

6. Question and answer

The question and answer technique can be used instead of lecturing. In order to use questions and answers effectively a checklist of the questions and answers should be prepared to ensure that all aspects of the topic have been covered by the end of the lesson. The questions must be properly planned beforehand to make sure that all the information necessary for the lesson or workshop has been obtained from the students.

Law teachers, when using the question and answer technique, should wait for a few seconds (eg at least about five seconds) after asking the question, in order to give students an opportunity to think before answering.

Instructors should be careful to ensure that more confident students do not dominate the question and answer session.

7. Simulations

Simulations require students to act out a role by following a script. They are not open-ended like role-plays, and are carefully scripted to ensure that the objectives of the exercise are achieved.

Simulations usually require more preparation than role-plays because the students need time to prepare to follow the script. The instructor should tell students about the persons or situation they are simulating before they act out the scene to give them time to rehearse. Simulations can be combined with case studies, moots and mock trials.

The procedure for conducting a simulation is similar to that for a role-play. (See above para G5)

8. Debates

Debates should involve relevant controversial issues such as abortion, prostitution, legalisation of drugs, capital punishment, etc. A controversial issue means that there should be a substantial number of students in favour of and against the proposition.

The students may be divided into two groups, or small groups, to prepare arguments for one or other side in the debate. The groups help the persons on each side who are chosen to debate on behalf of the group. The debate is conducted and the participants then vote in favour of or against the proposition.

The law teacher can use the following steps to conduct a debate:

Step 1: Allocate the debate topic to groups of students and choose which groups will argue for and against the proposition.

Step 2: Get the groups to prepare their arguments and to choose two debaters to present their arguments (one, the main debater, to present the group's arguments, and the other, a replying debater, to reply to the opposing group's arguments).

Step 3: Allow the main debaters who are in favour of the proposition to present their arguments first within the designated time frame (eg 5 minutes).

Step 4: Allow the main debaters who are against the proposition to present their arguments within the designated time frame (eg 5 minutes).

Step 5: Allow the replying debaters who are in favour of and against the proposition to briefly reply to their opponents within the designated time frames (eg 1 minute for each side).

Step 6: Ask all the students to vote on which side presented the best arguments and deserved to win the debate.

A variation of the debate is 'mini-debates'. Here all the participants are divided into triads (groups of three) to conduct mini-debates with debaters for and against the proposition in each triad, together with an adjudicator who controls the debate, decides who the winner is, and reports back to all the other students.

9. Games

Games are a fun way for people to learn because most people, whether they are adults or children, enjoy playing games. Games may be used as 'ice breakers' but they may also be used to teach important topics in the law. Games can illustrate complicated legal principles in a simple experiential format. Where games are used to teach about the law they should not just be fun but should also have a serious purpose.

An example of a game that can that can be used to teach values and knowledge and introduce students to the need for law and types of laws that exist in democratic societies is what the present writer calls the 'Pen game' (see below para 1.1.2 page 39). There are many variations of this game. It is sometimes called the 'No Rules Game'.

Law teachers should ensure that games are structured in such a way that they meet the learning outcomes for the exercise. Not only should the game cover the various principles to be learnt but the law teacher should ensure that during the debriefing all the outcomes have been achieved. Games can be used to teach knowledge, skills and values.

10. Hypothetical problems

Hypothetical problems are similar to case studies, except that they are often based on fictitious situations. They can be more useful than case studies in the sense that a particular problem can be tailor-made for the purposes of the lesson. Furthermore, they are often based on an actual event (eg a newspaper report), even though it is not an officially reported legal case. The advantage of hypothetical problems is that appropriate changes can be made to the facts depending on the purposes of the exercise.

Hypothetical problems are particularly useful when teaching about human rights in an anti-human rights environment, because reference does not have to be made directly to the home country. Even though the facts may be identical to those in the home country the hypothetical problem can present them as occurring in a foreign country.

When dealing with hypothetical cases, just as in case studies, students should be required to argue both sides of the case and then to reach a decision. To this end law teachers can use the same procedures as for case studies (see above para G4).

11. Moots

Moots involve case studies in which students are required to argue an appeal on a point of law. Moots are different from mock trials because there is no questioning of witnesses, accused persons or experts as there is in mock trials. All the questioning would have been done at the trial stage. The moot is the appeal stage after the trial has been heard. The only people the appeal court sees and hears are the lawyers who argue the appeal.

In law faculties moots are usually conducted formally and students dress in robes and argue the appeal in a simulated moot court environment. Law students are required to carry out the preparation work on an individual basis and to present their arguments individually as legal counsel.

A variation used in Street law-type clinics is for students to prepare arguments in small groups, as is sometimes done with case studies, and then to elect a representative to present the arguments of the group. The same procedure as for case studies can be used for these types of moots. (See above para G4).

Another method of presenting moots in street law-type clinics is to use 'mini-moots' where students are divided into groups of three with a lawyer on each side and a 'judge' to control the proceedings, give a judgment and report back to all the other students.

12. Mock trials

Mock trials are an experiential way of learning that teaches students to understand court procedures. Mock trials take a variety of forms. In law school programmes teaching criminal or civil proceedings, the trials can be spread over a full semester with students being carefully coached on each aspect of the trial. Law students are required to prepare and participate on an individual basis.

In Street law large numbers of students can be used in mock trials. For example, mock trials using five witnesses and an accused can involve up to 28 participants – eight lawyers for the plaintiff or prosecution team and eight for the defence team, three judges, five witnesses, an accused, a registrar, a court orderly and a time-keeper. One lawyer on each side can make an opening statement, each lawyer can question one witness or the accused, and one lawyer on each side can make a closing statement. The chief judge can control the proceedings, each judge can question one witness or the accused, and one judge can be responsible for giving the judgment. The registrar calls the case, court orderly keeps order in court and the time-keeper keeps the time.

Students are taught the different steps in a trial. They are also taught basic skills like how to make an opening statement, how to lead evidence, how to ask questions and how to make a closing statement. Students play the role of witnesses, court officials, judges and lawyers.

Generally, on how to conduct a Street law-type mock trial. (See below para G26).

13. Open-ended stimulus

Open-ended stimulus exercises require students to complete unfinished sentences such as: 'If I were the judge ...' or 'My advice to the Minister of Justice would be . . .'.

Another method of using an open-ended stimulus is to provide students with an untitled photograph or cartoon and require them to write a caption.

Students may also be provided with an unfinished story and asked to give their own conclusion or to act out the conclusion in a role-play. (See above para G5).

14. Opinion polls

An opinion poll allows students to express their opinion on the topic of study. A poll allows for a spread of opinions (for example, strongly agree, agree, undecided, disagree, strongly disagree). Opinion polls can (a) serve as the basis for discussion; (b) give the law teacher feedback on the values, attitudes and beliefs of the students; and (c) can be used to assess changes in attitudes.

To conduct an opinion poll, the law teacher should ask each student to express privately his or her opinion on the subject (eg by individually writing the opinion down). The law teacher should then ask students for their individual views and record them on a blackboard or flip chart in a table that reflects the views of all the students. This can be done by a simple show of hands. For example, how many strongly agree with statement number 1? Students should then be asked to justify their opinions and to listen to opposing points of view. If no one takes an opposing point of view, the law teacher can ask students what arguments can be made for the opposing position.

The law teacher can use various poll items to check the consistency of students' beliefs and may wish to follow the opinion poll with a case study on the subject being discussed. For example, if during an opinion poll a number of students say that criminals should be rehabilitated and not punished, the poll could be followed by a case study about a violent criminal with a long history of offences. The students could then be asked whether they think that the particular criminal should be punished or whether they still believe in rehabilitation.

15. Participant presentations

Students can be given a topic to prepare for presentation. For example, students may be asked to research the topic formally (eg by consulting book, magazine, journal or newspaper articles on the subject), or informally (eg by asking parents, relatives or friends about particular aspects of the law and how it has affected their lives). Students can then be called upon to make a presentation to all the other students. Thereafter, the presentations are discussed by all the students.

16. Taking a stand

Taking a stand requires students to stand up for their point of view by physically standing up and verbally justifying their position. A controversial topic should be chosen.

As an example, students might be asked who are in favour of and who are against the death penalty. Students would then have to take a stand under a placard stating 'In favour', 'Against' or 'Undecided', and would have to articulate their opinions on the death penalty.

The following procedure can be followed:

Step 1: Prepare placards with headings: 'In favour', 'Against' and 'Undecided' or other suitable headings.

Step 2: Introduce the controversial topic on which the students will be required to take a stand (eg the death penalty, legalisation of drugs or prostitution etc). Tell students that they may move their position if they hear a particularly good or bad argument.

Step 3: Request students to take a stand under the placard that reflects their point of view.

Step 4: Get students to justify their position by making a single argument – alternatively give students under each placard an opportunity to express their point of view.

Step 5: Get any students who moved their position to give their reasons for doing so.

Step 6: Test the consistency of the students' positions by introducing questions involving extreme examples (eg in a death penalty debate check whether those against would say that even Adolf Hitler, who was responsible for killing millions of people, should not be given the death penalty – had he been caught alive).

Step 7: Summarise the discussion and conclude.

To assist the students in articulating their viewpoints in a logical manner they may be required to use a formula like the PRES formula (see below para G17).

Taking a stand not only teaches students the skill of articulating an argument but also requires them to clarify their values.

17. The PRES formula

The PRES formula has been developed to help students, particularly law students, to construct a logical argument when asked to think on their feet.

The **PRES** formula requires students to present their arguments by expressing the following: (a) their **P**oint of view; (b) the **R**eason for their point of view; (c) an **E**xample or **E**vidence to support their point of view; and (d) to **S**ummarise their point of view.

For example, opinions on the death penalty could be articulated as follows using the PRES formula:

1. Argument in favour of the death penalty for murder
    My <u>P</u>oint of view is that I am in favour of the death penalty for murder.
    The <u>R</u>eason is that I believe that if you unlawfully take someone's life you deserve to lose your own.
    The <u>E</u>vidence for my point of view is the Old Testament of *The Bible* that says 'An eye for an eye and a tooth for a tooth'.
    Therefore in <u>S</u>ummary I am in favour of the death penalty for murder.

2. Argument against the death penalty for murder
    My <u>P</u>oint of view is that I am against the death penalty for murder.
    The <u>R</u>eason is that judges can make mistakes.
    An <u>E</u>xample is the English case of Timothy Evans who was found to have been innocent after he had been executed.
    Therefore in <u>S</u>ummary I am against the death penalty for murder.

3. Undecided argument on the death penalty for murder
    My <u>P</u>oint of view is that I do not know whether I am in favour or against the death penalty for murder.
    The <u>R</u>eason is that I do not know whether it makes any difference to the murder rate in a country.
    For <u>E</u>xample in the United States of America where some states have the death penalty and others do not the murder rate stays the same.
    Therefore in <u>S</u>ummary I do not know whether I am in favour or against the death penalty for murder.

Steps when teaching the PRES formula:

Step 1: Introduce and explain the PRES formula.

Step 2: Demonstrate the PRES formula.

Step 3: Pose questions to individual students on controversial issues and ask them to immediately use the PRES formula.

Step 4: Debrief and conclude on the value of the PRES formula.

The PRES formula can be combined with other learning methods such as 'taking a stand' (see above para G16). If students are required to make submissions rather than to express a point of view the PRES formula can become the **SRES** formula (Submission, Reason, Evidence/Example and Summary). The PRES formula teaches the valuable skill of being able to think on one's feet.

18. Problem solving

When solving a legal problem law students can construct a logical framework by using the FIRAC formula. The FIRAC formula refers to the following:

F = Facts
I = Issues
R = Rule of law
A = Application of rule of law to facts
C = Conclusion

Step 1: Ascertaining the Facts
The relevant facts concerning the case or problem must be identified: For example, the question may involve a detailed description of how a doctor behaved during an operation that was conducted negligently. The relevant facts that point to negligent conduct must be identified.

Step 2: Ascertaining the Issues
The issues or legal questions to be answered must be identified: For example, the question might be: Did the doctor act negligently?

Step 3: Identifying the Rule of Law
The relevant rules of law must be discussed – if there are conflicting rules these should be mentioned: For example, the rule of law regarding negligence by a doctor is that the doctor failed to exercise the degree of skill and care of a reasonably competent doctor in his or her branch of medicine (ie a reasonably competent doctor would have foreseen the likelihood of harm and would have taken steps to guard against it).

Step 4: Applying the Rule of Law to Facts
The rule of law must be applied to the facts: for example, the rule of law regarding negligence by doctors must be applied to the facts in order to determine whether or not on the facts the doctor was negligent. On the given facts, did the doctor's conduct measure up to that of a reasonably competent doctor in his or her branch of medicine?

Step 5: Reaching a Conclusion
After applying the rule of law to the facts, a conclusion should be reached on whether, for example, the doctor's conduct was negligent.

The FIRAC formula can also be used to write opinions and to answer problem questions in written examinations.

19. Values clarification

Values clarification exercises encourage students to express themselves and to examine their own values, attitudes and opinions as well as those held by others. Thus, students are given an opportunity to examine their attitudes and beliefs. At the same time they are asked to consider other points of view. A value clarification exercise promotes communication skills and empathy for others.

Value clarification is important for promoting the development of the ability of students to listen, as well as their communication skills, their empathy for others, their ability to solve problems and make decisions, their reasoning and critical thinking skills, and their ability to maintain consistency regarding their attitudes and beliefs.

The steps that can be used by law teachers to teach values clarification are the following:

Step 1: Ask students to express their opinions (ie identify their position on an issue).

Step 2: Ask students to clarify their opinions (ie explain and define their positions).

Step 3: Ask students to examine the reasons for their opinions (why they believe something; the reasons for their position; and the arguments and evidence that support their position).

Step 4: Ask students to consider other points of view (eg by asking students who hold opposite viewpoints to present their views, or asking students to write down the arguments for opposing viewpoints, or by the law teacher presenting opposite views for discussion).

Step 5: Ask students to analyse their position and other points of view (eg by asking students to identify the strongest and weakest arguments in support of their position, and the strongest and weakest arguments of students opposed to their opinion).

Step 6: Ask students to make a decision on the issue (ie students should re-evaluate and resolve the conflict between the various points of view to find the best result).

Step 7: Conduct a general discussion and summarise.

20. Fishbowl

'Fishbowls' can be used for observations of case studies, simulations, role-plays or any other lawyering activity where students are required to critically analyse what has transpired during the activity. They are also useful when dealing with values and attitudes. For instance, in gender-sensitivity exercises fishbowls can be used to enable students to observe the differences between how women relate to each other in given situations as opposed to what men do in similar circumstances.

An example of the steps in a fishbowl is the following:

Step 1: The law teacher introduces the exercise by mentioning that the students will be divided into small groups to prepare for a role-play.

Step 2: The law teacher divides the students into small groups of lawyers interviewing a client and clients who are about to be interviewed – with not more than five students in each group.

Step 3: The lawyers in the small groups prepare the questions they will ask during the interview and the clients in their groups prepare the questions they will ask and what they will tell the lawyer.

Step 4: The law teacher calls for volunteers from the groups to role-play the interview between the lawyer and the client in front of all the other students. The remaining members in the groups are told that they are observers and the law teacher gives them a checklist of things to look out for during the role-play.

Step 5: The role-play is conducted and the observers make notes.

Step 6: At the end of the role-play the law teacher asks the observers what they observed.

Step 7: The law teacher conducts a general discussion and concludes the exercise.

Fishbowls can be used to teach knowledge, values and skills in combination with a number of other learning methods.

21. Jigsaw

The jigsaw method is useful for introducing students to procedures such as legislative or law commission hearings where special parliamentary or law commission committees listen to representations from different interest groups regarding proposed changes in the law. The jigsaw is used to enable the different interest groups to consult with each other before they make representations to a parliamentary law commission or other committee that is hearing arguments from people or organisations that have different interests.

Jigsaws can be conducted using the following steps:

Step 1: Brainstorm ideas to select two interest groups in favour of the proposed changes to the law and two that would be against.

Step 2: Divide students into two groups in favour of the change, two groups against the change ('home groups'), and a group of parliamentary or law commission committee members.

Step 3: The home groups meet to discuss the arguments they will make to the parliamentary or law commission committee. At the same time the parliamentary or law commission committee discusses the issues and the questions they will ask the home groups.

Step 4: The home groups subdivide into multi-interest groups with representatives from each home group joining a multi-interest group to hear each other's viewpoints. The parliamentary or law commission committee continues its discussions.

Step 5: The multi-interest group members return to their home groups, report back to their colleagues, and in the light of what they have learned from the other groups, the home groups refine their arguments for the parliamentary or law commission committee. The home groups elect two representatives to present their arguments to the parliamentary or law commission committee: one to make the arguments, the other to deal with questions. The parliamentary or law commission committee continues its discussions.

Step 6: The home groups each have a limited time frame (eg two minutes each) to present their arguments to the committee. The committee has a limited period for questions (eg one minute per home group).

Step 7: The parliamentary or law commission committee has a limited time frame (eg two minutes) to consider its decision and to present it (eg a further two minutes).

Step 8: The law teacher debriefs the lesson and summarises.

The jigsaw is a fairly complicated procedure and the time frames need to be carefully managed by the law teacher.

22. Each one teach one

Each one teach one is a technique that requires all the students to become involved in teaching each other about a particular area of the law. Each student teaches another student a section of the law to be covered so that by the end of the exercise all the students would have learned about the whole topic.

The following steps may be followed when using the each one teach one technique:

Step 1: The law teacher prepares a number of cards with statements on them that cover different areas of the topic (eg certain legal definitions). A sufficient number of cards must be prepared to ensure that the topic is covered in accordance with the desired outcomes.

Step 2: The cards are distributed to the students and the students are told that they must teach their fellow students what is on the cards.

Step 3: The students move around the room teaching each other what is on their cards.

Step 4: Once all the students have taught each other what is on their cards the law teacher ends the exercise.

Step 5: The law teacher checks with the students to ensure that they have all learned what was on the cards.

Step 6: The law teacher debriefs the lesson and summarises.

The each one teach one procedure must be carefully controlled to make sure that all the information on the different cards has been transferred to all the students.

23. Visual aids

Visual aids take the form of photographs, cartoons, pictures, drawings, posters, videos and films. Photographs, cartoons, pictures and drawings can be found in text books, newspapers, magazines, etc. Videos and films are usually available online, in libraries and resource centres or from the organisations that produce them.

Visual aids can be used to arouse interest, recall early experiences, reinforce learning, enrich reading skills, develop powers of observation, stimulate critical thinking and encourage values clarification. Students can be required to describe and analyse what they see, and through questioning, to apply the visual aid to other situations.

When using visual aids the law teacher may use the following steps:

Step 1: Students describe what they see (focus on the elements of the visual aid and describe everything seen, including any symbols).

Step 2: Students analyse what they see (eg how the elements of the picture relate to each other; the point the photographer or artist is trying to make; the meaning or theme of the picture; and what the figures or people represent).

Step 3: Students apply the idea of the visual (ie apply the idea to other situations by thinking about what the picture reminds them of; whether they can think of other events similar to it; and how the idea applies to local people and communities).

Step 4: Students clarify their beliefs (ie express their opinions on the visual aid, eg whether they agree or disagree with the photographer's or artist's point of view, how they feel about the idea; and what they think should be done about the problem shown in the visual aid).

24. Inviting experts

Inviting experts can provide students with a wide variety of information, materials and experience not available in any books. The use of experts can give students valuable insights into how the law and social justice issues operate in practice.

Law teachers should use the following steps when using experts:

Step 1: Select an appropriate expert (eg a lawyer, community leader, judge, ex-offender or a government official).

Step 2: Prepare the speaker and the class (tell the expert and the students about the outcomes for visit, eg ask the students to prepare questions beforehand).

Step 3: Conduct the class (get the expert to give a short talk, or get them to play their normal role – eg a judge in a mock trial or to comment on students playing their role).

Step 4: Debrief the visit (students should be asked what they learnt from the expert; whether he or she answered all their questions; and how what they heard from the expert relates to what they had previously learnt about the topic).

25. Field trips

Field trips are useful because law teachers can choose both interesting and relevant places for students to visit. The trips should be arranged so that the experience of the students is consistent with the learning outcomes for the exercise.

Students should be prepared before the visit, and told to look out for specific things. They should also be asked to record their reactions on an observation sheet that should be prepared beforehand. The sheets can form the basis of a discussion when the students return from the field trip.

Law teachers should use the following steps when arranging field trips:

Step 1: Decide where to go (eg, the courts, prisons, police stations, hospitals, government offices etc).

Step 2: Plan the visit (students and hosts should be prepared for the visit: eg students should have observation sheets, and hosts prepared for briefings).

Step 3: Conduct the visit (students should observe the activities; ask questions; comment on specific things; and complete the observation sheets).

Step 4: Debrief the visit (students should report back on what they saw; how they felt; what they learnt; and, how what they learnt related to previous knowledge).

26. Mock trials

Mock trials are enactments of judicial proceedings. They may be based on historical events, cases of contemporary interest, school situations or hypothetical facts. The format can be either formal or informal. The format chosen depends upon the objectives of the class and the sophistication of the learners.

26.1 Purpose

Mock trials develop an insider's perspective on courtroom procedures. For example, they give a basic understanding of legal mechanisms through which society resolves many of its disputes. They sensitise learners to the substantive issues of the trial. Mock trials develop an appreciation for persons involved in lawsuits. They also develop critical skills, greater fluency in English, critical analysis of problems, strategic thinking, listening and questioning skills, oral presentation, on-the-spot argument, and skills in preparing and organising material. Mock trials promote co-operative learning and affect attitudes towards the legal profession. Learners are prepared for possible future involvement as parties and witnesses in trials. This lessens fear of the courts, and provides the knowledge needed to perform these roles effectively.

26.2 Preparations for a mock trial

1. **Distribute the mock trial materials to the class:** All learners should read the entire set of materials, including the facts of the case, legal authorities, witness statements and any other materials.

2. **Assign or select learners for the various roles in the mock trial:** Depending on the type of trials, learners should be selected to play the roles of lawyers, witnesses, registrar or clerk, orderly and court observers. For the role of judge, it is often helpful to invite a resource person, such as a lawyer, law student, or real judge. If this is not possible, an educator from another class or even a learner may act as judge.

3. **Prepare participants for the trial:** To expedite preparation for the actual enactment and involve the maximum number of learners, it is useful to divide the class into training groups:

   3.1 Divide participants (lawyers and witnesses) into a plaintiff's team (a prosecution team in a criminal trial) and a defence team. Each team has the responsibility for preparing its side of the case.

   3.2 Further divide the participants into task groups. Groups can be assigned to prepare each of the various tasks in a trial.

26.3 Steps in a trial

A number of events occur during a trial, and most trials must happen in a particular order. We will use a criminal trial as an example. (In a civil trial the plaintiff or his or her counsel would bring the case instead of the prosecutor.)

1. Court is called to order by the orderly.
2. Judge enters and takes the bench.
3. Registrar calls the case.
4. Prosecutor makes an opening statement.
5. Defence may set out basis of defence in a written statement.
6. Prosecutor presents the case.
   (a) Prosecutor calls first witness and conducts examination-in-chief.
   (b) Defence cross-examines the witness.
   (c) Prosecutor conducts re-examination if necessary.
   (d) Judge may ask questions.
   Steps (a), (b) and (c) are completed for each of the prosecution's other witnesses.
7. Prosecutor closes the case.
8. Defence presents the case in same manner as prosecutor in 6 above, with prosecutor cross-examining each witness. Accused must be called as first witness for defence if he or she is going to give evidence.
9. Defence closes the case.
10. Prosecutor makes closing argument.
11. Defence makes closing argument.
12. Prosecutor may offer replying argument but only on the law raised by the defence, not the facts.
13. Judge deliberates.
14. Verdict of judge.
    In a criminal case these next steps occur when an accused is convicted. (These do not occur in a civil case. In a civil case the judge decides in favour of one, or the other, or neither of the parties, and makes an appropriate court order – eg defendant must pay compensation.)
15. If accused is convicted, defence offers evidence in mitigation (reasons why the sentence should be reduced), and prosecution may reply.
16. Judge sentences convicted accused.

26.4 Simplified rules of evidence

So that each party to a trial can be assured of a fair hearing, certain rules have been developed to govern the types of evidence that may be introduced in a trial, as well as the manner in which evidence may be presented. These rules are called the 'rules of evidence'. The lawyers and the judge are responsible for enforcing these rules.

Lawyers do this by making 'objections' to the evidence or procedure wrongly employed by the opposing side. When an objection is raised the lawyer stands up and says, 'I object' and gives the reasons for the objection. The lawyer against whom the objection is raised will usually be asked by the judge to respond. A response should tell the judge why the question or the witness' answer was not against the rules of evidence.

The rules of evidence used in real trials can be very complicated. A few of the most important rules of evidence have been adapted for mock trial purposes, and these are presented below.

Rule 1: Leading questions

Leading questions may not be asked in the examination-in-chief. Leading questions may be used in cross-examination. A leading question is one which suggests the answer desired by the questioner, usually by stating some facts not previously discussed and asking the witness to give a 'yes' or a 'no' answer.

Example: 'So, Braam Afrika, you never heard or saw Koos Smit tell his younger brother that the plan was to steal the typewriter, did you?'

If counsel asks leading questions of his or her own witness, the opposing lawyer should object:

Objection: 'Objection, my Lord. Counsel is leading the witness.'

Possible response: 'My Lord, leading is permissible in cross-examination' or 'I'll rephrase the question'. So the example of the leading question would not be leading if rephrased as 'What, if anything, did you hear Koos Smit tell his younger brother about the plan to steal the typewriter?' This form of the question does not ask for a 'yes' or 'no' answer.

Rule 2: Witness goes beyond the question

Witnesses' answers must be in response to the questions. Answers that go beyond the questions are objectionable. This occurs when the witness provides much more information than the question calls for:

Example: Question: 'Shirley Govender, where do you work?'

Witness: 'I am a teacher at the Three Trees' High School. On 15 August 2003, I saw the two boys holding the new Olympia typewriter. I knew that they were stealing the typewriter. Koos Smit, who was at the school door, obviously was the mastermind behind the theft.'

Objection: 'Objection, my Lord. The witness is going beyond the question.'

Possible response: 'My Lord, the witness is telling us a complete sequence of events.'

Rule 3: Relevance

Questions or answers that add nothing to the understanding of the issue in dispute are objectionable.

Questions and answers must be related to the subject matter of the case. This is called 'relevance'. Those that do not relate to the case are 'irrelevant':

Example: In a theft case: 'Sergeant Msinga, how many wives do you have?'
Objection: 'My Lord, this question is irrelevant.'
Possible response: 'My Lord, this series of questions will show that Sergeant Msinga's first wife was a teacher at Three Trees' School and was once assaulted by a learner'. (If Sergeant Msinga does not have such a wife, the response should be: 'I'll withdraw the question'.)

In practice, the judge usually gives some freedom to the lawyers to ask questions, relying on the lawyers' good faith to ask questions that relate to the case.

Rule 4: Hearsay

With certain exceptions, statements that are made outside of the courtroom by persons not called as witnesses are not allowed as evidence if they are offered in court to show that the statements are true.

There are many exceptions to the hearsay rule, but the only two that apply in mock trials are:
1. A witness may repeat a statement made by the accused provided that the witness actually heard the statement.
2. Statements made by the accused which go against his or her own interest may be used as evidence:

Example: Koos Smit says, 'Hennie Smit told our mother that he would get his school fees somehow.'
Objection: 'Objection, My Lord. This is hearsay.'
Possible response: 'My Lord, since Hennie is the accused, the witness can testify to a statement he heard Hennie make.' Or, 'My Lord, this is a statement against his own interest.'

Rule 5: First-hand knowledge

Witnesses must testify about things that they themselves have seen, heard or experienced:

Example: Shirley Govender testifies, 'Hennie and Braam must have entered the typing room first.'
Objection: 'My Lord, the witness has no first-hand knowledge of who entered the typing room.'
Possible response: 'My Lord, the witness talked to the accused after the theft and discovered what had happened.'

Rule 6: Opinion

Unless a witness is qualified as an expert in the area under question, the witness may not give an opinion about matters relating to that area (Example 1). However, if the evidence is about something in common experience (Example 2), an ordinary witness may give an opinion:

> **Example 1:** 'Juvenile delinquency will continue to grow unless we put juvenile offenders in prison on a regular basis' is an objectionable opinion unless given by an expert on juvenile delinquency.
>
> **Example 2:** 'Hennie seemed to be very frightened' is within the common experience of an ordinary witness.
>
> **Objection:** 'My Lord, the witness is giving an opinion.'
>
> **Possible response:** 'My Lord, the witness may answer the question because ordinary persons can tell if someone is frightened.'

Rule 7: Beyond the scope of cross-examination

In cases where the lawyer has reserved time to re-examine a witness after cross-examination, on re-examination, the lawyer may only ask questions related to topics that the opposing lawyer asked about during cross-examination:

> **Example:** After cross-examination of Sergeant Msinga, in which the defence counsel only asked about the argument between the accused and his brother, the prosecutor in re-examination asks, 'Sergeant, at what time did the teacher contact you from Three Trees' High School?'
>
> **Objection:** 'Objection, My Lord, my learned friend is raising matters not covered in cross-examination.'
>
> **Possible response:** 'My Lord, by inquiring into the argument between the brothers, counsel opened the topic of the entire arrest process.' Or, 'I'll withdraw the question.'

Rule 8: Beyond the scope of the problem in the mock trial

Questions that ask for significant facts not contained in the mock trial problem are objectionable. However, minor details regarding a character's role may be asked and added:

> **Example:** 'Koos Smit, where did you attend secondary school?'
>
> **Objection:** 'Objection, My Lord. This is beyond the scope of the problem.'
>
> **Possible response:** 'My Lord, the witness is giving minor details to describe his person to the court, and the facts do not have a significant impact on the outcome of the trial.'

26.5 Special procedures

Procedure 1: Introduction of physical evidence

The lawyers may wish to offer as evidence, written documents or physical evidence, such as a stolen typewriter or a murder weapon. Special procedures must be followed before these items can be considered by the judge as evidence. In the case of physical evidence, like the typewriter, the prosecutor must use the last person having custody of the typewriter to get the evidence admitted to court. This person must then testify to the events to show that the typewriter has been under his or her control since the time the typewriter was brought to the police station.

After testifying to this 'chain of custody', the lawyer must ask the judge to admit the typewriter as Exhibit No 1. Things other than documents are marked with numerals (eg 1, 2, 3, etc); documents are marked with the letters of the alphabet (eg A, B, C, etc).

Procedure 2: Accomplice witnesses

Witnesses who are alleged to have participated in the crime prosecuted in the trial, but who have not yet been charged, are called 'accomplice' witnesses. Their evidence against one of the others charged with participating in the crime has to be used with great care. This is because they have a reason to lie and because they also may face prosecution themselves for the same crime. Making them give evidence, which could then be used against them in a later prosecution, violates the Constitution.

Therefore, a special procedure is used which allows accomplice witnesses to testify. If such a witness testifies satisfactorily, the judge will order the prosecutor not to charge the witness with that crime. This is called granting the witness 'immunity'.

The prosecutor must inform the judge that the witness is being offered as an accomplice witness. The judge will say to the witness, 'I'm informed that you took some part in the offence charged here. If you give satisfactory evidence, I will order that you should not be prosecuted, and the things you say will not get you into trouble in any way. Are you willing to be sworn in and to testify under these conditions?'

Procedure 3: Dishonest or confused witnesses

In cross-examination, the lawyers may want to show that the witness should not be believed. This can be achieved by showing that the witness has said something different in the past from what the witness is now saying. The witness may have said something different when giving evidence earlier or may have made an affidavit to the police which contradicts the evidence subsequently given.

For example, if a state witness gives evidence different from that given in the sworn statement, the prosecutor may hand the statement to the defence and allow the defence lawyer to cross-examine the witness on the affidavit. This could be done as follows:

Step 1: Ask the witness if he or she recognises the affidavit.
Step 2: Ask the witness to read the section that differs from the present answer:

> **Example:** Defence lawyer: 'Now, Miss Govender, you testified in the examination-in-chief that Hennie acted very nervously when you found the boys at the school on the night of 15th August, didn't you?'
>
> **Teacher:** 'Yes, that is what happened.'
>
> **Defence lawyer:** 'Do you know what this paper is? Please tell the judge what it is.'
>
> **Teacher:** 'Yes, that is my sworn statement to the police.'
>
> **Defence lawyer:** 'Will you please read the second-last line of this paragraph?'
>
> **Teacher:** 'I thought that Hennie seemed quite open and natural about having the typewriter.'
>
> **Defence lawyer:** 'That is sufficient, thank you.'

26.6 Conducting the trial

1.   Lay out the classroom

It is important for learners to be familiar with the physical setting of the courtroom. The following diagram depicts the layout of a typical courtroom:

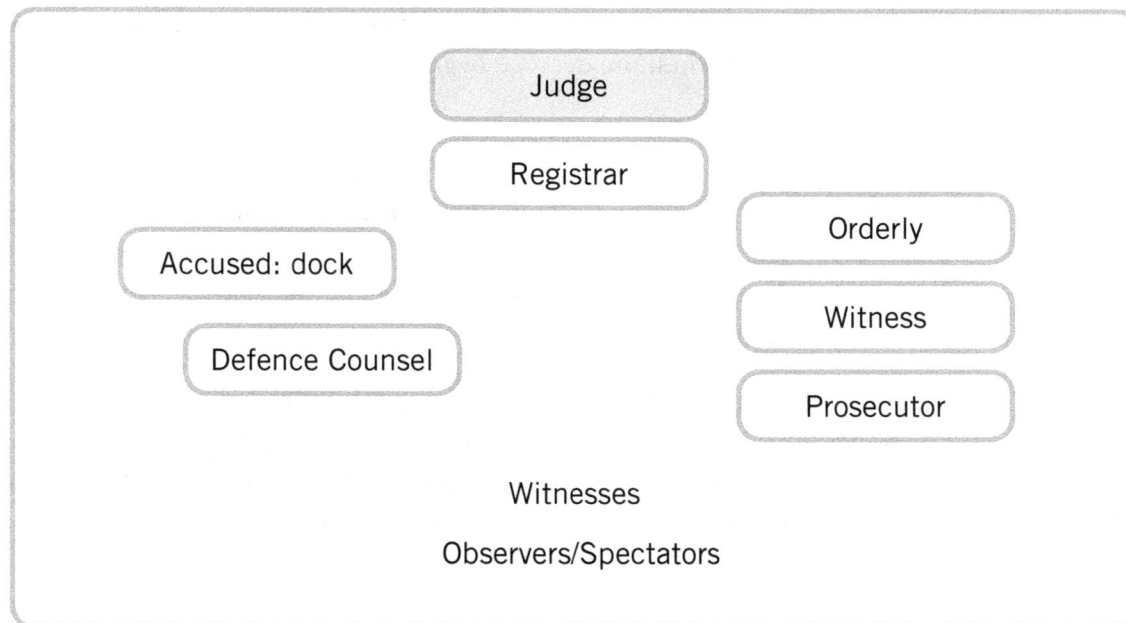

```
┌─────────────────────────────────────────────────────────┐
│                         Judge                            │
│                        Registrar                         │
│                                        Orderly           │
│          Accused: dock                                   │
│                                        Witness           │
│             Defence Counsel                              │
│                                        Prosecutor        │
│                                                          │
│                       Witnesses                          │
│                  Observers/Spectators                    │
│                                                          │
└─────────────────────────────────────────────────────────┘
```

Lawyers conduct the trial while standing at their places at counsel's table. Each lawyer remains seated while the other lawyer conducts his or her case. They do not stand or walk around.

2.   Have participants take their places

Participants include the judge, lawyers, parties, witnesses, registrar, orderly and courtroom observers (spectators).

3.   Orderly calls the court to order

As the judge is about to enter the courtroom, the orderly stands and says in a loud voice, 'Silence in court'.

4.   The registrar then informs the judge of the case

'My Lord, I am calling case (*give name and number*) for hearing.'

5.   In a criminal case

The judge asks the accused to stand, 'Will the accused please stand?' The judge says to the accused, 'Are you (name of the accused)? You are charged with the crime of (mention of crime and circumstances of the crime). How do you plead; guilty or not guilty?'

6.   Introduction of counsel

The judge asks counsel to introduce themselves, 'Who appears?'

7.   Opening statement

The opening statement is the introduction to the case. Usually it is only done by the prosecutor, who says what the charges are and what evidence will be led. Sometimes, but not necessarily, the defence lawyer sets out the basis of the accused's defence. The defence may hand in a 'section 115 statement' if the accused pleads 'not guilty' or a 'section 119 statement' if he or she pleads 'guilty'. The prosecutor always begins.

8. Prosecution case

The process of 'leading the evidence' begins. First, the prosecutor's team presents its witnesses and evidence, then the defence team presents its witnesses and evidence. If the accused is going to give evidence, he or she must be called first when the defence begins its case.

Each time a witness is called to the witness stand, the orderly administers the oath, by raising the right hand, and asking the witness to raise his or her right hand and asking, 'Do you swear that the evidence that you are about to give is the truth, the whole truth and nothing but the truth? Raise your right hand and say, 'So help me God.' The witness should respond 'So help me God'. A witness who does not wish to make an oath may make an affirmation, 'Do you affirm that the evidence you are about to give is the truth, the whole truth and nothing but the truth?'

The prosecutor or lawyer who called the witness asks a series of questions called 'examination-in-chief'. These questions are designed to get the witness to tell a story, reciting what he or she saw, heard, experienced or knows about the case. The questions must be asked only to establish the facts – not to give opinions (unless the witness has been declared an 'expert' in the area under question, or is giving an opinion about things in common experience).

In addition, the prosecutor or lawyer may only ask questions and may not make any statements about the facts, even if the witness says something wrong. When the examination-in-chief is completed, the lawyer for the other side then asks questions to show weaknesses in the witnesses' evidence through a process called 'cross-examination'.

The purpose of the cross-examination is to show the judge that the witness who gives unfavourable evidence should not be believed because the witness: (1) cannot remember facts; (2) did not give all of the facts in the direct examination; (3) told a different story at some other time; (4) has a special relationship with one of the parties (maybe a relative or a close friend); or (5) bears a grudge against one of the parties. The cross-examination questions are designed to bring out one or more of these factors.

Sometimes, the witnesses called by one side give evidence that helps the other side. The lawyer for the side receiving the unexpected help should remember to use that evidence in the closing argument. After cross-examination, the prosecutor may 're-examine' the witness about matters that are raised in the cross-examination. No further cross-examination is permitted after the re-examination.

When the prosecutor has closed the prosecution case, the defence opens its case.

9. Defence case

The procedure is the same as in the prosecutor's case except that the defence calls witnesses for the examination-in-chief and the prosecutor cross-examines. If the accused is going to give evidence, he or she must be called as the first witness. Again the defence may re-examine the witnesses but the prosecutor may not cross-examine them again.

10. Closing argument

The purpose of the closing argument is to convince the judge that the evidence presented entitles that side to win the case. The closing argument should include: (1) a summary of the charges against the accused and what the law requires to be proved; (2) a summary of the evidence presented that is favourable to the presenting lawyer's case; and (3) a summary of how the law, when applied to the evidence and facts in the case, should enable the judge to rule in favour of the presenting lawyer's case. New information may not be introduced in the closing argument. In a criminal case, the prosecutor closes first, then the defence, after which the prosecutor may reply to any new legal points raised by the defence.

11. Deliberation and decision

In making a decision, the judge considers the evidence presented and decides which witnesses are the most credible or believable.

To ensure that the mock trials are completed within a reasonable time, the following time limits are suggested:

- Opening statement   –   3 minutes each.
- Examination-in-chief –   7 minutes each.
- Cross-examination   –   4 minutes each.
- Closing argument   –   3 minutes each.
- Reply   –   1 minute.

If, during examination-in-chief or cross-examination, a lawyer objects to a question or an answer, this time should not be counted against the allocated time. This means that the length of time that the lawyers argue about the objection until the judge makes a ruling does not count towards the seven minutes of examination-in-chief or four minutes of cross-examination.

The prosecution or defence may 'reserve' time in order to obtain a second chance to ask questions. So, for example, if the prosecutor reserves two minutes to re-examine one of the witnesses, he or she will only get five minutes for the examination-in-chief. The defence counsel is allowed four minutes of cross-examination, and the prosecutor has an additional two minutes for re-examination. There is no further cross-examination after re-examination.

If time limits are used, the registrar should have time cards that read '2 min'; '1 min'; '0'. For each part of the trial that is timed, the registrar should hold up the appropriate card to the judge and to the lawyers, when they are asking questions, to let them know how much time is left.

1. Introduction to South African law and the legal system

CONTENTS

PART ONE

Introduction to South African law and the legal system

1.1 Street law and law in general

Outcomes

After completion of this section learners will be able to:

1. Explain the purpose and meaning of Street law and law in general

Assessment criteria

1. An explanation is given of the purpose and meaning of Street law and law.

2. The relationship between law and everyday life is identified.

3. A set of facts is examined and a decision is taken on whether or not the accused were guilty of murder.

4. The relationship between law and morality is identified.

5. The reasons for having laws in society are identified.

1.1.1 What is Street law? *(Learner's Manual p 5)*

Problem 1: The case of the silent radio *(Learner's Manual p 6)*

AIM: This case is meant as an example of what might happen in everyday life, and as a preliminary introduction to learners of the purposes of Street law and why it is important to know their legal rights and duties. The facts of the case should start learners thinking about law and legal principles based on common sense and logic rather than knowledge of the law. The problem also establishes whether learners can recognise a legal problem when they come across one.

PROCEDURE	TIME	
1. Ask the class as a whole what the problem is.	Identifying problem:	5 min
2. Divide the class into small groups of five each.	Group discussions:	10 min
3. Ask group 1 to discuss question 2, group 2 to discuss question 3, group 3 to discuss question 4 and group 4 to discuss question 5. Repeat for additional groups.	Reports back:	15 min
	Discussion and summary:	15 min
4. Get a report back from each group.	**TOTAL:**	**45 min**
5. Conclude with general class discussion and summary.		

1. Some learners might say that Mrs Khumalo can do nothing because the radio worked when she left the shop. Most, however, will probably say that the problem is that the radio does not work and the shop should fix it, replace it or give Mrs Khumalo her money back. The legal problem is whether a seller is obliged to repair, replace or give a refund for a second-hand radio which 'works well' in the shop, and is described as 'as good as new' by the salesman, but fails to work after it is taken from the shop. This is a consumer law problem which involves the question of the false representations by a salesman when he said 'it works well' and is 'as good as new'. It also involves hidden defects in the products. The law says that when something is sold, it should be free of defects unless described otherwise. Mrs Khumalo would be entitled to get her money

back. As a favour to the shop, however, she could agree to allow the shop to fix it or give her a replacement – but she does not have to. (See *Learner's Manual* Part 3 Consumer law.)

2. Some learners might say that, in Mrs Khumalo's position, they would have become very angry. They might have shouted at the salesman or argued with him. Others might have complained to the owner or threatened to warn other people about the shop. Mrs Khumalo is entitled to claim her money back and return the radio if it stopped working through no fault on her part. She could, however, allow the shop to replace or repair it. If the salesman refuses to help her, she may ask for the manager and tell him her problem. If the manager also refuses to help, she can consult an advice office, go to the small claims court (see *Learner's Manual* para 1.5.2) or, if she is poor, to a university law clinic (see *Learner's Manual* para 1.4.1.4.3). The claim would be too small for her to consult a lawyer.

3. Her friend could go with her as a witness to the discussions with the salesman or manager. The friend could also help by supporting Mrs Khumalo when she talks to the owner of the shop. She could also act as a witness in the small claims court (see *Learner's Manual* para 1.5.2) or give a statement to a legal aid clinic.

4. Learners will probably decide the case in favour of Mrs Khumalo and this would be correct. If they do, they should give reasons for their answer. If they decide against her, they would have to argue that she broke the radio herself or that it was sold 'as is', which is usually the case with second-hand goods. If, however, the radio was sold 'as is' and the salesman knew that it did not work, and this is proved, Mrs Khumalo could get her money back. The reason for finding in Mrs Khumalo's favour would be that if a person sells something to another and says that it 'works well' or is 'as good as new', the thing should measure up to its description. Even if no statement is made concerning the thing sold, the rule is that it should be fit for the purpose for which it is sold. (See *Learner's Manual* Part 3 Consumer law.)

5. The answers to this question will depend upon whether the learners have experienced or have heard of similar cases. The educator should assist the learners in deciding whether these are legal problems and whether the people concerned could have used the law to solve their problems (eg by going to a legal aid clinic, a lawyer or the small claims court). Were the problems solved satisfactorily?

Note: At this stage the educator should not expect very informed answers but should try to guide the learners to a correct answer (if there is one) and generate interest in the course. The educator will not be able to state the law in all the situations but can make a note of the questions and ask a lawyer or a law student later. The educator can give the learners the correct answer next time they meet. Lawyers or law students should also be invited at a later stage to visit the class and discuss problems with the learners.

Problem 2: A few general questions
(Learner's Manual p 7)

AIM: The purpose of this problem is to discover whether learners understand the value of learning Street law. There is no right or wrong answer, provided learners give good reasons for their answers.

PROCEDURE	TIME	
1. Divide class into small groups of five each.	Group discussions:	10 min
2. Ask each group to discuss one question.	Reports back:	15 min
3. Get reports back from each group.	Discussion and summary:	5 min
4. Conclude with general class discussion and summary.	**TOTAL:**	**30 min**

1. There are several possible answers to this question apart from those that appear in the *Learner's Manual*; for instance:
    (a) Street law shows learners that even though many people think that the law is always against them, sometimes it can be used for their protection.
    (b) Street law teaches learners survival skills 'on the street' by helping them to understand the law so that they can avoid difficulties with the law and know what can happen if they get into trouble. It also teaches them how to get legal assistance when they need it so that they know what can be done to protect their interests.
    (c) Street law enables learners to take legal knowledge back to their homes and to share it with other members of their families and community.
2. Again there are a variety of answers. Some may be the following:
    (a) No. Because if only lawyers knew about the law, people would not know if they had legal problems which were worth taking to lawyers. They also could not take action on their own to solve their own problems, eg by complaining or going to the small claims court.
    (b) No. Because if ordinary citizens know about the law, they can help each other in making sure that the law is properly enforced. For example, they can direct people who are the victims of unlawful acts or omissions to agencies or people who can help them.
    (c) No. Because 'prevention is better than cure', and if people know about the law they can protect themselves against people who harm or threaten them by breaking the law; for example, by not signing a contract they have not read, even though a salesperson says the contract is in their favour.
    (d) No. Because if people know what is wrong with the law, they may be better able to put pressure on politicians, community leaders and others to make the government change the laws.
    (e) Maybe it could be argued that because lawyers are legally trained 'officers of the court' they should be given a monopoly of legal knowledge as they will play a strong enough role in protecting society from people who break the law? Is this likely?
3. Again, the answers will depend upon the experiences of the learners. The educator should guide them in determining whether the trouble involved the law and whether knowledge of Street law would have helped the persons concerned. If the experiences lead to complicated legal questions educators should tell learners that they will attempt to deal with these later on in the course or refer them to legal advice outside of class. The exercise should be used to create general interest rather than provide detailed legal answers to the problems raised.

1.1.2   What is law? *(Learner's Manual p 7)*

Some time could be spent discussing definitions of law and the reasons for law. How does law differ from rules? Do parents make 'the law' at home? In South Africa, laws are made by Parliament, government organisations and town authorities.

Problem 3: Did the law touch you today? *(Learner's Manual p 7)*

AIM: The purpose of this activity is to show how the law affects every aspect of our daily lives, and to indicate that the law is usually more concerned with protecting people than punishing them.

<table>
<tr><td>

PROCEDURE ☰

1. Ask learners to write down the first activity they did in the morning.
2. Ask them to share their answers.
3. Record their answers on the blackboard or flipchart using the headings given below.
4. Ask learners if they think that there is any law affecting the activity; if so, which?
5. Ask them the reason for the law.
6. Ask them if the law should be changed.
7. General discussion and summary.

</td><td>

TIME 🕐

Individual work:	2 min
Question and answer:	38 min
Discussion and summary:	5 min
TOTAL:	**45 min**

</td></tr>
</table>

Note: Instead of using the Procedure mentioned above, the educator could show the learners a photograph or picture (eg of a busy street scene) and ask them to point out everything that they think is law related: for example, the educator could use the cartoon for Problem 5 at the end of para 1.1.2 in the *Learner's Manual*.

Write up the following headings across the blackboard or flipchart and record the learners' reactions under each heading:

Activities	**Reasons**
Affected by law?	Should the law be changed?
How?	Why or why not?

Problem 4: The case of the shipwrecked sailors   *(Learner's Manual p 8)*

AIM: The questions are designed to develop reasoning skills and to show learners how the law would be argued in a murder case. The educator should ask questions to make sure that at the end all sides to each question are brought out during the discussions.

<table>
<tr><td>

PROCEDURE ☰

1. Ask class as a whole what the facts are.
2. Divide class into small groups of five each.
3. Ask group 1 to prepare arguments for the prosecution, group 2 to prepare arguments for the defence, group 3 to imagine they are the judges, group 4 to imagine that they are sentencing experts and group 5 to be legal philosophers. Repeat for additional groups.
4. Ask group 1 to present arguments for the prosecution.
5. Ask group 2 to present arguments for the defence.
6. Ask group 3 to give their judgments.
7. Ask group 4 to give their sentences, assuming that the sailors were found guilty of murder.
8. Ask group 5 to explain the link between law and morality in the case.
9. Conclude with general class discussion and summary.

</td><td>

TIME 🕐

Identifying facts:	10 min
Group preparations:	10 min
Group presentations:	15 min
Discussion and summary:	10 min
TOTAL:	**40 min**

</td></tr>
</table>

1. Learners may argue that Dan and Sam should be charged with murder because they intentionally killed another person. Those who disagree may argue that because of the special circumstances, their acts did not constitute a serious crime. Rather, they should be charged with a less serious crime (eg manslaughter or 'culpable homicide' – see Part 2 Criminal law below) or not charged at all.

2. The lawyer (in this case, an 'advocate' – see *Learner's Manual*, para 1.4.1.2.1) acting for Dan and Sam could argue that the special circumstances must be taken into account and even though they killed a person, because of their situation, they should not be punished further. The lawyer could argue that because Dan and Sam went without food for 25 days, their minds had been affected and they could no longer distinguish between right and wrong (like insanity). It could also be argued that Bob had made an agreement (a 'contract', or even a law, that they had all agreed to, which he should not have broken). The lawyer could also argue that, in order for Dan and Sam to survive, it was necessary for them to kill Bob. ('Necessity' is sometimes recognised as a defence in criminal law – see Part 2 Criminal law.)

3. The lawyer acting for the State (the 'prosecutor') could argue that human life is sacred and that a person who kills another must be tried for breaking the law and to discourage others from committing murder (deterrence). If this were not done, society would be condoning what had happened. The state prosecutor could also argue that Bob had withdrawn his consent before the killing. In any event, maybe Bob's mind was so affected by his weakness and lack of food that he could not give a proper consent.

4. When considering whether or not they should be punished, the purposes of punishment should be kept in mind. These are usually listed as:
   (a) Retribution – punishment to satisfy the outrage of society.
   (b) Deterrence – punishment to stop the criminal from doing the act again or to frighten other people into not doing the act.
   (c) Rehabilitation – treatment of the criminal to change his or her behaviour so that he or she will not commit the crime again (generally, see below para 2.13.3 in *Learner's Manual*).
   (d) Incapacitation – keeping the criminal in an institution (eg a prison) to prevent him or her from harming society by committing crime again. (Generally, see below para 2.13.3 in *Learner's Manual*).
   (Note: Encourage learners to give reasons for their different approaches to the question of punishment. After discussing the questions, learners might be interested to learn the actual verdict and sentence mentioned below.)

5. Ask learners how the different purposes of punishment – retribution, deterrence, rehabilitation and incapacitation – would be served by convicting Dan and Sam. It could be argued that punishing them would not really serve as a deterrent because the situation was unique. Furthermore, there is no strong argument for rehabilitation since Dan and Sam would probably never commit such a crime again. Likewise, incapacitation is unnecessary. The only purpose of punishment here is retribution.

6. Traditional ideas of morality prohibit taking the life of another person under almost any circumstances but there are also moral arguments in favour of taking life, eg in self-defence or defence of another to save life (in this case, to save their own lives). There are also legal questions on both sides of the case – but they tend to be technical rather than moral ideas of right and wrong (eg were Dan and Sam insane? What law applied in the lifeboat?). Learners will have their own ideas as to why they think it was, or was not, morally wrong for Dan and Sam to kill Bob. Was it moral for Bob to withdraw his consent after he had lost the toss?

7. Learners should try to think of acts that may be legal but immoral, or moral but illegal. For example, a person who sees a crime being committed but does not report it may be acting legally but immorally. Likewise, a person living under the apartheid regime who laid a complaint with the police that someone of the 'wrong' race was living in their neighbourhood might have been acting legally but immorally in the eyes of many South Africans and people in other parts of the world. Similarly, people living under apartheid who were engaged in civil disobedience (eg demonstrating, attending prohibited funerals or peaceful meetings) while exercising their human rights, may have been acting illegally under South African law even though their actions may have been moral according to the views of many other people. Sometimes, people make decisions to disobey laws that they personally believe are immoral, and suffer the consequences of their acts.

Note: This case will be of great interest to learners. For information on how to use case studies in *Street law* see above para G4. This case raises important moral questions: Should Dan and Sam be punished for what they did? Was their conduct excusable? Was the agreement to kill one of them moral?

Learners may have seen films or TV shows or read books or newspapers about similar cases which raise these issues (eg when a ship is sinking and not everyone can fit into the life boat, who should be saved?).

Some of the issues which can be discussed in answering the specific questions involve:
(a) The historical, moral and religious reasons for prohibiting the killing of human beings.
(b) The relationship of law to society: did the sailors in their small boat far away from anyone constitute their own society? Did they make their own laws? Do certain laws, for example, those against killing, supersede manmade laws?
(c) The effect of the agreement: did they make a legally enforceable contract?
(d) Is cannibalism (eating people) acceptable to society (or any societies)?
(e) The decision by the court in the real case:
The problem is based on the old English case of *Regina v Dudley & Stephens* reported in 1884, where the court found both men guilty of murder and sentenced them to death. There was a public outcry and soon after the verdict, Queen Victoria changed the sentence to six months in prison.

Problem 5: Imagine there were no laws   *(Learner's Manual p 10)*

AIM: The object of this exercise is to make learners aware of the need for laws of some kind in any community.

PROCEDURE		
1. Ask class as a whole to answer question 1.		
2. Divide class into small groups of five each.		
3. Ask group 1 to discuss question 2, group 2 to discuss question 3, group 3 to discuss question 2 and group 4 to discuss question 3. Repeat for additional groups.		
4. Get reports back from each group.		
5. Conclude with general class discussion and summary.		

TIME	
Identifying problem:	5 min
Group discussions:	10 min
Reports back:	15 min
Discussion and summary:	15 min
TOTAL:	**45 min**

1. If large cities did not have traffic lights, there would be traffic hold ups at intersections. This would be especially so during peak hours in the mornings and evenings when people are trying to go to, and from, work. There would be traffic jams all over the cities and chaos on the roads. There would probably also be many more accidents as people race each other to get through the intersections first. There are, however, laws that say that motorists must slow down at intersections and keep a proper lookout.

   If there were traffic lights but no laws against going through a red light, there would also be chaos on the roads. People would not know when to stop, and even if they did, might try to go through the red lights when they were in a hurry. They would be tempted to do this because they could not be fined or punished for going through red lights. This might lead to an increase in accidents. There is, however, a law which says that motorists must keep a proper lookout and slow down at intersections.

2. If there were no laws against stealing, people might not respect each other's property. People might be tempted to take or use other people's things without asking for permission. Many more people are likely to steal if they know that they will not be criminally prosecuted. This cannot be taken too far, however, since many poor people steal out of desperation or need.

   Most people would probably agree that if there were no laws against stealing, there would probably be far more thieves in society.

3. Some learners may think that people are selfish and will only do what is fair or moral if the law tells them to do so. People are human beings who have faults and do not always do what is right. This is illustrated by an American case where a woman was viciously beaten and raped in a street while people in nearby flats watched for a long time before calling the police. Other learners may believe in the 'inherent goodness' of human nature and that people subscribe to the idea of 'love your neighbour as yourself'. They would argue that basically all human beings are good and will do what is moral for their fellows without the law requiring them to do so.

The Pen game (optional)

AIM: The Pen game helps to show why it is necessary to have laws or rules that include ideas of fairness and certainty and are not retrospective. It also raises problems of discrimination. The game can be easily adapted to meet the needs of the participants.

PROCEDURE
1. Tell the participants they will play a game.
2. Divide participants into teams of five each.
3. Appoint team captains for each team.
4. Tell the participants to start playing the game.
5. Stop the game and change the rules after each explanation of a new rule.
6. Arbitrarily choose a winning team.
7. Conclude by relating the rules of the game to laws in a democratic society.

TIME	
Introducing the game:	2 min
Dividing into teams and appointing team captains:	3 min
Playing the game:	5 min
Linking the rules of the game to laws in a democratic society:	5 min
Discussion and summary:	5 min
TOTAL:	**20 min**

The Pen game is played as follows:

Step 1: The teacher announces that the need for some sort of legal system will be illustrated by playing a game.

Step 2: The teacher checks that each student has a pen (or a paper clip, a match stick, sweet or any other suitable object). Once the teacher is satisfied that each student has a pen (or other object) the teacher informs them that they will be playing the 'pen' (or some other object) game.

Step 3: The teacher tells the students that as it is a game they need to be in teams and divides them into teams using small groups, or by rows if they are in a class room setting.

Step 4: The teacher tells the students that as they have teams they need to have team captains and designates the students on the right hand side of each group or row as the team captains.

Step 5: The teacher checks that the students know who is in their teams, who their team captains are and that they are playing the Pen game.

Step 6: The teacher tells the students to start playing the Pen game – ignoring any requests for rules.

Step 7: The teacher allows the students to make up their own rules regarding the game for a couple of minutes but then tells them that they are not playing the game properly.

Step 8: The teacher tells the team captains to pass the pen to the team members on their left and restarts the game. After a minute or so the teacher stops them and tells them that they are not playing the game properly.

Step 9: The teacher tells the team captains to hold the pen in their right hands and then to pass it to the team member on their left. After a minute or so the teacher again stops them and tells them that they are not playing the game properly.

Step 10: The teacher tells the team captains to hold the pen in their right hands, pass it to their left hand, and then pass it to the team member on their left. After a minute or so the teacher again stops them and tells them that they are not playing the game properly.

Step 11: The teacher tells the team captains to hold the pen in their right hands, pass it to their left hand, and then pass it to the right hand of the team member on their left. After a minute or so the teacher again stops them and tells them that they are still not playing the game properly.

Step 12: The teacher tells the team captains to hold the pen in their right hands, pass it to their left hand, pass it to the right hand of the team member on their left – but not to any members wearing spectacles (or any other distinguishing feature such as rings or clothes of a certain colour). After a minute or so the teacher again stops the game and arbitrarily chooses one of the teams as the winners.

Step 13: The teacher debriefs the game to find out how the students felt about it, why they felt the way they did, and what they learnt from the game.

Step 14: Summary and conclusion: The teacher checks that the students understand why society needs laws to prevent confusion and chaos, laws should not work retrospectively, laws should not discriminate against people, people should have access to impartial courts that apply the rule of law, citizens should participate in the lawmaking process.

The Pen game teaches knowledge and values – students not only learn why we need laws in society but also appreciate why laws are necessary.

When the 'winners' are announced, most of the remaining learners are likely to be dissatisfied about how the game was run. This dissatisfaction is used as a basis for discussion. The teacher can begin with the following questions: What made you dissatisfied about the way the game was played? Why was it unfair?

The answers should be directed to emphasise five main elements:

(a) A game cannot be enjoyed without a clear and consistent set of rules announced to all players before it begins. For example, the courts in South Africa will sometimes refuse to enforce laws that are written in an unclear way or are too vague.

(b) The rules cannot be changed in the middle of the game without feelings being hurt. For example, laws cannot be changed to make previously lawful conduct unlawful without warning people about the change beforehand. People cannot be charged with doing something that only became a crime after they did it. This applies in most democratic countries.

(c) Certain groups of individuals should not be arbitrarily discriminated against. Everyone should be treated equally. This applies in most democratic countries. In South Africa under apartheid laws discriminated against people on the grounds of race. This is now specifically outlawed in terms of the Constitution.

(d) Decisions regarding disputes should not be made arbitrarily. People should have access to independent and impartial persons or bodies who apply the rules fairly when making a decision. (This applies to access to courts in democratic countries.)

(e) Some learners might observe that the manner in which the game was played was undemocratic because the rules were imposed upon the participants without consultation. Such learners would be raising the question of being allowed to vote for representatives who make the laws that govern their society.

The class should be encouraged to see the relationship between the rules of the Pen game and laws in a society. Before leaving the game, the teacher should try to develop a definition of what law should be, based on the class experience in the game. Obviously the theory of what the law 'should be' is not always what 'it actually is' in practice. The difference between theory and practice will often come up in studying Street law.

A simple definition of law might be: 'The set of rules a group or community uses to control the conduct of the people within it'. These rules should be clear, consistent, fair, should not change without notice, should treat people equally, and should not be applied arbitrarily. People who are governed by rules should have the right to elect representatives responsible for making such rules.

1.2 Where law comes from, how it is made, and the different kinds of law

Outcomes

After completion of this section learners will be able to:

1. Demonstrate an understanding of where law comes from, how it is interpreted, and the different kinds of law.

Assessment criteria

1. An explanation is given of where South African law comes from and how it is made.

2. An explanation is given of how the Constitution operates.

3. Sets of facts are examined and decisions are taken on whether any rights in the Bill of Rights have been violated.

4. A set of facts in a case is examined and a decision is taken on whether the Constitutional Court should have abolished corporal punishment for juvenile offenders.

5. A set of facts is examined and a decision is taken on how the court would interpret the law.

6. A set of facts in a case is examined and a decision is taken on whether the judge calculated the damages correctly.

7. A set of facts is examined and a decision is taken on which acts were crimes and which were civil wrongs.

1.2.1 Where South African law comes from *(Learner's Manual p 11)*

Problem 1: The origin of South African law *(Learner's Manual p 12)*

AIM: The purpose of these questions is to make learners aware of the origins of South African law and how law evolves over time.

PROCEDURE	TIME	
1. Introduce the topic.	Introduction:	2 min
2. Divide class into small groups of five each.	Group discussions:	10 min
3. Ask group 1 to discuss question 1, group 2 to discuss question 2, group 3 to discuss question 3 and group 4 to discuss question 4 – repeat for additional groups.	Reports back:	15 min
	Discussion and summary:	3 min
	TOTAL:	**30 min**
4. Get reports back from each group.		
5. Conclude with general class discussion and summary.		

1. South African law comes from a mixture of legal systems. It is mainly Roman-Dutch, but there have been English influences especially in court procedures, and the law relating to companies, banks, insurance and shipping. Many of these influences are found in statute law, which is based

on English statutes. The common law in South Africa, however, is mainly Roman-Dutch law. The new democratic Constitution now requires that all law in South Africa, no matter where it comes from, must be in line with the provisions and values of the Constitution.

2. The legal system that has had the greatest influence on South African law in terms of the common law is Roman-Dutch law. This is probably because the Dutch ruled the Cape for about 150 years before it was taken over by the British. By that time Roman-Dutch law had become firmly rooted as the common law of the Cape Colony. It was then taken by the Dutch settlers to the interior of the country when the 'Voortrekkers' left on the 'Great Trek' to escape the Cape Colony's laws prohibiting slavery.

    Roman-Dutch law was used in the former Boer republics including those that eventually became the provinces of the Orange Free State and the Transvaal after the Union of South Africa in 1910. Since then it has been accepted throughout South Africa as the common law of the country.

3. Learners might argue that customary law is no longer so important because South African society has moved from a subsistence agricultural-based economy to a sophisticated farming, industrial and highly technological society. What was once a large number of simple village communities has now been replaced by large city populations. The extended family has been replaced by the nuclear family. African families were broken up under apartheid by the migrant labour system and influx control, which prevented families from living together in the cities. Customary law is generally unsuitable in a technological and commercial society that needs to protect its citizens from the dangers of modern technology (eg cars and machines) and exploitation in the market place. However, customary law is still important for rural communities living in family groups. Some might argue that Africans were better off under customary law when they lived in small villages. If in future African family groups again begin to live together, there may be a demand for the revival of customary law. Learners opposed to customary law would argue that it is an old-fashioned legal system that should be replaced with modern South African law. The new Constitution now requires that all customary law must be in line with the values and provisions of the Constitution.

4. Here learners should recognise how law is essentially imposed by whoever the rulers of a country are during a particular period in history. Before the Dutch arrived, customary law was used by the different African rulers. When the Dutch took power, they introduced the Roman-Dutch legal system. When the English took over, they left the Roman-Dutch law intact but influenced it by appointing judges trained in England and passing statutes based on English law. After Union in 1910 there was a move towards a 'South African' legal system based on Roman-Dutch law principles. Our laws are largely based on a European model. Some people argue that in time a more African legal system will develop. For instance, in Zimbabwe community courts and traditional medicine are recognised by the law. However, in most countries in Africa (eg Zimbabwe, Nigeria) and Asia (eg Hong Kong, India, Sri Lanka) the European legal systems have been retained because they are necessary for commerce and industry in a modern technological society. The new Constitution will affect how laws are interpreted in South Africa. If the laws are unconstitutional they will be declared invalid by the courts.

1.2.2　How South African law is made
(Learner's Manual p 13)

Problem 2: Some questions on the Constitution　_(Learner's Manual p 14)_

AIM: The object of this exercise is for learners to understand the nature of the South African Constitution, the meaning of concepts such as 'sovereign' and 'separation of powers', and to appreciate the difference between living under a democratic Constitution and what life would have been like under apartheid.

PROCEDURE ☰	TIME 🕐	
1. Introduce the exercise.	Introduction:	2 min
2. Divide the learners into small groups of five people each.	Group discussions:	10 min
3. Ask each group to answer one question.	Reports back:	15 min
4. Get reports back from each group.	Discussion and summary:	3 min
5. Conclude with general class discussion and summary.	**TOTAL:**	**30 min**

1. The doctrine of 'separation of powers' refers to the distinction between the legislature (the parliament), the executive (the President and Ministers) and the judiciary (the judges). Each has functions that are independent from the others. The legislature passes laws, the executive implements the laws, and the judiciary interprets the laws. The separation of powers is important because if one branch of government (eg the executive) were to take over all the powers of the other two branches (eg parliament and the judiciary), the result would be a dictatorship instead of a democracy.

2. Some learners might say that having a Constitution and a Bill of Rights protects them from being subjected to the abuses that existed under apartheid such as institutionalised racial discrimination, detention without trial and blatant interferences with their family life such as laws stating where they could live, where they had to go to school or university, whom they could marry and with whom they could have sex. These laws could be passed under a 'sovereign' Parliament because there was no Constitution and Bill of Rights to allow the courts to say that such laws were against the Constitution and invalid. However, others might say that things were better under an apartheid 'sovereign' parliament because, even if there was racial discrimination, at least there was much less crime and the death penalty could be imposed on murderers and rapists who could not rely on a Bill of Rights to protect them.

Problem 3: Which rights in the Bill of Rights were violated?　_(Learner's Manual p 16)_

AIM: The aim of the exercise is for the learners to identify which rights in the Bill of Rights of the people in the different scenarios have been violated.

PROCEDURE ☰	TIME 🕐	
1. Introduce the cases.	Introduction:	2 min
2. Divide the learners into small groups of five people each.	Group discussions:	10 min
3. Ask each group to answer one question.	Reports back:	15 min
4. Get reports back from each group.	Discussion and summary:	3 min
5. Conclude with general class discussion and summary.	**TOTAL:**	**30 min**

1. The right violated here is the right not to be refused emergency medical treatment. The private hospital may not refuse to treat a person who is seriously injured and requires an urgent blood transfusion – even if the person is unemployed and cannot afford to pay for the hospital's services. The private hospital must stabilise the person and then refer him to a public hospital for treatment (s 27).

2. The right violated here is the right to bail if the interests of justice permit, subject to reasonable conditions. The foreigner is legally employed and resident in South Africa so it is not likely that he will leave the country. A reasonable condition might be that he has to surrender his passport and report to the police station once a day (s 35).

3. The right violated here is the right not to be arbitrarily deprived of property. The police should have given the craftsman a receipt and a chance to recover his property if he is not charged with and convicted of a crime. The right to choose one's trade, profession or occupation freely is limited to citizens, but does not mean that foreigners are not entitled to work if they are permanent residents, are refugees or have work permits.

4. The rights violated here are the right not to be unfairly discriminated against and the right to fair labour practices. It would be unfair discrimination to dismiss a domestic worker solely on the basis of her HIV status. It would also be an unfair labour practice.

5. The right violated here is the child's right to life. The other rights violated here are the right of the child to basic health services and not to be refused emergency medical treatment. In any event the courts and the Children's Act state that parents or guardians of children may not refuse medical treatment for children solely on religious grounds.

Problem 4: A case about corporal punishment   *(Learner's Manual p 17)*

AIM: The object of this exercise is for learners to understand which rights in the Constitution are violated by sentencing juveniles to corporal punishment and to decide whether they believe that corporal punishment should be allowed.

PROCEDURE	TIME	
1. Introduce the case.	Introduction:	2 min
2. Divide the learners into small groups of five people each.	Group discussions:	10 min
3. Ask each group to answer one question.	Reports back:	15 min
4. Get reports back from each group.	Discussion and summary:	3 min
5. Conclude with general class discussion and summary.	**TOTAL:**	**30 min**

1. The answer is in the *Learner's Manual*. The Constitutional Court in the *Williams* case held that juvenile whippings violate the rights to dignity, not to be subjected to torture, and not to be subjected to cruel, inhuman or degrading punishment.

2. The court held that the violation of the above rights is not justifiable because other more creative humane forms of punishment could be used. An example of this would be community service where juveniles could be sentenced to do something to assist the community. Furthermore, there is no evidence that whipping would prevent juveniles from committing crimes any more than other forms of punishment.

3. Some learners may agree with the Constitutional Court decision and others may not. Some learners may suggest that if juveniles are convicted of a violent crime they should be subjected to violence themselves. Others may say that violence just leads to more violence and that attempts should be made to reform juveniles rather than punish them with whipping.

Problem 5: Statute law and common law (Learner's Manual p 18)

AIM: The questions are aimed at ensuring that learners know the difference between common law and statute law and how these laws can be changed.

PROCEDURE	TIME	
1. Introduce the questions.	Introduction:	2 min
2. Divide the learners into small groups of five people each.	Group discussions:	10 min
3. Ask each group to answer one question.	Reports back:	20 min
4. Get reports back from each group.	Discussion and summary:	3 min
5. Conclude with general class discussion and summary.	**TOTAL:**	**35 min**

1. The answer is in the *Learner's Manual*. Statute law is made by Parliament (the highest law-making body) or some other law-making body like a provincial legislature, or a municipality. Statute law is written and published in the *Government Gazette*. Common law comes from the old Roman and Roman-Dutch law writers and judgments in court decisions that have interpreted what the old writings mean. Nowadays, both statute and common law must be in line with the Constitution, otherwise they may be declared invalid by the Constitutional Court.

2. The common law can be changed by Parliament, the Supreme Court of Appeal or the Constitutional Court. Parliament can pass a statute changing the common law. The Supreme Court of Appeal or the Constitutional Court can establish a precedent and give the common law a new meaning.

3. Statute law can be changed by Parliament or the law-making body or person who made the law, or it can be declared invalid by the Constitutional Court if it conflicts with the new Constitution. If Parliament has given other bodies or people the power to make laws, Parliament itself can still change laws made by them or even take away their power. The Constitutional Court can declare statutes that conflict with the Constitution invalid. Judges will now interpret statute law against what they think the Constitution intended. Judges will ensure that Parliament does not take away people's common law and statutory rights which are guaranteed by the Constitution.

4. If a town council passes an unfair by-law, the law could be changed by the council itself making a new law or by the Province or Parliament making a new statute, or by the Supreme Court or Constitutional Court holding that it conflicts with the Constitution. In addition, a court may be asked to interpret the law in such a way as to give it a fair meaning. A court may also be asked to decide whether the town council has exceeded its powers. If the court finds that it has, the law will not be enforced. But if a town council was given the power to make such a by-law, it may be legal even though it is unfair, as long as it does not conflict with the Constitution.

Problem 6: A case of pain and suffering

(Learner's Manual p 19)

AIM: This problem is designed to help learners understand what is meant by a precedent and the binding effect of precedents on other courts.

PROCEDURE		TIME	
1. Introduce the case.		Introduction:	2 min
2. Divide the learners into small groups of five people each.		Group discussions:	10 min
3. Ask each group to answer one question.		Reports back:	15 min
4. Get reports back from each group.		Discussion and summary:	3 min
5. Conclude with general class discussion and summary.		**TOTAL:**	**30 min**

At the outset it should be pointed out to learners that the case was decided in 1949 when the rand was worth a lot more than it is now. For instance, a rand in 1949 was probably worth 100 times or more what it is today. In this case Radebe had been severely wounded in his private parts. He had been in hospital for 10 days and had suffered severe pain for three months. He would continue to suffer some pain and scarring for the rest of his life.

1. The precedent set was that a court which awards damages for pain and suffering must not be influenced by the race, culture or economic position of victims. In other words, a person's race, culture, class or wealth does not affect the amount of pain suffered.

2. As this was an Appellate Division (now Supreme Court of Appeal) decision, it has to be followed by all the courts in the land including the High and magistrates' courts.

3. If this precedent had been set by the Natal Provincial Division it would have to be followed by all the courts in KwaZulu-Natal. It would not be binding on courts in the other provinces, although they may be influenced by it.

4. Parliament, or the Supreme Court of Appeal itself, can change a precedent made by the Supreme Court of Appeal. The latter may occur if another similar case is brought before it.

5. Learners should argue both sides of the case. Learners deciding in favour of Radebe may argue that all human beings (except perhaps those used to pain, like boxers and wrestlers) suffer the same amount of pain and their race or culture should make no difference. Also whether people are rich or poor should not affect the amount of pain they suffer. Those in favour of Hough might say that money is the only thing that the courts can use to compensate people for pain and suffering and other damages, and the court should consider how much that money will be worth to the person claiming it. Therefore, a little money will mean a lot more to a poor person than to a rich person. Another argument might be that people of different cultures have different standards of living and some classes of people need less money than others. As a general rule, however, the courts believe it is unfair that a particular race or class of people who happen to be wealthier than others should receive more damages for pain and suffering. They would, of course, be able to claim higher damages if their injuries resulted in lost wages because they would be earning more and therefore have actually lost more wages. The 'equality clause' in the new Constitution means that everybody now has to be treated equally irrespective of their race, gender, creed, etc (see the box in *Learner's Manual* para 1.2.2.1).

Problem 7: No vehicles in the park! (Learner's Manual p 21)

AIM: This exercise is aimed at showing learners how a written law can be given different interpretations depending on whether the people interpreting the law base their arguments on:

(a) The letter of the law.
(b) What they think the intention of the lawmakers is.
(c) Their own sense of what they think the law should be.

The courts usually follow (a) and (b) above.

PROCEDURE	TIME	
1. Ask the learners to read the exercise.	Reading the exercise:	5 min
2. Divide class into small groups of five each.	Group discussions:	10 min
3. Allocate one case to each group to decide whether or not the vehicle should be allowed in the park.	Reports back:	20 min
4. Get reports back from each group and record on blackboard grid.	Discussion and summary:	5 min
5. Conclude with general class discussion and summary.	**TOTAL:**	**40 min**

Tell each group that it will be expected to give reasons for its answers. Groups may wish to appoint a spokesperson for the whole exercise or have different spokespersons to record the answers and reasons for each case study.

Other problems may be added like an ice cream seller pushing an ice cream cart or a person pulling a riksha. Each group will need about 10 minutes to arrive at their answers for their case. The educator should check that the groups are working properly and then record the answers and reasons for them on the blackboard, eg:

Groups	1	2	3	4	5	6
Cases	**Examples**	**Examples**				
1. Wheelchair	Allowed – Intention of law	 – Does not disturb				
2. Rubbish trucks	Not allowed – Disturb park – Letter of law	Allowed – Keeps park clean – Intention of law				
3. Police cars	Allowed – Emergency – Intention of law – Own feelings	Not allowed – Police can't break law				

4. Ambulance	Allowed – Emergency – Intention of law	Not allowed – Will die anyway – Letter of law				
5. Bicycles & skateboards	Allowed – Children should play – Intention of law	Not allowed – Disturb others – Letter of law				
6. Pram	Allowed – Not disturbing – Intention of law – Letter of law	Not allowed – Disturb people on grass				
7. Army truck	Not allowed – Spoil park – Own feeling against war	Allowed – Commemorating dead – Intention of law				

Once the groups have arrived at their answers, the educator should ask spokespersons from each group to give their decisions in each case and then record the responses on the blackboard. The reasons for the decisions should also be recorded for each group. The educator should point out how the decisions of the group reflect reasons based on: (a) the letter of the law; (b) what they thought the intent of the law-makers was; and (c) their own sense of values.

At the end the educator should ask the learners if the law could be rewritten to avoid the problems they have discussed. Should law be written in detail so that citizens can predict accurately what it means? Should laws be flexible so that they can meet changing situations? Can they be both?

How should 'emergency' situations be provided for in the law? Who should determine what constitutes an emergency?

What is an appropriate penalty for breaking this law? Should the penalty be included in the law? Is there any remedy for citizens if the police break the law? (Probably only if they have been injured by the police – although they could lay a complaint against the police themselves.)

1.2.3 Kinds of law

(Learner's Manual p 23)

The difference between criminal and civil law is often difficult for learners to understand, particularly where some breaches of the law involve both criminal and civil law. For instance, in an assault case, the wrongdoer may be punished criminally by the state for breaking society's law against people assaulting one another, and made to pay civil damages for compensation to the person injured. Likewise, negligent drivers of cars may be criminally liable for breaking a traffic law (eg by going through a red traffic light), but will only be civilly liable if they injure other people or their property.

Problem 8: The case of the juvenile delinquents (Learner's Manual p 23)

AIM: The object of this exercise is for learners to recognise which acts are unlawful, which are crimes, which are civil wrongs, and which are both.

PROCEDURE ≣		TIME ⊙	
1. Introduce the case study.		Introduction:	2 min
2. Divide the learners into small groups of five people each.		Group discussions:	10 min
3. Ask each group to answer one question.		Reports back:	15 min
4. Get reports back from each group.		Discussion and summary:	3 min
5. Conclude with general class discussion and summary.		**TOTAL:**	**30 min**

1. The following acts are unlawful:
   (a) stealing bicycles;
   (b) riding through a red traffic light;
   (c) selling a radio that does not work properly;
   (d) knocking over an old woman; and
   (e) assaulting the dishonest shopkeeper.
   (What about if they had run away from school for the day? They might be punished by their principals, and threatened with expulsion if they continue to absent themselves.)
   It would not be unlawful for the boys to damage their own property, unless they then tried to defraud the shopkeeper by saying that the radio did not work after they had broken it.

2. The following acts are crimes (see *Learner's Manual* Part 2 Criminal law):
   (a) stealing bicycles (crime of theft);
   (b) riding through a red traffic light (crime of disobeying a traffic law);
   (c) knocking over the old lady (crime – if the bicycle was ridden negligently ie dangerously, so that John ought to have foreseen that he would have run someone over if he did not take care); and
   (d) assaulting the shopkeeper (crime of assault).
   (Note: Technically, it would be the crime of fraud knowingly to sell a radio that does not work. The police, however, are unlikely to act unless the shopkeeper is doing this to a lot of people).

3. The following acts are civil wrongs:
   (a) the shopkeeper selling a radio that does not work properly (the boys can claim their money back);
   (b) knocking over the old woman and injuring her (she may claim damages for her injuries and for the damage to her property. This may also be criminal – see above); and
   (c) assaulting the dishonest shopkeeper (the boys would have to pay for any medical expenses, lost earnings, and injuries suffered by him – this is also a criminal act).
   (Note: The fact that the boys were angry because they had been sold a radio which did not work does not excuse their conduct. However, this fact may be taken into account by the court to reduce the punishment in a criminal case.

4. The following acts are both crimes and civil wrongs:
   (a) knocking over the old woman and injuring her; and
   (b) assaulting the dishonest shopkeeper.
   (Note: If John and Peter had damaged the stolen bicycles, they could also have been sued civilly by the owners for the value of the damage to the bicycles.)

1.3 The courts and settling disputes outside of the courts

Outcomes

After completion of this section learners will be able to:

1. Demonstrate an understanding of how the courts and other dispute resolution mechanisms work

Assessment criteria

1. An explanation of the different courts in South Africa is given.
2. A decision is taken on how magistrates should be appointed.
3. A set of facts in a case is examined and a decision taken on whether people were entitled to take the law into their own hands.
4. A stated problem is solved using negotiation, mediation and arbitration.
5. Sets of facts are examined and a decision is taken on the best method of resolving different disputes.

1.3.1 The different courts in South Africa *(Learner's Manual p 25)*

Problem 1: How should magistrates be appointed? *(Learner's Manual p 29)*

AIM: The object of this exercise is for learners to think about how magistrates are appointed and their role on the bench.

PROCEDURE
1. Introduce the exercise.
2. Divide the learners into small groups of five people each.
3. Ask group 1 to discuss question 1, group 2 to discuss question 2, group 3 to discuss question 3, and group 4 to discuss question 4 - repeat for additional groups.
4. Get reports back from each group.
5. Conclude with general class discussion and summary.

TIME	
Introduction:	2 min
Group discussions:	10 min
Reports back:	15 min
Discussion and summary:	3 min
TOTAL:	**30 min**

1. Some learners may say that it is better that magistrates are appointed by the Magistrates Commission because it gives the magistrates more independence. If they are appointed by the Minister of Justice, they would not be regarded as independent because he or she is the government Minister in charge of the prosecutors. However, magistrates are still regarded as civil servants. Thus the same learners may argue that in criminal cases many of the statutory crimes have been created by the government and it would be unfair for a government-appointed officer to decide whether or not a person is guilty.

   Other learners might argue that South Africa is no different from most other countries in Africa, Europe and Asia where magistrates are also government officials. A more relevant argument may be that it is appropriate for the lower courts to be manned by civil servants as long as there is an independent High Court to watch over them. In any event, magistrates should be there to find the truth, not to convict people. (In England magistrates are private people and not career civil servants.)

2. Arguments in favour of the present system of appointing magistrates are to be found in the *Learner's Manual*. They include the fact that magistrates are now appointed by the Magistrates Commission and not the Minister of Justice. In any event magistrates are trained to be 'independent' and usually have experience as prosecutors with training in how to find the truth. Another argument may be that even if some magistrates tend to favour the State and impose heavy sentences of imprisonment or fines on unrepresented accused persons, their cases will go on automatic review to the High Court (see *Learner's Manual* para 1.3.1.7).

3. Arguments against the present system are to be found in the *Learner's Manual*. These include the fact that even if magistrates are appointed by the Magistrates Commission they are still civil servants and are likely to be prejudiced in favour of the government because most magistrates have trained as prosecutors. Magistrates should also be required to obtain experience as defence lawyers so that they have seen both sides of the criminal process.

4. Learners may decide whether they think the system should be changed or not depending on their responses in 1–3 above. Magistrates have been given more independence by being appointed by the Magistrates Commission instead of the Minister of Justice. Some senior magistrates are also being appointed from private practitioners.

Problem 2: Should there be separate traditional courts for Africans?
(Learner's Manual p 31)

AIM: The object of this exercise is for learners to think about whether there should be separate courts for Africans or whether the system should be changed.

PROCEDURE	TIME	
1. Introduce the exercise.	Introduction:	2 min
2. Divide the learners into small groups of five people each.	Group discussions:	10 min
3. Ask each group to discuss both questions.	Reports back:	15 min
4. Get reports back from each group.	Discussion and summary:	3 min
5. Conclude with general class discussion and summary.	**TOTAL:**	**30 min**

1. Some learners may argue that separate courts should be used, particularly in the rural areas where chiefs and headmen still control their communities. In many of the remoter villages there are no magistrates' courts and chiefs and headmen can settle disputes themselves. If the parties are not satisfied with the decision of a chief or headman, they can appeal against it or bring a new action in a magistrate's court.

   Others might argue that separate courts for Africans reinforce tribalism, and that instead of sitting in a court, chiefs and headmen should act as 'mediators' (see *Learner's Manual* para 1.3.2.2). As far as possible, the same courts should be used for all South Africans irrespective of race. A solution, however, may be for proceedings in all courts to be simplified so that they can be used more cheaply.

2. Whether or not the courts should be changed will depend upon which arguments appeal to the learners. There is no right or wrong answer:

(a) Some of the arguments against separate courts were discussed in question 1. For instance, chiefs' and headmen's courts reinforce tribalism and apartheid by emphasising the difference between Africans and other South Africans. Other arguments are that most chiefs and headmen are not legally trained and would be better suited to act as mediators than judicial officers or arbitrators. There are also no proper written records of their court proceedings. (Dissatisfied parties, however, may begin afresh in the magistrate's court.)

(b) The arguments in favour of separate courts have also been discussed in question 1. These include the fact that separate courts make the law more accessible to Africans in rural areas. Other arguments may be that proceedings in these courts are simple, cheap and quick. It might also be argued that rural people are more at home in a chiefs' or headmen's court than in a magistrate's court.

Problem 3: Which court should be used? *(Learner's Manual p 33)*

AIM: The purpose of these exercises is to make learners aware of the different courts that can be used by people wishing to go to court. In some cases there is more than one court available to parties (eg the small claims court instead of the magistrate's court). Generally, learners should be encouraged to use and suggest that people use the cheapest and quickest court. Sometimes, however, it may be better to use a slower, more expensive, court to obtain justice, for example, in cases where, with the assistance of a lawyer, there is better chance of winning. Learners should be reminded that many cases can be settled out of court (see *Learner's Manual* para 1.3.2).

PROCEDURE
1. Introduce the exercise.
2. Divide the learners into small groups.
3. Ask each group to discuss one question.
4. Get reports back from each group.
5. Conclude with general class discussion and summary.

TIME	
Introduction:	2 min
Group discussions:	10 min
Reports back:	15 min
Discussion and summary:	3 min
TOTAL:	**30 min**

1. Mary is likely to be charged with theft and tried in the Durban Magistrate's Court. If she is convicted she can appeal to the KwaZulu-Natal High Court in Durban. If she cannot afford a lawyer and is likely be sentenced to imprisonment with the option of a fine and would not be likely to pay the fine within two weeks of being sentenced, she will be given a lawyer by Legal Aid South African. If she is not represented by a lawyer and is sentenced to a fine of more than R2 500 or imprisonment of more than three months by a magistrate of less than seven years' experience, her case will be automatically 'reviewed' by a judge. All the necessary court records and documents will be sent to the judge by the clerk of the court. The judge will check to see that Mary was properly convicted on the evidence.

2. John will be charged with rape and tried in the Pretoria Regional Magistrate's Court. Because rape is a very serious charge he will be provided with a lawyer by Legal Aid South Africa if he cannot afford one. If he is convicted he can appeal to the North Gauteng High Court (Pretoria).

3. Govan would be charged with murder and tried in the KwaZulu-Natal High Court. Because he has been charged with a crime that may result in life imprisonment, Legal Aid South Africa will provide him with a lawyer if he cannot afford one. The judge will also be assisted by two 'assessors' when hearing the case. If he is convicted he could appeal to the Supreme Court of Appeal in Bloemfontein.

4. Bheki could approach a lawyer to help him bring a case against the shop in the Durban Magistrate's Court. It would be easier and cheaper, however, to bring an action in the Durban Small Claims Court where he could bring the case himself without a lawyer because he is suing for less than R15 000. If he uses the magistrate's court and loses, he could appeal to the KwaZulu-Natal High Court in Durban, but this would be very expensive as he would need an advocate and attorney. If he uses the small claims court and loses, he would not be able to appeal. (Educators should find out the address of their local small claims court in the telephone directory.)

5. Peter could sue for his R50 000 in the Johannesburg Magistrate's Court. He would need to consult an attorney to do so. If he loses the case he could ask his lawyer to appeal to the South Gauteng High Court, but this is very expensive. His claim is too big to bring in the small claims court.

6. The cheapest way for Vusi and Ernest to solve their dispute is to approach their local chiefs' court. If they are not satisfied with the chief's decision they could approach the magistrate's court in the district where they live and appeal or begin a new court action.

7. Mary would have to sue her husband in the Cape Regional Court or the Cape High Court.

8. Sipho could bring an action in the High Court. This is because his case is a constitutional case to have parts of a statute declared invalid and must be brought in a High Court. If he loses in the High Court he can appeal to the Supreme Court of Appeal, and then to the Constitutional Court, or the High Court may refer his case there.

Learners should be reminded that a person can only appeal to another court if he or she can show that the magistrate or judge in the trial court made a decision based on wrong facts or wrongly interpreted law. A person may appeal automatically against a decision in a criminal case in the magistrate's court. An appeal from a High Court to the Supreme Court of Appeal requires the permission of the judge who heard the case. If a person appeals to another court in a criminal case, there is the danger that the higher court may impose a heavier sentence on the person who has been convicted.

The High Courts may also refer matters involving constitutional issues directly to the Constitutional Court. A person wishing to appeal to the Constitutional Court must get permission to do so from the Constitutional Court.

1.3.2 Settling disputes outside of court *(Learner's Manual p 36)*

Because of the emphasis on court cases in newspapers, television and radio, most people see the courts as the normal, or only, way of solving disputes between people. This section encourages learners to think of other methods of solving disputes without going to court. An obvious method of settling disputes outside of the courts is for the parties to take the law into their own hands. This may, however, have disastrous effects for society. There are a number of structured methods of problem solving outside of the courts such as negotiation, arbitration and mediation.

Problem 4: If people took the law into their own hands (Learner's Manual p 37)

AIM: The aim of these exercises is to make learners aware of the consequences that may follow if people are allowed to take the law into their own hands. In most cases the law disapproves of people taking the law into their own hands, but sometimes this is allowed (eg in self-defence).

PROCEDURE	TIME	
1. Introduce the cases.	Introduction:	2 min
2. Divide the learners into small groups.	Group discussions:	10 min
3. Ask each group to discuss one question.	Reports back:	20 min
4. Get reports back from each group.	Discussion and summary:	3 min
5. Conclude with general class discussion and summary.	**TOTAL:**	**35 min**

1. Clearly Paul has acted wrongfully in the eyes of society. Society does not tolerate people destroying each other's lives or property because somebody has cheated them. Even if the cheating is on a large scale people would expect victims to use lawful means of protecting themselves (eg by approaching an advice officer or a lawyer – through a legal aid clinic or a Legal Resources Centre if they are poor). Paul could have consulted an advice office or law clinic or threatened to take the case to the small claims court. (see *Learner's Manual* para 1.4.1.4.)

2. It is likely that Benny's act was unlawful because there is other action that he could have taken. For example, he could have caught the dog and sent it to the 'pound'. (The pound is a place where trespassing animals are sent until their owners pay for them to be released.) He could have called the police if the dog was very vicious and asked them to destroy it. If it was a very valuable dog, Benny could have asked a court to order Ahmed to stop allowing his dog to come onto his property. Could Benny have fenced off his property and charged Ahmed for the price? (Probably not – he might have to pay half the cost if he had warned Ahmed beforehand. Maybe Ahmed should have fenced his property to stop the dog trespassing?)

3. It is murder to kill another person intentionally, except perhaps in self-defence. Therefore, the people who killed Sharkie could be found guilty of murder if they acted intentionally and unlawfully. Even if Sharkie was a drug dealer who paid off the police so that he was not charged, the people had no right to kill him. If they thought that the police were corrupt, they could have reported them to the station commissioner in charge of the police station, the Independent Police Investigative Directorate or even to a newspaper. People do not like drug dealers. However, the law does not allow one to take the law into one's own hands and kill someone.

4. It is very difficult for people to decide what to do if the police are unable to protect them against crimes. Physically attacking the other group or its property might just accelerate the violence and lead to further 'pay-backs'. Instead, maybe a community leader or lawyer could be used to act as a go-between. The second group could perhaps approach the leader or a lawyer and ask him or her to persuade the police to patrol the area. If the second group can identify particular members of the group threatening violence, maybe they could get a court order preventing this. To get such a court order, the applicants would have to show that: (a) there was an immediate danger to them; (b) there was no other remedy, because the police would not help; and (c) they were entitled to a court order to protect themselves and their property. Should they form 'vigilante' groups to

protect themselves or appoint people to guard their property? The courts have recently ordered vigilante groups to stop using violence. If vigilante groups use violence against other people, they may be prosecuted for assault or murder (if they kill anyone).

5.   Whether or not Logan's acts were justified will depend upon whether he was in immediate danger of death or severe bodily injury. If he was in such danger, he could argue that he acted in self-defence. If, however, he could have driven away or could have aimed at a part of the man's body that would not have resulted in his death, a court might find that it was not necessary for him to shoot and kill the hijacker. It might also be argued that a knife is not as big a threat as a gun in this case and thus he used excessive force in killing the hijacker instead of driving away or shooting him in a part of his body which would not have caused him to die. If, however, he could not drive away because he was obstructed by other cars, the knife was a threat to his life, and he could not have aimed the gun anywhere else, he would have been justified in shooting and killing the hijacker (see *Learner's Manual* Part 2 Criminal law). Learners can make up their own minds regarding whether people should carry guns to protect themselves.

6.   Bob was trying to defend himself. He had attempted to run away. The law says that you may sometimes use reasonable force to save your or another's life. Technically, Bob could be charged with murder or culpable homicide (manslaughter) but if he can show that he was defending himself from an immediate threat of death, it might be a good defence (see Part 2 of *Learner's Manual*). The fact that he tried to run away is in his favour.

Problem 5: The case of Maria Mchunu   *(Learner's Manual p 39)*

AIM: The purpose of this role-play is to demonstrate: (a) how negotiation is done; (b) that disputing parties may be able to reach an agreement through negotiation; and (c) the advantages of using negotiation to settle disputes.

PROCEDURE

1.   Get learners to read the scenario.
2.   Divide the learners into pairs of (a) paralegals acting for Maria and (b) those acting as Mondi.
3.   Divide the learners acting as paralegals into groups of five or less and do the same for the learners acting as Mondi.
4.   Get the groups to discuss their strategies to prepare for the negotiation.
5.   Put the members of the groups back into their original pairs and get them to conduct their negotiations.
6.   Get feedback from the groups on the results of their negotiations.
7.   Discuss and summarise the results of the negotiation exercise.

TIME

Reading the case study:	5 min
Group discussions to prepare for the negotiation:	10 min
Conducting the negotiation:	25 min
Reports back:	15 min
Discussion and summary:	5 min
TOTAL:	**60 min**

The negotiators should follow the Negotiation Guidelines in the box in para 1.3.2.1 of the *Learner's Manual,* and try to reach an agreement. The person acting as the paralegal representing Maria Mchunu should try to get Mondi Mchunu to focus on his interests (eg his love for his wife and children and his wish for them to return) and to move away from his position (eg that he did not have an affair with Thandi and believes that he is entitled to unprotected sex with his wife).

The advantage of negotiation is that if people are flexible and prepared to move from their positions to their interests they will reach an agreement that satisfies both sides. For instance, Maria may agree to return to their home if Mondi undertakes an HIV test; stops drinking; agrees not to have affairs with other women; and undertakes not to assault her or the children again. Mondi may agree to have an HIV test provided Maria also has one. He may also agree to drink less; not to have affairs with other women; not to force Maria to have unprotected sex with him if he tests positive for HIV; and not to assault Maria and the children again. Maria may agree to unprotected sex with him if he is not HIV positive.

Problem 6: Hospital workers v hospital management   (Learner's Manual p 41)

AIM: The purpose of this role-play is to demonstrate: (a) how mediation is done; (b) that disputing parties may be able to reach an agreement through mediation if attempts at negotiation fail; and (c) the advantages of using mediation to settle disputes.

PROCEDURE
1. Get the learners to read the facts of the case.
2. Divide the learners into small groups of three: 1, 2 and 3.
3. Number 1s are hospital workers; number 2s are mediators; and number 3s are hospital management.
4. Place all the number 1s together, the number 2s together, and number 3s together in groups.
5. Subdivide the groups of number 1s and number 3s into small groups of not more than five to discuss the arguments for their points of view.
6. Bring the number 2s together, take them out of the training room, and check that they understand the steps in mediation by taking them through the procedure.
7. Reconstitute the students in their original groups of 1s, 2s and 3s and get them to begin their mini-mediations in groups of three.
8. Obtain a report back from each group.
9. Conclude with general class discussion and summary.

TIME	
Introduce the facts of the case:	10 min
Divide participants into 3 large groups and then into small groups:	5 min
Prepare for mediation:	10 min
Conduct mini-mediations:	25 min
Reports back:	10 min
TOTAL:	**60 min**

The mediators should follow the Steps in a Mediation in the box in para 1.3.2.2 of the *Learner's Manual*, and try to assist the hospital workers and hospital management to reach an agreement. The mediator's job is to assist them to reach their own agreement and not to decide the solutions for them. The person acting as the mediator should try to get the workers and management to focus on their interests (eg the workers do not want to lose their jobs if the hospital has to close because of thefts; the management does not wish to dismiss its workers) and to move away from their positions (eg the workers refuse to be searched; management insists that they are searched). For instance, maybe everyone, including management can be searched, or maybe security cameras can be installed.

The advantage of mediation, like negotiation, is that if people are flexible and prepared to move from their positions to their interests they will reach an agreement that satisfies both sides, eg the workers may agree to be searched if management is also searched.

Problem 7: Public Service health workers v Minister of Health

(Learner's Manual p 42)

AIM: The purpose of this role-play is to demonstrate: (a) how arbitration is done; (b) that disputing parties may have to resort to arbitration if they cannot reach an agreement; and (c) the advantages of using arbitration instead of the courts to settle disputes.

PROCEDURE

1. Get the learners to read the facts of the case.
2. Divide the learners into small groups of three: 1, 2 and 3.
3. Number 1s are the Public Service health workers ; number 2s are arbitrators; and number 3s are the representatives of the Minister of Health.
4. Place all the number 1s together, the number 2s together, and number 3s together in groups.
5. Subdivide the groups of number 1s and number 3s into small groups of not more than five to discuss the arguments for their points of view.
6. Bring the number 2s together, take them out of the training room, and check that they understand the guidelines for arbitration by taking them through the procedure.
7. Reconstitute the learners in their original groups of 1s, 2s and 3s and get them to begin their mini-arbitrations in groups of three.
8. Obtain a report back from each group.
9. Conclude with general class discussion and summary.

TIME

Introduce the case	5 min
Divide participants into 3 large groups and then into small groups:	5 min
Prepare for arbitration:	10 min
Conduct mini-arbitrations:	25 min
Reports back:	10 min
TOTAL:	**55 min**

The arbitrators should follow the Arbitration Guidelines in the box in para 1.3.2.3 of the *Learner's Manual,* and decide on a suitable solution for the dispute between the Public Service health workers and the Minister of Health. The person acting as the arbitrator may try to get the workers and the Minister to focus on their interests (eg the workers do not want to lose jobs if fewer can be employed because the wage increase is too high; the Minister does not wish hospitals to be short-staffed) and to move away from their positions (eg the workers and management insist that demands and offers are non-negotiable). However, if at the end of the day the parties cannot settle, the arbitrator's decision is final.

The advantage of arbitration is that is much cheaper and quicker than going to court.

Problem 8: Which is the best method of settling the dispute?

(Learner's Manual p 44)

AIM: The aim of these questions is to show learners that not all legal problems have to go to court. Learners should also realise that there is no one 'right' answer. Other factors learners should bear in mind are that the methods used may depend upon several things: whether negotiators, arbitrators and mediators are available; whether the legal problem is very complicated; and the amount of time and money involved.

PROCEDURE		TIME	
1. Introduce the exercise.		Introduction:	3 min
2. Divide the learners into small groups.		Group discussions:	10 min
3. Ask each group to discuss one question.		Reports back:	12 min
4. Get a report back from each group.		Discussion and summary:	5 min
5. Conclude with general class discussion and summary.		**TOTAL:**	**30 min**

1. The case could perhaps be best handled by an informal discussion between the father and daughter (negotiation). It may also be done by a mediator who knows and cares for the father and daughter (eg a mother, brother, sister or other relative). It might not be wise to involve strangers or lawyers. There may be a problem if the daughter is no longer under 21 years old. A court may be reluctant to say that the father should pay for her university education. But it may if he had promised to do so or had done the same for other children in the family. Maybe it was a breach of an agreement?

2. Before going to an outside person, Zo should try negotiating (speaking directly) with the store manager or owner (see *Learner's Manual* Part 3 Consumer law.) If this is unsuccessful, Zo should contact a legal aid clinic at one of the universities or an advice office to see if they will mediate for him. (Educators should try to establish which law clinics and advice offices are situated in their areas.) If this assistance is not available, Zo could go to a small claims court. (Educators should check with the local magistrates' court to see if there is a small claims court in their area.)

3. The tenant should try to solve the problem through informal discussion or negotiation with the town council's housing section. If this does not work, a law clinic or a Legal Resources Centre could be asked to mediate. The Legal Resources Centre would help if it was a case which affects hundreds of tenants (eg where a housing authority was not carrying out repairs). An advice office could be used, or if mediation fails, a case could be brought in a small claims court.

4. Labour disputes are often handled by arbitrators or negotiators. In some cases, a trade union and an employer will agree in advance to have disputes decided by arbitration. Even if there is no advance agreement, they will have to approach the Commission for Concilation, Mediation and Arbitration (CCMA) or a bargaining council before going to court (see *Learner's Manual* Part 6 Employment law).

5. People wanting a divorce often work out a settlement through negotiations between themselves. They may sometimes employ a lawyer to help. However, only the Regional Magistrate's Court or the High Court can grant a lawful divorce. If the couple are not sure whether or not they wish to divorce, it may be useful to call in a social worker or marriage guidance counsellor to help as a mediator.

6. Angela can approach the Commission for Conciliation, Mediation and Arbitration (CCMA) about arranging a meeting between her and Mogani to resolve the question through conciliation or mediation (see *Learner's Manual* Part 6 Employment law). If this does not work, the CCMA may hold an arbitration hearing and make a ruling in favour of either Angela or Mogani. If the CCMA rules in favour of Angela, it will order Mogani to re-employ Angela or to compensate her for losing her job.

1.4 Lawyers and the adversary system

After completion of this section learners will be able to:

1. Demonstrate an understanding of how lawyers and the adversary system work.

1. An explanation is given of when people are likely to need a lawyer.
2. A set of facts is examined and a decision is made on when a lawyer will be required.
3. A decision is taken on whether South Africa should have a divided legal profession.
4. An explanation is given of the qualifications and nature of the work of the different branches of the legal profession.
5. A set of facts in a case is examined and a decision is taken on who qualifies for legal aid.
6. A role-play of a consultation between a lawyer and a client concerning a motor collision is conducted.
7. An explanation is given of how the adversary system operates.
8. A role-play is conducted of a consultation between a lawyer and a client who admits that she is guilty of murder, and a decision is made on whether the lawyer should defend her.

1.4.1 Lawyers

(Learner's Manual p 45)

There are about 24 500 lawyers, of whom about 2 500 are advocates and 22 000 attorneys, who serve about 54 million people (see *Learner's Manual* para 1.4.1). Although *Street law* is designed to help learners identify, and in some cases solve, legal problems, learners should remember that, in certain cases, it is essential to have the assistance of a lawyer. Sometimes, it is important to contact a lawyer early to avoid making things more difficult later on (eg after arrest).

Problem 1: Is a lawyer necessary?

(Learner's Manual p 46)

AIM: The different scenarios are aimed at encouraging learners to consider when it may or may not be necessary to employ a lawyer. Learners should think about alternative means of settling the disputes if this is possible.

PROCEDURE
1. Introduce the exercise.
2. Divide the learners into small groups.
3. Ask each group to discuss one question.
4. Get a report back from each group.
5. Conclude with general class discussion and summary.

TIME	
Introduction:	2 min
Group discussions:	10 min
Reports back:	20 min
Discussion and summary:	3 min
TOTAL:	**35 min**

1. As long as your father's insurance company agrees to pay the total cost of repairs to your father's and the other person's car, there is probably no need to consult a lawyer. If, however, your father is sued for more than his insurance company will pay, he may need a lawyer.

2. This problem could probably be solved by you and your brother going to the police station and explaining what happened. If, however, the police have charged you and raise problems, it might be necessary to contact an attorney.

3. A person is only bound by a guarantee if it is drawn to the attention of the buyer at the time that the thing is bought. If you were not told about the 2-week guarantee when you bought the stereo, you have a common-law right to hand back the stereo and get a refund. Alternatively, you could, as a favour, allow the shop to repair or replace the stereo. If the shop still does nothing, it would be cheapest and quickest to go to the small claims court (see *Learner's Manual* para 1.5.2). If the small claims court is used, there is no need to contact a lawyer.

4. It is useful to get expert advice when buying a second-hand car (see *Learner's Manual* Part 3 Consumer law), but not necessarily from a lawyer. The car itself should perhaps be examined by a person with mechanical knowledge. The cheapest and most effective method is to ask the Automobile Association (AA) to test it for you. The AA will charge a fee but it is worth paying to avoid future problems with car. Just because a car has a COR (Certificate of Roadworthiness) does not mean that it is in excellent condition. If your brother is going to sign a credit agreement, he should make sure that he understands all its terms. If not, he should ask the seller to explain them to him.

5. You would certainly need an attorney or legal advice in this situation as you may be charged with a serious crime. Even though you did not take part in the robbery, you could be charged as an 'accessory' (see *Learner's Manual* Part 2 Criminal law and juvenile justice).

6. Before getting divorced, your parents should consider consulting a marriage guidance counsellor, social worker or a member of the clergy to see if one of them can help to solve their problems. If everything else has failed, and there is a dispute as to custody of the children and how the family property should be divided, it will be necessary for each to employ a lawyer. If there is no dispute and the case will not be opposed, one of them could bring the action himself or herself (see *Learner's Manual* Part 4 Family law). Ask the learners which court would be used for the divorce. (The answer is the Regional Court or the High Court.)

7. Wills have to comply with certain formalities and it is usually best to contact a lawyer – especially if your parents want to include some special clauses (see *Learner's Manual* Part 4 Family law). Sometimes banks will arrange for wills to be drawn up free for their clients as they hope to earn executors' fees when they deal with the estates of clients who have died.

Problem 2: The divided profession   *(Learner's Manual p 49)*

AIM: The object of this exercise is to make learners understand why there is a divided or dual profession and to consider whether it should be changed.

PROCEDURE		TIME	
1. Introduce the exercise.		Introduction:	3 min
2. Divide the learners into small groups.		Group discussions:	10 min
3. Ask each group to discuss one question.		Reports back:	12 min
4. Get a report back from each group.		Discussion and summary:	5 min
5. Conclude with general class discussion and summary.		**TOTAL:**	**30 min**

1. Learners might say that because South Africa was ruled by England and has English law influences, the divided profession was introduced by the English. Some of the other former English colonies like Canada, Australia, New Zealand, India, Pakistan, the West Indies, and those in Africa, were all subjected to the influences of English law. Many of these have now abandoned the divided profession (eg Canada, Australia and New Zealand, as well as most African Commonwealth countries). It has been suggested that the divided profession in South Africa should also be abolished.

2. The main advantage of the divided profession is said to be that, by specialising in court work, advocates are able to give people much better service than if they did not. Advocates also specialise in writing legal opinions and preparing arguments for court, whereas many attorneys find themselves solving administrative problems for their clients with little time to investigate the law in depth. Most complicated legal problems are referred by attorneys to advocates for an opinion.

   The main disadvantage of the divided profession is probably the high legal costs involved. Because usually only advocates appear in the High Court, a person bringing an action in that court has to employ an attorney and an advocate. Both lawyers have to be paid by the client. For example, people wishing to get divorced in the High Court with the assistance of lawyers may have to employ, and pay for, two lawyers each to represent them. This is very expensive. Previously, many highly trained and skilled attorneys were prevented from appearing in the High Court for their clients, but now they can do so.

   Learners can use the above arguments to decide whether or not they think the system should be changed.

3. Learners are likely to have their own views on whether they think that it is a positive development that certain attorneys may now appear in the High Court. One reason in favour could be that senior attorneys can now be appointed as High Court judges and, therefore, it is logical that they should also be allowed to appear in the High Court. Another is that many senior attorneys are likely to have much more experience in certain areas of the law than junior advocates. Arguments against the dual system could be that attorneys do not have the same training as advocates who are specifically trained to appear in the High Court. Another is that advocates have more time to think about the theory of the law than attorneys because the latter spend a lot of their time dealing with the day-to-day factual problems of their clients.

4. The answer to the question as to whether the division between the attorneys' and advocates' professions should be retained, now that certain attorneys can appear in the High Court, will depend upon which position the learners take in questions 2 and 3.

5. The same answers as those in questions 2 and 3 are likely to be given by students who are in favour of the Legal Practice Act doing away with the distinction between advocates and attorneys.

Problem 3: Some questions about the legal profession *(Learner's Manual p 51)*

AIM: The object of these questions is to enable learners to distinguish between attorneys, advocates, conveyancers and notaries public, to see that they understand what qualifications are required for the different branches of the legal profession and if they know where to find an attorney or advocate. They also require learners to discuss whether judges should only be appointed from senior advocates.

<table>
<tr><td>

PROCEDURE ≔

1. Introduce the exercise.
2. Divide the learners into small groups.
3. Ask each group to discuss one question.
4. Get a report back from each group.
5. Conclude with general class discussion and summary.

</td><td>

TIME 🕐

Introduction:	5 min
Group discussions:	10 min
Reports back:	25 min
Discussion and summary:	5 min
TOTAL:	**45 min**

</td></tr>
</table>

1. The main work of attorneys is set out in the *Learner's Manual* and includes commercial work such as drawing up contracts, registering companies, collecting money, drafting wills, winding up deceased people's estates, transferring land, doing court work (usually in the magistrate's court) and working with advocates. Only certain attorneys can appear in the High Court and none may appear in the small claims court and courts of chiefs or headmen. Many attorneys do not spend much time in court. Those who do, spend most of their time in the magistrates' courts. An attorney is like a general practitioner in the medical profession, as he or she deals directly with the public.

2. Conveyancers prepare documents for the transfer and registration of land and other immovable property, and the registration of mortgage bonds. Notaries public draw up special legal documents like ante-nuptial contacts and notarial deeds or bonds. Ante-nuptial contracts are entered into by people before they get married to set out how they want their property to be dealt with (see *Learner's Manual* Part 4 Family law). Notarial deeds and bonds are special documents used, for example, when people give others movable property as security for a loan. Thus, a person may give a bank some shares or an insurance policy as security for a loan.

3. The main work of advocates is appearing in court, writing legal documents (or 'pleadings') for court, and writing legal opinions to advise people. All advocates, unlike attorneys (where only some may), can appear in the High Court as well as in any other court except the small claims court and courts of chiefs and headmen. Advocates are like specialists in the medical profession as most do not deal directly with the public, but are consulted through attorneys who 'brief' them. Unlike many attorneys, most advocates spend a lot of time in court.

4. In order to become an advocate, a person requires an LLB degree from a South African university. If the advocate wants to join a Society of Advocates, he or she must also serve a 1-year period as a 'pupil' with a 'master' who is a practising advocate, and then pass the Bar Examination. While a person is a pupil, he or she cannot be paid for doing legal work except if the pupil is appointed to defend accused people in serious criminal cases. Although a person may be admitted by the High Court as an advocate after obtaining an LLB degree, he or she may not join a bar as a practising member without completing pupillage and passing the Bar Examination.

   In order to become an attorney, a person must also obtain an LLB degree. The person wishing to become an attorney must serve as an 'articled clerk' with a firm of attorneys or do 'community service' with a legal aid justice centre, a legal aid clinic or a Legal Resources Centre. This is an apprenticeship to be an attorney. Clerks are paid while they work, but not as much as when they qualify. The clerks may attend a Practical Training Course or a School for Legal Practice run by the Law Society of South Africa and must then write an Attorney's Admission Examination and complete a one- or two-year period of articles or community service before they are admitted as attorneys by the High Court.

5. The best way of finding an attorney or an advocate is to ask a friend who has used one successfully. If you do not know anyone who has consulted an attorney, you could look in the 'Yellow Pages' of the telephone book. Because individual attorneys tend not to advertise, you will not be able to establish which attorneys specialise in what cases. You could, however, telephone one of the attorneys' offices and ask if the firm does the type of work you require. You could also ask if the firm offers a 'fixed fee' for giving advice or does work 'on speculation'. (This means that you only pay a fee if you win the case.) Otherwise, you could consult a legal aid justice centre, a law clinic or an advice office, which might have a copy of the *Guide to Attorney's Services* published by a local law society. If you also need an advocate, a friend could advise you as to who would be suitable for your case. Employers, clergyman, school teachers, social workers or professional people may also be able to advise you as to which lawyer would be best for your case.

6. Some learners might think that judges should only be appointed from senior advocates because they have plenty of court experience and are specialists in the law. Senior advocates also have to practise on their own, without partnerships, and are independent. Advocates are usually more skilled in knowledge and application of the law than attorneys and other legal practitioners. Usually, judges are appointed from senior practising advocates who have had experience acting as judges, although in recent years judges have also been appointed from the attorneys' profession, academics and magistrates who have had similar experience.

Some members of the legal profession have suggested that judges should be appointed from the best and most senior legal practitioners, whether they are advocates or attorneys. Some civil servants have suggested that judges should also be appointed from among the senior magistrates. Judges in the Constitutional Court must be lawyers of at least 10 years' experience as advocates, attorneys or legal academics. This allows the best legal brains in the country to be appointed to the Constitutional Court.

Legal Aid South Africa has simplified its means test to provide legal aid for people who are single or separated – if they earn up to R5 000 per month, and, in the case of married people – up to R5 500 per month. There is no longer an allowance for the number of dependants (eg children) that a person has (see *Learner's Manual* para 1.4.1.4).

Problem 4: Some questions on legal aid　　　　(Learner's Manual p 53)

AIM: The object of this exercise is to encourage learners to think about why most of Legal Aid South Africa's budget is spent on legal aid in criminal cases and whether more money should be spent on civil legal aid.

PROCEDURE		TIME	
1. Introduce the exercise.		Introduction:	5 min
2. Divide the learners into small groups.		Group discussions:	10 min
3. Ask each group to discuss one question.		Reports back:	10 min
4. Get a report back from each group.		Discussion and summary:	5 min
5. Conclude with general class discussion and summary.		**TOTAL:**	**30 min**

1. Most learners are likely to say that most of Legal Aid South Africa's budget should be spent on criminal legal aid because the Bill of Rights specifically mentions legal representation at state expense in criminal cases where 'a substantial injustice would otherwise arise' if detained, arrested or accused persons are not provided with a lawyer. The reason that most of the legal aid budget is spent on legal aid in criminal cases is because South Africa has a very high crime rate, and lots of unemployed and poor people who require lawyers will have to be provided with legal aid in terms of the Constitution. Other learners might argue that most of the legal aid budget should not be spent on legal aid in criminal cases because more legal aid should be provided to unemployed or poor law-abiding people who need lawyers in civil cases.

2. Most learners are likely to say that Parliament should provide more money for legal aid in civil cases. This could be done by specifically providing that a certain amount of the legal aid budget (eg 30%) must be spent on civil cases, or by providing more money to Legal Aid South Africa which is specially allocated to civil cases. Others might argue that the Bill of Rights already provides that legal aid must be given to children in civil cases where 'a substantial injustice' will arise if they are not provided with legal representation. Children are the most vulnerable members of society and it is correct that they get legal aid when they need it. Adults can rely on other means of getting legal aid in civil cases, for example by entering into a 'contingency fee' arrangement with lawyers, or by bringing actions in the small claims court. Again others may argue, as was done in question 1, that more legal aid should be provided to poor people who obey the law but who need lawyers in civil cases.

Problem 5: Who qualifies for legal aid? *(Learner's Manual p 55)*

AIM: The object of this exercise is to enable learners to know when people who cannot afford lawyers can get legal aid. It will also help them recognise whether or not particular people will be entitled to legal aid and what alternative resources are available.

PROCEDURE	TIME	
1. Introduce the exercise.	Introduction:	2 min
2. Divide the learners into small groups.	Group discussions:	10 min
3. Ask each group to discuss one question.	Reports back:	15 min
4. Get a report back from each group.	Discussion and summary:	3 min
5. Conclude with general class discussion and summary.	**TOTAL:**	**30 min**

1. Mr Bona, who is married, would usually qualify for legal aid because he earns the 'means test' limit of R5 500. But because he is charged with a minor parking offence in a no-parking zone, he cannot get legal aid. He is in no danger of being sentenced to a period of imprisonment of three months without the option of a fine.

2. Mrs Green, who has been deserted, earns less than R5 000 per month. She therefore qualifies for legal aid. If she has not had a previous divorce paid for by Legal Aid South Africa, she will be given legal aid. Mrs Green could go to the local legal aid justice centre or to a university legal aid clinic which will direct her to the nearest legal aid office. She should take her pay slip, marriage certificate, and children's birth certificates with her.

3. Mr Samuels is a single person with no children and, as he is earning more than R5 000 per month he will not qualify for legal aid unless the head of the local legal aid justice centre uses his or her discretion and allows him to get legal aid. If the head of the local justice centre thinks that Mr Samuels's case is deserving he may give legal aid to him because he earns only R1 000 a month above the means test. As a lot of people have been cheated by the shop he could go to the nearest Legal Resources Centre and they would help him. If there is no Legal Resources Centre nearby, he could go to the local university legal aid clinic. The legal aid clinic would then help him to get his money back. If the furniture cost R15 000 or less, he could also bring an action for the return of his money in the small claims court – if there is one in his area. He can do this without going to a lawyer (see *Learner's Manual* para 1.5.2).

4. Mr Khuzwayo, who earns only R4 000 per month and is married, is entitled to earn up to R5 500 per month to qualify for legal aid. He should tell the lawyer how much he earns and ask him to get legal aid for him. If the lawyer refuses, Mr Khuzwayo should go to the nearest legal aid justice centre or a university legal aid clinic. He could also report the lawyer's refusal to the local law society. (In most provinces attorneys are not compelled to take legal aid cases. They are expected to do so, however, to ensure that the legal aid scheme works properly.)

5. Mrs Van der Merwe is married and earns R3 200 per month. Her husband earns R2 300 a month. Together they earn R5 500 a month which is the maximum allowed for a married couple to get legal aid. However, Mrs Van der Merwe cannot get legal aid because she wants to sue for defamation which is excluded from the scheme. Maybe a university legal aid clinic could write a letter of demand for her. The small claims court could also not be used even if she wished to claim less than R15 000, because she cannot sue for defamation in that court.

Problem 6: The case of the car crash
(Learner's Manual p 56)

AIM: This role-play is designed to:
1. Inform learners about the various factors to consider in selecting an attorney.
2. Inform learners about the nature of legal representation.
3. Sensitise learners to the type of information that they should obtain to assist their lawyers.

PROCEDURE	TIME	
1. Read the facts of the case and develop a checklist.	Introduce the case and checklist:	10 min
2. Divide learners into pairs of Tim and his attorney.	Divide participants into 2 large groups and then	
3. Divide the learners acting as Tim into groups of five or less and do the same for the learners acting as Tim's attorney.	into small groups:	5 min
4. Get the groups to discuss their strategies to prepare for the interview as mentioned in the *Learner's Manual*.	Prepare for interviews:	10 min
	Conduct interviews:	20 min
5. Put the members of the groups back into their original pairs and get them to conduct the interviews.	Reports back:	10 min
6. Get feedback from the groups on the results of their interviews.	**TOTAL:**	**55 min**
7. Discuss and summarise the results of the interview exercise.		

Learners should be given time to prepare for the role-play. Before the role-play, the educator should develop a checklist of issues with learners to cover in the interview – the types of information that Tim should ask for. During the preparations the groups playing Tim should work out the questions they will ask as Tim, and the groups acting as Tim's lawyer should prepare the replies they will to Tim's likely questions. These issues include fees (eg initial consultation fee, plus 10% commission on money collected, charges for extra consultations and further legal action); the lawyer's previous experience in this kind of problem (eg how much is Tim likely to get; is he likely to have to go to court?); providing the lawyer with all information pertinent to the case (eg details of the accident; did Tim have his car regularly serviced?; quotations for the repairs to Tim's car); and keeping the client informed of progress in the case.

After the role-play, the learners should discuss whether or not they would have retained the lawyer based on the initial consultation. Learners' decisions should be based on the lawyer's personality and trustworthiness, experience, communication skills and fees.

1.4.2 The adversary system (Learner's Manual p 58)

An understanding of the adversary system of justice is important throughout the Street law course. Although people may be critical of lawyers who represent 'guilty' persons, the system requires that lawyers represent their clients and do not take on the role of judges or magistrates.

Problem 7: Questions on the adversary system (Learner's Manual p 60)

AIM: The object of the questions is to make learners aware of the importance of the adversarial system and the need for the person trying the case to be independent from the contending parties. The questions also emphasise that a lawyer's role is to look after the interests of clients and not to take over the function of a judge or magistrate.

PROCEDURE	TIME	
1. Introduce the exercise.	Introduction:	2 min
2. Divide the learners into small groups of about five people each.	Group discussions:	10 min
	Reports back:	15 min
3. Ask each group to discuss both questions.	Discussion and summary:	3 min
4. Get a report back from each group.	**TOTAL:**	**30 min**
5. Conclude with general class discussion and summary.		

1. There is no right answer to this question. The *Learner's Manual* gives some of the arguments for and against the adversary system. In addition to these, the learners should think about the assumption that the system works because the parties to a dispute are supposed to be evenly matched. The same assumption is made when the parties are represented by lawyers. Some lawyers are better than others. What happens when one person has a lawyer and the other does not? For instance, in criminal cases in South Africa, the State is represented by a prosecutor while many accused are unrepresented. During the apartheid years, about 150 000 people a year were sentenced to imprisonment without being represented by lawyers. This has now changed

with the Constitution requiring legal aid at state expense to be given to accused persons who cannot afford lawyers where a 'substantial injustice' would otherwise result. The interpretation of a 'substantial injustice' is explained in the *Learner's Manual* para 1.4.1.4).

Studies have shown that people represented by lawyers have a much better chance of winning their cases than those who do not have lawyers. The result of a trial also depends upon the skill of the lawyers. Outstanding lawyers tend to charge higher fees, so people who have more money are able to hire the best lawyers. The adversarial system, however, is supposed to provide: (a) skilled representation for litigants; (b) an objective third party (eg a judge) to resolve disputes; (c) a set of procedural rules designed to ensure fairness; and (d) an opportunity to appeal against wrong decisions. In reality, many of these goals are not achieved – especially if one of the parties is unrepresented or one party has plenty of money while the other does not.

2.   The educator should make sure that learners understand the quote. He or she should then ask them if they agree or disagree with it and to give reasons for their answers. In practice, because of the difficulty of proving that a person is guilty 'beyond a reasonable doubt', it is probably true that many guilty people are found not guilty. Technically, guilty persons do not go free, because people are not 'guilty' unless and until they have been proven so. Some people who are found guilty may also 'go free' because they are given suspended sentences or put on probation.

The quotation probably also includes people who may have been found guilty if they had been caught by the police but were not. Obviously many of these morally 'guilty' people go free. Probably very few innocent people get convicted – although it is more likely to happen if they are not represented by lawyers.

Learners should be reminded that under the adversarial system, it is the court and not the lawyer who decides whether or not a person is guilty. Lawyers are not judges, but they are officers of the court. This means that they should never mislead the court.

At the same time, they must act in the best interests of their clients. If they cannot represent a client effectively, they should not undertake to do so. It is the criminal process that decides the guilt of the accused – not the lawyer.

Therefore even though the lawyer knows that a client is guilty, the lawyer can still wait and see whether the prosecutor proves the case against the client beyond a reasonable doubt. If there are weaknesses in the prosecutor's case, the lawyer is entitled to point them out to protect the client.

The lawyer should defend the client on other issues that do not depend on his client's possible guilt. What the lawyer cannot do is to lead the client or defence witnesses through evidence that the lawyer knows is false. Usually, a lawyer who knows that a client is guilty will persuade the client to plead guilty and then try to obtain a reduced sentence.

The client, however, is not obliged to follow the lawyer's advice. If lawyers feel that they cannot defend guilty people who will not admit their guilt, they should refuse to take the case. What would happen if guilty people could never get lawyers to defend them? They would all have to defend themselves.

Sometimes people think that they are guilty of crimes when technically they are not, because all the legal requirements for the crimes do not exist. These should be checked by the judge or magistrate before accepting a plea of guilty, but this does not always happen.

Problem 8: What should the lawyer do?

(Learner's Manual p 60)

AIM: • This role-play is designed to make learners aware of the moral dilemma facing a lawyer who is asked to defend a person who admits to having committed a crime.

PROCEDURE

1. Introduce the facts and the roles.
2. Divide participants into pairs.
3. Number 1s represent Mina; number 2s are the attorneys.
4. Place all the number 1s together and all the number 2s together.
5. Subdivide the number 1s and number 2s into small groups to discuss what they would do as Mina and as the attorney.
6. Reconstitute the learners into their original pairs and get them to begin their role-plays.
7. Obtain a report back from each group.
8. Conclude with general class discussion and summary.

TIME

Introduce the facts and the roles:	10 min
Divide participants into pairs and small groups:	5 min
Preparations for the consultation between Mina and the attorney:	10 min
Role-play the consultations:	10 min
Reports back:	10 min
TOTAL:	**45 min**

The learners playing Mina should be unrepentant and satisfied with the fact that she stabbed the deceased to death. The lawyers conducting the interviews should see if there are any grounds of defence (eg self-defence) or a reduction in sentence (eg provocation by insults to Mina and her mother). The lawyers should decide whether they would defend Mina, and give reasons why they would, or would not, take her case.

1.5 Civil courts and small claims courts

Outcomes

After completion of this section learners will be able to:

1. Demonstrate an understanding of how the civil courts and small claims courts work.

Assessment criteria

1. An explanation is given of how the civil courts and small claims courts operate.

2. A decision is taken on which courts it is necessary to employ a lawyer in.

3. A set of facts in a case is examined and a decision is taken on what steps will be followed in a civil case involving an assault on a worker by a foreman.

4. Sets of facts in a series of scenarios are examined and a decision is taken in each on whether the case should be heard in the small claims court.

5. A role-play concerning a consumer claim in a small claims court is conducted and a decision is made as to whether the consumer should recover his money.

Problem 1: When lawyers may and may not be necessary *(Learner's Manual p 63)*

AIM: The aim of the exercise is to make learners aware of why it is necessary to have a lawyer represent a person in court. Merely because people are innocent, does not mean that they will be found not guilty in criminal cases.

PROCEDURE	TIME	
1. Introduce the exercise.	Introduction:	2 min
2. Divide the learners into small groups of about five people each.	Group discussions:	10 min
3. Ask each group to discuss both questions.	Reports back:	15 min
4. Get a report back from each group.	Discussion and summary:	3 min
5. Conclude with general class discussion and summary.	**TOTAL:**	**30 min**

1. During a trial in which one or both of the parties are not represented by lawyers, the judge or magistrate will explain the procedural rules to them, but will not tell them how they should conduct their cases. The judge or magistrate is like a referee who sees that the rules are followed, but does not tell the parties which witnesses to call, or show them how to cross-examine or re-examine. If, however, witnesses are called, the judge or magistrate may join in the questioning to try to discover the truth. The judge or magistrate will also make sure that the parties or their lawyers do not ask unfair questions, or questions which are not allowed in terms of the court rules.

2. In the small claims court, it is not necessary to employ a lawyer because the proceedings are simplified. The clerk of the small claims court will help the parties draw up the necessary legal documents (eg letter of demand, summons). The Commissioner, who acts as a judge, will ask all the questions, so that it is not necessary for the parties to cross-examine witnesses. In any case, lawyers are not allowed to represent people in the small claims court (see *Learner's Manual* para 1.5.2).

Problem 2: The case of the assaulted worker   *(Learner's Manual p 67)*

AIM: The object of this case example is to make learners aware of the procedures used in a civil action. Learners will learn about procedures before the case goes to court, as well as what happens at a civil trial. Learners will also be asked to think about what might happen if a person still refuses to pay after being ordered to do so by the court.

PROCEDURE
1. Introduce the exercise.
2. Divide the learners into small groups of about five people each.
3. Ask each group to discuss one of the questions.
4. Get a report back from each group.
5. Conclude with general class discussion and summary.

TIME	
Introduction:	2 min
Group discussions:	8 min
Reports back:	12 min
Discussion and summary:	3 min
TOTAL:	**25 min**

1. Mr Dlamini's lawyer will ask Mr Dlamini to describe what happened and will take a statement about the incident. He will then write a 'letter of demand' to the foreman demanding that he pay the sum of R25 000 to Mr Dlamini within a certain number of days (eg 10 or 14 days). If the foreman rejects the demand or does not reply he will issue a 'summons'. The letter will usually be sent by registered post.

2. If the foreman ignores the letter of demand, the lawyer will issue a summons. The summons and two copies will be stamped by a court official called the 'clerk of the court' and sent to another court official called the 'sheriff of the court'. The sheriff will then take the summons and copies to the foreman and hand a copy to him (ie 'serve' the summons). The summons tells the foreman that he has a certain number of days (eg 7 or 10 days) to inform Mr Dlamini and the court that he intends to defend the case. If he does not defend it, 'default judgment' will be taken against him.

3. The case will only go to court if the foreman completes a 'Notice of Intention to Defend' and sends a copy to the court and one to Mr Dlamini's lawyer. There would then be a series of legal documents called 'pleadings' (eg Request for Further Particulars, Reply to Request for Further Particulars, Pleas, Notice of Set Down, etc) before the case comes to court. Eventually a trial date would be set and the case heard. Mr Dlamini's case would be presented first: his witnesses called; cross-examined by the foreman's lawyer; re-examined by Mr Dlamini's lawyer, and his case closed.

   Then the foreman would present his case: his witnesses would be called, cross-examined by Mr Dlamini's lawyer, re-examined by his lawyer, and the defence's case closed. The lawyer for Mr Dlamini first, and then the lawyer for the foreman, would each argue why their clients should win. Afterwards, the magistrate would give a judgment.

4. If the foreman fails to defend the case after he has received a summons, Mr Dlamini's lawyer will ask the court to grant a default judgment. This means that the court gives a judgment against the foreman in favour of Mr Dlamini. This judgment is given without any of the parties having to appear in court.

5. If the foreman refuses to obey a judgment telling him to pay Mr Dlamini, the latter will have to go back to court. His lawyer would ask the clerk of the court to issue a document called a 'Warrant of Execution.

    This allows a court official, called the 'sheriff of the court', to demand that the foreman pay the money owing. If the foreman still fails to pay, the sheriff will attach some of his property. This means that property worth enough to pay Mr Dlamini's claim (and the legal costs) will be pointed out by the sheriff. The foreman will be told that he cannot get rid of this property because it will be sold by the sheriff in the near future if Mr Dlamini's claim is not paid. Before he sells the property, however, the sheriff must advertise the sale.

6. If the foreman lost the case and thought that he should have won, he can appeal to the High Court against the judgment. This might, however, be very expensive and it might be cheaper for the foreman to pay out Mr Dlamini's claim.

Note: Mr Dlamini may not bring his claim in the small claims court since it is over the R15 000 maximum.

1.5.2 Small claims courts *(Learner's Manual p 68)*

Problem 3: The case of the cheap tape recorder *(Learner's Manual p 72)*

AIM: The purpose of the role-play is to show learners how a small claims court works.

The small claims court is less formal than a normal civil court and the rules of procedure are more relaxed. The commissioner asks all the questions and need not deal with the plaintiff and the plaintiff's witnesses first. The commissioner may ask witnesses and parties to give their evidence in any order. The commissioner may also stop the proceedings at any time if he or she is satisfied that there is enough evidence to give a judgment. This means that the commissioner may decide that it is not necessary to hear some of the witnesses. Usually, however, both parties will be allowed to have their day in court and all the witnesses will be heard. If the plaintiff or defendant wishes to ask each other or a witness a question, the question must be asked through the commissioner.

Role-play

The educator, a lawyer or a law student should play the part of the small claims commissioner. Learners should play the plaintiff, defendant and witnesses. The commissioner should question the parties and the witnesses about the facts and give a judgment. The participants should discuss the case to consider whether they thought it was a fair trial.

PROCEDURE	TIME	
1. Introduce the facts and the roles.	Introduce facts and roles:	2 min
2. Ask the learners to read through the roles and call for volunteers to play the different roles – if no volunteers are forthcoming, randomly select four students to play the different roles.	Students read roles:	5 min
	Allocate roles:	3 min
3. Conduct the role-play.	Conduct the role-play:	15 min
4. Conclude with general class discussion and summary.	Discussion and summary:	15 min
	TOTAL:	**40 min**

Steps in the role-play

1. Preliminary

(a) The commissioner should assume that he or she has a copy of the 'letter of demand' and 'summons' that has been sent to Tapes Galore.

(b) The commissioner should sit at a table in front of the class-room with the litigants seated at desks in front of the table and opposite each other. Each side's witnesses should sit beside them. There should be a court orderly sitting at a desk in front of the commissioner's table and between the table and the desks of the plaintiff and defendant. See diagram:

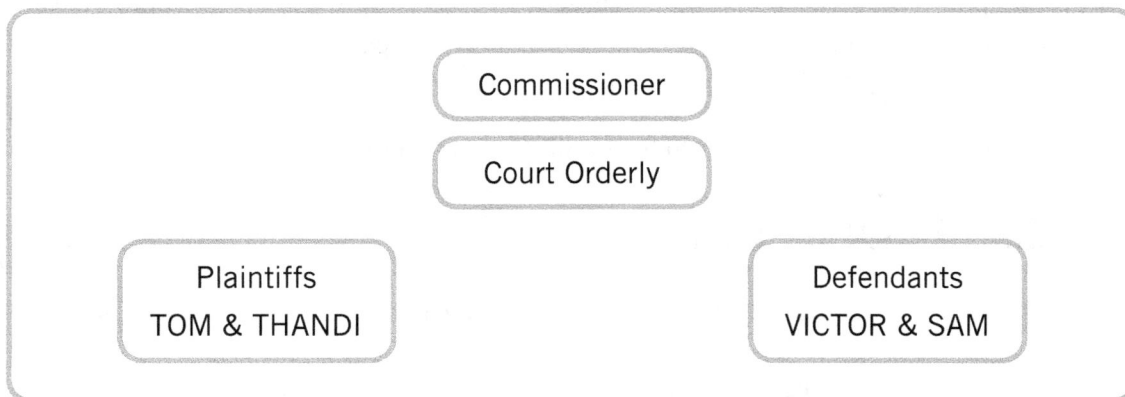

```
+-------------------------------------------------------+
|                                                       |
|                +-------------------+                  |
|                |   Commissioner    |                  |
|                +-------------------+                  |
|                +-------------------+                  |
|                |  Court Orderly    |                  |
|                +-------------------+                  |
|                                                       |
|   +-------------------+      +-------------------+     |
|   |    Plaintiffs     |      |    Defendants     |     |
|   |  TOM & THANDI     |      |  VICTOR & SAM     |     |
|   +-------------------+      +-------------------+     |
|                                                       |
+-------------------------------------------------------+
```

(c) Learners should be selected to play Tom and Thandi, Victor and Sam. They should try to memorise their evidence so that they do not have to read it.

(d) Tom should have a slip of paper which reads as an invoice, eg

---

25 Scurry Rd
DURBAN
4001

TAPES GALORE
(Suppliers of Top Quality Tape Recorders & Tapes)

1 Super Sound Special tape recorder
(Including V.A.T.)
R500.00

Note: This product is fully guaranteed for 5 days from the date of purchase. If defective, return it in the original box for credit towards another purchase.

Tom should also have an object that can be used as a tape recorder (eg a box or better still, a small tape recorder or 'walkman'). Tom should be told to think up an explanation for why he did not have the original box. He could say that his attention was not drawn to this on the invoice and that he did not think that the invoice would contain a 'guarantee').

2. Hearing

(a) The commissioner must control the proceedings by asking all the questions. The first thing the commissioner should do is 'swear in' the parties and witnesses, or ask them to make an affirmation to tell the truth. They should be asked to raise their right hands and say after the commissioner: 'I swear that the evidence that I shall give shall be the truth, the whole truth and nothing but the truth, so help me God'.

(b) The commissioner should also explain to the parties that he or she will ask all the questions, but that they may ask questions through him or her.

(c) The commissioner should then ask Tom to describe his problem and Victor to reply. He should ask Tom if he has a receipt and ask him to hand it to the orderly. The orderly should show it to Victor before giving it to the commissioner. The 'tape recorder' should also be handed in in the same manner.

The commissioner may ask Victor to respond to Tom's statement that he did not take the tape recorder back immediately because his mother was sick. He might also ask Tom what happened to the box.

(d) The commissioner could ask Thandi to give her evidence next. Her evidence is important because it backs up Tom's story that the tape recorder did not work when he took it home. Was her mother sick at the time?

(e) The commissioner could then ask Victor to give his evidence. The Commissioner could perhaps ask what would happen if a person were too ill or otherwise prevented from returning the tape recorder within five days. Would not the shop out of 'goodwill' replace it? Would the money have been refunded if the tape recorder had been returned in a damaged box? He could also ask Victor whether a five-day guarantee means that the fault must emerge within five days or whether it means that the tape recorder must be returned within five days, or both. Victor can also be asked whether he told Tom that he had to bring back the tape recorder within five days.

3. Judgment

(a) The commissioner should deal with the facts that he or she is satisfied have been proved. For example, that: the tape recorder was not working after it was brought home; that Tom was told that it was guaranteed for five days; Tom did not know that the invoice contained a guarantee which said that it must be brought back in the original box. Tom was not told that the five-day guarantee meant not only that the defect in the tape recorder must happen within five days, but also that it must be returned within five days. Depending on what Tom's explanation is for the missing box, the commissioner may or may not agree with Victor and Sam that Tom had dropped the tape recorder and broken it. The commissioner may also consider whether Tom should have been told that a five-day guarantee means not only that the fault must happen within five days but also that the tape recorder must be returned within five days.

(b) The commissioner should then deal with the law. The law says that goods which are sold should be in proper working order and not suffering from hidden defects. If they are defective, a buyer is entitled to his or her money back. If, however, the goods are sold subject to a guarantee, the buyer is bound by that guarantee if his or her attention was drawn to it at the time of the sale. However, any guarantee must be interpreted very strictly, and if it is not clear it must be interpreted in favour of the consumer.

(c) The commissioner should then apply the law to the facts. Even if the commissioner finds that Tom did not drop the box, Tom was not bound to return the tape recorder in its original box because that condition was not drawn to his attention at the time of the sale. Furthermore, the tape recorder had a five-day guarantee, which meant that any fault in the tape recorder had to emerge within five days to fall under the guarantee. However, Tom was not told that the five-day guarantee also meant that the tape recorder had to be returned within five days. If his mother was sick, as a courtesy he could have told the shop about the fault in the tape recorder. However, provided he can prove that the fault emerged within five days, he is entitled to take it back to the shop and obtain a refund from Tapes Galore.

(d)   The Commissioner then gives judgment. He could find that Tom has proved that Tapes Galore must give him his money back, because the fault in the tape recorder happened within five days, and Tom was not told that the five-day guarantee meant that he had to return it within five days. Tom was also not told at the time that he had to return the tape recorder in its original box. If the commissioner believes Tom and his sister he will give a judgment in favour of Tom.

Discussion:

The participants should then discuss the case to consider whether they thought it was a fair trial. How do they feel about the fact that lawyers are not allowed in the small claims court? Is it good that only the commissioner can ask questions? What did they think of the judgment? (They will learn more about Consumer law in *Learner's Manual* Part 3.) Should there be an appeal from the small claims court? Would appeals allow people with more money to defeat the objectives of cost-effectiveness and speed?

Further reading

1.1 Street law and law in general

Grimes R, McQuoid-Mason D, O'Brien E & Zimmer J 'Street Law and Social Justice Education' in Frank S Bloch (ed) *The Global Clinical Movement: Educating Lawyers for Social Justice* (2011) Chapter 15.

Kleyn D & Viljoen F *Beginner's Guide for Law Students* 5 ed (2011) Chapter 1

Maisel P & Greenbaum L *Introduction to Law and Legal Skills* (2001) Chapter 2

McQuoid-Mason D & Palmer R *African Law Clinicians Manual* (2013) Chapter 3

R v Dudley and Stevens [1884] 14 QBD 273 (DC)

1.2 Where law comes from, how it is made, and the different kinds of law

Currie I & De Waal J *The Bill of Rights Handbook* 5 ed (2005)

Kleyn D & Viljoen F *Beginner's Guide for Law Students* 5 ed (2011) Chapter 2

Maisel P & Greenbaum L *Introduction to Law and Legal Skills* (2001) Chapter 4

Radebe v Hough 1949 (1) SA 380 (A)

S v Mafu 1966 (2) SA 240 (E)

S v Williams 1995 (3) SA 632 (CC)

1.3 The courts and settling disputes outside the courts

Kleyn D & Viljoen F Beginner's *Guide for Law Students* 5 ed (2011) Chapter 11

Maisel P & Greenbaum L *Introduction to Law and Legal Skills* (2001) Chapters 5 and 6

1.4 Lawyers and the adversary system

Kleyn D & Viljoen F *Beginner's Guide for Law Students* 5 ed (2011) Chapters 8 and 12

1.5 Civil courts and small claims courts

Kleyn D & Viljoen F *Beginner's Guide for Law Students* 5 ed (2011) Chapter 6

2. Criminal law and child justice

CONTENTS

PART TWO

Criminal law and child justice

2.1 The meaning, nature and causes of crime

Outcomes

After completion of this section learners will be able to:

1. Explain the meaning, nature and causes of crimes.

Assessment criteria

1. An explanation is given of what a crime is.
2. A set of facts is examined and a decision is taken on whether a person's act or failure to act is a crime.
3. Causes of crimes are identified.
4. Ways of preventing and reporting crimes are identified.
5. A set of facts is examined and a decision is taken on whether or not to report a crime.
6. A set of facts is examined and a decision is taken on which parties should be held criminally liable.
7. A set of facts is examined and a decision is taken on which actions by people can be regarded as crimes.
8. An explanation is given of the types of behaviour that can take place prior to the commission of a crime.

2.1.1 What is 'crime'?   *(Learner's Manual p 83)*

An introductory brainstorming session could be used here. Ask learners to list on the board all the crimes they can think of. Try to categorise the crimes into different groups, ie how some are like others; how some are different. Some groups might be crimes against persons, crimes against property, so-called 'victimless' crimes (eg drug offences, prostitution, public drunkenness), 'white collar' crimes (eg by professional people), and crimes against society. What makes these acts criminal? Why are some crimes considered more serious than others?

Problem 1: If you were a lawmaker   *(Learner's Manual p 84)*

AIM: This activity provides an opportunity to examine the grey area between legal, though immoral, behaviour and a criminal act. Learners can work in small groups (of 4 to 5) to rank each act as 'very serious (vs)', 'less serious (ls)', 'petty (p)' or 'no crime (nc)'.

EXAMPLE:

Groups	1	2	3	4	5	6
Problems						
1	vs	vs	vs	ls	vs	vs
2	ls	vs	ls	ls	ls	vs

PROCEDURE		TIME	
1. Introduce exercise.		Introduction:	5 min
2. Divide participants into small groups.		Group discussions:	15 min
3. Learners rank acts according to instructions.		Report back:	20 min
4. Report back.		General discussion:	5 min
5. General discussion.		**TOTAL:**	**45 min**

Learners should rank the crimes based on how serious they think each crime should be, not on how serious the law says it is. If the learners feel that the conduct should not be regarded as a crime, they should say so. Each group must be prepared to explain why they rank each act as they do. Learners should be encouraged to challenge the reasoning behind how their fellow learners rank each act. If time is short, each group can be allocated one scenario and asked to rank it as above.

This activity can also be used to inquire into the relationship between law and morals – as was done with the case of the shipwrecked sailors in para 1.1.2 of the *Learner's Manual*, for example, leaving the store with too much change (5); or not reporting a friend committing a crime (10), may be immoral but not illegal.

If learners are curious as to what the real attitude of the courts would be in these cases, they may be told the following:

1. Zol's conduct would probably be regarded as a 'very serious' crime. Selling or dealing in drugs can lead to a heavy term of imprisonment, for example, there is a minimum sentence of five years' imprisonment for people who are convicted of dealing in prohibited drugs other than dagga.

2. Xolani's crime of pickpocketing would probably be regarded as a 'less serious' crime. If, however, pickpocketing was rife in the area, the court might impose a heavier penalty to deter people from doing it. (Charles Dickens showed in *David Copperfield* that even severe sentences like public hangings for pickpockets in England during the nineteenth century did not deter pickpocketing. One of the busiest times for pickpocketing was while people were watching pickpockets being hanged!)

3. Jan's offence would probably be considered a 'very serious' crime. The state takes a very firm line on armed robbery where there is a danger to life.

4. Midas' crime of tax evasion is likely to be regarded as a 'very serious' offence. If done on a large scale, it could undermine government financing.

5. Pam's conduct is probably immoral rather than illegal. It could probably be classified as 'no crime'. If, however, she had intentionally misled the cashier, she may be guilty of the crime of fraud. (A shopkeeper who deliberately shortchanges a person is guilty of theft.)

6. Sheila's conduct is likely to be classified as 'petty' by the courts. Prostitution is something that societies have lived with for centuries. Some people consider prostitution very immoral and believe it should be a 'serious' crime. The Constitutional Court held in 2003 that prostitution is still illegal and that it is not unconstitutional to criminalise it. It is now covered by the Sexual Offences Amendment Act (see *Learner's Manual* para 2.8.2).

7. Ming's conduct is probably also a 'petty' crime. He would usually be able to pay an 'admission of guilt', as it is a traffic offence.

8. Many people believe that water pollution should be regarded as a 'very serious' crime. Sometimes, however, the courts have been criticised for giving factory owners lighter fines than the public expect. This is because the courts do not want to discourage factory production. Depending on how bad the pollution is, it might only be considered a 'less serious' offence.

9. Max will probably be regarded as having committed a 'very serious' crime because he has killed someone. The court would regard his drinking while driving as an aggravating factor.

10. Jane is probably under no legal duty to report her friend's shoplifting. Therefore, there is 'no crime'. Jane may, however, be under a moral duty to report the crime. Some people believe that it should be a crime not to report crime. Parliament, however, has made it a crime for the owner or a person in charge of a place of entertainment (eg a disco) not to report that people are using drugs there.

11. Swearing at Juliet may be a 'petty offence' if it is insulting to her dignity as a woman (eg calling her a 'bitch'). If Romeo, however, merely used meaningless swear words, calling her a 'bat' or a 'battle-axe', it would probably not be a crime.

12. The shopkeeper cheating on his value-added tax returns may be regarded as having committed a 'very serious' crime. Not only is he defrauding the Receiver of Revenue, but also consumers, who think that they are paying VAT to the Receiver.

13. Zola could argue on the basis of freedom of religion, as protected by the Constitution, that he has the right to practise his religious freedom. Presently in South Africa, it is illegal to smoke or to be in possession of dagga.

14. Devan has the right to carry a gun provided he has a licence for the gun. Shooting someone who is trying to steal your car would only be legal if the person was a threat to your life.

15. Smoking in public has been legislated against in South Africa. All restaurants are required to have designated smoking areas so that customers like William can smoke. Smoking in a restaurant with no designated smoking area is a petty crime.

16. The youth political leader's chant 'kill the boer' may be a 'very serious' crime as it is a serious violation of the dignity or privacy of another person. The national police commissioner's chant 'shoot to kill' may be a 'very serious' crime if it taken literally; however, there may be circumstances in which police officers may use deadly force to protect themselves or the public.

2.1.2 The nature and causes of crime *(Learner's Manual p 86)*

Problem 2: The causes of crime *(Learner's Manual p 88)*

AIM: The object of this exercise is to encourage learners to think about the causes of crime not mentioned in the *Learner's Manual*. They are also required to list the causes in the *Learner's Manual*, together with those in their own lists, in order of importance.

PROCEDURE		TIME	
1. Explain the task that learners have to do.		Introduction:	5 min
2. Divide learners into small groups.		Individual work:	20 min
3. Learners list the causes of crime.		General discussion:	10 min
4. Learners must rank the causes of the crime listed by them and provide reasons.		**TOTAL:**	**35 min**
5. Questions and discussion.			

1. Other causes not mentioned in the *Learner's Manual* may be:
   (a) some people are just bad;
   (b) mental illness;
   (c) ignorance of the law;
   (d) jealousy or enmity;
   (e) revenge;
   (f) attention-seeking people; and
   (g) attitudes formed by family and peer groups.

2. When learners rank the causes of crime, ask them for the reasons for their rankings. What solutions could be used to eliminate these causes? How expensive will these solutions be? Who should pay for them?

2.1.3 Victims of crime
(Learner's Manual p 88)

Problem 3: Preventing and reporting crimes
(Learner's Manual p 92)

AIM: The objective of this exercise is to make learners aware of how crime affects our everyday lives and the problems it causes. It also makes them think about crime prevention measures.

PROCEDURE		TIME	
1. Introduce the exercise.		Introduction:	5 min
2. Divide learners into small groups of five each.		Group work:	10 min
3. Add one question to each group.		Report back and role-play:	30 min
4. Group discussions by groups with questions 1 to 3 and 5 to 6.		Debrief and discussion:	10 min
5. Role-play preparation by groups with question 4.		**TOTAL:**	**55 min**
6. Report back by groups with questions 1 to 3 and 5 to 6.			
7. Role-play by one group with question 4.			
8. Debrief role-play and general discussion.			

1. Learners can discuss experiences they, or others, have had as victims of crime. The hardship that crimes cause individuals (eg loss of money, psychological fear and depression, injuries, etc) should be stressed.

2. A number of crime-prevention programmes have been developed in South Africa and in other countries. Some are sponsored by the police (eg pamphlets and talks on what to do and what not to do to prevent crime), and others by organisations such as the National Institute for Crime Prevention and the Reform of Offenders (NICRO). The educator could contact the local police or NICRO for information on crime-prevention programmes in his or her area. Other methods are 'neighbourhood watch' schemes where neighbours keep an eye on each other's properties and report strange or criminal conduct in their neighbourhood to the police. Several South African towns are now introducing 'crime watch' programmes. (Is there a crime-watch programme in your neighbourhood?) Church and youth clubs can also develop crime prevention programmes. Wealthier neighbours have also introduced 'street patrols' by security guards.

   A number of crime-prevention techniques are listed in the text which can be referred to by the learners. People can lessen their chances of becoming victims by: (a) not walking in isolated or unlit areas at night; (b) not opening the doors or windows of their houses to strangers; (c) not accepting lifts from strangers; (d) not leaving doors or windows of houses unlocked when going out; (e) installing burglar bars; (f) not letting other people see that they are carrying money or valuables; and (g) always being on their guard in crowded places where people brush up against them. Can the learners think of any other methods?

The importance of reporting crime should always be stressed.

3 & 4. These questions are aimed at seeing how willing learners are to report crimes, and their understanding of how to do so. Learners playing the role of the suspicious neighbour should give the police all the necessary information. Learners playing the role of the police should ask the questions, and obtain the information needed to respond to the crime. This information should include: where, when, and how the crime was committed; what happened; who might have done it; and any other relevant facts.

5. Learners should discuss their knowledge about people who have been victims of crime. If learners themselves say that they have been victims but had not reported it, the class should explore the reasons why. The educator should stress the importance of reporting crime.

6. Learners' views will differ. Arguments against making it a legal obligation to report crimes might be: (a) it would be an interference with the freedom of people who do not wish to become involved; (b) it might force people to report conduct which they do not regard as criminal; and (c) it encourages people to spy on each other. It might also have a disastrous effect on social relationships in non-democratic countries where there are many political crimes.

Arguments in favour of imposing a legal obligation to report crime are: (a) it will reduce criminal activity if people know they will be reported; (b) failure to report a crime is a selfish and uncaring attitude towards the victims of crime; (c) it makes it easier for the police to apprehend criminals; and (d) it encourages people to protect each other against criminals.

2.1.4 What makes an act a crime? *(Learner's Manual p 93)*

This section briefly sets out the main elements of most crimes. The elements of individual crimes are to be found in the *Learner's Manual* at paras 2.2 to 2.9.

2.1.5 People who may be charged with crimes *(Learner's Manual p 93)*

Problem 4: The bank robbery *(Learner's Manual p 95)*

AIM: The object of this exercise is to enable learners to distinguish between the different parties to a crime.

PROCEDURE		TIME	
1. Introduce the facts of the case study.		Introduction:	5 min
2. Divide participants into small groups.		Group discussions:	20 min
3. Group discussions.		Report back:	15 min
4. Report back.		General discussion:	5 min
5. General discussion.		**TOTAL:**	**45 min**

1. Joe is a 'perpetrator' and will be charged with robbery. He is a perpetrator because he carried out the robbery. If he had talked Mary into joining him and Carl into helping, he might also have been guilty of 'conspiracy' (see *Learner's Manual* para 2.1.7).
2. Mary is a 'co-perpetrator'. Even though she did not carry out the robbery herself, the fact that she drove the van and kept a lookout makes her a co-perpetrator. Therefore, she can be charged with robbery in the same way as the perpetrator, Joe.
3. Carl is an 'accomplice' and can be charged with the same crime as the perpetrator, Joe, even though he was not present at the crime. He is an 'accomplice' because he helped Joe and Mary plan the robbery by giving them inside information about how busy the bank was, and when it would have the most money.
4. Bob is an 'accessory after the fact' and can be punished for the separate crime of obstructing the course of justice. He cannot be charged with robbery. Bob is liable because he knew about the robbery and then helped Joe and Mary get away.
5. David might have a moral obligation to take some action but he is not criminally liable for failing to report the crime. (What do the learners think about this? Should the law be changed to require witnesses to report crimes?)

2.1.6   Crimes of omission
(Learner's Manual p 95)

Although the courts more readily recognise a duty to act in the situations listed in para 2.1.6 of the *Learner's Manual*, the Appellate Court in *Minister van Polisie v Ewels* suggested that there might be a wider basis for liability. In *Ewels'* case, the court said that if the social convictions of the community would be outraged if a duty were not imposed in certain circumstances, then legal liability may be imposed. This principle, however, has not as yet been applied outside of the situations mentioned in the *Learner's Manual*.

Problem 5: Was there a duty to act?
(Learner's Manual p 96)

AIM: The object of this exercise is to make learners think about when the law ought to impose a duty to act. Learners should give reasons for their answers. The *Ewels* principle should be mentioned to the learners as an option.

PROCEDURE	TIME	
1. Divide class into small groups.	Introduction:	5 min
2. Each group should discuss one case.	Group discussions:	10 min
3. Groups report back.	Report back:	30 min
4. General discussion.	General discussion:	5 min
	TOTAL:	**50 min**

1. Busi may be morally obliged to do something, but in law she is probably not obliged to do anything. There is no link nor relationship between Busi and the blind man. (Would the community be outraged if no duty was imposed? Should she be charged with culpable homicide? See *Learner's Manual* para 2.2.1.2.)

2. Eunice may be morally obliged to do something; in law unless the legal convictions of the community would be outraged she would not be obliged to do anything. Would they? The same considerations apply as in Busi's case.

3. Ndaba had a legal duty to act because he was in control of dangerous property – the 'live' electricity cable. He would be guilty of culpable homicide. (See *Learner's Manual* para 2.2.1.2.)

4. Jacob had a legal duty to act because of the 'special relationship' that exists between a husband and wife. He would be guilty of culpable homicide. (See *Learner's Manual* para 2.2.1.2.)

5. Donald has a moral duty to help Graham. He might also have a legal duty if it is argued that a doctor holds a public office. (People holding public office are people who, because of their professions, hold themselves out as giving assistance, or providing a service to the public.) It could also be argued that, according to medical ethics, doctors should help injured people in emergencies. Donald's omission might not be criminal, but he could nonetheless be disciplined by the Health Professions Council. (Graham may also be able to sue Donald for damages if he could prove that Donald had had a legal duty to act, and he suffered extra injuries, pain and suffering as a result of Donald's failure to help.)

6. Francisco had a legal duty to fence the machine. The duty was imposed by a statute. His failure to fence the machine may be a crime in terms of the statute. (Silvia would be able to recover compensation from the Compensation Commissioner – see *Learner's Manual* para 6.3.5.)

2.1.7 Preliminary crimes

(Learner's Manual p 98)

Problem 6: Which crimes have been committed? *(Learner's Manual p 99)*

AIM: The object of this exercise is to make learners aware of the difference between mere preparation for and attempt to commit a crime, and the separate crimes of incitement and conspiracy.

PROCEDURE		TIME	
1. Introduction.		Introduction:	5 min
2. Divide learners into small groups.		Group discussions:	10 min
3. Give each group one question to answer.		Report back:	15 min
4. Group discussions.		General discussion:	5 min
5. Report back.		**TOTAL:**	**35 min**
6. General discussion.			

1. Lionel would not be liable for the crime of attempted theft. (For 'theft' see *Learner's Manual* para 2.6.3.) While he had done considerable preparation, he did not take any concrete substantial step towards committing the theft. He would, however, be guilty of inciting Dora to commit the crime.

2. Graham would be liable for attempted theft. (See *Learner's Manual* para 2.6.3.) The fact that Sarah did not have any money on her does not matter. The law is concerned with Graham's mental state – did he intend to commit a crime? – and his physical act – did he go beyond mere preparation?

3. In this situation, both Vernon and Mdlolo seem to have taken steps beyond mere preparation, but their acts so far (buying a gun and stealing a car) are probably not enough to prove their intent to commit a robbery (see *Learner's Manual* para 2.6.4).

   This is a borderline case but it is unlikely that they would be charged with attempted robbery. It appears that Vernon has not yet committed an illegal act, except perhaps conspiracy to commit robbery. Mdlolo can be charged with stealing the car.

4. Annie would be liable for attempted arson (the unlawful burning of property – see *Learner's Manual* para 2.6.1). She had done everything except obtain the matches and light the petrol. Spreading the petrol was a clear indication of her intention to commit the crime of arson.

Outcomes

After completion of this section learners will be able to:

1. List and explain the different crimes against people.

Assessment criteria

1. The elements of murder and culpable homicide are identified.

2. A set of facts is examined and a decision is made on whether the person was guilty of murder or culpable homicide.

3. Active euthanasia is distinguished from passive euthanasia.

4. A decision is made on whether active euthanasia should be regarded as a crime.

5. The legal position regarding suicide is explained.

6. The crime of assault is defined.

7. Common assault is distinguished from assault with intent to do grievous bodily harm.

8. A set of facts is examined and a decision is made on the kind of assault that has taken place.

9. Criminal insult (crimen injuria) is defined and discussed, with examples.

10. Kidnapping is defined and discussed.

2.2.1 Homicide – the unlawful killing of a person *(Learner's Manual p 100)*

Problem 1: The case of the jealous husband *(Learner's Manual p 102)*

AIM: The object of the problem is to show learners the difference between murder, culpable homicide and a non-criminal act resulting in death.

PROCEDURE
1. Introduce the case.
2. Divide learners into small groups.
3. Group discussions.
4. Report back.
5. General discussion.

TIME	
Introduction:	5 min
Group discussions:	20 min
Report back:	15 min
General discussion:	5 min
TOTAL:	**45 min**

1. If Nico was driving at a safe speed and the collision was unavoidable, he cannot be found guilty of murder or culpable homicide. It is not unlawful to drive a car at a safe speed if there was no fault on his part. He did not intend to kill the pedestrian, nor was his conduct negligent. Even though he intended to kill his wife and did actually kill her, the killing came about in a very different way from that which he intended. He thought that he had knocked down somebody else. In order to be guilty of murder, he must, at the time, have had a particular person or persons

in mind when he killed them. (This situation can be compared with two others:

(i) Nico goes to his wife's lover's house and shoots through the window at a figure he believes is his wife. The figure is in fact a dummy dressed in her clothes. Nico is guilty of attempted murder.

(ii) Nico arrives at the house, shoots at his wife, but misses her and hits her lover. As he did not intend to kill the lover, Nico would be guilty of culpable homicide. If, however, he ought to have foreseen that if he fired at his wife he might also hit her lover, and he did not care whether he shot him or not, Nico would be guilty of murder.)

2. If Nico was driving too fast and the collision was avoidable, he has killed her unlawfully and is guilty of culpable homicide. His conduct in driving fast and not avoiding the collision means that he has been negligent. Nico ought to have foreseen that if he drove too fast he might harm someone (eg collide with somebody), and he should have taken steps to avoid the collision. Even though he did not intend to harm anybody, because of his negligent conduct, he is guilty of culpable homicide.

3. If Nico deliberately drove over his wife, even though he did not know it was her, he will be guilty of murder. It is unlawful deliberately to drive over a person and he must have realised that he might kill her. (A car is like a dangerous weapon.) If he did not care whether or not she would be killed, he is guilty of murder – even if he did not know at the time that the person was in fact his wife.

Problem 2: The Oscar Pistorius trial
(Learner's Manual p 102)

AIM: The aim of this exercise is to indicate to learners that it is not always easy to prove that a person had the specific intention to kill someone in a murder case.

PROCEDURE	TIME
1. Brief the learners on the facts of the case.	Divide into groups of prosecutors, lawyers and judges: 5 min
2. Divide learners into small groups of prosecutors, lawyers for Oscar and judges.	
3. Prepare arguments as prosecutors and lawyers for Oscar and judgments as judges.	Prepare arguments and judgments: 20 min
4. Prosecutors and lawyers present arguments.	Present arguments: 10 min
5. Judges give judgments.	Give judgments: 5 min
6. General discussion.	General discussion: 10 min
	TOTAL: 45 min

Prosecutors may argue that Oscar had the necessary intention to kill Reeva because he had 'eventual intention' (*dolus eventualis*) in that he knew that his shooting at someone in a small bathroom and toilet might risk causing their death but did not care whether or not he did cause their death.

Lawyers for Oscar may argue that Oscar loved Reeva and did not intend to kill her. He thought that he was about to be attacked by a burglar and shot to protect himself and Reeva. Therefore he should be found guilty of culpable homicide not murder.

The judges can decide which argument they find persuasive.

[Note: In the actual case the judge, in a very controversial judgment, found Oscar guilty of culpable homicide – not murder and sentenced him to five years in prison. The state appealed on the basis that he should have been found guilty of murder.].

Problem 3: People who kill themselves or ask others to kill them
(Learner's Manual p 104)

AIM: The object of this problem is to make learners aware of the difficulties involved in the question of 'mercy killing' (euthanasia) and suicide.

PROCEDURE		TIME	
1. Introduce *Learner's Manual* para 2.2.1.3.		Introduction:	5 min
2. Divide learners into small groups.		Group discussion:	10 min
3. Allocate one question to each group.		Report back:	20 min
4. Report back.		General discussion:	10 min
5. General discussion.		**TOTAL:**	**45 min**

1.   Learners' views are likely to differ markedly. Learners in favour of euthanasia might argue that as these people will soon die anyway, they should be killed with their consent to end their suffering. Provided the person is terminally ill and has consented, euthanasia should be allowed. Such learners might also say that a person who carries out a mercy killing should not be guilty of a crime. (If euthanasia is allowed, should the person and his or her relatives sign a written consent? What if the relatives do not wish to consent?)

Learners against euthanasia might say that the sanctity of human life comes first. Nobody should be allowed to take another's life – even with that person's consent. If a person is going to die anyway, nature must take its course. All that can be done is to relieve pain. Any person who kills another in these circumstances is guilty of murder, or maybe murder with extenuating circumstances.

2.   Many people believe that attempted suicide is still a crime even though it is not. Some learners might feel that it should be a crime in order to deter people from trying to take their own lives. Those in favour of the present position might say that making it a crime will not deter people who attempt or commit suicide because they are emotionally disturbed and will not be influenced by whether or not it is a crime.

3.   The present practice concerning 'suicide pacts' is that a person who assists another to die is guilty of murder. It does not matter that the other person wishes to die. Where one party survives the killing, it is similar to 'active' euthanasia and is regarded as murder. Learners who place the sanctity of human life above everything else will argue that a survivor who assists with the death should be guilty of murder.

Those against the survivor's being tried for murder might argue that he or she is guilty of murder with extenuating circumstances because there was consent by the deceased. (Generally, however, in most cases consent is not a defence to a crime – certainly not murder.) The accused might be able to show that his or her mind was as emotionally disturbed as that of the deceased, and that he or she did not really know what he or she was doing. Therefore, there was no proper intention and the accused cannot be convicted of murder. He or she may, however, be guilty of culpable homicide.

2.2.2 Assault

(Learner's Manual p 105)

Problem 4: The wife's revenge

(Learner's Manual p 106)

AIM: The object of this problem is to show learners how the court will distinguish between common assault and assault with intent to do grievous bodily harm. It also makes them think about when an assault might be justified and when the fault of the accused will be reduced.

PROCEDURE	TIME	
1. Introduce the facts of the case.	Introduce case study:	5 min
2. Divide learners into small groups.	Prepare arguments and judgments:	15 min
3. Prepare arguments as defence lawyers, prosecutors and magistrates.	Present arguments:	10 min
4. Defence lawyers and prosecutors present arguments.	Give judgments:	10 min
5. Magistrates give judgments.	General discussion:	5 min
6. General discussion.	**TOTAL:**	**45 min**

This problem may be conducted as a mock hearing with learners appearing in small groups as prosecutors, defence lawyers and magistrates. They can then argue and decide if it was a crime or self-defence.

1. Prosecutors would probably charge Devi with assault with intent to do grievous bodily harm. Very hot cooking oil can cause serious injury to a person, and even permanent disfigurement. The fact that Shan had to spend a week in hospital indicates that his injuries were severe. However, the prosecutor might sympathise with Devi because of the previous assaults by Shan. The prosecutor may decide not to charge her, or to charge her only with common assault.
   Defence lawyers could argue that Devi had been consistently provoked and brutalised by Shan and that she had acted as a result of provocation.
   In any event, she did not use boiling oil and did not throw it in his face. She should be convicted of common assault, not assault with intent to do grievous bodily harm.

2. Learners acting as magistrates might find Devi guilty of assault with intent to commit grievous bodily harm. Her act was planned in advance and the method used could have caused very severe bodily injuries. The fact that she did not throw the hot oil in Shan's face, and attacked him after being frequently assaulted by him, might be taken into account by the court when passing sentence. Also, the fact that she did not use *boiling* oil, which would have caused even more serious injuries, and possibly death, might also count in her favour. The magistrate would weigh up the circumstances in which Devi assaulted her husband and the interests of society in protecting people from assaults. Although Devi might be convicted of assault with intent to commit grievous bodily harm, her sentence is likely to be reduced because of Shan's past conduct.

3. If Devi could show that she had acted in self-defence, and had thrown the oil at Shan during a fight in order to protect herself, she might be found not guilty. The court would take into account the fact that she was probably physically weaker than Shan, and had been frequently assaulted by him in the past. In the circumstances, her method of defending herself might have been reasonable.

2.2.3   *Crimen injuria* (criminal insult)   *(Learner's Manual p 106)*

Problem 5: Was it a violation of dignity or a violation of privacy?   *(Learner's Manual p 109)*

AIM: The object of this exercise is for learners to understand what constitutes the crime of *crimen injuria*. Learners will also decide whether the different situations are sufficiently serious cases of violations of dignity or privacy that they amount to *crimen injuria*.

PROCEDURE	TIME	
1. Introduce exercise.	Introduction:	5 min
2. Divide participants into small groups.	Group discussions:	15 min
3. Each group may consider all six problems, or each group could be given one problem (if time is short).	Report back:	20 min
	General discussion:	5 min
4. Report back.	**TOTAL:**	**45 min**
5. General discussion.		

1. The actions of the people of the village are a violation of the dignity of the mentally disabled person.
2. Although this is a violation of privacy, it may not be seen as a serious violation.
3. This is a violation of the privacy of the men even though the men are not aware that the woman is spying on them.
4. This is a clear case of a violation of privacy.
5. This is a very serious violation of the weightlifter's dignity as he was humiliated in front of other spectators.
6. This is very insulting for the junior police officers and is an example of insulting and humiliating language.

2.2.4   Kidnapping   *(Learner's Manual p 112)*

Problem 6: Was it kidnapping?   *(Learner's Manual p 112)*

AIM: The object of this exercise is for learners to understand what constitutes the crime of kidnapping. Learners will also decide whether the people in the different situations can be convicted of kidnapping.

PROCEDURE	TIME	
1. Introduce *Learner's Manual* para 2.2.4.	Introduction:	5 min
2. Divide learners into small groups.	Group discussion:	10 min
3. Allocate one question to each group.	Report back:	20 min
4. Report back.	General discussion:	10 min
5. General discussion.	**TOTAL:**	**45 min**

1. The boyfriend can be guilty of the crime of kidnapping as he has violated the control exercised over the young girl by her parents, even though she has consented to her removal by running away from home. However, the young girl cannot legally give a valid consent.

2. The crime of kidnapping can be committed even if there is no physical removal of a person. The father has deprived his daughter of her freedom of movement and will be guilty of the crime of kidnapping.

3. The action of the followers of the rival politician has not permanently deprived the son of his movement. To be guilty of the crime of kidnapping it is sufficient that they intended to release the boy upon the boy's father agreeing to support the motion of the rival politician in Parliament. The conduct of the alleged kinappers was unlawful and they violated the control exercised over the child by his parents and carers.

2.3 Sexual crimes

Outcomes

After completion of this section learners will be able to:

1. List and explain the different sexual offences.

Assessment criteria

1. The legal definition of rape and compelled rape is explained.

2. A set of facts is examined and a decision is made on whether the people were guilty of rape.

3. The procedures that should be followed after a rape attack are explained.

4. Some questions about rape are answered.

5. An explanation is given of sexual assault, compelled sexual assault and compelled self-sexual assault and a set of facts is examined and a decision is made on whether the people were guilty of sexual assault.

6. An explanation is given of sexual crimes against children.

7. A set of facts is examined and a decision is made on whether the people were guilty of statutory rape of children.

8. A set of facts is examined and a decision is made on whether the people were guilty of statutory sexual assault of children.

9. A set of facts is examined and a decision is made on whether the people were guilty of sexual exploitation of children.

10. A set of facts is examined and a decision is made on whether the people were guilty of sexual grooming of children.

11. The duty to report sexual offences against children is explained.

12. An explanation is given of sexual offences against mentally disabled persons and the duty to report sexual offences against them.

13. A set of facts is examined and a decision is made on whether the people were guilty of attempt, conspiracy, incitement or inducing another person to commit a sexual offence.

14. An explanation is given of the services available to victims of sexual assault and compulsory testing of sex offenders.

15. Other sexual offences are identified.

16. Trafficking of persons for sexual purposes is explained.

17. A set of facts is examined and a decision is made on whether the people were guilty of trafficking of persons for sexual purposes.

2.3.1   Rape

(Learner's Manual p 115)

Learners will find rape a delicate and interesting topic for discussion. They might want to consider whether rape should be abolished as a crime against women, and be replaced by non-sex-specific assault laws, as has been done in some countries (eg several states in the United States), as has been suggested by the South African Law Commission.

Learners might be surprised to learn that a man can be guilty of statutory rape even though the female 'consents'. The educator could arrange for a speaker from the local 'rape crisis clinic' (if there is one) to address them.

Problem 1: Was it rape?

(Learner's Manual p 115)

AIM: The object of this exercise is for learners to understand what constitutes the crime of rape. Learners will also decide whether the people in the different situations can be convicted of rape.

PROCEDURE	TIME	
1. Introduce *Learner's Manual* para 2.3.1.	Introduction:	5 min
2. Divide learners into small groups.	Group discussion:	10 min
3. Allocate one question to each group.	Report back:	20 min
4. Report back.	General discussion:	10 min
5. General discussion.	**TOTAL:**	**45 min**

1. The man can be guilty of rape if he intentionally and unlawfully commits an act of sexual penetration with the woman without her consent. In terms of law sexual penetration includes an act which causes penetration by the genital organs (private parts) of one person into or beyond the genital organs, anus (backside), or mouth, of another person. In this case the man had forced his penis into the woman's mouth.

2. The man can be guilty of rape if he intentionally and unlawfully commits an act of sexual penetration with the other man without his consent. In terms of the law the act of sexual penetration includes any act which causes penetration by any other part of the body (including a finger) of one person into or beyond the genital organs or anus of another person.

3. The man can be guilty of rape if he intentionally and unlawfully commits an act of sexual penetration with the woman without her consent. In terms of law sexual penetration includes an act which causes penetration by the genital organs (private parts) of one person into the anus (backside) of another person. The man had forced the prostitute to have sex, and the fact that the woman is a prostitute is no defence to the crime of rape.

4. The woman can be guilty of rape if she intentionally and unlawfully commits an act of sexual penetration with the woman without her consent. In terms of law sexual penetration includes any act which causes penetration by any object into or beyond the genital organs of another person. The woman's insertion of an artificial penis into another woman's vagina against her will is an intentional and unlawful act of sexual penetration.

5. The man can be guilty of rape if he intentionally and unlawfully commits an act of sexual penetration with the woman without her consent. In terms of law sexual penetration includes

any act which causes penetration by any other part of the body of one person into or beyond the genital organs of another person. The man's use of his tongue in the woman's vagina against her will is an intentional and unlawful act of sexual penetration.

2.3.2   Compelled rape

(Learner's Manual p 116)

Problem 2: Some questions about rape

(Learner's Manual p 117)

AIM: The objective of this exercise is for learners to understand why so few rape cases are reported, why there is the crime of 'statutory rape' and why rapes should be reported as soon as possible.

PROCEDURE	TIME	
1. Introduce the exercise.	Introduction:	5 min
2. Divide learners into small groups.	Group discussions:	10 min
3. Allocate one question for discussion by each group.	Report back:	20 min
4. Groups report back.	General discussion:	10 min
5. General discussion.	**TOTAL:**	**45 min**

1.   Many women feel that police treatment of rape victims in the past has been insensitive, although this is being remedied by the employment of sympathetic policewomen to assist victims.
Women also fear the type of questions asked by the police during their investigations, and by the prosecutor during the trial.
The conduct of defence lawyers, however, is one of the factors which makes many women reluctant to report a rape. Defence lawyers in an adversarial system (see *Learner's Manual* para 1.4.2) will use every method they can to discredit the victim's story. Even though it might not be relevant, they may try to pry into her private life, her previous relationships and sexual habits. They will usually try to persuade the court that either she consented to the act, or she led the accused to believe that she had consented. A more sensitive approach by the police and the courts, and the establishment of more rape crisis clinics, would encourage more women to report rape cases.

2.   Learners should be allowed to express their own opinions. In terms of the court procedures and rules of evidence, a woman's past sexual relationships should only be examined if they are relevant; for example, these may be used to show that he or she is likely to have consented to intercourse with the accused because he or she had previously had intercourse with him or her. Generally, however, it is not relevant that she has had sexual relations with people other than the accused. In any event, in a rape case, the fact that a person is a prostitute is not a defence. It may, however, be an indication of his or her attitude towards sex. Prostitution, however, is a defence to 'statutory rape'.

3.   Learners may agree with the law that allows husbands to be convicted of raping their wives – the Family Violence Act states that sex with any woman against her wishes is rape. If a husband or wife has sex with his or her wife or husband without his or her consent, he or she may lay a charge of rape against him or her at the nearest police station.

4.   A girl who is a victim of a rape should tell her parents or a friend immediately and should be examined by a doctor. This is to ensure that she has not been exposed to HIV infection, has not

contracted venereal disease and is not in danger of falling pregnant. She should also contact a rape crisis clinic, if there is one in the area, and the police. The sooner rape is reported, the more likely it is that precautions may be taken against HIV infection and that an accurate statement can be made to the police. It will also make it easier for the police to arrest the rapist and to obtain good medical evidence. A court hearing concerning a rape case might be positively influenced by the fact that the rape is reported 'without undue delay'.

2.3.3 Sexual assault
(Learner's Manual p 117)

Problem 3: Was it sexual assault?
(Learner's Manual p 118)

AIM: The object of this exercise is for learners to understand what constitutes the crime of sexual assault. Learners will also decide whether the people in the different situations can be convicted of sexual assault.

PROCEDURE	TIME	
1. Introduce *Learner's Manual* para 2.3.3.	Introduction:	5 min
2. Divide learners into small groups.	Group discussion:	10 min
3. Allocate one question to each group.	Report back:	20 min
4. Report back.	General discussion:	10 min
5. General discussion.	**TOTAL:**	**45 min**

1. The woman will be guilty of sexual assault if the man did not consent to the act, which includes any act which causes direct or indirect contact between the breasts of a woman and any part of the body of another person.

2. The man may be guilty of sexual assault if the woman did not consent to the act, which includes the direct contact between genital organ or anus of a person or breasts and any object resembling or representing the genital organs.

3. The man can be guilty of sexual assault if he kisses the woman's breasts without her consent. Sexual assault includes any act that causes direct or indirect contact between the mouth of one person and the breasts of a female.

4. The man can be guilty of sexual assault if he kisses the woman's mouth without her consent. Sexual assault includes any act which causes direct or indirect contact between the mouth of one person and the mouth of another person.

5. Sexual assault happens when a perpetrator unlawfully and intentionally sexually violates a victim without his or her consent. The woman could be found guilty of sexual assault, as sexual assault includes any act which causes direct or indirect contact between the mouth of one person and any other part of the body of another person, other than the genitals or anus of that person, which could cause sexual arousal or stimulation.

6. The man could be found guilty of sexual assault, as sexual assault includes any act which causes direct or indirect contact between the mouth of one person and any object resembling the genital organs. In this case the man is forcing the woman to suck on a banana and to pretend she is sucking a penis.

2.3.6 Sexual crimes against children (Learner's Manual p 119)

Problem 4: Was it statutory rape? (Learner's Manual p 120)

AIM: The object of this exercise is for learners to understand what constitutes the crime of statutory rape. Learners will also decide whether the people in the different situations can be convicted of statutory rape.

PROCEDURE	TIME	
1. Introduce *Learner's Manual* para 2.3.6.1.	Introduction:	5 min
2. Divide learners into small groups.	Group discussion:	10 min
3. Allocate one question to each group.	Report back:	20 min
4. Report back.	General discussion:	10 min
5. General discussion.	**TOTAL:**	**45 min**

1. The man commits an act of sexual penetration with the consent of the 11-year-old girl and in terms of the law is guilty of consensual penetration of a child (statutory rape). He cannot raise any kind of defence, as the girl is under the age of 12 years.

2. Both the boy and girl involved are older than 12 years but were under the age of 16 years at the time the consensual sex took place. According to the Sexual Offences Amendment Act, with the written authorisation of the National Director of Public Prosecutions the prosecution can charge both of them with consensual sexual penetration with a child. However, in *Teddy Bear Clinic for Abused Children v Minister of Justice and Constitutional Development* the Constitutional Court said that this section in the Act is discriminatory and unconstitutional. If the boy had been older than 16 years, only the boy would be charged.

3. The woman has committed an act of sexual penetration with the consent of the boy, who is older than 12 years but under the age of 16 years, and is guilty of consensual sexual penetration with a child. However, the woman may raise the defence that she was deceived by the boy into believing that he was 18 years old, and that she reasonably believed that the boy was 18 years old.

4. The boy, who is 16 years of age, has committed an act of consensual sexual penetration with the girl, who is 15 years of age. The boy is 16 years old, so only he can be prosecuted. However, before he is prosecuted there must be written authorisation from the National Director of Public Prosecutions. Although in *Teddy Bear Clinic for Abused Children v Minister of Justice and Constitutional Development* the High Court said that this section of the Sexual Offences Amendment Act is discriminatory and unconstitutional, the Constitutional Court left the matter open and referred it to Parliament for it to consider amending the legislation to conform with the Constitution.

Problem 5: Was it statutory sexual assault? (Learner's Manual p 121)

AIM: The object of this exercise is for learners to understand what constitutes the crime of statutory sexual assault. Learners will also decide whether the people in the different situations can be convicted of statutory sexual assault.

<table>
<tr><td colspan="2">

PROCEDURE

1. Introduce *Learner's Manual* para 2.3.6.2.
2. Divide learners into small groups.
3. Allocate one question to each group.
4. Report back.
5. General discussion.

</td><td colspan="2">

TIME

Introduction:	5 min
Group discussion:	10 min
Report back:	20 min
General discussion:	10 min
TOTAL:	**45 min**

</td></tr>
</table>

1. The man is guilty of the crime of statutory sexual assault, as his act is that of consensual sexual violation with a child. The man can raise a defence by showing that: (a) the child deceived him into believing that she was 16 years old at the time of the alleged commission of the offence and (b) that he reasonably believed the child was 16 years old at the time due to her appearance and what she said.

2. Both the boy and girl were involved are children under 16 years of age. In *Teddy Bear Clinic for Abused Children v Minister of Justice and Constitutional Development* the Constitutional Court said that this section in the Act is discriminatory and unconstitutional.

3. The woman may be guilty of statutory sexual assault as she has consensual sexual violation with a child. She can raise a defence to the charge of statutory sexual assault by showing that: (a) the boy deceived her into believing that he was 18 years old at the time of the alleged commission of the offence and (b) that she reasonably believed the child to have been 18 years old at the time.

Problem 6: Was it sexual exploitation of children? *(Learner's Manual p 124)*

AIM: The object of this exercise is for learners to understand what constitutes the crime of sexual exploitation of children. Learners will also decide whether the people in the different situations can be convicted of sexual exploitation of children.

<table>
<tr><td colspan="2">

PROCEDURE

1. Introduce *Learner's Manual* para 2.3.6.3.
2. Divide learners into small groups.
3. Allocate one question to each group.
4. Report back.
5. General discussion.

</td><td colspan="2">

TIME

Introduction:	5 min
Group discussion:	10 min
Report back:	20 min
General discussion:	10 min
TOTAL:	**45 min**

</td></tr>
</table>

1. In terms of the Sexual Offences Amendment Act the man is guilty of sexual exploitation of children as he unlawfully and intentionally engages the services of a child, with the consent of such child, for financial reward of R100, which is paid to the child for the purpose of engaging in a sexual act with the child. It is a crime if the man commits a sexual act with the child and it's also a crime if the sexual act does not take place, but the services of the child were obtained.

2. In terms of the Sexual Offences Amendment Act the taxi driver is guilty of the offence of sexual exploitation of children. The taxi driver has committed the offence as he (a) intentionally and unlawfully offers the services of a child to the tourist, (b) without the consent of such child, (c) for financial compensation of R300, (d) to the child. The taxi driver is guilty of the crime of

promoting, encouraging or facilitating the commission of a sexual act with the child for purposes of the commission of a sexual act with the child by the tourist.

3. In terms of the Sexual Offences Amendment Act the parents of the girl are guilty of the crime of furthering the sexual exploitation of a child. They are guilty of the crime as they have intentionally or knowingly allowed the 50-year-old man to commit a sexual act with their child, without the consent of the child. The parents, who have intentionally allowed their girl child to be kidnapped in terms of the *ukuthwala* custom as they assisted the man to take their child to his house, may be found guilty of furthering the sexual exploitation of a child.

In terms of the Sexual Offences Amendment Act the parents may be guilty of the crime of benefiting from the sexual exploitation of a child, as they may have received financial compensation for the commission of a sexual act with a child by the man, without the consent of the child. As the crime is based on intentionally receiving benefits from a sexual act with a child, parents or guardians who intentionally allow their girl children to be abducted in terms of the *ukuthwala* custom in exchange for *lobolo* may be convicted of benefiting from the sexual exploitation of children. The man who forced the girl to have sex with him is guilty of statutory rape.

Problem 7: Was it sexual grooming or using children for, or benefiting from, child pornography?
(Learner's Manual p 127)

AIM: The object of this exercise is for learners to understand what constitutes the crime of sexual grooming of children or using children for, or benefiting from, child pornography. Learners will also decide whether the people in the different situations can be convicted of sexual grooming of children or using children for, or benefiting from, child pornography.

PROCEDURE		TIME	
1. Introduce *Learner's Manual* para 2.3.6.4.		Introduction:	5 min
2. Divide learners into small groups.		Group discussion:	10 min
3. Allocate one question to each group.		Report back:	20 min
4. Report back.		General discussion:	10 min
5. General discussion.		**TOTAL:**	**45 min**

1. The Sexual Offences Amendment Act provides a definition of sexual grooming of children (see *Learner's Manual* para 2.3.6.4.2).

The parents are guilty of the crime of promoting the sexual grooming of their children as they have facilitated the production of a film that promotes or is intended to be used in the commission of a sexual act with or by a child. They have also supplied child pornography or film to a syndicate on the Internet with the intention to encourage, enable, instruct or persuade. The parents are also guilty of using the children for child pornography as they have (a) unlawfully and intentionally used the children, (b) with or without the children's consent, (c) for the purposes of creating, making or producing or in any manner assisting to create, make or produce any image, publication, depiction, description or sequence in any manner whatsoever of child pornography.

The parents are also guilty of the crime of benefiting from child pornography as they have knowingly and intentionally gained financially from compensation as a result of selling the video or child pornography.

2. The person is guilty of sexual grooming of children as he or she has shown the children how to use a vibrator to sexually stimulate themselves with the intention of encouraging or persuading such children to perform an act of self-masturbation in his or her presence.

3. In terms of the Sexual Offences Amendment Act it is a crime to unlawfully and intentionally expose or display child pornography or pornography to a child, either with or without the consent of the child. The person who invites and shows the street children such pornography is guilty of the crime of exposure or display of child pornography or pornography to children.

4. The man may be guilty of the crime of sexual grooming if he commits any act with a child with the intention to encourage or persuade such child or to reduce any unwillingness on the part of such child to perform a sexual act with the man. If the man's intention in buying the girl lots of gifts is to reduce her unwillingness to perform a sexual act with the man, then he will be guilty of the crime of sexual grooming. This may be so, as he has asked her 'to be nice' to him.

5. The man may be guilty of the crime of exposing or displaying the exposure or display of genital organs or anus to the children. The man has exposed his private parts to the group of children. However, this offence will not be committed by a person who commits such acts as part of a legitimate cultural practice, which may not be the case in this scenario because the man exposed his private parts to a group of street children.

2.3.8 Attempt, conspiracy, incitement or inducing another person to commit a sexual offence *(Learner's Manual p 130)*

Problem 8: Was it an attempt, conspiracy, incitement or inducing another person to commit a sexual offence? *(Learner's Manual p 130)*

AIM: The object of this exercise is for learners to understand what constitutes the crime of attempting, conspiring, inciting or inducing another person to commit a sexual offence. Learners will also decide whether the people in the different situations can be convicted of attempting, conspiring, inciting or inducing another person to commit a sexual offence.

PROCEDURE	TIME	
1. Introduce *Learner's Manual* para 2.3.8.	Introduction:	5 min
2. Divide learners into small groups.	Group discussion:	10 min
3. Allocate one question to each group.	Report back:	20 min
4. Report back.	General discussion:	10 min
5. General discussion.	**TOTAL:**	**45 min**

1. In terms of the Sexual Offences Amendment Act it is a crime for the man to (a) attempt; (b) conspire with any other person; or (c) aid, abet, induce, incite, instigate, instruct, command, counsel or procure another to commit a sexual offence in terms of the Act. The man has clearly

conspired with the foreign women and assisted them and arranged for his house to be a place where they sell sex.

2. The Sexual Offences Amendment Act makes it a crime for the woman to conspire with other persons and to aid, abet, induce, incite, instigate, instruct, command, counsel or procure another to commit a sexual offence in terms of the Act. By arranging the visas and meeting the women at the airport so that the women can become sex workers, the arrested person was helping to aid and procure them to commit sexual offences in terms of the Act.

3. In terms of the Sexual Offences Amendment Act the man is guilty of a crime as he has attempted to and has offered money to procure the sex worker to commit a sexual offence in terms of the Act.

2.3.10 Other sexual offences (*Learner's Manual p 132*)

Problem 9: Was it trafficking for sexual purposes? (*Learner's Manual p 134*)

AIM: The object of this exercise is for learners to understand what constitutes the crime of trafficking for sexual purposes. Learners will also decide whether the people in the different cases can be convicted of trafficking for sexual purposes.

PROCEDURE	TIME	
1. Introduce *Learner's Manual* para 2.3.10.1.	Introduction:	5 min
2. Divide learners into small groups.	Group discussion:	10 min
3. Allocate one question to each group.	Report back:	20 min
4. Report back.	General discussion:	10 min
5. General discussion.	**TOTAL:**	**45 min**

1. In terms of the Sexual Offences Amendment Act the people who meet the woman from Thailand are guilty of the crime of trafficking in persons for sexual purposes as they have trafficked the woman from Thailand without her consent under the pretence that she will be employed as a secretary in South Africa.

   The people who meet the woman from Thailand are also guilty of the crime of involvement in trafficking in persons for sexual purposes as they have, for sexual purposes, (a) organised, controlled or directed trafficking; (b) performed any act aimed at committing, causing, bringing about, encouraging, promoting, contributing towards or participating in trafficking; and (c) commanded, aided, recruited, or encouraged the woman to participate in trafficking.

2. In terms of the Sexual Offences Amendment Act the woman from the Philippines is guilty of the crime of involvement in trafficking in persons for sexual purposes, as she consented to and participated in trafficking.

2.4 Domestic violence

Outcomes

After completion of this section learners will be able to:

1. Explain what is meant by domestic violence.

Assessment criteria

1. The different types of domestic violence are identified.
2. The duty to report child abuse and children in need of care and protection is explained.
3. The duty to report abuse of older persons in the home and elsewhere is explained.
4. A set of facts is examined and a decision in made on whether the abuse must be reported to the authorities.

2.4.3 Duty to report abuse of older persons *(Learner's Manual p 136)*

Problem 1: Was there a duty to report? *(Learner's Manual p 136)*

AIM: The object of this exercise is for learners to understand when there is a legal duty to report child and elder abuse. Learners will also decide whether the people in the different cases have a duty to report the abuse.

PROCEDURE	TIME	
1. Introduce *Learner's Manual* para 2.4.	Introduction:	5 min
2. Divide learners into small groups.	Group discussion:	10 min
3. Allocate one question to each group.	Report back:	20 min
4. Report back.	General discussion:	10 min
5. General discussion	**TOTAL:**	**45 min**

1. The Children's Act provides that a medical practitioner who on reasonable grounds concludes that a child has been abused in a manner causing physical injury, sexually abused or deliberately neglected, must report such conclusion in the prescribed form to a designated child protection organisation, the provincial department of social development or a police official. According to the Act there is a mandatory duty on designated categories of persons such as the doctor to report instances of abuse or neglect to the relevant authorities. If the doctor fails to comply with this duty he would be guilty of a criminal offence which may also result in civil liability for damages if the child concerned suffers further injury as a result of failure to report.

2. The Children's Act provides that a minister of religion who on reasonable grounds concludes that a child has been abused in a manner causing physical injury, sexually abused or deliberately neglected, must report such conclusion in the prescribed form to a designated child protection organisation, the provincial department of social development or a police official. According to

the Act there is a mandatory duty on designated categories of persons such as the priest to report instances of abuse or neglect to the relevant authorities. If the priest fails to comply with this duty it would be a criminal offence and may also result in civil liability for damages if the child concerned suffers further injury as a result of failure to report.

3. The Children's Act provides that a traditional leader who on reasonable grounds concludes that a child has been abused in a manner causing physical injury, sexually abused or deliberately neglected, must report such conclusion in the prescribed form to a designated child protection organisation, the provincial department of social development or a police official. According to the Act there is a mandatory duty on designated categories of persons such as the traditional leader to report instances of abuse or neglect to the relevant authorities. If the traditional leader fails to comply with this duty it would be a criminal offence and may also result in civil liability for damages if the child concerned suffers further injury as a result of failure to report.

4. The Children's Act provides for discretionary reporting by anyone who on reasonable grounds believes that a child is in need of care and protection, and may report that belief to the provincial department of social development, a designated child protection organisation or a police official. The school teacher has the discretion to report the child's need for care and protection. As the reporting duty regarding children in need of care and protection is discretionary, there is no criminal liability for deciding not to report that a child is in need of care. But where a failure to report that a child needs care and protection results in foreseeable harm to the child it may be a breach of a common-law duty on the person concerned to prevent such harm. This is due to the special relationship the teacher has with the child. Thus the injured child may institute a civil action for damages.

    Upon reporting the child abuse or neglect, the teacher must justify his or her conclusion or belief to the relevant provincial department of social development, a designated child protection organisation or a police official, and if he or she does, he or she will not be liable for any civil action if the report was made in good faith. The teacher in this case has enough information, as the child's parents cannot afford to look after her and she misses classes to go out with 'sugar daddies'.

5. The Older Persons Act states that that any person who is involved with an older person in a professional capacity and who on personal observation concludes that the older person is in need of care and protection must report such conclusion to the director-general of social development. Doctors are clearly involved with their patients in a professional capacity so there would be a legal duty on the doctor to report the abuse of his patient to the authorities.

2.5   Cyber crimes

Outcomes

After completion of this section learners will be able to:

1.   Explain what is meant by cyber crimes.

Assessment criteria

1.   The different types of cyber crimes are identified.

2.   Some sexting terms are listed and explained.

3.   A set of facts is examined and a decision in made on whether the conduct was cyber bullying.

4.   How a person may be protected against cyber crime is explained.

5.   A set of facts is examined and a decision in made on whether what was posted on Facebook violated a person's human rights.

2.5.1   Cyber bullying

(Learner's Manual p 138)

Problem 1: Was it cyber bullying?

(Learner's Manual p 140)

AIM: The object of this exercise is for learners to understand what constitutes the crime of cyber bullying. Learners will also decide whether the people in the different cases can be convicted of cyber bullying.

PROCEDURE
1. Introduce *Learner's Manual* para 2.5.
2. Divide learners into small groups.
3. Allocate one question to each group.
4. Report back.
5. General discussion.

TIME	
Introduction:	5 min
Group discussion:	10 min
Report back:	20 min
General discussion:	10 min
TOTAL:	**45 min**

1.   Cyber bullying is the use of information technology on computers and cell phones to harass, threaten, embarrass, or target another person. Cyber bullying can take place when a person sends hurtful and hateful SMSes to another person. The boy's act of sending a threatening SMS to another boy can be a form of cyber bullying.

2.   Cyber bullying can take place through password stealing. Password stealing happens when a person steals another person's password and then pretends to be that person or locks the person out of his or her account. Cyber bullying occurs if the person pretending to be another does things that harm the other person's dignity or reputation or prevents him or her from using his or her account. The girl using another girl's password is guilty of an offence, as she stole the password to download pornography from the Internet, knowing that it's against the school's rules and will prevent the other girl from using her account.

3. Cyber bullying can take the form of blogs. Blogs allow a person to send a message to a large number of people at once using an online journal. When used in cyber bullying blogs invade another person's privacy or say things that will damage the person's reputation or dignity. The boy using the blog has harmed the dignity of the boy going out with his ex-girlfriend by posting a message that the boy is gay.

4. Cyber bullying can happen where teenagers create an Internet poll inviting fellow teenagers to vote on something that harms another person's dignity or reputation. The girl has created an Internet poll inviting other girls to nominate and send photographs of boys for 'Stud of the Year Award' and some of the boys nominated have had their dignity or reputation harmed as they are embarrassed, upset and angry.

Problem 2: The story of Desiree

(Learner's Manual p 143)

AIM: The object of this exercise is to make learners think about when the law ought to impose a duty to act. Learners should give reasons for their answers.

PROCEDURE		TIME	
1. Introduce the facts of the case study.		Introduction:	5 min
2. Divide participants into small groups.		Group discussions:	10 min
3. Group discussions.		Report back:	30 min
4. Report back.		General discussion:	5 min
5. General discussion.		**TOTAL:**	**50 min**

1. Learners can identify that Desiree's rights to dignity and privacy have been infringed. They can say that Desiree's right to dignity was violated when she was described as a lesbian on Facebook. Learners can say that Desiree's right to privacy was infringed when James copied all their private discussions into his chats with his friends. By so doing James was disclosing private information to his friends.

2. Some learners can argue that Cassandra's right to freedom of expression allows her to say nasty things about Desiree, as the right includes the freedom of imparting information or ideas. Others can argue that Cassandra's right to freedom of expression does not include the freedom to advocate hatred that is based on gender. Therefore, freedom of expression does not allow Cassandra the freedom to say nasty things about Desiree on Facebook.

3. Learners can identify that James infringed the right to privacy and the right to dignity. The right to privacy includes the right not have the privacy of one's communications infringed. James should not have shared his private conversations with Desiree with his friends.
   The right to dignity provides that everyone has inherent dignity and the right to have his or her dignity respected and protected. The right to human dignity requires all of us to acknowledge the value and worth of human beings as members of society. The right to dignity is linked with other human rights, eg equality and privacy. The right to a good name and reputation forms part of the right to dignity.

4. Learners should discuss and draft a plan of action with reference to the information on 'protecting yourself against cyber crime' below. Learners may come up with different plans of action depending on what they are exposed to.

Protecting yourself against cyber crime

1. Places like Facebook, MySpace and Twitter are public spaces.
2. Make sure you do not post anything that you do not want the world to know.
3. Avoid posting your address, contact details or specific whereabouts.
4. Make sure that you report harassment, hate speech and inappropriate content to your Internet service provider, or to your social media provider.
5. Do not post anything that will embarrass you later.
6. Think twice before posting photographs or information that you would not want your parents or friends to see.
7. Do not lie about your age.
8. Make sure you create a strong password that you update regularly – strong passwords are usually at least eight characters with a number and a special character such as an '&' or '@'.
9. Keep different passwords for different online accounts.
10. If a phisher gains access to your e-mail account he or she can request that your password be sent via a 'forgotten password' feature.
11. Make sure that you are on an authentic website when logging into your social media account.
12. If you are asked to log into your account for a second time you may have been redirected to a phishing site.
13. If you receive an e-mail asking you to verify your account and/or giving you a time limit to respond you can assume that the e-mail is fraudulent and is part of a phishing scam – do not respond to such an email in any way.
14. Do not click on unknown links embedded in an e-mail.
15. Install anti-virus and anti-spyware filters, and be sure to keep your operating system updated with the latest patches and firewall software.
16. If a person is attacking you in an electronic public forum, block that person (eg on Facebook you can unfriend a person who is harassing you).
17. Customise your privacy settings to reflect the amount of information you want to share with your online friends.

Note: Parents and older people often find it difficult to keep up with technology – they should get their children or young friends to teach them the basics of online social media.

2.6 Crimes against property

Outcomes

After completion of this section learners will be able to:

1. List and explain the crimes against property.

Assessment criteria

1. The different crimes against property are identified.

2. A set of facts is analysed and a decision is taken on whether any crimes against property have been committed.

3. The elements of the crimes of arson; malicious injury to property; theft; robbery and housebreaking are explained.

Problem 1: Which crimes have been committed? *(Learner's Manual p 149)*

AIM: The object of this exercise is to enable learners to determine whether, in the different circumstances, a crime has been committed.

PROCEDURE	TIME	
1. Introduce exercise.	Introduction:	5 min
2. Divide learners into small groups.	Group discussions:	20 min
3. Each group may consider all seven problems, or	Report back:	15 min
4. each group could be given one problem (if time is short).	General discussion:	5 min
5. Report back.	**TOTAL:**	**45 min**
6. General discussion.		

1. Paul has committed the crime of theft if he takes the radio with the intention of stealing it. If he only intends to borrow it, and knows that Pam will object, he may be guilty of unauthorised borrowing.
2. Sarel is guilty of arson if the building has been damaged by fire (eg, the floor has been scorched). He will also be guilty of malicious injury to property for the damage caused to the carpet.
3. Zo is guilty of housebreaking with intent to commit theft. Even though he did not force his way in, the fact that he pushed the door further open means that there has been a 'breaking'.
4. Ashwin is guilty of malicious injury to property. It is not arson because he did not set fire to a building or immovable structure.
5. Bobby has committed the crime of unauthorised borrowing. If, however, Bobby was friendly with Betty and thought that she would not mind, he would not be guilty of unauthorised borrowing.
6. Vuka is guilty of robbery. Even though Vuka does not use a weapon, he will still be guilty of robbery. A threat of force is sufficient for him to be guilty.
7. If Ismeralda knew that the ring was stolen, she would be guilty of receiving. If she did not know but suspected that it was stolen, she might still be guilty. If Ishmael stole the ring he would be guilty of theft. If he did not know that the ring was stolen, but thought that it might be, he would be guilty of receiving stolen property.

2.7   Crimes against the state

Outcomes

After completion of this section learners will be able to:

1.   List and explain the crimes against the state.

Assessment criteria

1.   Crimes against the state are identified and explained.

2.   The reasons why the state recognises these crimes are identified.

3.   A set of facts is analysed and a decision is taken on which crime against the state has been committed.

Problem 1: Crimes against the state

(Learner's Manual p 152)

AIM: The object of this problem is to encourage learners to think about arguments against, and in favour of, the law being used to suppress political opposition.

PROCEDURE
1. Introduce the exercise.
2. Divide learners into small groups.
3. Allocate one question to each group for discussion.
4. Report back.
5. General discussion.

TIME	
Introduction:	5 min
Group discussions:	10 min
Report back:	15 min
General discussion:	10 min
TOTAL:	**40 min**

1.   The members of the right-wing organisation could be charged with high treason. A democratically elected government should be able to use a crime like high treason to prevent itself from being removed by undemocratic means. The crime of high treason may be used to protect the government from being removed by force. If a parliamentary means of bringing about change in government is fair and open to the majority of people in a country, then clearly it is reasonable for the government to protect itself against treason. There may also be other points of view.

2.   Answers will differ. Some learners might reject public violence as a solution for any problem, except perhaps where the public themselves are the victims of unjustified violence. Therefore it might be argued that if a government uses 'public violence' to maintain itself in power, the public might be justified in using violence to protect themselves from the government. Other learners might argue that, no matter how a government comes to power, its main concern must be law and order. They might say that this is especially true where a government is trying to make reforms. Therefore, the authorities are entitled to prosecute people who disturb the peace or security of others or invade their rights – for whatever reason. They would say that under no circumstances can public violence be condoned. Other arguments may also be raised.

3. Learners who favour freedom of the individual might argue that people should be able to plan together in order to defy, undermine or attack the authority of a government. Indeed, in most democratic countries, the crime of sedition is seldom used. Learners who prefer a more authoritarian approach might say that people should not be able to plan against the authority of the state. If they wish to oppose a government, they should do so through the ballot box. Others might argue that this cannot apply where people do not have the vote – as used to be the case under apartheid. Again, there may be other arguments.

4. The members of the right-wing organisation may be charged with sabotage because they have intentionally endangered public safety and interrupted the movement of rail traffic.

5. Learners in favour of anti-terrorism legislation might say that terrorism requires special measures and that these should be introduced even if it might undermine certain fundamental rights. They might argue that saving human life is more important than protecting civil liberties. Learners against anti-terrorism legislation might argue that the existing measures in the law are sufficient and that the hard-won rights in the Bill of Rights should not be watered down.

Outcomes

After completion of this section learners will be able to:

1.   Explain the crimes against morality involving sexual conduct.

Assessment criteria

1.   The crimes against morality are identified and questions about them are answered.

2.   Incest as a crime is explained.

3.   An explanation of prostitution is provided.

4.   An explanation of bigamy is provided.

5.   An explanation of bestiality is provided.

6.   The crime of sexual acts with a corpse is explained.

7.   The legal position regarding abortion is explained.

8.   The legal position relating to drug offences is explained.

9.   Arguments about whether there should be crimes against morality are advanced.

10. Some questions on the rights of gays and lesbians are answered.

Crimes against morality are controversial because they involve situations where people consent to harm, but society or the state shows its disapproval by labelling their acts as criminal.

Problem 1: Crimes against morality   (Learner's Manual p 156)

AIM: The object of this problem is to make learners think about whether society should use the criminal law to impose moral values on its members for conduct done in private between consenting adults, and if so, when this should be done.

PROCEDURE
1. Introduce the exercise.
2. Divide learners into small groups.
3. Allocate one question from 1–5 to each group for discussion.
4. Report back.
5. Take a stand on question 6.
6. General discussion.

TIME	
Introduction:	5 min
Group discussions on questions 1–5:	20 min
Report back:	10 min
Take a stand on question 6:	10 min
General discussion:	5 min
TOTAL:	**50 min**

1.   The answers to these questions will vary. Some learners might argue that society as a whole should set certain standards of behaviour and its members should be required to abide by them. Others might argue that the state has a protective role and should protect weaker members of

society from their own conduct which will harm them. Some people are weak and likely to be exploited by the unscrupulous if the state does not protect them; for example, people with emotional or other problems might be led into drug addiction. Vulnerable women might be sexually exploited as prostitutes.

Learners in favour of complete individual freedom might say that people should be able to do as they like with their lives, provided they do so in private and do not harm others.

Some will argue that these issues are not the governments' business. Therefore, people should be allowed to indulge in drugs or prostitution in the privacy of their homes.

2. In terms of the law, people who drink alcohol or smoke cigarettes are engaged in using legally acceptable drugs. The consumption of alcohol is also socially accepted, although the smoking of cigarettes is becoming less so. The use of dagga, however, is illegal and is still generally frowned upon by society. Many argue that dagga is worse than alcohol because it makes people lose interest in working, going to school, or leading a useful life. There are, however, some sections of society who would regard the use of dagga as socially acceptable and not harmful. They would also argue that there is no logical reason for distinguishing between alcohol and dagga, as both have effects which can be detrimental to individuals or their families. At present, however, alcohol is socially acceptable but dagga is not. Before the arrival of the European colonists in many parts of the world, dagga was socially acceptable. Today it is not. Recently in the United States of America some states have decriminalised possession of dagga.

3. The learners' responses will depend on their personal attitudes towards prostitution. Some might argue that even though people are punished for prostitution, they do not stop committing it. If prostitution were to be abolished, they would argue, it would make little difference – provided it was done in the privacy of people's homes. They might say that it could still be a crime to engage in such conduct in public. Those in favour of regulating the moral conduct of society might argue that by making prostitution a crime, the social stigma and punishment attached to it acts as a deterrent. They believe that people are influenced by the fact that there is always the danger that if they engage in such conduct, they may be convicted as criminals.

    Some learners might argue that prostitution should be a crime because it leads to the sexual exploitation of women. Others might say that since prostitution is probably the 'oldest profession' in the world, it could be properly controlled by zoning and health regulations. Learners against legalisation of prostitution might argue that most people do not want open prostitution. Its legalisation would weaken the moral fibre of society. Furthermore much prostitution is controlled by organised crime.

    In *S v Jordan*, the Constitutional Court held that making prostitution a crime was not unconstitutional.

4. Learners might say it depends on the age of the children. If the children are under 10 years old, they cannot be prosecuted. Some learners may suggest that this law should be changed. Children from 10 to 14 years are usually presumed to be incapable of forming the intention to commit a crime unless the prosecutor proves otherwise.

    Learners against such children's being prosecuted might argue that young children are impressionable, easily tempted and vulnerable – especially if they come from poor families or broken homes. They would probably say that it is the people who sexually exploit children who should be punished, not the children themselves. The latter should be seen as 'victims' of crimes by adults.

Learners in favour of children who sell sexual favours being punished might argue that if the children know that what they are doing is wrong, and they are old enough to be criminally liable, the ordinary criminal law should apply. Therefore, they should be convicted as accomplices. Furthermore, punishing the children will act as a deterrent to prevent other children from doing the same thing. In terms of the Sexual Offences Act if people over the age of 16 years have sex with such children they can be prosecuted (see above para 2.3.6)

5. Most learners would probably agree that incest should be a crime because it is disruptive of family life, leads to abuse of children and may result in physically or mentally disabled children being born. A minority of learners might suggest that, as long as incest occurs between consenting adults, and precautions are taken against pregnancy, it should be allowed.

6. Learners should be required to line up underneath three signs: on the left a sign stating 'In favour of legalising prostitution'; on the right a sign stating 'Against legalising prostitution'; and in the middle, 'Undecided'. Learners should then be asked to make arguments in favour of their positions and to justify their reasons using the PRES formula (see above Part 1 para G17).

Problem 2: The rights of gays and lesbians   *(Learner's Manual p 157)*

AIM: The object of these exercises is to enable learners to understand the rights of gays and lesbians in the light of the Constitution.

PROCEDURE	TIME	
1. Introduce the case.	Introduction:	5 min
2. Divide learners into small groups.	Group discussions:	10 min
3. Allocate one question to each group.	Report back:	15 min
4. Report back.	General discussion:	5 min
5. General discussion.	**TOTAL:**	**35 min**

1. According to the common law, it was a crime for men to engage in sodomy (ie anal intercourse). Furthermore, according to the Sexual Offences Act 23 of 1957, it was a crime for a man to commit any act which was intended to stimulate sexual passion in another man.

2. The Constitutional Court found that the above two offences violated the right to equality in that they unfairly discriminated against gay men on the basis of sexual orientation. Also, the right to human dignity was found to be violated as gay men were seen to be degraded and devalued by the offences. The right to privacy was also violated as the offences criminalised private conduct between two consenting adults.

3. Learners might agree with the decision of the court if they agree that the rights of equality and dignity are closely related in the present case. This conveys the message that gays and lesbians cannot share family life in a same-sex relationship that is respected or protected by law, and constitutes an invasion of their right to dignity. The Sexual Offences Act was held to discriminate unfairly against gays and lesbians on the overlapping grounds of sexual orientation and marital status, and seriously limited their equality rights and their rights to dignity. It did so in a way which was not reasonable and justifiable in an open and democratic society based on human

dignity, equality and freedom. Learners might disagree with the decision if they feel it is morally wrong for persons of the same sex to be in a physical/intimate relationship.

4. Learners in favour of more rights for gays and lesbians will argue that they should have the same rights as other people. The failure to allow them to marry or adopt children would be against their rights to equality and dignity and would amount to unfair discrimination based on sexual orientation.

Learners against more rights for gays and lesbians will argue that the Constitution allows for limitation of rights, provided the limitations are reasonable and justifiable. They might argue that not many free, open and democratic countries allow for gay and lesbian marriages or adoption by same-sex couples. South Africa does, however, allow these. The Civil Union Act now allows for unions of same-sex couples (see *Learner's Manual* para 4.1.3).

2.9   Crimes involving alcohol and drugs

Outcomes

After completion of this section learners will be able to:

1.   List and explain the crimes of abusing alcohol or possessing or dealing in illegal drugs.

Assessment criteria

1.   Offences in terms of the National Road Traffic Act are identified and explained.

2.   Offences in terms of the Drugs and Drug Trafficking Act are identified and explained.

2.   The reasons why the state recognises these crimes are identified.

3.   A set of facts is analysed and a decision is taken on which crimes involving drugs and alcohol have been committed.

2.9.2   Drug offences   *(Learner's Manual p 159)*

Problem 1: Was it a crime involving alcohol or drugs?   *(Learner's Manual p 160)*

AIM: The object of this exercise is to enable learners to determine whether, in the different circumstances described, crimes involving drugs and alcohol have been committed.

PROCEDURE		TIME	
1. Introduce exercise.		Introduction:	5 min
2. Divide participants into small groups.		Group discussions:	15 min
3. Learners determine acts according to instructions.		Report back:	20 min
4. Report back.		General discussion:	5 min
5. General discussion.		**TOTAL:**	**45 min**

1.   In terms of the National Road Traffic Act the man has committed a crime as he occupied the driver's seat of a vehicle with its engine running on a public road, while under the influence of intoxicating liquor.

2.   The student may be guilty of drinking in public as he was walking on a public road.

3.   In terms of the Drugs and Drug Trafficking Act no person shall use or have in his or her possession any undesirable dependence-producing substance (eg dagga), unless there are statutory grounds of justification. The students have committed a crime.

4.   In terms of the Drugs and Drug Trafficking Act no person shall use or have in his or her possession any undesirable dependence-producing substance (eg dagga), unless there are statutory grounds of justification. The woman may be guilty of the crime of possession of dagga. However, she can raise the defence that she did not have criminal intent as she did not know that the plant was a dagga plant.

5. In terms of the Drugs and Drug Trafficking Act no person shall use or have in his or her possession any undesirable dependence-producing substance (eg dagga), unless there are statutory grounds of justification (eg where X is a patient who has bought drugs on prescription from a pharmacist). The Rastafarian will be guilty of the crime if he or she is unable to provide a legal ground of justification. In *Prince v President, Cape Law Society* the Constitutional Court held that Rastafarians could not be allowed to possess and use dagga for religious purposes.

6. A registered traditional healer may be allowed to prescribe dagga to cure a patient's illness and it may be a legal ground of justification.

Outcomes

After completion of this section learners will be able to:

1.   Identify and explain the different defences to crimes.

Assessment criteria

1.   Defences to crimes are identified.

2.   A situation when no crime has been committed is identified.

3.   A set of facts is examined and a decision is made on whether the person used reasonable force to prevent a crime.

4.   An explanation is given of when a criminal act is committed, but excused or justified.

5.   An explanation of private defence and necessity is given.

6.   Lack of criminal responsibility is explained.

7.   A set of facts is examined and a decision is made on whether there was a defence to each of the crimes.

Problem 1: The use of force to prevent crimes   *(Learner's Manual p 164)*

AIM: The aim of this exercise is to enable learners to determine whether or not the conduct of the persons concerned is excusable or justified.

PROCEDURE		TIME	
1. Introduce the exercise. 2. Divide learners into small groups. 3. Each group to answer both questions. 4. Report back. 5. General discussion.		Introduction: Group discussions: Report back: General discussion: **TOTAL:**	5 min 15 min 10 min 5 min **35 min**

1.   Petrus' conduct is unlawful because he has not acted in self-defence. The burglar was already fleeing. If the burglar was carrying the radio, he could have called on him to drop it. It is unlikely that the court would hold that he was entitled to kill the thief to save his radio. A more successful defence might be raised if the man threatened him with serious bodily injuries and the only way to protect himself was to shoot. Unless the attempt at arrest is proved, however, Petrus would have to be found guilty of unlawfully killing the burglar. The crime would probably be culpable homicide, unless he intended to kill him or shot at him recklessly.

2.   The shop owner can use reasonable force to protect his or her property. Usually deadly force cannot be used to protect property – except in special circumstances. Certainly it cannot be used to stop the theft of a tape recorder – unless perhaps the person threatened the life of the shop owner. The owner could, however, use reasonable force to arrest and detain the shoplifter until

the police arrive. When carrying out a citizen's arrest, the shop owner must tell the shoplifter that he or she is being arrested.

Problem 2: What defences are available? *(Learner's Manual p 166)*

AIM: The object of this exercise is to enable learners to determine whether or not the people concerned had the mental capacity to commit a crime.

PROCEDURE	TIME	
1. Introduce the exercise.	Introduction:	5 min
2. Divide learners into small groups.	Group discussions:	10 min
3. Each group to discuss one question.	Report back:	15 min
4. Report back.	General discussion:	5 min
5. General discussion.	**TOTAL:**	**35 min**

1. Depending on how serious the threat was, the 17-year-old may be able to plead 'duress'. He would have to show that the threat to assault him and his family was real, and would have endangered his life or that of his family or would have caused them serious bodily injury.

2. A six-year-old boy is presumed to be too young to form the mental intent necessary to commit malicious injury to property. He can never be guilty of a crime as he is under 10 years of age. The law would presume that his 13-year-old brother is unable to form the necessary criminal intent – unless the prosecution could prove beyond a reasonable doubt that he intended unlawfully to smash the door. If the latter was proved, he would be guilty of malicious injury to property. The closer a youth is to the age of 14 years, the more likely it is that the prosecution will succeed in proving that he or she had the necessary criminal intent.

3. The man may be regarded as not responsible for his actions. This is because the law recognises that people who are mentally ill should not be punished as they might not have formed the intention to commit the crime. The man could raise the defence of insanity if it can be shown that he could not tell the difference between right and wrong, or could tell the difference between right and wrong but could not act in accordance with this appreciation.

4. Unless the husband was so drunk that he did not know what he was doing, he will be guilty of assault. If his intention to assault was caused by alcohol, it might reduce his punishment. If, however, he knew that if he drank, he would get angry and assault his wife, his drunkenness might be an aggravating factor. If he was so drunk that he could not form the intention to assault her, he would not be guilty, and intoxication would succeed as a defence.

5. The stranger could argue that the man made him so angry by insulting him about his mother that he did not appreciate or know what he was doing. This could succeed as the defence of provocation if it can be shown that the stranger did not have the criminal intention to punch the man in the face.

6. The woman could rely on the defence of mistake if she is able to prove that she genuinely thought that the bundle of clothing contained her clothes.

2.11 Powers of the police and bail

Outcomes

After completion of this section learners will be able to:

1. Understand the powers of the police and what constitutes bail.

Assessment criteria

1. The powers of the police to question are explained.
2. The aim of arrest is explained.
3. A set of facts is examined and a decision is made on what a person should do when stopped and questioned by the police.
4. The powers of the police to arrest with or without a warrant are explained.
5. A set of facts is examined and a decision is made on whether the arrest was lawful.
6. A set of facts is examined and a decision is made on whether the police were entitled to use deadly force.
7. A set of facts is examined and a decision is made on whether a citizen's arrest could be made.
8. The rights of arrested people from the time of arrest are explained.
9. A distinction is drawn between police bail and court bail.
10. An explanation is provided on what to tell the court when applying for bail in court.
11. A set of facts is examined and a decision is made on whether a person should be granted bail.

Learners should be made aware that the police are not above the law or a law unto themselves. They must act within their powers and failure to do so may result in criminal and civil action against them. The police, however often have difficult work to do, particularly when exposed to danger or required to enforce unpopular laws.

2.11.1 Powers of the police to question (Learner's Manual p 167)

Problem 1: The second-hand clothes arrest (Learner's Manual p 169)

AIM: The object of this exercise is to show learners that people who are stopped by the police do not have to tell the police more than their names and addresses. (They may, however, have to produce their identity documents.) Such people do not have to give explanations or make statements. Sometimes, however, it might be wise to do so.

<table>
<tr><td>

PROCEDURE ≔

1. Introduce the facts of the case.
2. Select learners to role-play question 1.
3. Conduct the role-play.
4. Debrief the role-play.
5. Divide the learners into small groups to discuss questions 2–4.
6. Allocate a question to each group.
7. Report back.
8. General discussion.

</td><td>

TIME 🕐

Introduction:	5 min
Select volunteers for role-play:	5 min
Conduct role-play:	5 min
Debrief role-play:	5 min
Group discussions:	10 min
Report back:	10 min
General discussion:	5 min
TOTAL:	**45 min**

</td></tr>
</table>

1. The role-play is designed to teach learners not to become angry or insulting to the police even if they are being harassed. They should be firm but polite when asserting their legal rights. The learner playing Mr Msomi should carry a box or schoolbag when he is accosted by the learner playing the policeman.

    In the street (in front of the class), Mr Msomi's replies to the policeman should be firm but polite. The same should apply to his request for the policeman to identify himself. The learner playing the policeman should adapt a more aggressive approach as Mr Msomi becomes more unco-operative.

    At the police station (with a desk being used as an office counter), Mr Msomi should still request identification before he answers any questions. If the policeman identifies himself, Mr Msomi should give his name and address. He should also ask to contact his lawyer before making a statement. In any event, he cannot be forced to make a statement. The policeman might say that Mr Msomi cannot contact his lawyer because he has not yet been arrested. Mr Msomi should then say he wants to leave as he is not under arrest. If the police refuse to let him go, he should say that if they are detaining him, he wants access to a lawyer. He might also say that if they do not let him contact his lawyer, he will mention it in court.

    At the end of the role-play, the class should analyse how the policeman dealt with Mr Msomi and how he reacted to him. Was the policeman persuasive? Was Mr Msomi obstructive? What should each of them have done?

2. Technically, Mr Msomi is obliged to give his name and address only if the person requesting them is identified as a policeman. In the street, unless the plain-clothes person identifies himself by showing his identity document, Mr Msomi is not obliged to give him any information. At the police station, if the plain-clothes policeman refuses to show his identity, Mr Msomi should ask the station commissioner to tell him to do so. At this stage, however, if he is in a police station, it may be wise just to give his name and address and nothing more. Mr Msomi might, however, decide to answer questions concerning how he came to be in possession of the clothes. He might also tell the police the name of his employer and ask them to check his story. (If they refuse to do this, the police will be acting unreasonably and may subsequently be sued for wrongful arrest.) By answering these questions, Mr Msomi might be released earlier by the police. If he is obstructive, he may be detained for much longer than is necessary to clear up the matter.

3. Some learners might argue that once Mr Msomi knows that the person requesting the information is clearly a policeman, he should provide his name and address. Other learners might argue that whilst Mr Msomi is being harassed by the police, he should in turn confront

them by requesting to see proof of identity as he is entitled to by law. The first group might also say that as Mr Msomi is innocent, he should tell the police where he obtained the clothing and ask them to check with his employer (eg by telephoning the employer). This might save him being held at the police station and having to contact his lawyer. Those against co-operation with the police would argue that Mr Msomi should insist on his legal rights and contact his lawyer to sort matters out.

Others would say that this is unrealistic as most people in South Africa do not have lawyers or the money to hire them. Legal aid, however, may be available if Mr Msomi asks for it when he appears in court.

4. Learners in favour of people having the right to refuse to answer questions by the police might argue that the liberty of citizens can only be protected if people are not obliged to answer such questions. People should be given access to lawyers before they are required to say anything which may prejudice them in a criminal case. If this is not done, people might make damaging statements, based on ignorance or representations by the police, which might result in their being convicted of crimes they may not have committed.

Learners against people having the right to refuse to answer questions by the police might argue that, if people are going to tell the truth, they should not be afraid to do so when questioned by the police. Only 'guilty' people benefit by not having to answer questions by the police. The right to refuse to answer questions benefits guilty people who are then given a chance to make up a story which will allow them to escape a criminal conviction.

If people have the right to keep quiet, the police should tell them about it because many people do not know what their legal rights are. If people do not know their rights and the police do not tell them that they may remain silent, the rule is meaningless. Many people believe that they have to answer questions by the police, and might make damaging statements before they have access to lawyers.

2.11.2 Powers of the police to arrest   *(Learner's Manual p 170)*

Arrests by policemen in films and on television seldom show them using warrants. In practice, however, in most cases, warrants of arrest are used – except where people are arrested when there is a reasonable suspicion that they have committed a serious crime, or they are actually committing a crime and there is no time to obtain a warrant.

It is important to emphasise that being aggressive towards, or not co-operating with, the police when stopped by them could be problematic. It might result in the police treating the person in a worse manner. But this does not mean that a person has to consent to a search or answer incriminating questions. If the police violate a person's rights, the person arrested should try to remember everything, and, after being released from police custody, write it down as soon as possible. The statement should then be taken to an attorney.

Problem 2: Were the arrests lawful?   *(Learner's Manual p 171)*

AIM: the object of this exercise is to make learners aware of when an arrest is, and is not, lawful. They should be able to analyse the case studies and decide what the legal position is in respect of each case.

PROCEDURE		TIME	
1. Introduce the case studies.		Introduction:	5 min
2. Divide learners into small groups.		Group discussions:	15 min
3. Each group to answer all questions.		Report back:	20 min
4. Report back by spokesperson.		General discussion:	10 min
5. General discussion.		**TOTAL:**	**50 min**

1. The arrest of the man without a warrant may be lawful if the police are acting with a reasonable suspicion that the man committed a serious crime. The police arrested the man upon information by an anonymous caller. Unlawful arrests might happen if the police fail to obtain a warrant of arrest when one is required, do not have a reasonable suspicion for an arrest without a warrant, or do not have lawful reasons for the arrest. In this case, it could be argued that the police acted on a suspicion not based on lawful reasons by arresting the man. If the arrest was unlawful, the man may bring an action against the police or the Minister of Safety and Security for damages.

2. The police may lawfully arrest the driver and the passengers if they can show that they reasonably suspected the men of stealing the vehicle. The men and the vehicle fitted the description. Therefore, the police had a reasonable suspicion that they were the people mentioned in the tip-off. They were reasonably suspected of having stolen the VW Beetle.

The need for a 'reasonable suspicion' before issuing a warrant of arrest, or arresting a person without a warrant, is illustrated by Problem 3 below:

Problem 3: The case of the fleeing car thieves   *(Learner's Manual p 173)*

AIM: the object of this exercise is to make learners aware of when police may use force to effect an arrest.

PROCEDURE		TIME	
1. Introduce the exercise.		Introduction:	5 min
2. Divide learners into small groups.		Group discussions:	10 min
3. Each group to answer one question.		Report back:	15 min
4. Report back.		General discussion:	5 min
5. General discussion.		**TOTAL:**	**35 min**

1. The police are allowed by law to use force when arresting suspects only in limited situations. The use of force must be reasonably necessary and proportionate in the circumstances. This means that police may only use the force that is necessary. Learners might argue that the police in this matter used unlawful force as there was no use of life-threatening violence, nor a strong likelihood that the men were to going to cause serious bodily harm to anyone. The police may also use deadly force if they are protecting another police officer who is making an arrest, or any other person, from death or serious bodily harm.

2. The police may use the force necessary to protect a police officer making an arrest. If the suspect is resisting arrest and is threatening the life of the police officer, the police officer may use deadly force in self-defence.

Grounds for arrest				
1	2	3	4	5
no information	suspicion	reasonable suspicion	proof beyond a reasonable doubt	absolute certainty

Note:
Stage 5 is the ideal ground for securing a warrant of arrest or an arrest without warrant.
Stage 3, however, will suffice.
Stage 4 is sufficient for a conviction in a criminal court.
Stages 1 and 2 are not sufficient to justify the arrest of a person.

3. Hijacking a car is a serious crime and in most cases the perpetrators would use life-threatening violence when carrying out the hijacking. In this case, the police officer may use deadly force while the suspect is committing the crime. This is because the police are allowed to use deadly force when the crime is of such a nature that it involves the use of life-threatening violence, or there is a strong likelihood that it will cause serious bodily harm.

Problem 4: The use of force by private citizens   *(Learner's Manual p 174)*

PROCEDURE
1. Introduce the exercise.
2. Divide learners into small groups.
3. Each group is to answer one question.
4. Report back.
5. General discussion.

TIME
Introduction:	5 min
Group discussions:	10 min
Report back:	15 min
General discussion:	5 min
TOTAL:	**35 min**

1. The foreman as a citizen only has the power to arrest in certain situations. Two of these situations are when the person has committed, or is suspected of having committed, a serious offence, or is fighting. An ordinary assault is not a serious offence. The fight between the two employees happened two days previously. Sam was not fighting with Jovu at the time that the foreman tried to arrest him. Thus, the arrest is unlawful, as is the shooting. Even if they were fighting, the shooting would probably be regarded as excessive force and unlawful. The foreman would probably be ordered by the court to pay Sam damages.

2. The shooting of the youths was not lawful unless the youths were threatening the night watchman's life. The law says that if a serious offence has been committed, and there is no other way of arresting the person, the police or a citizen may use reasonable force to arrest the person. Housebreaking is seen as a serious offence. The two youths were resisting arrest by trying to escape. However, unless they were a threat to the night watchman's life or had threatened him with violence, he would not be entitled to shoot them.

2.11.3 The rights of arrested people

(Learner's Manual p 174)

Problem 5: Should an accused be let out on bail?

(Learner's Manual p 177)

AIM: The object of this exercise is to make learners aware of the factors taken into account by the courts when allowing, or refusing, bail.

PROCEDURE		TIME	
1. Introduce the exercise.		Introduction:	5 min
2. Each group is to discuss one scenario in question 1 or question 2.		Group discussions:	10 min
		Report back:	20 min
3. Divide learners into small groups.		General discussion:	5 min
4. Group discussions.		**TOTAL:**	**40 min**
5. Report back.			
6. General discussion.			

1. (a) Most learners would probably argue that Jannie should stay in prison. He stays in a boarding house, has no job and five previous convictions. His previous convictions all concern theft and housebreaking. If Jannie was let out of prison, he may run away or even commit another crime. It is most unlikely that he would return to stand trial if he were released.

   (b) Learners would probably allow Moona out on bail subject to certain conditions. Because he owns a large house and has several businesses, they would probably set the bail very high. As Moona owns a house, is married with children, and owns businesses, it is unlikely that he would fail to stand trial. Learners might suggest, however, that Moona should be required to surrender his passport so that he cannot leave the country and should report to the Westville police station once a week. Dealing with drugs is a serious offence and Moona's release might be strenuously opposed by the state.

   (c) Most learners would probably allow Vuma out on a warning or a nominal amount of bail. Vuma committed the killing during an argument. He lives at home with his family, is a good learner, and has not previously been in trouble with the law. Even if he is let out on a warning, it is likely that he will stand trial on the day his case is heard.

2. Learners in favour of keeping arrested people in prison before trial might argue that many accused persons commit crimes while they are out on bail. They might also argue that by keeping people in prison, the court can make sure that they stand trial on the date set down. Learners against keeping accused persons in prison before trial might argue that statistics show that only a small percentage of these people will in fact be sentenced to a term of imprisonment by the court if found guilty. This means that the taxpayer's money is wasted by keeping such people in prison, because they will be released by the court. Also, first-time accuseds should not be allowed to mix with common criminals as they will learn criminal habits. In any event, it is the courts that should punish people by imprisoning them, not the prosecuting authorities. Learners in favour of pre-trial imprisonment might argue that it should be more difficult to get out of prison before trial. Learners against pre-trial imprisonment might argue that it should be made less difficult because of the reasons mentioned above.

Problem 6: The case of the unlucky couple

(Learner's Manual p 178)

AIM: The object of the exercise is to make learners aware of how they are likely to react to the police in certain situations. It also gives them an opportunity to understand the difficulties facing the police when enforcing the law.

PROCEDURE
1. Introduce the facts of the case.
2. Select volunteers for the role-play in question 1.
3. Conduct the role-play.
4. Debrief the role-play.
5. Divide learners into small groups to discuss questions 2–4.
6. Allocate one question to each group.
7. Group discussion.
8. Report back.
9. General discussion.

TIME	
Introduction:	5 min
Select volunteers for role-play:	5 min
Conduct role-play:	10 min
Debrief role-play:	10 min
Group discussions:	10 min
Report back:	10 min
General discussion:	5 min
TOTAL:	**55 min**

1. The role-play is designed to show how the police and citizens interact, as well as to develop skills for use in police/citizen contacts. Learners playing the roles of Logan and Sandy should be reminded that it is best not to provoke the police by swearing or struggling.
   Nevertheless, they should remain firm about their legal rights concerning questioning, the right to a lawyer and the right to apply for bail. Likewise, the learners playing the roles of constables Van der Merwe and Sibiya should appear firm and polite, rather than aggressive and bullying. The learners' role-play will be coloured by their personal experiences and perceptions of how the police behave. In some schools, it may be possible to arrange for a police officer to observe the role-play and participate in the debriefing by explaining how the police would handle such a situation. In many schools, this will not be possible and a lawyer or law student could be used for the debriefing.

2. The police would certainly have a reasonable suspicion for stopping the car and investigating further. If they thought that Logan and Sandy were armed, they might have told them to get out of the car and searched them for weapons. Whether or not the police have sufficient suspicion for an arrest at this stage is unclear. The extent of their suspicion would be important in determining the type of search they could make. It is not certain whether Logan and Sandy could be arrested on a reasonable suspicion for burglary at the time that the police approached the car.

3. Learners will have their own opinions as to how they think that constables Van der Merwe and Sibiya would act.

4. If they are mistakenly arrested as burglars and the police have acted unreasonably, Logan and Sandy may bring a civil action against them. They may also bring a civil action for wrongful arrest if the police acted without reasonable suspicion, or malicious arrest if they acted out of malice. Constables Van der Merwe and Sibiya, however, would have a good defence. They could say that they made a mistake in good faith based on a reasonable suspicion. If necessary, the police are allowed to use reasonable force to effect an arrest, but if they used excessive force Logan and Sandy could successfully sue for assault. They would not, however, be allowed to resist a good-faith arrest, even if the police made a mistake. If they were abused or mistreated by the police, they could sue them for insult (*injuria*) and, if physically threatened or injured, for assault.

2.12 Search and seizure

Outcomes

After completion of this section learners will be able to:

1. Understand the legal principles applicable to search and seizure.

Assessment criteria

1. The powers of the police to search and to seize property are explained.
2. A set of facts is examined and a decision is taken on whether the evidence should be admitted.
3. Searches with and without warrants are explained.
4. A set of facts is examined and a decision is made on whether the searches carried out were legal.
5. The powers of the police to stop and search vehicles at roadblocks are explained.

2.12.1 The powers of the police to search and seize property
(Learner's Manual p 180)

Problem 1: A case involving the exclusionary rule   *(Learner's Manual p 181)*

AIM: The object of the exercise is to make learners aware that the courts will exclude evidence that is obtained unconstitutionally which will bring the administration of justice into disrepute.

PROCEDURE		TIME	
1. Introduce the facts of the case.		Introduction:	5 min
2. Divide participants into small groups.		Group discussion:	10 min
3. Allocate one question for discussion to each group.		Report back:	20 min
4. Report back.		General discussion:	10 min
5. General discussion.		**TOTAL:**	**45 min**

1. Learners presenting arguments as advocates for the accused might argue that the Constitution guarantees that everyone has the right to privacy. The Constitution also regulates how the police are to collect evidence. Thus, it states that if the police obtain evidence in a manner that violates any rights in the Bill of Rights, that evidence may not be admitted in court if it would make the trial unfair or detrimental to the administration of justice. If the evidence is admitted, it might give the public the impression that the courts tolerate illegal methods of investigation and human rights violations by the police. Also, the administration of justice would be brought into disrepute.

2. Learners presenting arguments as prosecutors might argue that the duty of the police is to ensure that necessary evidence about criminals is collected in order to protect society against crime. When people commit serious crimes, it is the duty of the police to ensure that they are arrested and tried in a court of law. The police should be allowed to use different methods, including the reasonable invasion of privacy of citizens in order to collect evidence that will ensure that

dangerous criminals do not go free. The admission of the evidence would assist the functioning of the administration of justice.

3. Some learners might agree with the court's decision as the court made it clear that the right to privacy is a fundamental right in the Constitution and also that the admission of the evidence would give the public the impression that the courts tolerate illegal methods of investigation and human rights violations.

   Other learners might disagree with the court's decision because if the evidence is excluded, the criminals would go free and the administration of justice would be hampered. In addition, this would not send a good message to the public, which expects the police to play a major role in administration of justice.

4. The Constitution is supreme and any law or conduct inconsistent with it is invalid. This means that all individuals, including the police, should abide by the provisions set out in the Constitution. The Constitution protects the human rights of all individuals, including the police. If the evidence collected by the police was admitted in court, the Constitution itself would be undermined because it would allow the police to mislead the courts in order to obtain a conviction.

Problem 2: Searches by the police (Learner's Manual p 184)

AIM: The object of these case studies is to enable learners to distinguish between situations where the police may search premises with search warrants, without search warrants, and when they may not search the premises.

PROCEDURE		TIME	
1. Introduce the exercise.		Introduction:	5 min
2. Divide learners into small groups.		Group discussions:	10 min
3. Allocate one question for discussion by each group.		Report back:	15 min
4. Report back by spokespersons.		General discussion:	5 min
5. General discussion.		**TOTAL:**	**35 min**

1. The search was legal even though there was no search warrant because Elsa, Hendrik's mother, consented to his room being searched.

2. The search was unlawful. Even though the police had a search warrant, they should have shown it to Brad when he requested them to do so. It was also unlawful because it was unreasonable for the police to search the house, and in places like dressing table drawers and the refrigerator, for stolen cars. They should have confined their search to the garage and outside premises. Brad could sue the police for invasion of privacy.

3. The search was legal because a warrant had been issued for Raj's arrest. No search warrant is necessary if a person has been arrested.

4. The search is illegal. The police had no search warrant and Muzekile did not consent to the search. Also, the police had no reason to believe that Muzekile had committed a crime. She could sue them for invasion of privacy.

AIM: The object of this problem is to show learners the powers of the police when manning roadblocks.

PROCEDURE		TIME	
1. Introduce the exercise to the learners.		Introduction:	5 min
2. Each learner is to consider the problem individually.		Individual work:	15 min
3. Report back.		Report back:	20 min
4. General discussion.		General discussion:	5 min
		TOTAL:	**45 min**

The police did not have reasonable grounds for suspecting that the car contained the escaped prisoners because it was a different make and colour from that described in the police alert. It is a criminal offence for a vehicle to fail to stop at a roadblock after being directed to do so by the police. The driver can be fined or imprisoned. It is not, however, a serious offence like those listed in the *Learner's Manual* para 2.2.1. Therefore, the use of deadly force in this case is unlawful. In a similar case, where this actually happened, the policeman who fired shots that injured people in the car was found guilty of assault with intent to do grievous bodily harm.

Outcomes

After completion of this section learners will be able to:

1. Demonstrate an understanding of the criminal trial and sentencing process.

Assessment criteria

1. The procedures to be followed in a criminal process are explained.
2. A set of facts is examined and a decision is made on what steps will be taken during an arrested person's trial.
3. The different types of sentences are identified.
4. A set of facts is examined and a decision is made on what would be an appropriate sentence.
5. The arguments for and against the death penalty are explained.
6. The meaning of vigilantism is explained.
7. A decision is taken on the effectiveness of community policing forums.

2.13.1 The criminal process
(Learner's Manual p 186)

Problem 1: Making the prison population smaller
(Learner's Manual p 187)

AIM: The object of these questions is to encourage learners to think about: (a) how the prison population can be reduced; (b) whether it is practical to provide a lawyer for every accused person who might be sent to prison; and (c) whether or not they would change the law regarding legal representation for an accused person who might be sent to prison.

PROCEDURE		TIME	
1. Explain the exercise.		Explanation:	5 min
2. Divide learners into small groups.		Group discussions:	10 min
3. Allocate one question for discussion to each group.		Report back:	15 min
4. Report back.		General discussion:	5 min
5. General discussion.		**TOTAL:**	**35 min**

1. Methods of reducing the large number of awaiting trial and sentenced prisoners might be by: (a) making them aware of their right to a lawyer from the time of their arrest; (b) simplifying bail application procedures; (c) requiring the police to tell arrested persons that they have a right to a lawyer, bail and legal aid, if they are poor; (d) requiring the court to ensure that unrepresented accused persons are informed of their right to a lawyer, bail or legal aid if they qualify; and (e) reducing the number of criminal offences – especially petty crimes.

2. Arguments in favour of making sure that every accused person who might be sent to prison, if found guilty, is given a lawyer are: (a) it would ensure that the adversary system works properly;

(b) as the state is represented by a lawyer (the prosecutor), the accused should also be represented by a lawyer; (c) accused persons in criminal cases cannot represent themselves properly as they do not know how the criminal justice system works; (d) accused persons represented by lawyers have a better chance of being acquitted; (e) unrepresented accused might not feel that they have had a fair trial; and (f) it would give the criminal justice system more credibility in the eyes of the community.

Arguments against making sure that every accused person who may be sent to prison, if found guilty, is given a lawyer are: (a) there are not enough lawyers to defend all accused persons; (b) judges and magistrates are trained to discover the truth; (c) the adversarial system is designed to ensure that people have a fair trial; (d) accused persons are presumed innocent until proved guilty; (e) there is a heavier burden on the state to prove that an accused is guilty than on the accused to prove his or her innocence; and, (f) it is less likely that a guilty person will be found guilty than that an innocent person will be wrongly convicted.

3. Learners' responses will vary according to which of the above arguments they favour. Learners wishing to introduce a new law might include provisions that require the following:

   (a) Every accused person who is faced with the possibility of a prison sentence must be represented by a lawyer, unless he or she knowingly decides not to be so represented.

   (b) On arrest, people must be told by the police that they have the right to consult a lawyer, and, if they cannot afford one, that they may obtain legal aid.

   (c) On arrest, people must be told by the police that they may apply for bail.

   (d) Accused people who appear in court must be told by the court that they have a right to a lawyer and may apply for legal aid if they cannot afford a lawyer.

   (e) Accused people who appear in court must be asked by the court if they wish to apply for bail.

   Most of these rights are provided for in the Constitution.

2.13.2 The criminal trial
(Learner's Manual p 187)

Problem 2: The case of the stolen car
(Learner's Manual p 191)

AIM: The object of this case example is to encourage learners to understand what people should do when they are charged with crimes. It also makes them think about the court procedures involved and what can be done if a person is convicted. Learners are also given an opportunity to discuss whether they think that Jay was guilty of a crime.

PROCEDURE	TIME	
1. Introduce the facts of the case.	Introduction:	5 min
2. Select volunteers for role-play in question 1.	Select volunteers for role-play:	5 min
3. Conduct role-play.	Conduct role-play:	10 min
4. Debrief role-play.	Debrief role-play:	10 min
5. Divide learners into small groups to discuss questions 2–6.	Group discussion:	20 min
6. Allocate one question to each group.	Report back:	5 min
7. Report back.	General discussion:	5 min
8. General discussion.	**TOTAL:**	**60 min**

1. Learners should first role-play what they think Jay and the police are likely to do at Jay's house. Thereafter, they should role-play what they think should happen if Jay is taken to the police station. Learners playing Jay should remember what his rights are if he is questioned and arrested by the police.

   The first thing that Jay should do after being arrested is to request to contact his lawyer. The law says that he is entitled to a lawyer from the moment of his arrest. If the police refuse to let him contact a lawyer, he should tell this to the magistrate when he is brought to court. He should also ask the police if he can have bail. As he has been arrested for a minor offence, the police should let him out on bail. Jay will be asked to make a statement, but need only give his name and address. He should say that he will make a statement only if his lawyer is present.

2. Unless Jay is arrested on a Friday, in which case he will have to wait until the Monday, Jay should appear before a magistrate within 48 hours.

3. When Jay is first brought to court, he will be charged and asked to plead. If he has not been allowed to contact his lawyer, he should tell the magistrate that he wants to consult a lawyer. If he cannot afford a lawyer, he should tell the magistrate that he wants legal aid. If he has been abused by the police (eg they would not let him contact a lawyer, or assaulted him), he should bring this to the attention of the magistrate. If he is asked to plead, he should say that he is not guilty. If the magistrate asks him to explain his defence, he should say that he mistakenly got into the wrong car. It is not necessary for him to go into details and he should not do so. If he does, it might make it difficult for his lawyer to defend him. He should say that he does not wish to plead until he has consulted a lawyer. If he is not out on bail, Jay should ask the magistrate to give him bail. Usually, the court will allow people bail if they have permanent addresses and jobs. Bail is a deposit paid to the court which is lost if the person to whom it applies fails to come to court on the date set down for trial. The bail money will be returned to Jay if he appears in court as required.

4. At the trial, Jay will again be asked to plead. If he pleads not guilty, the prosecutor will call the State witnesses. The main witness is likely to be Roy, who will tell the court his story. Jay's lawyer will then cross-examine Roy, who may be re-examined by the prosecutor. After all the State witnesses have given their stories, been cross-examined and re-examined, the prosecutor will close his case. Jay's lawyer will then call his witnesses. The main witness will be Jay. He will have to give his evidence before the other witnesses for the defence. Jay will tell his story and then be cross-examined by the prosecutor.

   Jay's lawyer will then re-examine him to clear up any problems that may damage his defence. After all the defence witnesses have been called, cross-examined and re-examined, Jay's lawyer will close the defence's case. The prosecutor will then argue why Jay should be found guilty, and Jay's lawyer will argue why Jay should be found not guilty. The magistrate will listen to the arguments and give a judgment.

5. It is the crime of 'unauthorised borrowing' to take a person's car without permission. It might be a defence, however, for the person taking the car to show that he or she made a genuine mistake and thought that the car belonged to him or her. The law would probably accept that a genuine mistake by Jay would be a good defence to theft or the crime of unauthorised borrowing. If Jay had found out about this mistake when he arrived home, should he not have tried to contact the real owner, or taken the car back to the car park? Do you think that the court would believe his story that he did not know that the car was not his after he had driven it for a while?

6. If Jay is found guilty of stealing the car or of using it without the permission of the owner, he may appeal to the High Court (see *Learner's Manual* para 1.3.1.7.2). In order to appeal, he would have to show that the magistrate made a mistake about the facts of the case or applied the law wrongly. In this case, he could argue that the magistrate made a mistake about the law. In other words, the magistrate should have found him not guilty because he did not intend to steal or use the car without the owner's permission. He made a genuine mistake.

Problem 3: Giving evidence and being defended   *(Learner's Manual p 192)*

AIM: The object of this exercise is to make learners think about whether accused persons should give evidence in a trial and why it is necessary for accused persons to be represented by lawyers.

PROCEDURE ⸭	TIME ◷	
1. Introduce the aim of the exercise.	Introduction:	5 min
2. Divide learners into small groups.	Group discussions:	15 min
3. Allocate one question to each group for discussion.	Report back:	20 min
4. Report back.	General discussion:	5 min
5. General discussion.	**TOTAL:**	**45 min**

1. Arguments in favour of an accused not having to give evidence in a criminal case might be: (a) an accused is presumed innocent until proved guilty; (b) the duty is on the state to prove the accused's guilt; (c) there is no duty on accused persons to assist the state in proving their guilt; and, (d) if the State's case is weak, an accused should be able to apply for a discharge after the State has closed its case, without having to lead evidence in defence (eg as in the Shrien Dewani case). Arguments against an accused not having to give evidence might be: (a) the court has no opportunity to discover whether or not the accused is telling the truth; (b) if an accused is innocent, he or she should not be afraid to give evidence; (c) an accused who refuses to go into the witness box gives the impression that he or she has something to hide; and (d) a failure by the accused to give evidence may prevent the court from discovering the truth, and allow a guilty person to escape conviction.

2. The advantages of allowing accused persons to give evidence are that, if they are articulate and honest, they will make a good impression on the court. Furthermore, if the accused persons are innocent and candid with the court, it will assist the court in coming to a decision in their favour. The disadvantages of allowing an accused to give evidence are that, if the accused is inarticulate and unlikely to be an impressive witness, it might be best not to put such a person in the witness box. This applies even if the accused are innocent, because if they become confused and make a bad impression, they might not be believed by the court. As a general rule, however, innocent accused should give evidence. If the accused are guilty, it might be unwise to let them give evidence, since a defence lawyer cannot mislead the court by leading evidence that is false or untrue. It might be tactically better to attack the State's case and destroy the credibility of its witnesses, instead of running the risk of the accuseds' guilt being exposed by their evidence. If, however, the accused plead guilty, there may be no need to give evidence except to say why the sentence should be reduced.

3. The reaction of the learners will vary according to how they feel about the arguments mentioned in 1 above. An accused in a criminal trial has the right to remain silent and to let the prosecution prove his or her guilt. The State must prove the guilt of the accused beyond a reasonable doubt. If there is any doubt, the prosecutor will not have proved the accused's guilt. In general, therefore, a judge or magistrate should not draw any inference from the accused's failure or refusal to give evidence, as he or she would merely be exercising the right to remain silent. Where, however, the State has proved facts which, if not disproved by the accused himself or herself, would establish the guilt of the accused, the latter cannot afford to remain silent. In this case, if there is no contrary evidence in favour of the accused, he or she might be obliged to give evidence, otherwise there will be a finding of guilty.

4. Even if accused persons are innocent, because the judge or magistrate does not help the accused (or prosecutor) to run their cases, the accused might not know when it is necessary to call certain witnesses. The accused might also not know how and when prosecution witnesses should be cross-examined or when defence witnesses should be re-examined. Because accused persons often do not know the legal requirements for the crime charged and the possible defences to it, they might not know how to go about defending themselves. They cannot simply stand up in court and say that they are innocent. The court will expect them to lead some evidence to confirm this.

This is usually done by calling defence witnesses or destroying the State's case by showing that the prosecution witnesses are unreliable or not telling the truth. This can only be done by proper cross-examination, which is difficult for people who are not used to court procedures. If prosecution witnesses are able to get away with telling lies, or with less than the whole truth, an innocent person could be found guilty of a crime.

2.13.3 The sentencing process

(Learner's Manual p 192)

Problem 4: The death penalty case

(Learner's Manual p 194)

AIM: The object of these questions is to encourage learners to understand the arguments on both sides concerning the death penalty and whether it should still be applied in South Africa. Learners are also required to consider whether there should be minimum penalties for some crimes.

PROCEDURE
1. Explain the facts of the case.
2. Divide learners into small groups.
3. Allocate one question to each group for discussion.
4. Report back.
5. Take a stand on question 5.
6. General discussion.

TIME	
Explanation:	5 min
Group discussion:	10 min
Report back:	20 min
Take a stand:	10 min
Discussion:	5 min
TOTAL:	**50 min**

1. The answer is in the *Learner's Manual* in para 2.13.3.2. In addition, learners in favour of the death penalty might contend that it is morally justifiable to take the life of one who has taken

the life of another. They might also say that it acts as a deterrent to discourage people from murdering each other or committing treason or other dangerous crimes against the state. Another argument might be that it costs too much to keep convicted murderers in jail for long periods of time. Furthermore, keeping political prisoners in jail, rather than executing them, raises the danger of their being used as bargaining chips for exchanging hostages kidnapped by 'terrorists'. (If the death penalty is allowed, maybe it should be limited to crimes where people have intentionally and unlawfully killed others? Learners may express their own views.)

2. The answer is in the *Learner's Manual* in para 2.13.3.2. In addition, learners against capital punishment might argue that it is morally wrong to take the life of anyone convicted of a crime. They might also argue that the death penalty does not discourage crime any more than life imprisonment. Studies show that most murders result from fear, passion, mental disorder or the anger of the moment. Furthermore, where political offenders may be executed because of unlawful acts motivated by political considerations, their execution might glorify the deeds and causes for which they were condemned to death. The death penalty might occasionally be imposed on an innocent person. Unlike other sentences, the death penalty cannot be reversed if new evidence is found.

3. The answer is in the *Learner's Manual* in para 2.13.3.2. The Constitutional Court eventually decided that the death penalty is unconstitutional and that people in South Africa may no longer be sentenced to death. The court felt that the death penalty infringes the rights to life, dignity and not to be subjected to cruel, inhumane or degrading punishment. It also said that the death penalty is arbitrarily imposed and there was no evidence that it acted as a deterrent. Some judges said that it was against the principle of *ubuntu* common to traditional indigenous customs.

4. Learners can make up their minds as to whether or not they agree with the Constitutional Court. They should be required to give reasons for their answers.

5. Learners should be asked to take a stand on the death penalty by lining up under signs reading 'In favour', 'Against', and 'Undecided'. Learners should then be asked to argue in favour of their positions and to justify their reasons using the PRES formula (see above Part 1 para G17).

Problem 5: How would you have sentenced the criminal? *(Learner's Manual p 197)*

AIM: The object of this exercise is for learners to understand the factors a court takes into account when sentencing a person convicted of a crime.

PROCEDURE		TIME	
1. Explain the aim of the exercise.		Explanation:	5 min
2. Divide learners into small groups.		Group discussions:	15 min
3. Allocate one question to each group for discussion.		Report back:	20 min
4. Report back.		General discussion:	5 min
5. General discussion.		**TOTAL:**	**45 min**

When choosing a sentence, learners should take into account the different aims of sentencing (*viz* retribution, deterrence, rehabilitation or incapacitation). In determining these aims, they should also consider the interests of the criminals, the victims and the needs of society.

1. Petrus is an 18-year-old youth who is unrepentant because he says that he did not commit the crime. He comes from a broken home, but is a good scholar who has been misled by a gang of older boys. Two years previously, he had been convicted of theft. The watchman he stabbed is paralysed for life. The watchman and society are likely to be outraged if Petrus is not punished for his crime. They would demand retribution. Because of his previous conviction, it might also be necessary to deter him from committing any further crimes. It might also be desirable to try to rehabilitate him. There is no evidence requiring that he should be imprisoned for a long period of time to protect society.

    Learners who favour the retribution approach might argue that he should go to prison for a fairly long term (eg five years), because of the severe injury caused to the watchman.

    Learners more concerned with deterrence and rehabilitation might argue that he should be given a suspended sentence, combined with an order that he should at first assist, and then, when he begins working, pay compensation to the watchman. A compromise might be a sentence of, say, five years in prison, four years of which are suspended on condition he gives assistance and compensation to the watchman for his lost earnings.

2. Jopie is a 56-year-old 'white-collar' criminal. He has defrauded a number of banks of R100 000 but is sorry for what he has done. He has also co-operated with the police during their investigations. He has been a useful member of society, and is able to support himself and his wife.

    Learners who favour retribution might argue that because Jopie was an accountant, a respected person, and a church-goer who committed a large fraud on a number of banks, he should be severely punished (eg seven years in prison). Learners who prefer deterrence might argue that he should be given a suspended sentence (eg seven years, six of which are suspended).

    Those who favour rehabilitation might suggest that the suspended sentence should be conditional upon community service (eg by providing free accounting services to several welfare organisations), together with a compensation order in favour of the banks. Most learners will probably agree that there is no purpose in sending Jopie to prison as he would lose his job. The state would then have to support his wife.

2.13.4 Vigilantism
(Learner's Manual p 197)

Problem 6: A vigilante case study – a murder accused has his bail paid by vigilantes
(Learner's Manual p 199)

PROCEDURE	TIME	
1. Introduce the facts of the case.	Introduction:	5 min
2. Divide learners into small groups.	Group discussions:	15 min
3. Each group is to discuss both questions.	Report back:	20 min
4. Report back.	General discussion:	5 min
5. General discussion.	**TOTAL:**	**45 min**

1. The learners' responses might vary. Some learners might argue that the actions of the residents were wrong. This is because the criminal justice system should have been allowed to take its course.

With violence and death as key vigilante objectives, this form of justice goes against the human-rights approach of the South African Constitution. The action of the residents does not allow the alleged offender to defend himself, nor does it allow for a fair trial.

It also goes against the presumption of innocence. What is to be done if it is found that the victim of vigilante action was innocent?

Other learners might argue that the actions of the residents are justified by the failure of the criminal justice system. Also, there are not enough police to do the proper work of tracing and arresting offenders. The residents might also feel that it is better for them to administer their own justice equivalent to the violent death the alleged murderer had caused his victim.

2. The Constitution does not allow people to take the law into their own hands. The Constitution sets out the rules for the working of the government and how the government must relate to the people. It also sets out the rules regarding the treatment of persons who are accused of crimes. The Constitution also has a Bill of Rights which lists the rights of individuals, such as the right to life, human dignity and the right to equality. The Constitution is the most important law in South Africa and law or conduct inconsistent with it is invalid.

2.13.5 Community policing forums *(Learner's Manual p 200)*

Problem 7: Questions on community policing forums *(Learner's Manual p 200)*

PROCEDURE		TIME	
1. Introduce the aim of the exercise.		Introduction:	5 min
2. Divide learners into small groups.		Group discussions:	10 min
3. Each group is to discuss both questions.		Report back:	15 min
4. Report back.		General discussion:	5 min
5. General discussion.		**TOTAL:**	**35 min**

1. Some learners might know, and others might not, if their area, or some other area, has a community policing forum. CPFs were introduced in South Africa during the period of transition from apartheid to democratic rule.

2. CPFs were intended to be broadly representative of the local community. They can be seen to have played a positive role in providing channels for social concern about crime and the establishment of networks of cooperation within communities.

   Some learners might argue that CPFs have enabled the police to establish relationships only with particular sections of local communities. Their voluntary nature has also, in part, been a problem, with the poorer communities less able to sustain this type of participation. Even the cost of travelling to and from meetings is an impediment to the functioning of CPFs in some areas.

   Some learners might also argue that, in several areas, the communities have lost faith in their CPFs because no matter how much they complain about the inefficiencies of the police, nothing is done. At the end of the day, it is the quality of the leadership and dedication of the police officers that makes a difference, not whether or not there is a CPF. Others will argue that efficient and effective police officers would ensure that the CPF is taken seriously.

Outcomes

After completion of this section learners will be able to:

1. Explain what is meant by child justice.

Assessment criteria

1. An explanation is given of who is regarded as a child in conflict with the law.
2. An explanation is provided on what is meant by the criminal capacity of children.
3. A set of facts is examined and a decision made on whether a child can be charged with a crime.
4. An explanation is given of how probation officers assess children in conflict with the law.
5. An explanation is given of a preliminary inquiry and how it works.
6. An explanation is given of how diversion works and the different types of diversion.
7. A set of facts is examined and a decision made on whether the child should be diverted out of the criminal justice system.
8. An explanation is provided regarding the operation of child justice courts.
9. The different sentences that are usually used for children in conflict with the law are identified.
10. A discussion is held on whether children in conflict with the law should be rehabilitated or punished.
11. A set of facts is examined and a decision made on whether or not the proceedings should be stopped and the child referred to a children's court.

2.14.2 Criminal capacity of children   *(Learner's Manual p 202)*

Problem 1: The case of the jealous child   *(Learner's Manual p 203)*

AIM: The object of this exercise is to show that children under the age of 10 years of age are regarded as incapable of committing crimes.

PROCEDURE	TIME	
1. Explain the facts of the case.	Explanation:	5 min
2. Divide learners into small groups.	Group discussions:	15 min
3. Each group is to discuss all questions.	Report back:	20 min
4. Report back.	General discussion:	5 min
5. General discussion.	**TOTAL:**	**45 min**

Damon will not be found guilty of murder because he is under 10 years of age and is presumed to be incapable of forming the criminal intention necessary for murder. As he is under 10 years of age the police may not arrest him but must hand him over to his parents. The police must also inform a probation officer that Damon, who is under the age of 10 years, is suspected of having comitted a crime.

Learners who think that Damon should be punished by the law might argue that, even though he was under 10 years of age, he knew that what he was doing was wrong. He deliberately killed his brother and sister so that he could have his parents' full attention.

Learners who think that Damon should not be punished by the law might argue that, because Damon was under 10 years of age, he was not really able to distinguish between right and wrong. In any event, it would be unfair to treat a child under the age of 10 years like an adult when it comes to deciding criminal intention.

Learners in favour of criminally punishing a child under the age of 10 years might argue that the law should be changed to be the same law that applies to criminal acts by children of 10 to 14 years of age. The law could be worded as follows:

'Any child under the age of 14 years shall be presumed to be incapable of committing a criminal act, unless the State can show beyond a reasonable doubt that at the time the child committed the act he or she knew that it was wrong, and that it would have the results that it did'.

2.14.3 Assessment

(Learner's Manual p 204)

Problem 2: The case of the cruel boys

(Learner's Manual p 205)

AIM: The object of this exercise is to make learners aware of what the duties of the police and probation officers are when faced with children older than 10 years who are alleged to have committed a crime.

PROCEDURE
1. Introduce the facts of the case.
2. Select volunteers for role-plays.
3. Conduct role-plays.
4. Debrief role-plays.
5. Divide learners into small groups to discuss role-plays.
6. Allocate one role-play discussion to each group.
7. Report back.
8. General discussion.

TIME	
Introduction:	5 min
Select volunteers for role-plays:	5 min
Conduct role-plays:	10 min
Debrief role-plays:	10 min
Group discussion:	20 min
Report back:	5 min
General discussion:	5 min
TOTAL:	**60 min**

1.   As the investigating police officer you should arrest Sam and Vusi and then refer them to a probation officer for an assessment report to be done on each so that the report can be presented to the magistrate at a preliminary inquiry. The police should also inform their parents or carers.

2.   As the probation officer to whom Sam and Vusi have been referred for assessment, you need to carry out the duties mentioned in para 2.14.3.1 of the *Learner's Manual* and prepare an assessment report on each of them. You then need to present the reports at the preliminary inquiry.

2.14.5 Diversion

(Learner's Manual p 207)

Problem 3: The case of the drug-taking school children *(Learner's Manual p 213)*

AIM: The object of this exercise is to understand how a preliminary inquiry works and how presiding magistrates decide on which diversion options would be appropriate.

PROCEDURE	TIME	
1. Introduce the facts of the case study.	Introduction:	5 min
2. Divide participants into small groups.	Group discussions:	10 min
3. Group discussions.	Report back:	30 min
4. Report back.	General discussion:	5 min
5. General discussion.	**TOTAL:**	**50 min**

1. The people who may attend the preliminary inquiry are the child, the child's parent or an appropriate adult, the probation officer and, if a diversion order is likely to be made, a diversion service provider identified by the probation officer.

2. Some learners acting as the magistrate at the preliminary inquiry might say that the children should be diverted away from the criminal justice system because they are school children who are merely experimenting, as teenagers do, and are not a danger to society. It would be unfair for them to receive a criminal record at this early stage in their lives. They may also raise other arguments.

    Others might argue that because drug-taking is a big problem at the school (and other schools) the children should be made an example of and punished by the law. If the children are not diverted they (and others) will think that what they did was not serious and may continue taking drugs. If they are subjected to the criminal justice system they (and others) will think twice about taking drugs in future. They may also raise other arguments.

3. The answer lies in para 2.14.5.1 of the *Learner's Manual*. It will depend upon the value of the drugs found on the children as to whether they qualify for a Level 1, Level 2 or Level 3 diversions. If they qualify for a Level 1 diversion – as the children are over 14 years of age – they can be given not more than 24 months of diversion. If they qualify for Level 2 or 3 diversions they cannot receive more than 48 months of diversion. Learners might suggest that the school children should be diverted to work at a drug rehabilitation centre on Saturday mornings and during their school holidays. Other suggestions could also be made.

2.14.6 Child justice court

(Learner's Manual p 214)

Problem 4: The hungry boy

(Learner's Manual p 216)

AIM: The object of this exercise is to understand how diversion works. Learners will decide on the different diversion options that could apply to the hungry boy.

<table>
<tr><td colspan="2">**PROCEDURE** ▶≡</td><td colspan="2">**TIME** 🕐</td></tr>
<tr><td colspan="2">1. Introduce the facts of the case study.</td><td>Introduction:</td><td>5 min</td></tr>
<tr><td colspan="2">2. Divide participants into small groups.</td><td>Group discussions:</td><td>10 min</td></tr>
<tr><td colspan="2">3. Group discussions.</td><td>Report back:</td><td>30 min</td></tr>
<tr><td colspan="2">4. Report back.</td><td>General discussion:</td><td>5 min</td></tr>
<tr><td colspan="2">5. General discussion.</td><td>**TOTAL:**</td><td>**50 min**</td></tr>
</table>

1. Some learners might argue that Thami is a good candidate for diversion because he is only 12 years old and should be kept out of the criminal justice system. He is also ignored by his parents and has to rely on his own resources to feed himself. They may also raise other arguments. Other learners might say that Thami is not a good candidate for diversion but should rather be sent to a children's court to determine if he is a child who needs care and protection. This is because his parents neglect him and he has to fend for himself. They may also raise other arguments.

2. The answer lies in para 2.14.5.1 of the *Learner's Manual*. It will depend upon the value of the money stolen as to whether Thami qualifies for a Level 1, Level 2 or Level 3 diversion. If Thami qualifies for a Level 1 diversion – as he is under 14 years of age – he cannot be given more than 12 months of diversion. If he qualifies for Level 2 or 3 diversions he cannot receive more than 24 months of diversion. Learners might suggest that Thami should be diverted to classes on Saturday mornings and during his school holidays so that he learns the importance of obeying the law and respecting the rights of others. Another suggestion might be that he does supervised car washing so that he can earn some money for food. Other suggestions could also be made.

2.14.7 Sentencing
(Learner's Manual p 217)

Problem 5: How would you sentence Barend?
(Learner's Manual p 221)

AIM: This problem raises questions regarding how a child accused whose case is not diverted and who goes to trial should be sentenced on conviction.

<table>
<tr><td colspan="2">**PROCEDURE** ▶≡</td><td colspan="2">**TIME** 🕐</td></tr>
<tr><td colspan="2">1. Introduce the aim of the exercise.</td><td>Introduction:</td><td>5 min</td></tr>
<tr><td colspan="2">2. Divide learners into small groups.</td><td>Group discussions:</td><td>15 min</td></tr>
<tr><td colspan="2">3. Each group is to discuss one question.</td><td>Report back:</td><td>20 min</td></tr>
<tr><td colspan="2">4. Report back.</td><td>General discussion:</td><td>5 min</td></tr>
<tr><td colspan="2">5. General discussion.</td><td>**TOTAL:**</td><td>**45 min**</td></tr>
</table>

1. The factors that should be taken into account before sentencing Barend are to be found in para 2.14.7.5 of the *Learner's Manual*. These are: (a) the seriousness of the offence, with regard to the amount of harm done or risked through the offence and the fault of the child in causing or risking the harm; (b) the protection of the community; (c) the severity of the impact of the offence on the victim; (d) the previous failure of the child to respond to non-residential

alternatives, if applicable; and (e) the desirability of keeping the child out of prison. All of these except (d) are relevant to Barend's case and learners can decide how they would apply them.

2. What would be an appropriate sentence for Barend? The victim indicated that she did not want to meet Barend. Learners can decide what they think an appropriate sentence would be – bearing in mind that most of the sentences that apply to adults apply to Barend because he is over 14 years of age. As he stole less than R2 500, his conviction for theft is a Schedule 1 offence and he cannot be sent to prison for this as there are no compelling reasons for doing so. However, rape is a Schedule 3 offence for which he can be imprisoned. Learners can decide what they think an appropriate prison or other sentence would be.

3. Learners must decide what they think the purpose of sentencing Barend should be: (a) to satisfy the outrage of society; (b) to punish Barend for what he has done; (c) to deter Barend (and others) from doing it again; (d) to protect society from Barend by keeping him out of society; (d) to rehabilitate Barend; (e) to make Barend do community service; (f) restorative justice etc. Learners can decide for themselves.

2.14.8 When criminal proceedings are stopped and the child is referred to a children's court *(Learner's Manual p 222)*

Problem 3: Would you stop the proceedings? *(Learner's Manual p 223)*

AIM: The object of this exercise is to let learners decide how they would have dealt with the child concerned if they were the presiding magistrate in a child justice court. Would they have stopped the proceedings and referred the child to a children's court?

PROCEDURE	TIME	
1. Introduce the aim of the exercise.	Introduction:	5 min
2. Divide learners into small groups.	Group discussions:	15 min
3. Each group is to discuss one question.	Report back:	20 min
4. Report back.	General discussion:	5 min
5. General discussion.	**TOTAL:**	**45 min**

1. Learners can make their own decisions, taking into account the factors mentioned in the box in the *Learner's Manual* para 2.14.8. If so, proceedings should be stopped and Gawie referred to a children's court. If not, the magistrate will try Gawie like any other criminal.

2. Likewise, learners should decide whether Sue falls into any of the categories in the box in para 2.14.8 of the *Learner's Manual*. Again, learners should make a decision whether to stop proceedings or to proceed with the trial in the ordinary way.

2.15 Mock trial

Outcomes

After completion of this section learners will be able to:

1. Conduct a mock trial.

Assessment criteria

1. A mock trial is defined.
2. The steps in an investigation are explained.
3. Steps in a trial are explained.
4. A set of facts is examined and a decision is taken on what the prosecution and defence must prove in the mock trial.
5. A set of facts is examined and teams of prosecutors and defence lawyers prepare and present questions and arguments.
6. A set of facts is examined and judgment is given in a mock trial.

S v Jozini has been included as a mock trial for use by educators should they wish to conclude their lessons on the criminal justice system with a court case simulation.

(See above Part 1 para G26 on how to conduct a mock trial.)

2.15.1 Procedure for conduct of *S v Jozini* mock trial

The case of the *S v Jozini* may be conducted as a mock trial in a classroom. It normally takes about six classroom lessons of at least 35 minutes each to complete the exercise. (Instructions for the conducting of a mock trial, together with simple rules of evidence, are to be found in the *Educator's Manual* para G26.)

The exercise could be conducted as follows:

(1) Lesson 1: State the rules of the mock trial, including the simple rules of evidence (see above *Educator's Manual* para G26), and go through the statement of facts with the learners. Require the learners to read the statements of the witnesses at home and to draw up a 'fact and time line'. Learners should be asked to prepare for the next lesson by reading the witnesses' statements and deciding which evidence in each statement will be useful to the prosecution case and which to the defence case.

(2) Lesson 2: The educator should draw up a 'fact and time line' on the blackboard and ask the learners to indicate which facts in the different statements are significant in order to reconstruct the events leading up to Jay Jozini's trial.
The educator should then go through each witness's statement with the class and ask them to mark which portions of the evidence are relevant to the prosecutor's case and which to the defence's case. Learners should be told that when preparing questions for leading evidence from, or cross-examination of, witnesses they should bear in mind which of the highlighted facts should be brought to the notice of the court.

Learners should then be divided into groups to play the parts of witnesses for the prosecution and defence, prosecutors and defence lawyers, evidence experts, a time-keeper and a court orderly.

(3) Lesson 3: Learners should work in teams to prepare their witnesses and practise leading evidence-in-chief, conducting cross-examination, delivering closing arguments and objecting on points of evidence. A lawyer or law student could be asked to sit in on the next three lessons to play the role of a magistrate while the mock trial is conducted.

(4) Lesson 4: Presentation of prosecution case.

(5) Lesson 5: Presentation of defence case.

(6) Lesson 6: Judgment of the court and discussion of the mock trial.

2.15.2 Role-players

Prosecution team

1. Prosecutor: Opening statement
2. Witness: Jermaine Jones
3. Witness: Sgt Jean Naidoo
4. Witness: Dr Silver Khoza, pathologist
5. Prosecutor: Examination-in-chief of Jermaine Jones
6. Prosecutor: Examination-in-chief of Sgt Jean Naidoo
7. Prosecutor: Examination-in-chief of Dr Silver Khoza, pathologist
8. Prosecutor: Cross-examination of Jay Jozini, accused
9. Prosecutor: Cross-examination of Johannes van Wyk
10. Prosecutor: Cross-examination of Pat Wung
11. Prosecutor: Closing argument

Defence team

1. Defence lawyer: opening statement
2. Witness: Jay Jozini, accused
3. Witness: Johannes van Wyk
4. Witness: Pat Wung
5. Defence lawyer: Examination-in-chief of Jay Jozini, accused
6. Defence lawyer: Examination-in-chief of Johannes van Wyk
7. Defence lawyer: Examination-in-chief of Pat Wung
8. Defence lawyer: Cross-examination of Jermaine Jones
9. Defence lawyer: Cross-examination of Sgt Jean Naidoo
10. Defence lawyer: Cross-examination of Dr Silver Khoza, pathologist
11. Defence lawyer: Closing argument

Court officials

1. Judge
2. First assessor
3. Second assessor
4. Court orderly
5. Time-keeper

2.15.3 Stipulated facts

The case involves a shooting that occurred on 15 June 2012 on the corner of Massgrave and Fountain Streets. The accused, Jay Jozini and the victim, Frank Williams, were in the Choices Club that evening. Around 23h00 they became involved in an argument which was broken up by the barman. The accused then left the club, followed by Williams. The accused shot and killed Williams in the street a short while later. The state has indicted the accused for murder and he has entered a plea of not guilty on the basis of self-defence.

2.15.4 Witnesses

The prosecution might call the following witnesses:
1.   Jermaine Jones
2.   Sgt Jean Naidoo
3.   Dr Silver Khoza, pathologist

The defence may call the following witnesses:
1.   The accused, Jay Jozini
2.   Johannes van Wyk
3.   Pat Wung

Exhibits and materials: the following may be available:
1.   Gun
2.   Box containing five cartridges and one empty cartridge case.
3.   Diagram
4.   Medico-legal post-mortem examination report

2.15.5 Indictment (Charge)

IN THE KWAZULU-NATAL HIGH COURT, DURBAN

THE STATE
vs
JAY JOZINI
A male aged 30 years
hereinafter called 'the Accused'

INDICTMENT

The Director of Public Prosecutions for the Province of KwaZulu-Natal presents and gives the Court to be informed that the Accused is guilty of the crime of:

MURDER

IN THAT upon or about 15 June 2012 at or near the Choices Club in the district of Durban, PROVINCE OF KWAZULU-NATAL, the accused did unlawfully and intentionally kill FRANK WILLIAMS by shooting him in the chest with a firearm.

N Padayachee
DIRECTOR OF PUBLIC PROSECUTIONS

2.15.6 List of witnesses

IN THE KWAZULU-NATAL HIGH COURT, DURBAN
REPUBLIC OF SOUTH AFRICA

THE STATE

vs

JAY JOZINI

LIST OF WITNESSES

---

1. JERMAINE JONES
    300 MANOR DRIVE
    MANOR GARDENS
    DURBAN

2. DETECTIVE WARRANT OFFICER JEAN NAIDOO
    MURDER AND ROBBERY UNIT
    SA POLICE SERVICES
    DURBAN

3. DR SILVER KHOZA
    SA MEDICO-LEGAL LABORATORIES
    86 GALE STREET
    DURBAN

4. JAY JOZINI
    500 MASSGRAVE STREET
    DURBAN

5. JOHANNES VAN WYK
    6 BEREA CRESCENT
    DURBAN

6. PAT WUNG
    ST GEORGES HOTEL
    ST GEORGES STREET
    DURBAN

2.15.7 Witness statements

1. Statement of Jermaine Jones: Prosecution witness

My name is Jermaine Jones. I am a bank manager. I live at 300 Manor Drive in Manor Gardens. On the evening of the 15th June 2012 at approximately 23h05 as I was walking along Massgrave Street towards

Fountain Street I heard shouting. I saw that about 30 metres in front of me, opposite the entrance to the Choices Club, two men were arguing. I could not hear what they were saying but they were obviously angry. The short thin man (the accused) had his back towards me, and the tall man (Williams) appeared to be moving towards him. They seemed to be about three metres apart. I did not want to become involved so I stopped where I was. Because of the light and distance I am not sure how far apart they were, but I would say it was about three metres. They seemed to get closer, almost a metre or two apart when a shot rang out and the tall man fell to the ground. The short man just stood there. People rushed out of the Choices Club. The short man dropped his gun and tried to run up the street, but they grabbed him and took him back to where the tall man had fallen. They held him until the police arrived.

I was able to see what happened because there is a floodlight outside the Choices Club. There is also a street light on the corner of Massgrave and Fountain Streets, as well as another street light between where I was standing and the two men.

2.   Statement by detective warrant officer Jean Naidoo: Prosecution witness
My name is Detective Warrant Officer Jean Naidoo. I live at 400 Lighthouse Road on the Bluff in the district of Durban. I joined the SAPS in 1985.

On the 15th June 2012 at about 23h10 I was on a routine motor patrol when I received a radio message that a man had been shot on the corner of Massgrave and Fountain Streets. I proceeded to the scene and observed several people holding a man, the accused, Jay Jozini. Another man, Frank Williams, was lying on the pavement with an apparent bullet wound in his chest. I called an ambulance and Williams was taken to Addington Hospital.

The corner of Massgrave and Fountain Streets is a business and residential area for people living in private houses. Fountain Street is a one-way street with five traffic lanes and two parking lanes. Fountain Street is approximately 25 metres wide and Massgrave Street is 12 metres wide. The street lighting is typical for a residential area. I searched the area and found a .38 calibre Smith and Wesson revolver, approximately one metre from Williams's head containing five unspent cartridges and one spent cartridge case. There was the smell of fresh gun powder. No other weapons were found in the area. Williams's body was lying on the pavement almost in front of the entrance to the Choices Club. No other weapons were found on or near Williams. The revolver was labelled, sealed and sent off as an exhibit.

I handcuffed the accused and put him in the rear of my squad car. I asked him what had happened and he said that he and Williams had got into an argument in the club but refused to say what the argument was about. He said that Williams had wanted to go outside and fight and that he, the accused, had acted in self-defence.

The accused said nothing further until at the police station. When he was being charged he said: 'You know, Williams threatened me last week too'. When asked to make a further statement he refused to do so.

3.   Statement of Dr Silver Khoza, senior government pathologist: Prosecution witness
My name is Dr Silver Khoza and I am a Senior Government Pathologist in Durban. I hold the MBCh (For Path) (UCT) degree. I live at 100 Northway, Durban North. On 16 June 2012 at 13h45 at the SAPS Medico-Legal Laboratory, Gale Street, Durban I examined the body of Frank Williams, a

deceased adult male. I completed a medico-legal post-mortem examination report in which I showed that death was caused by a single gun-shot wound through the heart and left lung.

My pathological findings were:
(1) A gunshot entry wound, at nipple level of chest, two centimetres to the right of the left nipple, perforating the chest muscles and thorax.
(2) A gunshot exit wound, at the third lumbar vertebrae (L3) level, 2 cm to the left of the spine, perforating the back muscles.
(3) The bullet had caused gunshot wounds to the following:
   (a) the heart, by perforating the left ventricle;
   (b) the lower lobes of the left lung; and
   (c) the left side of the diaphragm.

My additional findings and observations were the following :
(1) After analysis the blood showed the presence of 0.12g/100 ml alcohol.
(2) Around the area of the bullet entrance wound there were propellant (gunpowder) deposits causing tattooing.
(3) The right-hand knuckles of the deceased had clear bruises.

4.   Statement of Jay Jozini: Accused

My name is Jay Jozini and I live at 500 Massgrave Street in Durban. I am 30 years old and am employed as a Investment Broker by Simunye Investment Corporation. I have worked for them for the past eight years.

On 15 June 2012 I got off work late at 21h30 pm. After work I went home and changed and then walked down to the Choices Club, which is not very far from where I live.

At the bar I met Frank Williams, whom I had seen a week earlier when we were involved in an argument involving an import-export business deal. This was on 8 June 2012. On that occasion I had gone down to the club at about 22h00. Williams was already there and I had sat down on a bar stool not far away. He accused me of embezzling R50 000 that he had invested in a business deal involving our firm. I told him that the business deal had gone bad and there was nothing that I could do to retrieve his investment. He went into a rage calling me a liar and grabbed my arm and told me to give him back his money. Again I told him that there was nothing that I could do. The bar man Pat Wung told him to knock it off. He eventually went back to his stool. Later that night he said that he was going to 'make me pay for this'.

On the night of 15 June 2012 I also arrived at the club at about 22h00 and had a couple of drinks. Williams was there again. He kept saying things like 'When are you going to pay me back?' and 'Let's settle this outside'. I got tired of his nonsense and left at about 23h00.

I had just walked out of the club and was leaving the entrance when I heard the door open and Williams walked out. He shouted at me. 'Let us settle this you lousy crook' and 'You've had it coming'. I told him that I did not want to fight and backed away. He kept coming closer and closer. He then punched me and lunged at me with his hands. I thought he had a knife, so I pulled out my pistol and shot him. I had seen him with a knife before. Williams was a game hunter who often bragged about his exploits in the wild. He often used to demonstrate his hunting technique with a hunting knife. I honestly thought that he was going to stab me. That was the reason why I shot at him. He is known to become quite aggressive and brutish whenever he has been drinking. I once saw him beat up a guy outside the Choices Club a few months before I had had trouble with him.

I was once convicted of drunk driving when I was twenty years old and put on one year probation. I have never been convicted of any other crimes.

5. Statement of Johannes van Wyk: Defence witness

My name is Johannes van Wyk and I live at 6 Berea Crescent, Durban. I have known both Jozini and Williams for about two years. I am a social friend of Jozini and see him about once a week on average. I usually see him at the Choices Club because we are both regular patrons. Jozini works for Simunye Investment Corporation. I also knew Williams, but only because he was a regular at the Choices Club. I used to see Williams about once a month. He owned an abbattoir.

I know about the reputations of both Jozini and Williams. Jozini is a small slender man with a reputation at the Choices Club, and elsewhere, of being a quiet, soft-spoken, retiring type of person who 'would not hurt a fly'. My opinion of Jozini is the same. Williams was a huge muscular guy with a reputation at the club for being very aggressive. He became involved in arguments, particularly when he had drunk a lot. My experience of Williams was the same.

I have never seen Williams with a knife, nor have I ever been told that Williams had a knife. I was in the Choices Club the previous week, 8 June 2012, when Jozini and Williams got into an argument over money involving an investment deal. Williams walked over to Jozini, leaned over towards him and told him to give back the money he had invested in a deal. Jozini said that he could not give back the money and the barman eventually intervened to break up the argument. I never saw Williams grab Jozini but he looked very threatening.

On the night of 15 June 2012 I was in the club when Williams again began to pick on Jozini. This was at about 23h00. It was another argument concerning the investment deal. Jozini again denied that he had stolen any money and the barman had to tell them to calm down. Soon afterwards Jozini left and he was immediately followed by Williams. After a couple of minutes I heard a loud bang. We all ran outside and saw Williams lying on the pavement and Jozini standing over him with a gun. When he saw us Jozini ran away. He was caught by some of the patrons and held until the police came.

It is a shame that Jozini is being prosecuted because he is a quiet, decent person.

6. Statement by Pat Wung: Defence witness

My name is Pat Wung. I am the barman for the Choices Club and live at the St Georges Hotel, St Georges Street, Durban. I was in the Choices Club from about 21h00 on the evening of the 15th June 2012. The usual crowd came in from the neighbourhood. The club is quite smart and has snooker tables in the back. It serves cocktails and exotic foods like caviar and other delicacies.

When I arrived, Jozini and Williams were already there, as were several other people. Everyone was drinking socially. Jozini and Williams were mixing their drinks. I served them about four drinks each between 21h00 and 23h00. Around 23h00 Jozini and Williams got into an argument. I did not hear what they were saying, but they were definitely arguing about something. I went over and told them to knock it off, which they did. Things returned to normal. The previous week on 8 June 2012 I had had to break up a similar argument between them.

After a minute or two Jozini left, followed two or three minutes later by Williams. About a minute later I heard a loud bang. We all ran outside and I saw Jozini standing over Williams holding a gun. He looked at us, dropped the gun and started running up the street towards the parking garage. A few of the guys chased him and brought him back. He just stood there until the police arrived and did not try to resist. He never said anything except 'I didn't want to fight him'.

2.15.8 Applicable law

Private defence

Private defence includes self-defence, defence of property or defence of other people. A person who is unlawfully attacked by another man can use reasonable force in self-defence. The force used in private defence must be reasonable and must stop once the attack ends. If there is a way for the threatened person to flee instead of fighting, he or she should do so. In exceptional cases if killing the attacker is the only way of protecting oneself, then deadly force may be used. The courts, however, are very strict on the use of deadly force.

R v Zikalala

This case involved a man who was attacked by a gang of men in a crowded hall. The accused stabbed the deceased. The court approached the problem by weighing whether or not a reasonable person in a similar situation would have reacted like the accused. Here, the accused had been unable to run away because his path had been blocked.

R v Ratel

This case involved a man who saw his brother struck over the head with a hammer. The accused thought that he was the next one to be struck, so he pulled out a revolver and shot the deceased. The court ruled that, in emergency situations, a reasonable man might not act as rationally as usual. This is known as the sudden-emergency doctrine.

Further reading

2.1 The meaning, nature and causes of crime

Burchell J *Principles of Criminal Law* 3 ed (2005)

McQuoid-Mason D, Lotz L, & Natsylishvili A *Criminal law: Student book* (2009)

Milton JRL *South African Criminal Law and Procedure (Volume II) Common Law Crimes* 3 ed (1996)

Minister van Polisie v Ewels 1975 (3) SA 590 (A)

2.2 Crimes against people

Burchell J *Principles of Criminal Law* 3 ed (2005)

McQuoid-Mason D, Lotz L, & Natsylishvili A *Criminal law: Student book* (2009)

Milton JRL *South African Criminal Law and Procedure (Volume II) Common Law Crimes* 3 ed (1996)

2.3 Sexual crimes

McQuoid-Mason D 'The Children's Amendment Act and the Criminal Law (Sexual Offences and Related Matters) Amendment Act: Duty to Report Child Abuse and Sexual Offences against Children and Mentally Disabled Persons' 2008 *SA'Med J* 929–931.

Criminal Law (Sexual Offences and Related Matters) Amendment Act 32 of 2007

Masiya v Director of Public Prosecutions, Pretoria and Another 2007 (5) SA 30 (CC) – the Constitutional Court found that the common-law definition of rape was not unconstitutional, but that it needed to be appropriately adapted and that it had to be extended to include acts of non-consensual, intentional penetration of a penis into a female's anus.

S v Geldenhuys 2009 (1) SACR 1 (SCA) – it was held, while it was possible that certain children of 12 years of age might be regarded as competent to make rational decisions about their sexual activity, this did not mean it was unconstitutional to set the age of consent higher than 12. It was further held that the state is both constitutionally and internationally obliged to protect its children from all forms of abuse and that, by setting the legal age of consent to sexual activities above the age of 12 years, is in line with these obligations.

The Teddy Bear Clinic for Abused Children v Minister of Justice and Constitutional Development Case Number 733300/10, 14 January 2013, North Gauteng High Court, Pretoria (unreported); *Teddy Bear Clinic for Abused Children and Another v Minister of Justice and Constitutional Development and Another* 2014 (2) SA 168 (CC).

2.4 Domestic violence

Children's Act 38 of 2005

Domestic Violence Act 116 of 1998

Older Persons Act 13 of 2006

Minister of Safety and Security v Carmichele 2004 (3) SA 305 (SCA) – the Supreme Court of Appeal held that the respondent owed a legal duty to the appellant to take reasonable steps to prevent an escaped serial rapist from causing her harm.

S v Baloyi 2000 (2) SA 425 (CC) – the Constitutional Court held that the Constitution imposes a direct obligation on the state to protect the right of all persons to be free from domestic violence.

2.5 Cyber crime

Currie I & De Waal J *The Bill of Rights Handbook* 5 ed (2005)

http://kidshealth.org/parent/positive/talk/cyberbullying.html accessed on 6 September 2011

http://www.character.org/bullyprevention accessed on 6 September 2011

http://www.stopcyberbullying.org/how_it_works/direct_attacks.html#im accessed on 6 September 2011

http://www.collegeotr.com/college_otr/word_of_the_week_sexting_16399 accessed on 7 September 2011

http://www.esarcasm.com/347/25-more-sexting-acronyms-parents-should-know/ accessed on 7 September 2011

Constitution of the Republic of South Africa, 1996

Protection from Harassment Act 17 of 2011.

Le Roux v Dey 2010 (4) SA 210 (SCA) – learners found liable for manipulating and electronically posting a photograph that ridiculed and humiliated the deputy-principal of a school by falsely showing him to be involved in naked homosexual activity with the school principal.

National Coalition for Gay and Lesbian Equality v Minister of Justice 1999 (1) SA 6 (CC)

2.6 Crimes against property

Burchell *Principles of Criminal Law* 3 ed (2005)

McQuoid-Mason D, Lotz L & Natsylishvili A *Criminal law: Student book* (2009)

Criminal Procedure Act 51 of 1977

2.7 Crimes against the state

Burchell J *Principles of Criminal Law* 3 ed (2005)

McQuoid-Mason D, Lotz L & Natsylishvili A *Criminal law: Student book* (2009)

Criminal Procedure Act 51 of 1977

Protection of Constitutional Democracy against Terrorist and Related Activities Act 33 of 2004

2.8 Crimes against morality involving sexual conduct

Burchell J *Principles of Criminal Law* 3 ed (2005)

McQuoid-Mason D, Lotz L & Natsylishvili A *Criminal law: Student book* (2009)

Choice of Termination of Pregnancy Act 92 of 1996

Choice of Termination of Pregnancy Amendment Act 38 of 2004

Christian Lawyers Association of South Africa v Minister of Health 2005 (1) SA 509 (T); 2004 (4) All SA 31 (T) – minor's ability to consent to termination of pregnancy independently.

S v Jordan 2002 (6) SA 642 (CC) – the majority of the Constitutional Court confirmed the criminality of prostitution (sex for reward). It also stated that the customer of the prostitute may be guilty of being an accomplice or of incitement or conspiracy regarding the offence of the prostitute.

S v M 2004 (3) SA 680 (O) – the court confirmed the constitutionality of the crime of bestiality and correctly regarded the conduct covered by the crime as against legal convictions of the community (*boni mores*).

2.9 Crimes involving alcohol and drugs

J Burchell J *Principles of Criminal Law* 3 ed (2005)

McQuoid-Mason D, Lotz L & Natsylishvili A *Criminal law: Student book* (2009)

Criminal Procedure Act 51 of 1977

Drugs and Drug Trafficking Act 140 of 1992

National Road Traffic Act 93 of 1996

Prince v President, Cape Law Society 2002 (2) SA 794 (CC) – the Constitutional Court held that the Drugs and Drug Trafficking Act was not in conflict with the Constitutional right to freedom of religion by not granting Rastafari exemption to possess and use dagga for religious purposes.

2.10 Defences to crimes

Burchell J *Principles of Criminal Law* 3 ed (2005)

Child Justice Act 75 of 2008

Children's Act 38 of 2005

2.11 Powers of the police and bail

Burchell J *Principles of Criminal Law* 3 ed (2005)

Criminal Procedure Act 51 of 1997

2.12 Search and seizure

Boezaart T (ed) *Child law in South Africa* (2009)

Burchell J *Principles of Criminal Law* 3 ed (2005)

Mofokeng L *Legal Pluralism in South Africa: Aspects of African customary, Muslim and Hindu family law* (2008)

Criminal Procedure Act 51 of 1977

2.13 The criminal trial and sentencing process

Burchell J *Principles of Criminal Law* 3 ed (2005)

McQuoid-Mason D, Lotz L & Natsylishvili A *Criminal law: Student book* (2009)

Criminal Procedure Act 51 of 1977

South African Police Services Act 68 of 1995

S v Makwanyane 1995 (3) SA 391 (CC) – dealt with the constitutionality of the death penalty: the court abolished the death penalty and described the rights to life and dignity as the 'most important of all human rights, and the source of all other personal rights in the Bill of Rights'.

2.14 Child justice

Gallinetti J *Getting to know the Child Justice Act* (2009)

Coetzee L (ed) *Child Justice Act: Training Manual* (2nd Draft) (2009)

Brandt v S [2005] 2 All SA 1 (SCA) indicated that the traditional purpose of punishment, in respect of children, has to be re-appraised and developed to be in line with the South African Constitution.

Centre for Child Law v Minister of Justice and Constitutional Development and Others 2009 (6) SA 632 (CC) – declaring that minimum sentences are invalid for children aged 16 and 17 years old.

DPP, KwaZulu-Natal v P 2006 (1) SACR 243 (SCA)

Weber v Santam Versekeringsmaatskappy Bpk 1983 (1) SA 381 (A) – the court held that when determining capacity the test is subjective, whereas the test is objective when determining fault. When a child is found to have criminal capacity, the negligence or otherwise should be determined in accordance with the ordinary reasonable person.

3. Consumer law

CONTENTS

PART THREE

Consumer law

3.1 Consumer protection

Outcomes

After completion of this section participants will be able to:

1. Identify and explain the protection afforded to consumers in South Africa.

Assessment criteria

1. A decision is taken on whether a person was a wise consumer.
2. An explanation is given on how to prevent consumers becoming victims of dishonesty and fraud.
3. The main statutes protecting consumers and the common-law protection of consumers are listed.

Consumer protection is one of the most important parts of a practical law course. Most of us experience situations affected by consumer law many times each day (eg every time we buy something or use a service). Learners must be trained to be aware of themselves as consumers. Learners need to understand how consumer law intrudes into their everyday lives. When learners try to solve the problems raised in this chapter, they should be asking themselves: where could I obtain help? In the last couple of years the legislature has enacted the Consumer Protection Act 68 of 2008 and the National Credit Act 34 of 2005. Both of these pieces of legislation aim to improve the protection afforded to consumers in South Africa. The purpose of the Consumer Protection Act is to promote and advance the socio-economic welfare of South African consumers. The National Credit Act aims to promote a fair, transparent, competitive, sustainable credit market. It encourages responsible borrowing and promotes equity in the credit market.

3.1.2 Buying on the spur of the moment *(Learner's Manual p 234)*

Problem 1: Were you a wise consumer? *(Learner's Manual p 234)*

AIM: The aim of this exercise is to sensitise learners to impulse buying. They should be able to identify whether the product that they bought is a need or a want from the reasons that they provide for buying each particular product. The exercise must teach learners to evaluate what they are buying prior to entering into the transaction. Learners must also be made aware of the kind of things (eg advertising, peer pressure, etc) that influence our decision making.

PROCEDURE
1. Introduce exercise.
2. Allow learners to individually make a list of five products bought in the last week. Learners should provide the reasons for deciding to buy these products.
3. Ask for responses to questions 2 and 3 from a selection of learners.
4. Conclude with general discussion and summary..

TIME	
Introduction:	5 min
Individual listing of products bought and providing reasons for decision to purchase:	5 min
Report back from learners:	10 min
Discussion and summary:	15 min
TOTAL:	**35 min**

Problem 2: Some questions about consumers *(Learner's Manual p 235)*

AIM: The aim of this exercise is to conduct an opinion poll to stimulate learners' interest in consumer matters.

PROCEDURE	TIME	
1. Introduce exercise. 2. Ask learners to write out their answers to the questions. 3. Ask for responses to the questions from the learners and ask them to give reasons for their answers. 4. Conclude with general discussion and summary.	Introduction: Individual work: Vote by show of hands: Discussion and summary: **TOTAL:**	5 min 15 min 5 min 20 min **45 min**

The facilitator could ask the learners for their responses to each question, which could be given by a show of hands. For example, regarding each question, how many strongly agree (sa), agree (a), are undecided (u), disagree (d), strongly disagree (sd), etc?

Questions	(sa)	(a)	(u)	(d)	(sd)
1.	10	5	1	2	2
2.	5	4	2	4	5
3.	etc	etc	etc	etc	etc
4.					
5.					

Learners favouring one or other response should be asked to justify their opinions and to consider opposing points of view. Here are some possible arguments. There may be others.

1. Arguments against children making contracts without approval are:
    (a) children are immature and easily exploited;
    (b) children should be protected;
    (c) parents and guardians are there to protect children; and
    (d) children usually do not have their own money and have to rely on their parents or guardians for support.

    Arguments in favour of children making contracts without approval are:
    (a) children who know what they are doing should be allowed to enter into contracts;
    (b) it is impractical to require approval for every contract (eg buying an ice-cream, cool-drink or bus ticket);
    (c) some children are able to earn their own money (eg selling or delivering newspapers, or working in a supermarket), and should be allowed to spend it how they like; and
    (d) not all children are immature, especially those over 14 years old.

2. Arguments in favour of contracts in writing are:
    (a) written contracts are easier to prove than verbal statements;
    (b) people will be more careful if contracts are in writing; and

(c) people will know exactly what is agreed if it is in writing.

Some of the arguments against written contracts are:
(a) very often people are in a hurry and do not read the contracts that they sign, resulting in their not knowing the terms of the contract that they signed;
(b) where the parties decide that reducing the agreement to writing will be a pre-requisite for the contract, the contract will only be valid once it is written down and signed by the parties;
(c) sometimes the whole agreement is not contained in one document; and
(d) it is important (eg where people are buying every day things like groceries or other goods).

3. Arguments in favour of buying on credit are:
(a) people obtain ownership or use of the thing before they have fully paid for it;
(b) people who cannot usually afford to buy something are able to do so;
(c) people who buy under a credit agreement are protected from unfair discrimination (see *Learner's Manual* para 3.3);
(d) persons who were historically unable to access credit, eg black people, can now access credit; and
(e) people may pay a small amount each month and can plan their budgets accordingly.

Arguments against buying on credit are:
(a) people pay more for the thing because they must pay finance and interest charges;
(b) people very often buy things they do not really need;
(c) people are tempted to over-commit themselves and end up with financial problems;
(d) people who get into financial difficulties may become insolvent and may even have their estates sequestrated if they cannot pay their debts; and
(e) incurring too much credit might result in people becoming poorer.

4. Arguments in favour of dishonest sellers going to prison are:
(a) it will stop them cheating consumers;
(b) if a seller intentionally cheats another, the seller has committed the crime of fraud (see *Learner's Manual* para 2.6.8) and should go to prison;
(c) dishonest sellers might cheat thousands of customers out of a few cents each, but this may add up to a lot of money; and
(d) if consumers are sent to prison for shoplifting (see *Learner's Manual* para 2.6.3), dishonest sellers should also be sent to prison for stealing from consumers.

Arguments against dishonest sellers going to prison are:
(a) it would be better to make them repay the people they have cheated;
(b) it is difficult to generalise – maybe only those who commit a serious fraud should be sent to prison;
(c) giving them a heavy fine would be better than sending them to prison; and
(d) maybe people who do not use violence to steal from a consumer should not be sent to prison.

What should happen if both the seller and the buyer are dishonest? (For example, they sell and buy stolen goods.) The law might send the seller to prison for stealing and the buyer for receiving stolen property (see *Learner's Manual* para 2.6.6).

5. Arguments showing that most consumers are affected by television and radio advertising are:
   (a) sellers would not advertise on television and radio if it did not work;
   (b) studies show that many people believe what they see on television or hear on the radio;
   (c) audio-visual and audio advertisements are much more persuasive than those read in newspapers or magazines; and
   (d) advertisements on television or radio usually appear more than once a day for several days or weeks so that some people become 'brainwashed' by them.

   Arguments against most consumers being affected by television and radio advertising are:
   (a) people often ignore the advertisements and focus on the main programmes;
   (b) irritating interruptions by advertisements will make people consciously avoid buying the thing advertised;
   (c) viewers and listeners can take a break when the advertisements are being broadcast; and
   (d) consumers buy only what they need and not what the advertisements say they need.

6. Arguments in favour of repossession are:
   (a) sellers are able to reduce finance charges because they can repossess the goods;
   (b) sellers may save some of their losses if the buyer cannot afford to pay;
   (c) buyers can give the thing back if they cannot afford to keep it; and
   (d) sellers can only repossess provided the buyers have been given a warning to pay before the repossession is made.

   Arguments against repossession are:
   (a) the buyer still has to pay the balance of the purchase price after the goods have been repossessed;
   (b) finance charges are not usually lower for goods that can be repossessed (eg furniture and cars) than for those that cannot be repossessed (eg building alterations); and
   (c) sellers may be tempted to use 'strong arm' illegal tactics to repossess the goods.

7. Arguments in favour of the government prohibiting the sale of harmful items are:
   (a) the government should protect the health of the public;
   (b) people who are injured by harmful goods will become a burden on society;
   (c) sellers and manufacturers should not be allowed to make money out of goods that harm the public; and
   (d) many people are unable to protect themselves against harm, so the government must take steps to do it for them.

   Arguments against the government prohibiting the sale of harmful items are:
   (a) people should have the right to choose whether or not they wish to harm themselves;
   (b) in a 'free-enterprise' system people should be allowed to make and sell what they like, provided they take responsibility for their acts (eg compensate injured people);
   (c) sellers and manufacturers should be required to put warnings on their products (eg on cigarettes) rather than be prohibited from selling them; and
   (d) it is too difficult to decide what is 'harmful' (eg alcohol, cigarettes, coffee, salt, sugar, etc).

3.2 Consumer Protection Act of 2008

Outcomes

After completion of this section participants will be able to:

1. Identify and explain the protection give to consumers in South Africa by the Consumer Protection Act (CPA).

Assessment criteria

1. An explanation is given of the different rights of consumers under the Consumer Protection Act (CPA).
2. A decision is taken on whether a consumer was discriminated against.
3. A decision is taken on whether a person can 'opt out' of direct marketing.
4. A solution is recommended to problems relating to discrimination against consumers.
5. Advice is given to a supplier on 'bundling' of products.
6. A decision is taken on whether cancellation of an agreement can take place.
7. Advice is given to a consumer on whether a contract may be cancelled.
8. A decision is taken on whether a consumer can insist that broken goods be replaced.
9. A recommendation is provided about a consumer's duties in relation to goods sent in the post that were not ordered.
10. Labelling on products is analysed for correctness.

3.2.2 The right to equality

(Learner's Manual p 238)

Problem 1: Was the consumer unfairly discriminated against?

(Learner's Manual p 239)

AIM: The aim of this exercise is for learners to identify whether a consumer has been discriminated against and to assess whether the learners understand that a supplier is not allowed to unfairly exclude persons from accessing goods and services.

PROCEDURE		TIME	
1. Introduce exercise.		Introduction:	5 min
2. Divide class into groups of no more than five learners.		Group work:	10 min
3. Ask each group to discuss one question.		Groups report back:	15 min
4. Receive reports from each group.		Discussion and summary:	5 min
5. Discuss and summarise group feedback and explain correct legal position where necessary.		**TOTAL:**	**35 min**

1. Learners can argue that it is not clear on what grounds the local shop will refuse to serve anyone. They must further discuss whether, if a service is refused on one of the grounds listed in the

Constitution, it could amount to unfair discrimination. In this case the shop will have to show that it is reasonable and justifiable not to sell liquor to persons under 18 years of age. This would be easy because it is illegal in terms of the Liquor Act to sell liquor to people under the age of 18 years.

2. Learners should indicate that this constitutes unfair discrimination on the grounds of race. They need to appreciate that the bank is treating white low-income earners differently from black low-income earners. Race is a listed ground in the South African Constitution. It is unlikely that the bank can offer a reasonable and justifiable explanation for the difference in treatment.

3.2.3 The right to privacy
(Learner's Manual p 240)

Problem 2: Opting out from being contacted by direct marketers
(Learner's Manual p 242)

AIM: The aim of this exercise is for learners to identify that consumers may opt out of being contacted by direct marketing agencies, the most effective method of doing so and whether it is sensible to opt out from getting junk e-mail.

PROCEDURE	TIME	
1. Introduce exercise.	Introduction:	5 min
2. Divide class into groups of no more than five learners, or use same groups from previous exercise.	Group work:	10 min
3. Ask each group to select a scribe and someone that will report back.	Groups report back:	10 min
4. Ask each group to discuss one question.	Discussion and summary:	5 min
5. Receive reports from each group.	**TOTAL:**	**30 min**
6. Discuss and summarise group feedback and explain correct legal position where necessary.		

1. Learners need to explain that the direct marketer is contacting you outside the time allowed. No direct marketing is allowed between 19h00 and 08h00 the following day. You can opt out of any requests for donations.

2. Learners should suggest that people place a sign outside their front door indicating that direct marketers are not allowed. In addition to the questions posed in the *Learner's Manual*, educators may ask the groups to make the sign that they will put outside their house to advise direct marketers that they have opted out.

3. The groups should explain that where the e-mail has its origin in South Africa there should be an 'unsubscribe' option in the e-mail. However, if the e-mails originate outside of South Africa, the country where the e-mail originates might not have similar laws that allow persons to opt out of direct marketing.

3.2.4 The right to choose
(Learner's Manual p 242)

Problem 3: Simpiwe wishes to cancel his gym contract
(Learner's Manual p 245)

AIM: The aim of this exercise is to give learners the opportunity to discuss the reasonableness of the penalty charged by the supplier upon cancellation of the fixed-term contract.

<table>
<tr><td>

PROCEDURE ☰

1. Introduce exercise.
2. Divide class into groups of no more than five learners, or use same groups from previous exercise.
3. Ask each group to select a scribe and someone that will report back. Where you have more than one group activity it is recommended that you require groups to rotate the position of scribe and rapporteur every time they do group work.
4. Ask the groups to discuss Simpiwe's situation.
5. Receive reports from each group.
6. Discuss and summarise group feedback and explain correct legal position where necessary.

</td><td>

TIME 🕐

Introduction:	5 min
Group work:	10 min
Groups report back:	10 min
Discussion and summary:	5 min
TOTAL:	**30 min**

</td></tr>
</table>

Simpiwe needs to give Muscle Power Gym 20 business days' notice in writing of his intention to cancel the gym membership. Neither the CPA nor the regulations specify a percentage that can be charged. Learners need to debate the reasonableness of a 60% charge and whether charging 60% would make it worthwhile for the consumer to cancel the agreement.

Problem 4: The case of the costly quotation   *(Learner's Manual p 245)*

AIM: The object of this exercise is to make learners aware of what should be done when obtaining a quotation for repairs.

<table>
<tr><td>

PROCEDURE ☰

1. Introduce exercise.
2. Divide class into small groups of five learners each.
3. Ask each group to discuss Mavis's situation.
4. Get report back from each group.
5. Conclude with general discussion and summary.

</td><td>

TIME 🕐

Introduction:	5 min
Group work:	10 min
Groups report back:	15 min
Discussion and summary:	5 min
TOTAL:	**35 min**

</td></tr>
</table>

1. Mavis has done something wrong. She allowed the mechanic to give her an open-ended quotation. She should have asked for a written quotation and should have insisted that no work was to be done if its cost would exceed the original quotation.

2. If Mavis refuses to pay, the service station may keep her car until she pays or gives an undertaking to pay. In most cases a garage will have a lien over a car handed over to it for repairs. A lien means that the garage may keep the car until arrangements have been made to pay for the repairs, or security has been given to pay for them.

3. If additional costs are incurred because of repair work not requested by Mavis, she would only be liable for the cost of the materials used, not the cost of labour. This will apply if the additional repairs were necessary and useful (ie the repairs are necessary to keep the car roadworthy). If not, she could ask the garage to put the car back in the condition it was before the extra repairs were done. Then she would not have to pay for the cost of materials. If she had received a written quotation, it would have been easier to establish exactly what she had asked to be repaired.

Problem 5: Noluthando buys some waterless cooking pots
(Learner's Manual p 246)

AIM: The aim of this exercise is for learners to explain whether the consumer has a right to cancel an agreement during a cooling-off period.

PROCEDURE	TIME	
1. Introduce exercise.	Introduction:	5 min
2. Divide class into groups of no more than five learners, or use same groups from previous exercise.	Group work:	5 min
	Groups report back:	10 min
3. Ask each group to select a scribe and someone that will report back.	Discussion and summary:	5 min
	TOTAL:	**25 min**
4. Ask each group to discuss Noluthando's situation.		
5. Receive reports from each group.		
6. Discuss and summarise group feedback and explain correct legal position where necessary.		

Learners should identify that Noluthando has a cooling-off period of five business days during which she is allowed to change her mind about buying the pots. She has five business days to cancel the agreement – measured from either the date of conclusion of the contract or the date of the delivery of the pots, whichever date is the later. Noluthando does not have to provide reasons for her decision. If Noluthando made a payment when she agreed to buy the pots, the payment must be refunded in full within 15 business days of the date of cancellation of the agreement.

3.2.6 Consumer's right to return defective goods *(Learner's Manual p 247)*

Problem 6: The case of the faulty TV set
(Learner's Manual p 247)

AIM: The object of this exercise is to make learners aware of the interaction between salespeople and consumers at the time of purchase and later when consumers complain. It also teaches learners how to complain and how to negotiate a settlement.

PROCEDURE	TIME	
1. Introduce exercise.	Introduction:	5 min
2. Divide into groups of not more than five.	Group work:	5 min
3. Ask each group to select a scribe and someone that will report back.	Groups report back:	10 min
	Discussion and summary:	5 min
	TOTAL:	**25 min**
4. Ask each group to advise the Thodis.		
5. Receive reports from each group.		

For the purpose of the exercise, assume that the Thodis received no written guarantee.

The answer is in *Learner's Manual* para 3.2.6. The CPA protects consumers against defective goods and allows consumers to return the goods within 6 months without penalty and to get a refund. The

Thodis can decide if they want the TV replaced or wish to get their money back.

Problem 7: The case of the defective cell phone (Learner's Manual p 248)

AIM: The aim of this exercise is for learners to identify that the consumer, not the supplier, decides whether defective goods should be replaced, repaired or the money paid for them refunded.

PROCEDURE	TIME	
1. Introduce exercise.	Introduction:	5 min
2. Divide class into groups of no more than five learners.	Group work:	5 min
3. Ask each group to select a scribe and someone that will report back.	Groups report back:	10 min
	Discussion and summary:	5 min
4. Ask each group to advise you on your rights.	**TOTAL:**	**25 min**
5. Receive reports from each group.		
6. Discuss and summarise group feedback and explain correct legal position where necessary.		

When you buy something, the manufacturer, importer, distributor or retailer gives you an implied warranty that the goods you receive are quality goods fit for the purpose for which they are bought. Where the goods are defective within six months from the date of purchase, the purchaser may return the goods without any penalty. The consumer, and not the seller, may decide whether the goods must be replaced, repaired or the money paid for them returned to the consumer.

Problem 8: The case of the unwanted books (Learner's Manual p 248)

AIM: The purpose of this exercise is to assess whether learners can explain the legal position of unordered goods.

PROCEDURE	TIME	
1. Introduce exercise.	Introduction:	5 min
2. Divide class into groups of no more than five learners.	Group work:	5 min
3. Ask each group to select a scribe and someone that will report back.	Groups report back:	10 min
	Discussion and summary:	5 min
4. Ask each group to advise you on your rights.	**TOTAL:**	**25 min**
5. Receive reports from each group.		
6. Discuss and summarise group feedback and explain correct legal position where necessary.		

Learners need to explain that The Reader's Friend cannot charge for the unordered book. You may send the book back but you cannot be compelled to send it back. It is the duty of The Reader's Friend to collect the unordered book from you. Where The Reader's Friend has not collected the book within 20 business days of the books being delivered to the consumer or of the supplier being informed to collect the books, the consumer is entitled to keep them without paying for them.

3.2.7 The right to be given information *(Learner's Manual p 248)*

Problem 9: Did the shopkeepers break the law? *(Learner's Manual p 251)*

AIM The purpose of this exercise is to assess whether learners can identify whether a product is correctly labelled. The exercise further seeks to assess whether learners understand the difference between 'use by' and 'best before' date.

PROCEDURE	TIME	
1. Introduce exercise.	Introduction:	5 min
2. Divide class into groups of no more than five learners.	Group work:	10 min
3. Ask each group to select a scribe and someone that will report back.	Groups report back:	15 min
4. Ask each group to discuss one question.	Discussion and summary:	5 min
5. Receive reports from each group.	**TOTAL:**	**35 min**
6. Discuss and summarise group feedback and explain correct legal position where necessary.		

1. Learners must identify that a supplier may not mislead consumers about the contents of the orange juice. Learners should indicate that it would be better if the label read 100% fruit juice. As it is labelled currently, the label leads one to think that the juice contains 100% orange juice with nothing else added.

2. It is not illegal for the shopkeeper to keep goods on the shelf after the 'best before' date. The 'use by' date means the date by which the chocolates must be eaten or used. If not used by the 'use by' date, it becomes unhealthy to use the goods. The shopkeeper has not done anything wrong by keeping the chocolates on the shelf after the 'best before' date. The shopkeeper will have to remove the chocolates from the shelf in one month when the chocolates reach their 'use by' date.

Problem 10: Something to do in your community *(Learner's Manual p 252)*

AIM: The purpose of this exercise is to allow learners the opportunity to go to their local shops and determine whether the labelling complies with the law that they have been taught. The exercise further expects learners to identify 'grey goods' that are sold by shops in their areas.

PROCEDURE	TIME	
1. Introduce the exercise.	Introduction: Explain to learners what is expected from homework assignment	
2. Allow learners the opportunity to perform individual assignments in shops in their communities as 'homework'.	Allow learners opportunity to perform two tasks for homework	
3. Learners report back on the due date for homework and present their findings to the rest of the class.	Individual learners report back on their findings when homework is due:	30 min
4. Discuss and summarise feedback and explain the correct legal position where necessary.	Discussion and summary:	5 min
	TOTAL:	**35 min**

1. Learners should go to their favourite clothing or shoe shop and check whether the information on the labels of the clothing or shoes contains the information required by the Consumer Protection Act.
2. Learners should go to a furniture or electric appliances shop and find out if they sell 'grey goods'. They should ask the shop whether it provides a guarantee for the goods sold.

3.2.8 The right to fair and responsible marketing *(Learner's Manual p 252)*

Problem 11: Some questions about advertisements *(Learner's Manual p 252)*

AIM: The object of this exercise is to make learners aware of why some advertisements are effective and others are not. They are also encouraged to be aware of how their emotions are manipulated.

PROCEDURE	TIME	
1. You can take a number of magazines to the class and ask learners to identify advertisements that appeal to them and confuse or mislead them.	Introduction:	5 min
2. Alternatively, learners could be given homework the previous day in which they are asked to bring along copies of advertisements in print which appeal to them.	Individual work:	15 min
	Report back:	30 min
	Discussion and summary:	5 min
3. Allow learners to explain the advertisements that appeal to them and the reasons why.	**TOTAL:**	**55 min**
4. Ask learners to explain advertisements that they found misleading, unhelpful and or confusing.		
5. Discuss, summarise and explain correct legal position where necessary.		

As an introduction to the persuasiveness and effectiveness of advertising, particularly television advertising, facilitators should ask the learners to identify the product associated with certain advertising slogans, for example:

'Snap, Crackle and Pop' (RICE CRISPIES); 'Yebo Gogo' (Vodacom); 'Go all the way, LION LAGER'; 'It's the Gravy!' (DOGMOR); 'It's not inside, it's on top' (CREMORA); 'It washes whiter than white' (OMO/SURF).

Facilitators may include their own list of popular advertisements and make the above list more relevant to the community involved. Facilitators may also do the activity visually with symbols (eg the symbol of a make of car; or the logo from a company, manufacturer or retail store; or a brand of petrol) instead of slogans. They may show learners a copy of an advertising symbol or logo taken from a newspaper or magazine.

Learners need an opportunity to practise analysing visual advertisements, especially those they see on television or in newspapers or magazines. Ask learners to analyse different advertisements to determine the most effective and the least effective. Ask them to try to determine, perhaps working in small groups, the characteristics of the effective and less effective advertisements. Depending on their location, the learners may be told to focus on newspaper, radio or television advertisements in their community.

1. Some advertisements may appeal because they have a catchy tune, or make the listener feel good, or make people want to aspire to what the people in the advertisement represent (eg status, money, success).

    Learners will have their own reasons for why they find certain advertisements appealing. They should give reasons for why they would or would not buy the thing advertised.

2. These may include their ability to afford the thing. Whether or not they need it will also be important to the more discerning learners.

    Advertisements that do not appeal may be unhelpful, confusing or misleading because of the manner in which they are presented. They may also be boring or unattractive so that people do not like them. Such advertisements may be completely unrelated to the thing advertised in terms of its quality or make-up.

    If the product is necessary it may be bought despite its unappealing advertisements. Conversely, an advertisement that is unhelpful, confusing and misleading is less likely to stimulate an artificial need in consumers. Learners should be encouraged to give their own examples of advertisements.

Problem 12: Is the advertisement puffing or false and misleading?

(Learner's Manual p 254)

AIM This exercise requires learners to identify whether an advertisement is puffing or false and misleading.

PROCEDURE		TIME	
1. Introduce and explain the meaning of and difference between false and misleading advertising and puffing.		Introduction:	5 min
2. Ask learners in small groups to study the advertisements and to decide whether they are false and misleading, or merely puffing.		Group work:	10 min
		Report back:	15 min
3. Allow learners to explain their answers to each of the four statements provided.		Discussion and summary:	5 min
		TOTAL:	**35 min**
4. Discuss, summarise, and explain the correct legal position where necessary.			

1. This is false and misleading advertising. As the dresses are not hand sewn, the advertisement is based on a factual misstatement.

2. This is puffing. It is based on the seller's opinion and is not a claim on which a consumer would reasonably rely.

3. This language is almost border-line between puffing and false advertising. The statement is specific (like 'hand sewn') and not just an opinion (like 'famous').

    However, it is probably an example of puffing since a reasonable person would probably not rely on jogging shoes to be able to jump higher and run longer. This ability is more likely to be as a result of training, fitness and technique.

4. This is false and misleading advertising. It is based on a specific statement of fact that has the ability to mislead and confuse. Does it mean that a consumer will lose two to five kilograms in a week or less than a week? Or does it mean that a consumer will lose two to five kilograms or less in a week?

Problem 13: To whom do the advertisements appeal? *(Learner's Manual p 255)*

AIM: This exercise includes advertisements that use the techniques described in the *Learner's Manual* (para 3.2.8.1) as well as several other common techniques. As the techniques are identified, learners should be asked to give other examples of advertisements (from the printed, visual media or electronic media) that use the same techniques.

PROCEDURE	TIME	
1. Divide learners in groups of no more than five.	Introduction:	5 min
2. Groups discuss and agree on:	Group work:	15 min
(a) Which method of making people buy the product is used in each advertisement?	Report back:	15 min
(b) Identify the information that is missing from each advertisement.	Discussion and summary:	5 min
(c) Identify to which group of persons the advertisement is trying to appeal.	**TOTAL:**	**40 min**
6. Each group provides a report back.		
7. Discuss and summarise.		

1. This advertisement associates the product with the desire to be the 'first' to obtain something of value. Its appeal is to all drivers young and old. It does not mention the cost of or any facts important to the purchase of a car. There is also an element of sex appeal.

2. This advertisement uses fear or scare tactics. It also associates the product with protection of the family. It does not say what else the insurance covers or how expensive the cover is. It is trying to appeal to adult home owners.

3. This advertisement associates the product with the popular symbol of motherhood. It appeals to parents of babies. It fails to mention costs, ingredients, or effectiveness.

4. This advertisement tries to associate the product with sex appeal. It attempts to attract women customers. It does not mention cost or ingredients or the fact that perfume plays only a small role, if any, in getting that special man.

5. This advertisement attempts to associate the product with a famous sportsman. Its appeal is to sports fans who like beer. It fails to mention the alcohol content, quality, taste or the price.

Problem 14: The case of the TV switch *(Learner's Manual p 257)*

AIM: This problem gives learners ideas on how to handle a 'bait and switch' situation, and shows them how important it is to be a wise consumer.

PROCEDURE		TIME	
1. Introduce exercise.		Introduction:	5 min
2. Choose learners for the role-play and explain to them what is expected during the role-play.		Role-play preparation:	5 min
		Role-play:	5 min
3. Preparation and presentation of role-play.		Group discussions:	15 min
4. Divide learners into small groups of five each.		Report back:	15 min
5. Ask groups to discuss the questions listed in problem.		Discussion and summary:	5 min
6. Get report back from each group.		**TOTAL:**	**50 min**
7. Conclude with general discussion and summary.			

1. What should a consumer do in this situation? Is it possible that the advertised item is of lesser quality? How can the consumer know which item is better? The learners playing the Browns should be firm in their wish to buy a black and white television set. The learner playing the salesperson should try to carry out the selling instructions of the shop. The role-play gives learners another opportunity to discuss what wise consumers should do (eg avoid impulse buying; obtain objective information about other similar goods, etc).

2. This gives learners an opportunity to relate 'bait and switch' techniques from their own experience. They may also discuss whether they thought that the technique worked on them or whether they realised what was happening.

3. The use of aggressive selling methods does not always result in 'bait and switch' tactics. If, however, the seller disparages the advertised products, or claims to be out of them, this is likely to be a 'bait and switch' tactic. If the salesperson merely tries to sell a colour TV, instead of a black and white set, this is probably not a 'bait and switch' technique. Learners should discuss their own responses to aggressive selling, and what they think are the advantages and disadvantages to consumers and shops. Consumers may find it helpful to be pressurised by aggressive selling. A salesperson who supplies accurate information about a product may be more valuable to a consumer. From the shop's point of view, aggressive selling may result in more sales to some customers. But it may also put off people who do not like over-aggressive attention from salespersons.

Problem 15: The case of the wrong racquet sent by mail order
(Learner's Manual p 258)

AIM: The aim of this problem is for learners to know what remedies they have if they buy a product from a catalogue and the wrong product is delivered to them.

PROCEDURE		TIME	
1. Divide class into small groups of five each.		Introduction:	5 min
2. Ask each group to discuss the question.		Small group discussions:	10 min
3. Get report back from each group.		Debrief and report back:	5 min
4. Conclude with general class discussion and summary.		Discussion and summary:	5 min
		TOTAL:	**25 min**

The answer is to be found in the text of the *Learner's Manual* para 3.2.8.5 which sets out what the Consumer Protection Act requires sellers who use catalogues to do. In this case the picture makes an express representation that the product sold will be the same as in the picture. As the representation is false, Garp may cancel the sale and get his money back. Alternatively, he could, as a favour to the sellers, agree to accept a metal racquet in exchange for the wooden one sent to him.

Problem 16: The case of the wrong bicycle
(Learner's Manual p 258)

AIM: The aim of this exercise is to make learners aware of what a good consumer should do before buying a product, and subsequently, if something goes wrong with it.

PROCEDURE	TIME	
1. Introduce exercise.	Introduction:	5 min
2. Divide learners into small groups of five each.	Group discussions and	
3. Ask each group to discuss one question.	role-play:	10 min
4. Groups discussing question 2 should also conduct the role-play.	Report back:	15 min
5. Get report back from each group.	Discussion and summary:	5 min
6. Conclude with general discussion and summary.	**TOTAL:**	**35 min**

1. From the facts of the case, it seems that Harry reacted on impulse to the advertisement. He should have found out about the 'Chief' bicycle, and should have shopped around comparing prices, quality, warranties and service. At the time he bought the bicycle, Harry should have demanded a receipt showing that the R800 was for a 'Chief' bicycle.

2. His first step should be to talk to the salesperson at Ron's Speed Shop. If this is unsuccessful, he should talk to the manager or owner. If the manager does not help, Harry should write a letter. If he still obtains no satisfaction, he should contact a lawyer or, if he cannot afford one, a law clinic (see *Learner's Manual* paras 1.4.1.3 and 1.4.1.4). It would be cheaper, however, to contact the Small Claims Court if there is one in his area (see *Learner's Manual* para 1.5.2). A newspaper or a citizens' advice bureau could also be contacted before going to a lawyer or law clinic, but the latter might bring a quicker response.

   Learners role-playing Harry should insist on their right to be sent the bicycle they paid for. By sending a 'Chuffer' instead of a 'Chief', Ron's Speed Shop has breached the contract to deliver a 'Chief' bicycle. Harry should insist that he is given either a 'Chief' or his money back. Technically, if Ron's could not give him a 'Chief', in addition to his money back, Harry could claim any increase in the price he would have to pay if he had to buy a 'Chief' somewhere else. The salesperson might argue that the shop is unable to order any more 'Chiefs' as the suppliers are out of stock. The shop might also argue that the 'Chuffer' costs the same as the 'Chief' and is a good buy.

3. Learners could be asked to research the consumer agencies available in their town or neighbourhood. For example, is there a citizens' advice bureau, a consumer affairs division, a newspaper with a consumer column, a Chamber of Commerce, a legal aid clinic or a Small Claims Court in their area? Where are they situated? What are their telephone numbers? What help will they give?

   Learners should be encouraged to think carefully before they buy expensive products.

Problem 17: The competition to win a car *(Learner's Manual p 260)*

AIM: To determine whether the learners can analyse a set of facts and decide whether the Consumer Protection Act has been complied with.

PROCEDURE
1. Introduce exercise.
2. Divide learners into small groups of five each.
3. Ask groups to discuss the question.
4. Get report back from each group.
5. Conclude with general discussion and summary.

TIME	
Introduction:	5 min
Group discussions:	10 min
Report back:	15 min
Discussion and summary:	5 min
TOTAL:	**35 min**

Promotional competitions may not require that participants pay, either directly or indirectly, for participating in the competition. Where the competition requires the participants to enter the competition electronically, eg by sending an SMS, the entry fee cannot be more than R1,50.

3.2.9   The right to fair and honest dealing   *(Learner's Manual p 260)*

Problem 18: Were the representations false or misleading? *(Learner's Manual p 261)*

AIM: The object of this exercise is for learners to decide whether the representations of the sales assistants were false or misleading.

PROCEDURE
1. Divide the class into small groups of five people each.
2. Allocate one problem and role-play to each group.
3. Ask each group to prepare their role-play and to decide whether the representations were false or misleading.
4. Conduct role-plays — one for each question.
5. After each role-play, debrief and get a report back from groups that prepared it.
6. Conclude with general discussion and summary.

TIME	
Preparation of role-plays and answers:	10 min
Role-play 1:	5 min
Debrief and report back:	5 min
Role-play 2:	5 min
Debrief and report back:	5 min
Discussion and summary:	5 min
TOTAL:	**35 min**

1. An express warranty has been given that the dress may be washed in a washing machine. Debra told the sales assistant that she planned to use a washing machine to wash it and was informed that it was all right. The fact that the dress shrank when washed in the washing machine is a breach of the express warranty given by the shop assistant. Debra is entitled to cancel the contract and obtain a refund of her money.

2. Ivan's words, 'This is the best camera on the market', are an implied warranty against latent defects. His words, 'It will last for years' are not an express warranty, however. They are mere puffing. Therefore, the question is: is a lens that falls out after six months of ordinary quality? How long can a lens be expected to last?

Problem 19: Arno and his pension package

(Learner's Manual p 264)

AIM: This exercise assesses whether learners can identify that the offer by the People's Trust is a Ponzi scheme and that the offer by the bank to place the money in a money market account of the bank would be the better option.

PROCEDURE
1. Introduce exercise.
2. Choose learners for the role-play and explain to them what is expected during the role-play.
3. Preparation and presentation of role-play.
4. Divide learners into small groups of five each.
5. Ask the groups to discuss where they think Arno should invest his money.
6. Get report back from each group.
7. Conclude with general discussion and summary.

TIME	
Introduction:	5 min
Role-play preparation:	5 min
Role-play:	5 min
Group discussions:	10 min
Report back:	10 min
Discussion and summary:	5 min
TOTAL:	**40 min**

During the role-play the person playing the role of Arno must show that he is confused about what to do with his money. The person representing the investment business must try to convince Arno that investment with the People's Trust is the best option. The representative of the People's Trust must make a strong argument focussing on how much quicker Arno will earn interest if he invests in the Trust.

Learners should identify that an investment with the bank with which Arno has had a long-standing business relationship will be the best option.

Problem 20: 'Sorry ma'am, the flight has been over-booked'

(Learner's Manual p 265)

AIM: To enable learners to decide what can be done by the consumer and the seller when over-selling or over-booking takes place.

PROCEDURE
1. Introduce exercise.
2. Divide learners into small groups of five each.
3. Ask the groups to discuss the questions.
4. Get report back from each group.
5. Conclude with general discussion and summary.

TIME	
Introduction:	5 min
Group discussions:	5 min
Report back:	10 min
Discussion and summary:	5 min
TOTAL:	**25 min**

A supplier may not accept payment for goods and services if they intend not to supply it. Where the airline accepts a reservation it will be penalised if the woman cannot take the flight on which she reserved the ticket. Learners should identity that the woman (consumer) may demand a full refund of any amounts paid, with interest at fixed interest dates from the date of payment until the date she gets her money back.

Learners should advise that the airline should refund her and must have systems in place that will ensure that there are no over-bookings or should compensate consumers who are 'bumped off' flights because of over-booking.

3.2.10 The right to fair, just and resonable terms and condtions
(Learner's Manual p 265)

Problem 21: The 'fantastic Firebird' *(Learner's Manual p 266)*

AIM: The object of this exercise is to make learners aware of clauses which may not be included in credit agreements. If they are included, they are not enforceable by the seller.

PROCEDURE		TIME	
1. Ask volunteers from the class to prepare a role-play for the salesperson selling the car to Javu.		Preparation for role-play:	5 min
2. Conduct and debrief role-play.		Role-play:	5 min
3. Divide the class into small groups of five each.		Group discussions:	10 min
4. Ask the groups to discuss the questions.		Report back:	10 min
5. Get a report back from each group.		Discussion and summary:	10 min
6. Conclude with general class discussion and summary.		**TOTAL:**	**40 min**

1. Learners playing the salesperson should enthusiastically sing the praises of the 'fantastic Firebird', using the language mentioned in the text. Javu should be suitably impressed by the sales talk and agree to sign the credit agreement.

2. The clause is not valid and the courts will not enforce it. This is because it says that the seller has made no warranties or representations about the car. It also says that Javu buys the car 'as it stands'. This is a *voetstoets* clause which says that the seller is not liable for any latent defects in the car. The clause also says that Javu acknowledges that he has inspected the goods. All of these conditions are unenforceable under the CPA (see *Learner's Manual* para 3.2.10.1).
If the car breaks down because of a major fault, the *voetstoots* clause will not protect Shifty's Car Sales because the clause is invalid. Javu will be entitled to cancel the contract and obtain a refund. Alternatively, he could agree to Shifty's repairing the car for him. The choice is his.
If the car broke down and needed expensive repairs Javu might not want to cancel the sale, but might have paid a lesser price had he known what was wrong with it. In this case, he could sue Shifty's for a reduction in the purchase price equivalent to the cost of the repairs. Again the *voetstoots* clause would not operate against him.

3.2.11 The right to fair value, quality and safety *(Learner's Manual p 267)*

Problem 22: What should the buyer and seller do? *(Learner's Manual p 268)*

AIM: The aim of this exercise is to help learners recognise when a seller is regarded as having given a consumer an implied warranty against hidden defects. Learners must also decide whether the consumer is entitled to either a refund or a reduction in the purchase price.

<table>
<tr><td colspan="2">

PROCEDURE ⣿

1. Introduce exercise.
2. Divide learners into small groups of five each.
3. Ask the groups to discuss the questions.
4. Get report back from each group.
5. Conclude with general discussion and summary.

</td><td>

TIME 🕐

Introduction:	5 min
Group discussions:	10 min
Report back:	10 min
Discussion and summary:	5 min
TOTAL:	**30 min**

</td></tr>
</table>

1. Trusty's Second Hand Cars is regarded in law as having given Vos an implied warranty against latent defects. This is because there are no express conditions covering the sale. Vos would be entitled to ask for a reduction in the purchase price of R2 000 if he would still have bought the car had he known of the defective brakes, but would have paid R2 000 less so that he could have the brakes repaired. Vos might try to argue that he would never have bought the car had he known of the defective brakes and is entitled to a refund of R50 000. The court might, however, decide that this would be unreasonable.

2. Sally's supermarket is regarded as having given Natie an implied warranty that the 'whistling kettle' would whistle when the water boils. If Natie would never have bought the kettle had he known that it did not whistle, he would be entitled to get his money back. If he would have still bought the kettle, but would have paid R100 less had he known of the defect, he may claim a reduction of R100 in the purchase price.

Problem 23: Can the consumer claim damages? *(Learner's Manual p 270)*

AIM: The object of this exercise is to help learners recognise the circumstances in which consumers may claim damages in addition to a either refund of, or reduction in, the purchase price.

<table>
<tr><td colspan="2">

PROCEDURE ⣿

1. Introduce exercise.
2. Divide learners into small groups of five each.
3. Ask the groups to discuss the questions.
4. Get report back from each group.
5. Conclude with general discussion and summary.

</td><td>

TIME 🕐

Introduction:	5 min
Group discussions:	5 min
Report back:	10 min
Discussion and summary:	5 min
TOTAL:	**25 min**

</td></tr>
</table>

1. Mrs Tshabalala is entitled to recover damages from the butcher for her medical expenses and lost wages. This is because the CPA imposes strict liability on producers and seller of goods to compensate consumers for harm caused by defective products. She is also entitled to a refund of the purchase price.

2. Mr Smit could sue Jerry's General Store for damages for the same reasons as Mrs Tshabalala. A general-store dealer is a seller or retailer. Therefore, Mr Smit can sue the store for damages without proving fault (eg negligence) by them. Mr Smit would also be entitled to recover the purchase price, without proving fault. Mr Smith could sue the manufacturer of the electric drill instead if he wished. The damages he could recover would be for medical expenses incurred and lost wages for his week off work.

3. Mrs Nair would be entitled to sue Queen's Quality Furnishers for the broken tea set worth R1000 without proving fault by them for the same reasons as Mr Smit. Mrs Nair could also recover the purchase price of the sofa.

3.2.13   Payments in advance

(Learner's Manual p 271)

Problem 24: Buying a prepaid 1 gig data bundle

(Learner's Manual p 272)

AIM: This exercise seeks to assess whether learners know if a prepaid certificate can expire prior to its value being used.

PROCEDURE		TIME	
1. Introduce exercise.		Introduction:	5 min
2. Divide learners into small groups of five each.		Group discussions:	5 min
3. Ask the groups to discuss the question.		Report back:	10 min
4. Get report back from each group.		Discussion and summary:	5 min
5. Conclude with general discussion and summary.		**TOTAL:**	**25 min**

The CPA protects consumers where suppliers accept payment from them in exchange for a prepaid certificate or voucher. In terms of the Act a prepaid certificate will only expire when its full value has been used. If the full amount has not been used it will expire three years after the date on which it was issued, or after a longer period that the supplier has agreed to.

Problem 25: The two-year gym membership

(Learner's Manual p 273)

AIM: This exercise assesses whether the learner knows the rights and responsibilities of the consumer and the seller in a prepaid services transaction.

PROCEDURE		TIME	
1. Introduce exercise.		Introduction:	5 min
2. Divide learners into small groups of five each.		Group discussions:	10 min
3. Ask the groups to discuss the questions.		Report back:	10 min
4. Get report back from each group.		Discussion and summary:	5 min
5. Conclude with general discussion and summary.		**TOTAL:**	**30 min**

1. The money belongs to the consumer and the Swimming Academy may deduct the monthly membership fee each month.
2. Aquatic Swimming Academy may deduct R350 each month.
3. If the Aquatic Swimming Academy is going to close down it may provide Zintle with an alternative service. If it will not be providing an alternative service, the Aquatic Swimming Academy must give Zintle 40 business days' written notice of its intention to close down and any money due to Zintle must be repaid to her within five business days after the closing.

Problem 26: The untimely death of Eunice *(Learner's Manual p 274)*

AIM: This exercise seeks to determine whether learners know when the supplier is entitled to charge a termination fee upon cancellation of a lay-by.

PROCEDURE
1. Introduce exercise.
2. Divide learners into small groups of five each.
3. Ask the groups to discuss the questions.
4. Get report back from each group.
5. Conclude with general discussion and summary.

TIME	
Introduction:	5 min
Group discussions:	10 min
Report back:	10 min
Discussion and summary:	5 min
TOTAL:	**30 min**

Any money paid by Eunice will belong to her deceased estate. Get Fashions cannot treat any of the amounts paid by Eunice as its own till the dress is paid for and delivered. In the event of Eunice's death she is unable to complete the agreement. Get Fashions may not insist that Eunice's daughter pay the outstanding amount for the dress. The lay-by is terminated by Eunice's death. Get Fashions has to pay back all the money that Eunice paid into her estate and may not deduct a termination fee.

3.2.15 Steps consumers should take when complaining
(Learner's Manual p 276)

Problem 27: Who would you contact? *(Learner's Manual p 276)*

AIM: The object of this exercise is to test the learners' understanding of which agencies and organisations may be used to settle consumer problems.

PROCEDURE
1. Introduce exercise.
2. Divide learners into small groups of five each.
3. Ask groups to discuss questions listed in the problem.
4. Report back.
5. General discussion.

TIME	
Introduce exercise:	5 min
Group discussions:	20 min
Report back:	25 min
Discussion:	10 min
TOTAL:	**60 min**

1. You might complain to the shop about the toy and obtain your money back or a replacement. If you wish to complain about the advertisement being misleading, you could write to the Advertising Standards Authority in Johannesburg. If you believe the toy is dangerously defective, you could complain to the Consumer Affairs Division of the Department of Trade and Industry, the press and the manufacturers.

2. Apart from obtaining a refund of your money, you could contact the Department of Health. A health inspector would be sent around to check the hygiene of the café or shop selling the pie. People who fail to keep food products clean and healthy may be prosecuted.

3. You would be entitled to your money back and compensation for any illness, medical expenses and lost wages. If the supermarket does not refund your money and compensate you, you and your friends could possibly sue the supermarket or the manufacturer. This may, however, be expensive unless you obtain legal aid. You could also inform the local Department of Health which would take immediate steps to have the dangerous tins removed from the shelves.

4(a) Your parents might complain to the shop to obtain their money back or a replacement refrigerator. They could also complain to the Domestic Appliances Manufacturers' Association in Johannesburg or the South African Bureau of Standards that has a branch in all the major cities.

4(b) They could make sure that the next refrigerator will work by threatening to report the manufacturer to the South African Bureau of Standards if it does not. The Bureau has the power to withdraw its 'SABS' mark from the manufacturer of products that are not up to its standards.

5. You could write them a letter refusing to pay their fees and stating the reasons why. (You should always keep copies of any letters that could be used in a court case if your complaint is not resolved.) You could contact a law clinic or lawyer concerning the legal action against you. Maybe a newspaper consumer columnist would be prepared to publish the story. A complaint to the SA Direct Marketing Association may also cause the correspondence college to be censured and persuaded not to sue you.

6. You could telephone your travel agent and explain what happened and that you want your money back. If the agent does not refund your money you could us the Small Claims Court to recover your money. If you wish to complain about the agent's negligence you could write to the Association of South African Travel Agents in Johannesburg.

7. Your parents should contact the Automobile Association (AA) and ask them to give the car a thorough technical test. They could then take the list of defects provided by the AA to the seller. If the defects are so bad that your parents would never have bought the car if they had known, they are entitled to cancel the sale and obtain a refund of their money or obtain another car. If the defects are not so bad that they wish to cancel the sale, and your parents will be satisfied if the car is repaired, they should request the seller to carry out the repairs listed by the AA.

   If the seller does not satisfactorily replace or repair the car your parents could tell the seller that if the car is not satisfactorily repaired they will take the car elsewhere for repairs and hold the seller liable for the costs. If they wish to complain about the service provided by the seller or manufacturer they may contact the AA or the Retail Motor Industry in the nearest major city.

The case of the cheap tape recorder (Problem 3 in the *Learner's Manual* para 1.5.2.2) is a good example of a consumer case brought in the Small Claims Court.

The instructions for the conducting of a Small Claims Court mock trial are to be found in the *Educator's Manual* para 1.5.

3.3. Credit buying and credit agreements

Outcomes

After completion of this section learners will be able to:

1. Demonstrate an understanding of the law relating to consumer credit.

Assessment criteria

1. The advantages and disadvantages of credit are identified
2. A decision is taken on whether credit should be given to a specific person.
3. A decision is made on which costs may be charged when credit is incurred.
4. A decision is made on the type of credit that is provided in a specific transaction.
5. A decision is made on whether a consumer's rights were infringed.
6. How repossession works is explained.
7. What creditors may or may not do if debtors do not pay their debts is explained.
8. Sets of facts are examined and decisions are made on whether the debt collection was lawful, immoral or illegal.

3.3.2 National Credit Act

(Learner's Manual p 280)

Problem 1: Using credit

(Learner's Manual p 282)

AIM: This exercise requires learners to consider the advantages and disadvantages of using credit.

PROCEDURE
1. Introduce exercise.
2. You may require learners to complete the assignment individually or learners can be asked to answer the questions in pairs.
3. Get report back from each learner/pair of learners.
4. Conclude with general discussion and summary.
5. Learners could list different types of transactions, eg buying a car or a house, buying clothes on an account, buying groceries or other goods on a credit card.

TIME	
Introduction:	5 min
Individual work or work in pairs:	15 min
Report back:	10 min
Discussion and summary:	5 min
TOTAL:	**35 min**

1 and 2.   Examples of what students can mention are in the table below:

Type of thing bought on credit	Advantages	Disadvantages
Clothing for a special occasion	You will have the clothes you need immediately. You will have something to wear. You will be seen wearing the latest fashion wear.	By the time you have paid for the item it is already old. The balance of the accounts can become so high that you struggle to pay the instalments. If interest is charged on the account you pay much more for the item than when you paid cash.
University fees	You are able to go to university when your parents do not have the money to pay cash. You improve your education, which will help you get a better job.	The loan might be in your own name and when you start to work you will have a large debt to pay off.
A car to drive to work	You can get yourself to work without having to rely on public transport. You are able to buy something that most people do not have the cash for upfront. You can start a lift club with colleagues. Having your own car makes you more independent.	The monthly instalment will significantly reduce the money you have to live off. You pay much more for the car. It takes you a long time to pay off a car. A car always decreases in value and is not an investment.
A holiday	You get to go on a holiday that you cannot afford to pay cash for immediately.	The holiday will be long forgotten and you will still be paying off on it. The instalments that you have to repay will result in your not being able to save money for your next holiday. You have nothing to show for it after you come back from the holiday except photographs and debt.

3.   Some rules when deciding to buy on credit

Some of the rules that learners might mention are:

(a)   Make sure it is an item that you need and do not simply want.

(b)   Work out your budget to make sure you can afford it.

(c)   Shop around for the best deal.

(d)   Make sure you understand the provisions of the contract.

(e)   Get credit quotes from different service providers and choose the cheapest quote.

Problem 2: Was Nosethu unfairly discriminated against? *(Learner's Manual p 283)*

AIM: The aim of the exercises is for learners to decide whether, in terms of the Constitution and the National Credit Act, Nosethu was unfairly discriminated against.

PROCEDURE ☰		TIME ◷	
1. Introduce the exercise		Introduction:	5 min
2. Divide the class into small groups of five each.		Group discussions:	10 min
3. Ask the groups to discuss whether any of Nosethu's rights were infringed.		Report back:	10 min
		Discussion and summary:	10 min
4. Get a report back from each group.		**TOTAL:**	**35 min**
5. Conclude with general class discussion and summary.			

Groups need to decide whether the bank is treating people differently merely because of their skin colour. Having a policy that does not provide loans to black domestic workers will be unfair discrimination and S Bank should not be allowed to have such a policy.

Problem 3: Cameron applies for a personal loan *(Learner's Manual p 284)*

AIM: The aim of this exercise is for learners to decide whether, in terms of the National Credit Act, Cameron is entitled to a loan for the full amount that he wishes to borrow.

PROCEDURE ☰		TIME ◷	
1. Introduce the exercise		Introduction:	5 min
2. Divide the class into small groups of five each.		Group discussions:	10 min
3. Ask the groups to explain Cameron's rights.		Report back:	10 min
		Discussion and summary:	10 min
4. Get a report back from each group.		**TOTAL:**	**35 min**
5. Conclude with general class discussion and summary.			

The National Credit Act aims to correct the imbalances between consumers and credit providers when credit is being negotiated.

If Cameron is 18 or older he has the right to apply for credit. However, this right does not mean that he can force a credit provider to give him credit. A valid reason for refusing a consumer credit would be that the credit provider, after considering the application, came to the conclusion that the consumer cannot afford the credit. Cameron may approach B Bank and ask them to provide him with reasons why the bank is only prepared to lend him R5 000 instead of the R10 000 that he applied for.

Problem 4: Tiaan wants to pay off his bank loan early *(Learner's Manual p 285)*

AIM: The aim of this exercise is for learners to decide whether, in terms of the National Credit Act, Tiaan may pay off his bank loan earlier than originally agreed.

PROCEDURE

1. Divide the class into pairs.
2. Ask each pair to take turns role-playing a conversation between Tiaan and his lawyer.
3. The conversation in the role-play must include Tiaan explaining his situation to his 'lawyer', the lawyers must ask questions of clarity and the role-play must conclude with the lawyer explaining to Tiaan whether he may settle the balance of his account before the end date of the contract.
4. Learners must swap roles to allow each person the opportunity to play both roles
5. Get a report back from each pair.
6. Conclude with general class discussion and summary.

TIME	
Introduce exercise:	5 min
Divide learners into pairs:	5 min
Role-play including swapping of roles:	10 min
Report back:	10 min
Discussion and summary:	10 min
TOTAL:	**40 min**

Each learner must identify that Tiaan has the right to settle an account earlier than agreed without giving notice to the credit provider. Tiaan must ask the credit provider for a statement that contains the settlement amount. The credit provider must deliver such an account within five days of receiving the request and it will be binding on the credit provider for five days after its delivery.

Problem 5: Marelize's personal credit information is disclosed to her son's school
(Learner's Manual p 286)

AIM: The aim of this exercise is for learners to decide whether, in terms of the National Credit Act, personal information about Marelize should have been disclosed by a credit provider to her son's school.

PROCEDURE

1. Divide the class into small groups of five each.
2. Ask the groups to discuss whether any of Marelize's rights were infringed.
3. Get a report back from each group.
4. Conclude with general class discussion and summary.

TIME	
Introduce exercise:	5 min
Group discussions:	10 min
Report back:	10 min
Discussion and summary:	10 min
TOTAL:	**35 min**

The NCA requires people who receive personal information in terms of the Act to keep such information confidential. Therefore, the groups need to explain that Uptown Fashion Designers must protect the personal information that they have about Marelize's income and expenditure and are not allowed to give the school information about Marelize that is not generally known to the public. Uptown Fashion Designers have gone against the provisions of the NCA.

The educator could also mention that the South African Schools Act provides that a learner may not be refused admission to a public school on the grounds that his or her parents cannot afford to pay school fees, and School Governing Bodies of public schools are prohibited from doing credit checks on parents.

Problem 6: Neville checks his personal information in the credit bureau

(Learner's Manual p 287)

AIM: The aim of this exercise is for learners to decide whether, in terms of the National Credit Act, Neville can demand that the credit bureau correct the personal information about him that it has on record.

PROCEDURE :≡	TIME ⊙	
1. Divide the class into small groups of five each.	Introduce the exercise:	5 min
2. Ask the groups to explain to Neville his rights in terms of the NCA.	Group discussions:	10 min
3. Get a report back from each group.	Report back:	10 min
4. Conclude with general class discussion and summary.	Discussion and summary:	10 min
	TOTAL:	**35 min**

Groups need to explain that the credit bureau is forced to check the accuracy of the information that is submitted to it. The plumber should have informed Neville that he was going to submit negative information (slow payer) about Neville to the bureau. After inspection of his information Neville may lodge a complaint with the National Credit Regulator challenging the accuracy of the information.

Problem 7: Sally is not given a quotation

(Learner's Manual p 287)

AIM: The aim of this exercise is for learners to decide whether, in terms of the National Credit Act, Sally should have been given a quotation and to identify what Jaftha should do in future to protect the rights of consumers.

PROCEDURE :≡	TIME ⊙	
1. Ask volunteers from the class to prepare the role-plays.	Introduce the exercise:	5 min
2. Conduct and debrief role-play.	Preparation for role-play:	5 min
3. Divide the class into small groups of five each.	Role-play:	5 min
4. Ask the groups to explain Jaftha's duties to him in terms of the NCA.	Group discussions:	10 min
	Report back:	10 min
5. Get a report back from each group.	Discussion and summary:	10 min
6. Conclude with general class discussion and summary.	**TOTAL:**	**45 min**

1. The learner asking Sally questions needs to ask Sally whether she was given a written quotation by Jaftha. Sally must be asked if she received information in written format. If Sally admits to getting a written document before signing the agreement, she must be asked whether she read and understood the document. Sally must appear very ignorant about what she got from Jaftha.

2. The groups need to explain to Jaftha that the National Credit Act forces him to provide purchasers with written quotations before they enter into the contract. For details of what must be mentioned in the quotation see *Learner's Manual* para 3.3.2.12.

Problem 8: Mrs Hemraj buys a vacuum cleaner (Learner's Manual p 288)

AIM: The aim of this exercise is for learners to decide whether, in terms of the National Credit Act, the Hemrajs are entitled to cancel the sale during the 'cooling-off' period.

PROCEDURE ☰
1. Ask for volunteers to play roles of Arthur Goldmouth, Mrs Hemraj and Mr Hemraj.
2. Conduct and debrief role-play.
3. Divide the class into small groups.
4. Ask groups to answer questions 3 & 4.
5. Report back.
6. General discussion.

TIME ⊖	
Introduce the exercise:	5 min
Preparation for role-play:	5 min
Role-play:	5 min
Group discussions:	10 min
Report back:	10 min
Discussion and summary:	10 min
TOTAL:	**45 min**

Learners playing Arthur Goldmouth should sing the praises of the 'Super Sucker' vacuum cleaner, emphasising that it is 'the world's greatest vacuum cleaner'. They should also point out the reasonable terms of payment. Learners playing Mrs Hemraj should be tentative initially regarding the virtues of the 'Super Sucker', but eventually agree to buy it.

Learners playing Mr Hemraj should begin by being angry with Mrs Hemraj for buying the vacuum cleaner. Learners playing Mrs Hemraj should point out the advantages of the 'Super Sucker' and its reasonable price. After the discussion of their needs and financial position, however, the Hemrajs should decide that they do not want it.

1. The contract entered into is a credit agreement. Mrs Hemraj obtains possession of the vacuum cleaner immediately but has to pay a deposit. The rest of the purchase price together with finance charges will be paid off in instalments. The agreement was not entered into at the seller's business premises. It is a door-to-door sale. Where a contract was entered into at any place which is not the business premises of the credit provider, the consumer has a right to cancel the agreement within five business days from the date of signing this agreement. Mrs Hemraj has the right to return the vacuum cleaner and cancel the agreement within five business days from the date she signed the contract. She should deliver a written notice to the sellers saying that she is cancelling the agreement and wants a refund of her R400 deposit.

2. Arthur Goldmouth and the sellers must return Mrs Hemraj's R400. Mrs Hemraj will incur no expenses on cancelling the agreement, except perhaps for postage if she sends the notice by registered post. This is because she used the 5-day cooling-off period. Mr Goldmouth would have to arrange to collect the vacuum cleaner from her.

Problem 9: Michelle is retrenched (Learner's Manual p 289)

AIM: The aim of this exercise is for learners to decide whether, in terms of the National Credit Act, Michelle is entitled to return the TV set and get a refund.

PROCEDURE		TIME	
1. Divide the class into small groups of five each.		Introduce exercise:	5 min
2. Ask the groups to explain to Michelle her rights in terms of the NCA.		Group discussions:	10 min
		Report back:	10 min
3. Get a report back from each group.		Discussion and summary:	10 min
4. Conclude with general class discussion and summary.		**TOTAL:**	**35 min**

Groups need to advise Michelle that she may return the television. Once she returns it, it will be valued and sold and the proceeds will be deducted from the balance of her account. If the proceeds from the sale of the television are not enough to finish paying Michelle's account, she will still be responsible for paying the balance, even though she does not have the television any more.

3.3.4   Obtaining credit

(Learner's Manual p 291)

Problem 10: If you were the credit manager

(Learner's Manual p 292)

AIM: The aim of this exercise is for learners to decide whether, in terms of the National Credit Act, the bank manager is obliged to give the different people the loans they are requesting.

PROCEDURE		TIME	
1. Divide the class into small groups of five each.		Introduce exercise:	5 min
2. Get each group to discuss one case.		Group discussions:	15 min
3. Get a report back from each group.		Report back:	10 min
		Discussion and summary:	10 min
4. Conclude with general class discussion and summary.		**TOTAL:**	**40 min**

1. Groups should respond that Tilly has no income other than her children's maintenance. After paying her rent and other expenses from the maintenance she is only left with R100. It would be reasonable to assume that she will be unable to repay the loan. The bank manager would be justified in refusing to give her a loan.

2. Jannie cannot prove that he has a steady income. He is not employed full time. He might not be able to pay the bank if in a particular month he does not earn any income from odd jobs. He has only R200 left over after paying his monthly expenses. The bank manager would be justified in refusing him a loan.

3. If the bank gives Shadreck the student loan, details of the loan have to be recorded in the National Register of Credit Agreements. Shadreck has proved to be a good student and is in his final year. With a BComm he may become a successful businessman and may be a good investment as a future client of the bank. The bank manager may wish to make such an investment and, because it is a student loan, is not required to do an affordability test on him.

3.3.7 Credit transactions
(Learner's Manual p 295)

Problem 11: Identify the type of credit
(Learner's Manual p 298)

AIM: The aim of this exercise is for learners to decide what type of credit is involved in the different case studies.

PROCEDURE	TIME	
1. Divide the class into small groups of five each. 2. Get each group to discuss one case. 3. Get a report back from each group. 4. Conclude with general class discussion and summary.	Introduce exercise: Group discussions: Report back: Discussion and summary: **TOTAL:**	5 min 20 min 10 min 10 min **45 min**

1. The agreement that Aphele may enter into is a credit transaction because it is a low income housing agreement that includes a mortgage agreement.
2. Seni, Thando, Dennis and Luvuyo have entered into a stokvel agreement.
3. Melanie has entered into a secured loan agreement.
4. Zintle has entered into an instalment agreement.
5. Stoffel has entered into a student loan agreement.

3.3.10 Reckless credit granting
(Learner's Manual p 300)

Problem 12: What should Odette do?
(Learner's Manual p 301)

AIM: The aim of this exercise is for learners to decide whether Odette needs debt counselling and what she should do about her financial situation.

PROCEDURE	TIME	
1. Divide the class into small groups of five each. 2. Get each group to discuss one case. 3. Get a report back from each group. 4. Conclude with general class discussion and summary.	Introduce exercise: Group discussions: Report back: Discussion and summary: **TOTAL:**	5 min 20 min 15 min 10 min **50 min**

1. Odette must be advised to go to a registered debt counsellor to have a debt review done.
2. Odette needs to approach a registered debt counsellor who will do a debt review. The debt review means that the debt counsellor will help Odette work out what her monthly income and expenditure is and how much she owes. Odette will have to give the debt counsellor copies of her payslip and her statement of accounts. The debt counsellor will review Odette's financial affairs and decide whether Odette is unable to pay all her monthly expenses (whether she is over-indebted). If the debt counsellor is of the opinion that Odette is over-indebted, the debt counsellor may issue a proposal to the magistrate's court that Odette be placed under debt counselling.

3.3. Credit buying and credit agreements • 191

3. The retailer is compelled by the NCA, prior to granting credit, to take into account the consumer's income and expenditure and the consumer's previous repayment history. If the retailer granted Odette credit without asking for this information it is reckless credit granting, is wrong, and against the NCA.

4. Odette may approach a court for an order that the credit agreement is reckless credit granting. If the court is of the opinion that the agreement is reckless it may set aside the rights and obligations of Odette in terms of the agreement. If the credit agreement results in the Odette being over-indebted the court may suspend the reckless agreement to a date in the future, or the court may restructure the agreement. When restructuring the agreement the court may order that Odette does not have to make any payments in terms of the agreement or that Odette may not be charged interest, and may determine that the retailer may not enforce its rights in terms of the agreement.

5. If Odette lied or withheld information from the retailer, she may not rely on the protection afforded in connection with reckless credit granting.

3.3.12 What creditors may or may not do if debtors do not pay
(Learner's Manual p 303)

Problem 13: The case of the missing motorcycle
(Learner's Manual p 304)

AIM: The object of this exercise is to make learners aware of the procedures that should be followed if goods are unlawfully repossessed by a seller.

PROCEDURE
1. Ask volunteers to prepare a role-play where Willem complains to the manager of Price Busters.
2. Conduct and debrief role-play.
3. Divide the class into small groups of five each.
4. Ask the groups to discuss questions 2 and 3.
5. Get a report back from each group.
6. Conclude with general class discussion and summary.

TIME	
Preparation for role-play:	5 min
Role-play:	5 min
Group discussions:	10 min
Report back:	10 min
Discussion and summary:	10 min
TOTAL:	**40 min**

1. Willem should point out that he was given no warning notice by Price Busters that he was behind in his instalments and that the motorcycle would be repossessed if he did not pay. They had no right to send a man in the middle of the night to repossess the motorcycle. The manager of Price Busters should say that it was Willem's own fault. He should have told them about the funeral expenses, and they might have given him an extension. They repossessed the motorcycle because he had fallen behind in his payments without giving any reasons.

2. Price Busters might have been able to repossess the motorcycle lawfully if they had followed the proper procedures. In this case, however, their conduct was unlawful. It was a breach of the credit agreement by them. It could be argued that, because Price Busters have unlawfully deprived him of possession of the motorcycle, Willem is entitled to cancel the agreement and demand a refund of all monies paid by him. Alternatively, he may ask the court to order Price Busters to return the motorcycle if he pays the missing instalments.

Price Busters has two options if Willem falls behind in his instalments. Firstly, they could ask Willem to consent to repossession, and then repossess the motorcycle. Secondly, if Willem refuses to consent to repossession, Price Busters would have to apply to court. Before approaching the courts, Price Busters must send Willem a letter demanding payment within a period of not less than 30 days, and inform Willem that he has committed a breach of contract by not paying the instalment. Only then, if Willem still fails to pay, may Price Busters take legal steps by asking the court to grant a repossession order. If a repossession order is granted, the sheriff of the court will repossess the car.

3. Willem may recover the motorcycle by paying the arrear instalments within 30 days of the date it was repossessed. Price Busters must keep the motorcycle for 30 days before reselling it. If Willem pays all the arrear instalments, Price Busters must return the motorcycle to Willem, and the credit agreement remains in force.

Problem 14: Were the actions of the creditor lawful, immoral or unlawful?
(Learner's Manual p 305)

AIM: The object of this exercise is to enable learners to recognise lawful, immoral and unlawful debt-collection practices. Learners should also be encouraged to think about the remedies available for unlawful debt collection practices.

PROCEDURE
1. Introduction.
2. Divide class into small groups of five each.
3. Allocate one question and role-play to each group.
4. Group discussions and role-play preparation.
5. Reports back and role-plays by one group for each question.
6. Debrief and role-play.
7. Conclude with general discussion and summary.

TIME	
Introduction:	5 min
Group discussions and preparation for role-plays:	15 min
Reports back, role-plays and debriefs:	35 min
Discussion and summary:	5 min
TOTAL:	**60 min**

1. The seller's conduct in breaking into Sofala's home is housebreaking and trespass. Damaging the door and lock is malicious injury to property. The taking of the radio, for which she had paid in cash, is theft. Sofala could lay charges with the police for all these crimes. She could also bring a civil action against the seller for the damage to her door and for the return of the radio. Generally, credit sellers may only repossess property with the consent of the buyer, or court order, and may not use unlawful methods to repossess goods. In theory, Sofala could bring an action to force the seller to return the furniture to her because the repossession was unlawful. It was certainly immoral. It might be easier for her, however, to pay the arrear instalments within 30 days. The seller would then be legally obliged to return the furniture to her.

2. It is immoral for a creditor to use a fake summons that is drawn up to look like an official court document. Any document that is headed with the word 'Summons' will only be official if it has been rubber stamped by the magistrate's court or the High Court (if the amount of money is in excess of R200 000). Any document that does not have an official stamp from the magistrate's or High Court on it, and which is not signed by the clerk of the magistrate's court or the

Registrar of the High Court, cannot be regarded as a proper summons. A person may no longer be imprisoned for failure to pay her debts. A summons will usually only demand payment of money outstanding or order the debtor to do something. False legal documents are immoral and sometimes unlawful. It could be very difficult, however, to prove a criminal act by the television shop. Vloog should, take the document to the police station and ask whether he can lay a charge of fraud against the television shop concerned. If the police refuse to help, he could take the document to a legal aid clinic, Legal Resources Centre, a Consumer Affairs Division office, or even a newspaper consumer columnist. The latter could then warn the public about the television shop's immoral conduct.

3. It would be immoral and unlawful for the credit manager to threaten to tell Lucy's employers that she has not paid her clothes account for R3 000. If the credit manager did tell her employers, Lucy would have an action for the invasion of privacy. Unfortunately, if Lucy cannot afford a lawyer, she would not be able to obtain legal aid for such an action. Actions for 'sentimental' damages, like invasion of privacy, are excluded from the national legal aid scheme in terms of the *Legal Aid Guide*. If the threat is made Lucy should approach a university legal aid clinic, a Legal Resources Centre or a newspaper columnist. The latter could publicise the immoral and unlawful debt-collection practices of the clothes shop.

4. As in Lucy's case, it may be immoral and unlawful for the owner of the shop to tell other computer dealers about Arvin's failure to pay the R2000. It might be justified, however, if Arvin always runs up accounts with computer shops and then defaults on his payments. If this were the case, the owner of the computer shop could argue that she had a social, moral or legal duty to warn other computer shops against Arvin's practice of not paying his accounts. This would be regarded as a 'privileged occasion' and would be a good defence to an action by Arvin against the computer shop for invasion of privacy or defamation. (It is defamatory to say that a person does not pay his or her debts.) If this is the first time that Arvin has failed to pay his debts, he should consult a legal aid clinic, a citizen's advice office or a newspaper columnist if he cannot afford a lawyer. He could write a letter to the computer shop advising the owner that, if she proceeds with her threat, she will be sued for invasion of privacy or defamation.

5. The debt collector's threats are unlawful. Ferdie may lay a charge of assault against the debt collector. It is assault not only to harm a person physically but also to threaten to do so.

6. The sheriff's action was not unlawful because he had a warrant of execution issued by the court. The warrant of execution enables the sheriff to attach property even if Greg is not at home. Usually, the sheriff will give the debtor a chance to pay the debt and legal costs before attaching the property.

7. The manager's act was immoral and unlawful. If the shoes were sold to Dambuza on credit, and he became owner of the shoes and socks, the manager's act is theft. Dambuza could lay a charge of theft with the police and bring a civil action to recover his shoes and socks. The manager's act was also humiliating for Dambuza and he could bring a civil action for 'sentimental damages' for insult and hurt feelings. If he could not afford a lawyer, however, he would not obtain legal aid for an action for 'sentimental damages'.

3.4 Common-law protection of consumers

Outcomes

After completion of this section learners will be able to:

1. Demonstrate an understanding of the common-law protection of consumers when statute law does not apply, particularly under the law of contract.

Assessment criteria

1. The common-law protection of consumers when statute law does not apply, is explained.
2. The requirements for a valid contract at common law are explained.
3. A decision is taken on whether or not a contract has been entered into.
4. Different types of terms and conditions in contracts that may sometimes exclude liability are identified.
5. A decision is taken on whether a person may enter into a contract.
6. Five types of contracts that must be in writing are listed.
7. An explanation is given on what should be done before entering into a written contract.
8. Decisions are made on whether breach of contract has occurred.
9. The court's powers when a breach of contract occurs are explained.
10. A set of facts is examined and a decision is made on what order the magistrate should give.
11. Sets of facts are examined and decisions taken on whether or not the persons breaching the contracts are liable.

The common law protects consumers when they are not protected by the CPA or NCA because the sellers are not manufacturers, suppliers or distributors of goods. This section deals with the elements of a contract, illegal contracts, how minors are or are not able to enter into contracts, breach of contract and terms limiting liability in contract.

3.4.1 Requirements for a contract *(Learner's Manual p 308)*

Problem 1: Is there a contract? *(Learner's Manual p 309)*

AIM: The object of this exercise is to help learners understand whether a valid contract has, or has not, been entered into.

PROCEDURE	TIME	
1. Divide class into small groups of five each.	Introduction:	5 min
2. Ask each group to discuss one question.	Group discussions:	20 min
3. Get report back from each group.	Report back:	20 min
4. Conclude with general class discussion and summary.	Discussion and summary:	10 min
	TOTAL:	**55 min**

1. This is a valid contract. An offer of a reward is an offer to the whole world. The first person to accept the offer by carrying out its conditions is entitled to be rewarded. Chiman, by finding the child, accepts the offer and enters into a binding contract with the parents.

2. No contract has been made. Thandi has tried to make an acceptance, but there has been no valid offer. Lindiwe said she was 'going to sell' her bicycle for R4 000. She did not say that she was offering to sell it at that amount to Thandi.

3. This is a valid contract. Fanie's father's offer was conditional on Fanie reaching the age of 18. Fanie has fulfilled the condition and is entitled to his money.

4. This is a valid contract. John made an offer and Piet accepted it by fulfilling the condition. Even though Piet did not say anything he accepted the offer by walking across on the log.

5. This is not an enforceable contract because it is an agreement to do something illegal. Even though there is an offer and acceptance the courts will not enforce a contract which requires somebody to commit a crime.

6. No contract has been made. Dan makes an offer and Peggy accepts it. Neither of them know, however, that at the time Dan's car had been destroyed. This means that it would have been impossible for him to carry out the contract. The court will not enforce a contract that was impossible to carry out at the time that it was entered into.

7. No contract has been made. Tom's offer is too vague and does not contain any definite terms. No price is mentioned, and Tom does not say when he will buy the car.

8. No contract has been made. An agreement that prevents a person from entering into a marriage is not enforceable.

9. No valid contract has been entered into if you can prove that Lindi was so drunk that she did not understand that she was entering into a contract or that she did not understand the terms of the contract. Such a contract will be void.

3.4.2 Conditions that limit the liability of people in contracts

(Learner's Manual p 310)

Problem 2: Is the buyer bound by the terms and conditions?

(Learner's Manual p 310)

AIM: The object of this exercise is for learners to decide whether the buyers are bound by the exclusionary terms and conditions in the following contracts.

PROCEDURE		TIME	
1. Ask volunteers from the class to role-play the discussion between Ntombi and Frikkie		Introduction of exercise:	5 min
2. Debrief the role-play and make sure learners identified the correct legal question.		Preparation of role-play:	10 min
		Role-play:	5 min
3. Divide class into small groups of five each.		Debrief:	5 min
4. Ask each group to discuss the scenario and decide what the court should order.		Group discussions:	10 min
		Report back:	15 min
5. Get report back from each group.		Discussion and summary:	10 min
6. Conclude with general discussion and summary.		**TOTAL:**	**60 min**

The 'as is' clause in the contract between Frikkie and Ntombi will not be enforceable because Frikkie knew that the car had a faulty gearbox. When you know that there is something wrong with the car and you do not disclose it, it is fraud. If Frikkie did not know about the faulty gearbox then the 'as is' clause would have been valid and Ntombi would not be able to cancel the contract. The Consumer Protection Act will only be applicable if Ntombi bought the car from a business. When a consumer buys from a business/dealer then the agreement may not contain an 'as is' clause

Problem 3: What should the buyer and seller do?   *(Learner's Manual p 312)*

AIM: The aim of this exercise is to help learners recognise when a seller is regarded as having given a consumer an implied warranty against hidden defects. Learners must also decide whether the consumer is entitled to either a refund or a reduction in the purchase price.

PROCEDURE	TIME	
1. Divide class into small groups of five people each. 2. Allocate one problem and role-play to each group. 3. Ask each group to prepare their role-play and to decide whether the consumer had an implied warranty. 4. Conduct role-plays — one for each question. 5. After each role-play debrief and get a report back from groups that prepared it. 6. Conclude with general discussion and summary.	Preparation of role-plays and answers:	10 min
	Role-play 1:	5 min
	Debrief and report back:	5 min
	Role-play 2:	5 min
	Debrief and report back:	5 min
	Discussion and summary:	10 min
	TOTAL:	**40 min**

1.   Jack is regarded in law as having given Vos an implied warranty against latent defects. This is because there are no express conditions covering the sale. Vos would be entitled to ask for a reduction in the purchase price of R1 000 if he would still have bought the car had he known of the defective brakes, but would have paid R1 000 less so that he could have the brakes repaired. Vos might try to argue that he would never have bought the car had he known of the defective brakes and is entitled to a refund of R15 000. The court might, however, decide that this would be unreasonable.

2.   Winnie is not legally entitled to exchange the dress as it is not defective. She merely chose the wrong colour. If, at the time Winnie bought the skirt, Dorothy had said that she could exchange it if she was unhappy with the colour, she would legally be entitled to do so because it would have been a condition of the sale. In this case, Dorothy might, as a favour, agree to exchange it in order to make Winnie want to continue buying clothes from her.

Problem 4: Can the third party consumer claim damages?   *(Learner's Manual p 315)*

AIM: The object of this exercise is to show learners how to recognise situations in which third party consumers may claim damages from a seller or manufacturer.

PROCEDURE		TIME	
1. Divide the class into small groups of 5 people each.		Preparation of role-plays and answers:	5 min
2. Allocate one problem and role-play to each group.		Role-play 1 and small group discussions:	10 min
3. Ask each group to prepare their role-play and to decide whether the consumer can claim damages.		Debrief and report back:	5 min
4. Conduct role-plays – one for each question.		Role-play 2 and small group discussions:	10 min
5. After each role-play, debrief and get a report back from groups that prepared it.		Debrief and report back:	5 min
6. Conclude with general discussion and summary.		Discussion and summary:	5 min
		TOTAL:	**40 min**

1. Frans cannot claim damages because he was not injured, but he could try to negotiate with his neighbour on behalf of Robbie. The common law applies in this case because the contracting parties are private persons who are not conducting business as suppliers and manufacturers of goods and services. Frans therefore has to rely on the common-law remedies (see *Learner's Manual* para 3.4). Robbie is entitled to claim damages from the neighbour and the manufacturer of the cord if he can prove fault by them. He will have to prove that the seller knew that the item had a fault, or should have foreseen that it was defective. He is more likely to succeed against the manufacturers, unless he can prove that the seller knew that the cord was dangerous.

   If Robbie can prove fault by the neighbour or the manufacturer, he would be entitled to claim R3 000 for his hospital expenses and R700 for lost wages. He may also claim for pain and suffering. Frans may claim the purchase price from the neighbour. If Robbie had still been a minor and Frans was supporting him, Frans could have recovered the R3 000 hospital expenses.

2. Hluka's wife may claim against the manufacturer of the gas lamp if she can prove fault by them. The 'as is' condition applies to Hluka, but not his wife. Hluka's wife did not buy the lamp and is not bound by the condition. Hluka's wife may claim damages for pain and suffering, disfigurement and damages to her clothing and any other property. If she is working, she could claim for lost wages. Hluka may not claim for her medical expenses because he is bound by the 'as is' condition. If the condition applied only to the manufacturer, Hluka may be able to sue Hansa for the medical expenses. In any event, Hluka would be entitled to a refund of the purchase price from Hansa.

3.4.3 Minors and contracts
(Learner's Manual p 315)

The law concerning contracts with minors gives learners an opportunity to discuss the relationship between rights and responsibilities. As the *Learner's Manual* para 3.4.3 indicates, minors have less responsibility than adults for carrying out their part of the contract. Their rights, however, are limited because they usually need the assistance of their parents or guardians before a seller will deal with them.

Do learners think that this is unfair? If they do, ask them how they think it could be changed. Let the class explore possible alternatives.

If a minor continues making payments on a contract after turning 18 years old, he or she will be regarded as having ratified the contract. Once a contract has been ratified, it can no longer be cancelled at the option of the person who was a minor at the time the contract was entered into.

Problem 5: The case of the unassisted minor *(Learner's Manual p 316)*

AIM: The object of this exercise is to illustrate the legal position of minors who enter into contracts without the assistance of their parents or guardians.

PROCEDURE	TIME	
1. Divide class into small groups of five each.	Introduce exercise:	5 min
2. Ask the groups to discuss the questions in problem 5.	Group discussions:	15 min
3. Get report back from each group.	Report back:	15 min
4. Ask the groups to prepare a role-play of the meeting between Syd and the owner of Flash Bikes.	Role-play:	5 min
	Debrief role-play:	5 min
5. Ask one group to conduct the role-play.	Discussion and summary:	5 min
6. Debrief role-play.	**TOTAL:**	**50 min**
5. Conclude with general discussion and summary.		

1. There is no binding contract. If people under the age of 18 attempt to enter into contracts without the assistance of their parents or guardians no binding contracts arise. The contract could only be valid if Syd's parents or guardians or Syd ratified it. He could do this when he turns 18.

2. Syd could not be made to pay if he wished to change his mind unless his parents or guardian had ratified it or he had turned 18 and ratified it. Syd would have to return the motorbike to the seller if he changed his mind and did not pay.

3. If Syd wants to keep the motorbike he would have to pay for it. In order to make the contract legally binding he should ask his father to tell the seller that he consents to the sale. If Syd keeps the motorbike without paying, the seller could obtain an order for to make him return the motor-cycle. He may also be sued for damages for 'unjust enrichment' if he benefits from using the motor-cycle. If Syd wishes to cancel the contract he should tell Flash Bikes that he is cancelling the contract because he is a minor and did not have his father's consent. At the same time he should hand back the motorbike to Flash Bikes. Syd would then be entitled to his money back. If he had negligently or intentionally damaged the motorbike he might have to compensate Flash Bikes for any loss suffered. Also if Syd had intentionally misrepresented his age by saying that he was over 18, Flash Bikes could sue him for any loss suffered by selling the motorbike to him.

4. The learners playing Syd and the owner of Flash Bikes should discuss the points mentioned in 3 above.

3.4.5 Written and spoken contracts *(Learner's Manual p 317)*

Problem 6: The case of the broken promise *(Learner's Manual p 318)*

AIM: The object of this exercise is for learners to consider whether there is a legally binding contract in this case. The exercise also allows learners to discuss the difference between law and morals.

<table>
<tr><td>

PROCEDURE

1. Ask volunteers from the class to prepare a role-play of the meeting between Mr Brown and Mr Wilson.
2. Ask individual learners whether there is a legally binding contract.
3. Learners should explain their answers.
4. Conclude with general class discussion and summary

</td><td>

TIME

Introduce the exercise:	5 min
Role-play preparation:	5 min
Role-play:	5 min
Question & answer session:	10 min
Discussion and summary:	10 min
TOTAL:	**35 min**

</td></tr>
</table>

1. Learners playing Mr Brown should point out that Mr Wilson promised to sell his land to him and that there was a verbal agreement between them. They should argue that Mr Wilson was morally bound to accept Mr Brown's written offer to purchase the land at the agreed price of R450 000. Mr Wilson's decision to sell the land to Mr Green for R600 000 was immoral. Learners playing Mr Wilson could argue that an agreement to sell land has to be in writing. Until such time as there is a written acceptance by Mr Wilson of Mr Brown's offer there is no legally binding contract between them. Therefore Mr Wilson is entitled to change his mind and sell the property to Mr Green at a higher price.

2. According to the Alienation of Land Act, contracts for the sale of land must be in writing (see *Learner's Manual* paras 3.4.5.1 and 6.4.10.9). The only exception is land sold by public auction. In this case only the offer by Mr Brown was in writing. The acceptance was not made in writing. Therefore no legally binding contract was entered into.

   Did Mr Wilson act morally even if he did not act unlawfully? Is breaking a promise generally regarded as a violation of society's accepted code of conduct? Do learners think that the legal results of the case are fair? Do they agree that contracts for the sale of land should be in writing? Why or why not?

3.4.6   Breaking a contract   *(Learner's Manual p 318)*

Problem 7: Was there a breach of contract?   *(Learner's Manual p 319)*

AIM: The object of this exercise is for learners to decide whether or not there has been a breach of contract.

<table>
<tr><td>

PROCEDURE

1. Divide class into small groups of five each and allocate one question to each group.
2. Ask the groups to discuss whether breach of contract occurred in their given question.
3. Get report back from each group.
4. Conclude with general class discussion and summary.

</td><td>

TIME

Introduce the exercise:	5 min
Group discussions:	15 min
Report back:	15 min
Discussion and summary:	10 min
TOTAL:	**45 min**

</td></tr>
</table>

1. There has been a breach of contract. There was an offer by Andy and an acceptance by Bob. Therefore, there was valid contract. By selling his car to Chris, Andy has breached the contract of sale between himself and Bob. Bob could sue for damages. Bob's damages would be the increased price that Bob would have to pay to buy a similar car from somebody else. (This case differs from Problem 6 in the *Learner's Manual* para 3.4.5.1 because for the sale of a motorcar a verbal agreement is sufficient unless the car is sold under a credit agreement.)
   If Bob were going to buy Andy's car in terms of a credit agreement there would be no breach of contract. This is because all credit agreements have to be in writing. Bob would then have been in the same position as Mr Brown in Problem 6.

2. There has been a breach of contract. An agreement of sale is a contract. Fast Furnishers, in the agreement of sale, agreed to deliver the furniture within two weeks of Harriet signing the agreement. They failed to do this. Therefore, they breached the contract. Harriet may cancel the contract and get back any money she has paid.

3. There has been a breach of contract. Freddy's undertaking to deliver 1st grade potatoes is a term of the contract. By delivering 3rd grade potatoes, he has breached the contract. The restaurant may cancel the contract and sue for damages. The damages would be based on any loss of profits the restaurant suffered as a result of receiving 3rd grade instead of 1st grade potatoes.

Problem 8: What should the court order?

(Learner's Manual p 321)

AIM: The object of this exercise is to make learners aware of the different orders the court may make for a breach of contract.

PROCEDURE	TIME	
1. Divide class into small groups of five each and allocate one question to each.	Introduce the exercise:	5 min
2. Ask the groups to discuss whether breach of contract occurred in their given question.	Group discussions:	10 min
	Report back:	20 min
3. Get report back from each group.	Discussion and summary:	10 min
4. Conclude with general class discussion and summary.	**TOTAL:**	**45 min**

1. Harold breached the contract. Roberta may ask the court to order specific performance requiring Harold to repair the house. Alternatively, Roberta may cancel the contract and sue Harold for the return of her deposit and any other damages she may have suffered. These damages may include the extra cost another repair person would charge to do the same repairs to Roberta's house.

2. Sound Waves has breached the contract. The stereo should have been delivered without the scratch unless it had been pointed out to Fanyana and he was given a discount. If he wants to keep the stereo, Fanyana could ask for a reduction in the purchase price. If the scratch was so bad that he would never have bought the stereo if he had known, he may cancel the contract and ask for his money back.

3. Sammy's Service Station has breached the contract because Koos pointed out that the repairs had to be done urgently. Koos could cancel the contract and recover damages for his lost-delivery commission of R500. He would have to prove that he would have earned R500 commission.

4. Jadwat has breached his contract with Paruk. Paruk may apply to court for an urgent interdict (court order) to stop Jadwat delivering the car to Norma. At the same time, Paruk could obtain an order of specific performance compelling Jadwat to deliver the car to him. If the car had already been delivered to Norma, Paruk could sue Jadwat for damages for breach of contract. This is because when movable property is sold, ownership passes to the buyer on delivery. (When immovable property is sold, eg land or buildings, ownership passes only when the transfer has been registered at the Deeds Office; see below *Learner's Manual* para 5.6.4.10.9.) Paruk's damages will be the difference between the R40 000 Paruk would have paid Jadwat for the car, and what Paruk would have to pay another seller for a similar car. For example, if the reasonable cost of a similar car from somebody else was R41 000, Paruk could sue Jadwat for R1 000.

3.5 Cars and the consumer

Outcomes

After completion of this section learners will be able to:

1. Understand the legal rules applicable when buying a car.

Assessment criteria

1. The steps a wise consumer should follow when buying a car are explained.
2. Advice is given to a consumer about the things that should be done when test driving a car.
3. A distinction is drawn between warranties and guarantees.
4. An explanation is given on what to do when buying a car from a private seller.
5. The transfer documents that are necessary for a consumer to transfer ownership of a car are listed.
6. The different types of vehicle insurance are explained.
7. A description is given of how a 'no claim bonus' works.
8. A set of facts is examined and a decision made on the liability of the insurance companies of the different parties involved in a motor accident.
9. An explanation is given of what to do and not to do in the case of an accident.

Problem 1: Gerhard's dream

(Learner's Manual p 324)

AIM: The object of this exercise is to enable learners to understand what should be done by consumers when they decide to purchase a motorcar from either a dealer or a private person.

PROCEDURE
1. Introduce the exercise.
2. Divide class into small groups of five people each.
3. Allocate one question to each group.
4. Groups allocated questions 4 and 5 are to prepare role-plays.
5. Report back for questions 1 to 3.
6. Role-plays and debriefings for questions 4 and 5.
7. General discussion.

TIME	
Introduce the exercise:	5 min
Group discussions:	10 min
Report back and role-play:	25 min
Discussion and summary:	5 min
TOTAL:	**45 min**

1. Before going to Al Autos, Gerhard should shop around to discover what a reasonable price for a GT Sprint would be. He could do this by reading the classified section of the newspapers and by visiting dealers' showrooms. Before deciding on a GT Sprint, Gerhard should be satisfied that the Sprint is a reliable, economical and safe motorcar.

2. In addition to the purchase price, Gerhard should also consider the cost of insurance, petrol, general maintenance and repairs, interest charges, licensing and registration. (In big cities, if the car has to be parked in a parking garage, add the cost of parking.) However, before buying a car,

a consumer should consider whether there are alternatives like buses and trains which may be cheaper in the long run.

3. Insurance costs may be found by telephoning different companies listed in the *Yellow Pages*. Petrol costs may be estimated by working out how much driving will be done, the petrol consumption of the car and the present cost of petrol. The consumer should bear in mind, however, that the price of petrol might increase. An idea of the general maintenance and repair costs for a motorcar may be obtained from the Automobile Association which gives figures for the annual and monthly up-keep of different-sized motorcars. Interest rates may be obtained from the different finance companies (eg banks and finance houses) that offer assistance with the buying of motorcars. Licensing and registration costs may be obtained from the local licensing and registration offices.

4. The discussion between Gerhard and the A1 Autos salesperson should include questions about the things mentioned in the *Learner's Manual* paras 3.5.3–3.5.6; eg: (a) hidden costs such as finance charges, insurance costs, number-plate costs and licensing fees; (b) the availability of the petrol log book and service record (if they are not available, the fuel consumption and average service bill for the car, and the frequency with which it must be serviced); and (c) what warranty is given? Gerhard might also ask if the car could be tested by the Automobile Association (AA) – see *Learner's Manual*: 'Test-driving a used car: what to look for'.

    Otherwise, he should carry out the checks mentioned in the *Learner's Manual*: 'Buying a used car: what to look for'.

5. The discussion would be along similar lines to 4 above, except that the private seller would have a more intimate knowledge about the car. The private seller is also more likely to have a complete service and repair record as well as a petrol logbook.

Problem 2: Phewa and the minibus
(Learner's Manual p 328)

AIM: The object of this exercise is to make consumers aware of the need to check a vehicle carefully before buying it. They should not simply rely on the statements of the seller. They should also ensure that any warranties are confirmed in writing.

PROCEDURE
1. Introduce the exercise.
2. Divide the class into small groups of five each.
3. Allocate one question to each group.
4. Groups allocated question 4 are to prepare a role-play.
5. Report back for questions 1 to 3.
6. General discussion.

TIME	
Introduce the exercise:	5 min
Group discussions:	10 min
Report back:	20 min
Role-play:	5 min
Discussion and summary:	5 min
TOTAL:	**45 min**

1. Before agreeing to buy the minibus, Phewa should have done what Gerhard did in Problem 1 (see *Learner's Manual* para 3.5.4 Problem 1). He should also carry out an inspection of the minibus (see *Learner's Manual* box: 'Buying a used car: what to look for', or arrange for the AA to do so. Phewa should ask Babu's to give him a written guarantee, otherwise he could rely on his common-law rights which cannot be taken away if he enters into a credit agreement. Phewa

should also find out how much extra he will pay in finance charges and insurance if he allows Babu's to arrange the finance and insurance.

2. Learners should decide what they would have done if they were Phewa. Some might suggest that they ask the AA to test the minibus for them. Others might do it themselves and carry out the tests mentioned in the *Learner's Manual* box: 'Test driving a used car: what to look for'. The warranty given by Babu's is only for a short period of time, and it might be difficult to prove that the defects were not simply those one would expect in a second-hand minibus. It is advisable for Phewa to test the car properly or have it done by the AA. Even if the minibus is new, it is always best to test drive it to make sure that there are no obvious defects. Phewa should ensure that he is happy about the minibus he is going to buy. How easy is it to drive? What is the visibility like? Can he reach all the controls? How does it hold the road, etc?

3. The saleslady's words, 'This is the best minibus on the market. It will give you many years of good service', are probably more of a puff that a promise or term of the contract. The promise concerning repairs in the guarantee is a term of the contract. Therefore, a failure to honour the guarantee would be a breach of the contract.

4. Learners role-playing the conversation should include the representations made by the saleslady and the requests by Phewa.

3.5.7 Buying from private sellers *(Learner's Manual p 328)*

Problem 3: Car dealers v private sellers *(Learner's Manual p 329)*

AIM: The object of the exercise is to enable learners to compare the advantages and disadvantages of buying from used-car dealers with those of buying from private sellers.

PROCEDURE	TIME	
1. Divide the class into small groups of five each.	Group discussions:	15 min
2. Ask each group to discuss one question.	Report back:	15 min
3. Get a report back from each group.	Discussion and summary:	10 min
4. Conclude with general class discussion and summary.	**TOTAL:**	**40 min**

1. The advantages of buying from used-car dealers are that they usually: (a) provide written guarantees; (b) arrange finance and insurance; (c) do the paperwork concerning the transfer of ownership including obtaining a COR; and (d) have an address that may be easily traced if something goes wrong.
The disadvantages of buying from used car dealers are that:
(a) the cars cost more; (b) the guarantees reduce the buyer's common law rights; (c) the dealers may not always give an accurate picture of the history of the car; and (d) the dealers might not give an accurate estimate of the running costs of the car.

2. The advantages of buying from a private seller are that: (a) the car may cost less; (b) the seller will usually know about the history of the car; (c) the seller can give an accurate estimate of the running costs of the car; and (d) the seller might give a guarantee that does not take away the buyer's common-law rights.

The disadvantages of buying from a private seller are that: (a) the seller might not give a guarantee; (b) the buyer might have to do all the paperwork concerning the transfer of ownership including obtaining a COR; (c) the seller might not have enough money to compensate the buyer if anything goes wrong; (d) the seller might not have a fixed or long-term address; and (e) the seller might not have paid the full purchase price to the person from whom the car was originally bought.

3. The things that a consumer might have to do when buying a used car from a private seller which would not have to be done when buying from a dealer may include: (a) doing all the paperwork concerning the transfer of ownership; (b) arranging the necessary finance and insurance; (c) obtaining a COR for the car; and (d) checking that the private seller has paid the full purchase price to the previous owner of the car.

3.5.8   Transfer documents

(Learner's Manual p 330)

Problem 4: Anil wants to take ownership of a car   (Learner's Manual p 330)

AIM: The object of this exercise is to show learners what documents they will need in order to take ownership of a motorcar.

PROCEDURE	TIME	
1. Introduce the exercise.	Introduce the exercise:	5 min
2. Divide the class into small groups of five each.	Group discussions:	15 min
3. Ask the groups to make a list of documents that Anil will need and prepare the role-play.	Report back and role-play:	15 min
4. Get one grup to conduct a role-play	Discussion and summary:	10 min
5. Debrief role-play.	**TOTAL:**	**45 min**
6. Conclude with a general discussion and summary.		

1. Anil will need the following documents: (a) a registration certificate; (b) a certificate of road worthiness (COR); (c) a change-of-ownership form; (d) a detailed invoice and receipt; and (e) a licence disc.
2. The learner playing Anil should make sure that Jason has signed a change-of-ownership form and has handed over the registration certificate — the COR, a detailed invoice, receipt and the licence disc. Anil should also check that Jason has paid the previous owner the full purchase price.

3.5.9   Insuring a car

(Learner's Manual p 330)

Problem 5: Some questions on insurance   (Learner's Manual p 331)

AIM: The object of this exercise is to make learners think about why it is advisable for motorists to take out insurance against motor collisions.

PROCEDURE		TIME	
1. Divide the class into small groups of five each.		Group discussions:	10 min
2. Ask each group to discuss one question.		Report back:	10 min
3. Get a report back from each group.		Discussion and summary:	10 min
4. Conclude with a general class discussion and summary.		**TOTAL:**	**30 min**

1. Learners who think that it is necessary for people to take out insurance against accidents might argue: (a) if people are not insured and cause damage or injury to others, they might have to compensate the victims out of their own pockets; (b) an injured person might be able to sue a negligent uninsured driver for thousands of rands; (c) insurance companies will often provide insured drivers with legal assistance if they are criminally prosecuted or sued civilly; and (d) depending on the type of insurance taken out by them, insured drivers might be compensated by their own insurance companies for damage caused to their own property.

    Learners who think that it is unnecessary for people to take out insurance against accidents might argue: (a) insurance is too expensive; (b) the chances of having an accident are not very great; (c) if you are a careful driver, you will not be sued; and (d) if you injure people, they will be covered by the Road Accident Fund Act which requires all vehicles to be insured.

2. Insurance companies that cover people for injuries or death caused by accidents provide compensation for: (a) medical bills; (b) funeral expenses; (c) lost wages; (d) future medical expenses; (e) future lost wages; (f) pain and suffering; (g) disfigurement; (h) loss of amenities of life (eg, inability to play sport, shortened life expectancy); and (i) loss of support (eg where a widow and children sue for the death of a breadwinner).

Problem 6: Some questions on motor accidents   (Learner's Manual p 332)

AIM: The object of this exercise is to make learners think about what might happen to an innocent victim of an accident caused by a person who is not insured. It also gives learners an opportunity to discuss an accident involving themselves, their relatives or their friends.

PROCEDURE		TIME	
1. Introduction.		Introduction:	5 min
2. Divide learners into groups of five persons.		Group discussions:	10 min
3. Allocate one question to each group.		Report back:	15 min
4. Group discussions.		Discussion and summary:	10 min
5. Report back.		**TOTAL:**	**40 min**
6. Conclude with general discussion and summary.			

1. The answer to this question will depend upon the individual experiences of the learners.
2. The answer to this question is that if the learner was negligent or at fault and caused serious bodily injury to the driver or the other car, the latter would have an action against the learner if the learner's car were not covered by the Road Accident Fund Act. Most cars, however, are covered by the Act, which means that the insurer of the car which caused the collision will pay

compensation to the injured people. The damages payable to a person who can never walk again are likely to amount to thousands of rand. It is unlikely that the average motorist could afford to pay such damages. This is why the Road Accident Fund Act was introduced.

3. Most learners would probably say that it would be unfair if an injured person could only recover compensation where the person who caused the injuries could afford to pay damages. This is why the Road Accident Fund Act provides that insurers must pay damages to people injured in motor collisions. The idea is that all motorists are taxed on petrol sales and the proceeds of the sales are paid into the Road Accident Fund. Road accident insurance is an example of risk being spread amongst motorists to help the victims of road accidents.

Problem 7: The crash in the rain
(Learner's Manual p 334)

AIM: This problem gives learners an opportunity to analyse a set of facts and to determine which driver was at fault.

PROCEDURE ☰		TIME ☉	
1. Introduction.		Introduction:	5 min
2. Ask the groups to discuss questions and prepare a role-play.		Group discussions:	15 min
3. Get one group to conduct a role-play.		Role-play and debrief:	10 min
4. Debrief role-play.		Discussion and summary:	10 min
5. Conclude with general class discussion and summary.		**TOTAL:**	**40 min**

1. The answer is not clear. If Micky was speeding, Donald might not have been able to estimate when Micky would reach the intersection. Usually, a driver in the position of Donald who turns across the path of a driver like Micky, must yield to Micky's vehicle. If, however, Micky speeded up rather that slowed down when the light turned orange, he would be negligent. He would also be negligent if he had not kept his brakes in proper working order by having his car regularly serviced. In our law, the person who is at fault has to pay the medical bills and car repairs of the innocent people involved in the motor collision. This applies, for example, if the Road Accident Fund Act and comprehensive insurance do not cover the motor vehicle that caused the accident. In most cases, however, motorists are insured under the Road Accident Fund Act and by their own private insurance. This means that usually insurance companies pay for repairs resulting from car accidents. Where, however, guilty drivers are not insured, they might have to pay for the repairs out of their own pockets.

2. Micky's attorney might argue that, as Donald turned in front of Micky's car, Donald was responsible for the accident and should pay all Micky's damages. Donald's attorney could argue that, because Micky was going too fast in the rain, and his brakes did not stop the car, Micky caused the accident and should pay Donald compensation.
Donald's injuries will be paid for by the Road Accident Fund. The attorneys might eventually negotiate a settlement; for example, each driver might be regarded as having been 50% at fault. This would mean that Micky will have to pay 50% of Donald's R4 000 damages (ie R2 000), and Donald would have to pay Mickey 50% of his R8 000 damages (ie R4 000). As Mickey has balance-of-third-party insurance, his insurance company will pay out the R2 000 to Donald. But because Donald was uninsured, he will have to pay R4 000 damages to Micky out of his own pocket.

AIM: The object of this exercise is to show learners how insurance companies settle claims incurred by insured persons who have caused harm to other people.

PROCEDURE	TIME	
1. Introduction.	Introduction:	5 min
2. Divide the class into small groups of five each.	Group discussions and preparation	
3. Allocate one question to each group.	for role-play:	10 min
4. Group discussions by groups with questions 1, 2 and 4.	Role-play and debrief:	15 min
5. Role-play preparation by groups with question 3.	Report back:	15 min
6. Report back by groups with questions 1, 2 and 4.	Discussion and summary:	10 min
7. Role-play by one of groups with question 3.	**TOTAL:**	**55 min**
8. Debrief role-play.		
9. Conclusion and discussion.		

1. The problem assumes that Micky was at fault. Therefore Micky's comprehensive insurance company would have to pay the amount that Micky is insured for in respect of Donald's hospital expenses and car repairs. The insurer of Micky's car would only pay Donald's hospital and medical expenses if these are not paid for by the Road Accident Fund. As Micky had a comprehensive insurance policy, his insurance company would pay for Donald's car repairs.

2. Micky's insurance company would be responsible for his car repairs because he was comprehensively insured. (If he was not comprehensively insured, he would not receive anything from his own insurance company.) As regards Micky's hospital and medical expenses, he would not be covered by the compulsory motor accident insurer of his own car because the 'third-party' insurance company only has to pay out the claims of third parties. His comprehensive insurance company may, however, pay these expenses. If Micky could show that Donald was also at fault, Micky could claim for his hospital expenses from the Road Accident Fund. If Donald was also at fault, his comprehensive insurance company would compensate Micky for damage to his car.

3. The learners role-playing Donald's and Micky's insurance companies could negotiate on the same basis as the attorneys in Problem 7 question 2.

4. Micky would have to pay his R1 000 excess and the insurance company would pay the remaining R3 000. Donald would receive R1 000 damages. In practice, Micky would probably pay the R1 000 to his insurance company and the insurance company would pay out the full R4 000 to Donald.

3.5.10   What to do in the case of an accident *(Learner's Manual p 335)*

Problem 9: The motorcycle accident *(Learner's Manual p 337)*

AIM: This exercise is designed to make learners aware of the various questions and issues that drivers should keep in mind after an accident.

PROCEDURE		TIME	
1. Introduction.		Introduction:	5 min
2. Divide the class into small groups of five each.		Group discussion and preparation	
3. Allocate one question to each group.		for role-play:	15 min
4. Group discussions by groups with questions 1 and 2.		Report back:	15 min
5. Role-play preparation by groups with question 3.		Role-play and debrief:	10 min
6. Report back by groups with questions 1 and 2.		Discussion and summary:	5 min
7. Role-play by one of groups with question 3.		**TOTAL:**	**50 min**
8. Debrief role-play.			
9. Conclusion and discussion.			

1. In addition to the points of information listed in the *Learner's Manual* para 3.5.10.1, Sabelo's list should include information on: (a) where the cars were damaged; (b) the time of day; (c) the fact that there were no apparent injuries; and (d) a reference to the fact that Kippie's eyes were bloodshot.

2. Sabelo should inform the police about the accident and immediately contact his insurance company. If Sabelo is not insured, he should obtain three or more quotations for repairs from panel beaters and repairers and then consult an attorney. The quotations will be used to indicate that Sabelo is claiming the 'reasonable and necessary costs' of repairs to his motorcycle.

3. The role-play should be used to show learners the importance of exchanging information (names, addresses, telephone numbers, licence numbers and registration numbers) without: (a) telling the other driver the extent of their insurance; (b) confessing any guilt; (c) signing any statement that they are not injured; or (d) saying that their insurance company will take care of things.

Further reading

3.1 Contracts

Boezaart T *Child Law in South Africa* (2009) p 197

Hutchison D et al *The Law of Contract in South Africa* (2009)

Children's Act 38 of 2005

Joubert WA *The Law of South Africa* 2 ed, Vol 5 Part 1 (2010)

Sesing v Minister of Police 1978 (4) SA 742 (W) 745

Consumer Protection

Consumer Protection Act 68 of 2008 and Regulations in terms of the Consumer Protection Act 68 of 2008

Electronic Communications and Transactions Act 25 of 2002

Department of Trade and Industry *Your Guide to Consumer Rights and How to Protect Them* (2009)

Van Eeden E A *Guide to the Consumer Protection Act* (2009)

Van Eeden E A *Commentary on the Consumer Protection Act 2008* (2011)

Badler, H *What are my consumer rights?* http://www.bizcommunity.com/Article/196/160/17811.html accessed on 11 October 2011

Joubert WA *The Law of South Africa* 2 ed, Vol 5 Part 1 (2010)

http://www.michalsons.co.za/grey-goods-under-the-consumer-protection-act/8162 accessed on
13 January 2012

http://www.southafrica.info/services/consumer/consumer.htm accessed on 11 October 2011

3.2 Consumer Protection Act of 2008

Consumer Protection Act 68 of 2008 and Regulations in terms of the Consumer Protection Act 68
of 2008

Electronic Communications and Transactions Act 25 of 2002

Department of Trade and Industry *Your Guide to Consumer Rights and How to Protect Them* (2009)

Van Eeden E A *Guide to the Consumer Protection Act* (2009)

Van Eeden E A *Commentary on the Consumer Protection Act 2008* (2011)

Joubert WA *The Law of South Africa* 2 ed, Vol 5 Part 1 (2010)

Badler H *What are my consumer rights?* http://www.bizcommunity.com/Article/196/160/17811.html
accessed on 11 October 2011

http://www.michalsons.co.za/grey-goods-under-the-consumer-protection-act/8162 accessed on
13 January 2012

http://www.southafrica.info/services/consumer/consumer.htm accessed on 11 October 2011

3.4 Credit buying and Credit Agreements

National Credit Act 34 of 2005 and Regulations in terms of the National Credit Act 34 of 2005

Promotion of Equality and Prevention of Unfair Discrimination Act 4 of 2000

South African Schools Act 84 of 1996

Campbell N & Logan S *The Credit Guide: Manage your Money with the National Credit Act* (2008)

Joubert WA *The Law of South Africa* 2 ed, Vol 5 Part 1 (2010)

Scholtz JW et al *Guide to the National Credit Act* Service Issue 2

Bregman R & Logan S (Law Society of South Africa) *The National Credit Act 43 of 2005 A Basic
Guide for Attorneys*, http://www.un.org/esa/sustdev/publications/consumption_en.pdf accessed on
11 October 2011

Goodwin-Groen RP *The National Credit Act and its Regulations in the Context of Access to Finance in
South Africa*, http://www.amfisa.org.za/Downloads/Finmark%20Trust%20paper%20on%20NCR.
pdf accessed on 30 April 2012

http://www.ncf.org.za/services/complain.html accessed on 11 October 2011

http://www.ncf.org.za/main.php?include=about/history.html&menu=menus/about.html accessed on
11 October 2011

http://www.un.org/esa/sustdev/publications/consumption_en.pdf accessed on 11 October 2011

http://www.investorwords.com/620/bundling.html#ixzz1jJywG2tc accessed on 12 January 2012

http://www.southafrica.info/services/consumer/consumer.htm accessed on 11 October 2011

http://www.ncf.org.za/services/complain.html accessed on 11 October 2011

National Credit Regulator v C Bornman and Others case no NCT/656/2010/57(1)(a)(c)(P), National
Consumer Tribunal (unreported)

Nedbank v National Credit Regulator 2011 (3) SA 581 (SCA)

Wesbank v Papier 2011 (2) SA 395 (WCC)

Street law

4. Family law

CONTENTS

4.1 The family, marriage and civil unions

Outcomes

After completion of this section learners will be able to:

1. Demonstrate an understanding of the different types of marriages and families recognised in South African law.

Assessment criteria

1. The meaning of 'family' is explained.

2. An explanation is given as to why the definition of the nuclear family is not a good definition of the modern South African family.

3. Different types of marriages and civil unions are identified.

4. A set of facts is given and a decision is made on who may and may not marry or enter into a civil union.

5. A set of facts is given and a decision is made on whether or not the marriages or civil unions are valid.

6. A description is given of how a marriage or civil union is entered into.

7. The requirements for entering into a valid marriage or civil union are given.

8. The customary marriage is explained.

9. The status of Muslim and Hindu marriages is explained.

4.1.1 The family

(Learner's Manual p 346)

Problem 1: What is a family?

(Learner's Manual p 349)

AIM: The object of this exercise is to make learners think about what is meant by 'a family'. Learners should also be encouraged to consider the different types of families and whether there is such a thing as an ideal family.

PROCEDURE	TIME	
1. Explain the concept of family.	Explanation:	5 min
2. Divide the learners into small groups.	Group discussions:	15 min
3. Allocate one question to each group for discussion.	Report back:	15 min
4. Report back.	General discussion:	10 min
5. Summarise learners' responses.	**TOTAL:**	**45 min**
6. General discussion.		

1. A method for obtaining the learners' response to the question is to divide the class into small groups and to ask them to come to a group decision as to what is meant by a family. They could consider the following: what are the characteristics of a family? Is a family a certain number of

people? Is it a group of people with a special relationship to each other? Is their relationship based on blood, marriage, or some other relationship? Who are the members of the family? Does the law give special protection to members of a family? Each group could then be asked to discuss its conclusions with the rest of the class.

2. A nuclear family is one where just the parents and their children live together without other relatives. Young couples from different families get married and set up their own small family, which usually includes only themselves and their children. In South Africa, the nuclear family concept may generally apply to people living in cities and towns, but not to those in rural areas, who live according to their traditional customs.

3. The question raises issues like the following: what are the different kinds of family arrangements? How has the traditional type of family changed in recent times? Do people who live together, but are not married, constitute a family? Other questions are: is it unconstitutional to deny legal privileges, which traditional families have, to people who choose other living arrangements? If legal privileges are granted to non-traditional families, will this undermine traditional marriages or families?
Another issue that might be raised is: what benefit to society do families provide? Answers could include:
   - an orderly setting for sexual conduct;
   - childbirth in a stable and economically secure environment;
   - socialisation and moral and physical development;
   - companionship and psychological support in times of need;
   - economic security and potential for dividing responsibilities, for obtaining income, for looking after the home, and child-rearing;
   - a form of insurance because members of the family can help each other in sickness, accidents, old age, poverty, etc.

These benefits may be useful in leading onto the next section and the question: why do people get married or enter into civil unions?

4.1.4 Marriages and civil unions *(Learner's Manual p 350)*

Problem 2: Getting married or entering into a civil union *(Learner's Manual p 350)*

AIM: This question is designed to help learners become aware of the importance of the decision to get married or enter into a civil union and the complexity of the factors and issues which must be considered.

PROCEDURE	TIME	
1. Divide learners into small groups to discuss the first three questions.	Group discussions:	15 min
2. Ask groups to nominate spokespersons to report back.	Report back:	10 min
3. Select two learners from each group to role-play question 4 for their groups.	Role-play and report back:	15 min
4. Learners conduct the role-play.	General discussion:	5 min
5. Report back.	**TOTAL:**	**45 min**
6. Summarise responses.		
7. General discussion.		

1. The class could be divided into small groups and each group required to rank the different considerations, giving reasons for their rankings. Group spokespersons could be elected to present the groups' findings on a flip chart, or the educator could write them up on a blackboard.

2. This problem helps learners develop an appreciation of the types of issues their parents could have discussed when they were considering getting married. Some of the questions that learners might list are: where should we live? Should we have children? If so, how many children? Are our finances sufficient to support a marriage or civil union? Should we both work? Are we likely to live happily together because we get on with each other? Learners will probably list a number of other factors.

3. This problem reinforces how the law affects our daily lives and again emphasises the importance of studying family law. If, for example, the learners listed the questions mentioned above, they may be interested to know that the law says the following: generally, the husband may decide where the spouses live, but the decision should preferably be made by both parties, as is the case in civil unions. If parents have children, they have to support them. Both parents are bound to contribute towards the maintenance of their family.

   If the husband or one of the civil union partners cannot earn sufficiently to support them, the wife or other civil union partner is also obliged to help with supporting the family. If the spouses or partners do not get on or are incompatible, this may lead to a breakdown in the marriage or civil union, which could result in divorce.

4. The learners in the role-play could raise the issues discussed in 1 and 2 above.

Problem 3: Restrictions on certain people marrying or entering into civil unions
(Learner's Manual p 352)

Aim: The object of this exercise is for learners to learn who may not marry or enter into a civil union with whom, and to think about the age requirements for marriage and civil unions.

PROCEDURE	TIME	
1. Divide learners into small groups.	Group discussions:	15 min
2. Allocate one question to each group.	Report back:	15 min
3. Ask each group to discuss their question.	Discussion:	15 min
4. Report back.	**TOTAL:**	**45 min**
5. General discussion.		

1. The answer to this question is in the text. Usually people related to their common ancestors within the first degree of relationship (eg parents, grandparents, great-grandparents, children, grandchildren, etc) may not marry. For instance, people may not marry their children, parents, grandparents, great-grandparents, brothers, sisters, uncles, nieces, or nephews. Cousins may, however, marry because they are related to each other in the second degree.

2. Even if the parents of William and Miro consented to the marriage, the couple could still not marry because William is under 18 years old. William would have to obtain the written permission of the Minister of Home Affairs. This can be done through a lawyer. The Minister

will grant his permission if he considers the marriage desirable. In addition to the Minister's consent, it would be necessary for William and Miro to have their parents' consent.

3. There are probably two main reasons for having a minimum age for marriage. These are:
    (a) Marriage involves legal and financial obligations for which a minor may not be responsible enough – although legally when you marry you become a major.
    (b) Marriage involves a serious commitment which requires a certain degree of maturity and judgment not usually found in young children. Therefore minors are often considered to be risky marriage candidates. Learners should discuss whether setting a minimum age for marriage does anything to ensure these legal and personal obligations. If the learners think that there should be a minimum age, they should discuss what they think it should be and why.

4. Learners will say that the Constitution guarantees the right to equality. Therefore, it is unconstitutional to deny minors of the same sex the right to exercise the ministerial consent to marry if minors in a heterosexual relationship are given an opportunity to marry by obtaining ministerial consent. Learners may add that the Constitution prohibits discrimination on the basis of sexual orientation; as a result it is discriminatory to deny Pauline and Bridget the right to obtain ministerial consent and conclude a civil union.

    Learners against same-sex marriages may raise moral, religious and ethical questions regarding the recognition of such marriages. For example, they might argue that it is against the laws of nature that two people of the same sex should be allowed to marry irrespective of age, or that it is God's will that one man and one woman marry so that they may have children together, etc.

5. This question should be used to provoke learner responses to the different treatment of men and women by the law. One reason why females have a lower age limit is because previously they were not responsible for supporting the household. Today, however, things have changed, with more equal responsibility between husbands and wives. It is also believed that a woman's body develops sooner than a man's does.

    It is generally more acceptable for a man to marry a younger woman than for a woman to marry a younger man.

    In South Africa the age of puberty is regarded as 14 years for boys and 12 years for girls. The age of majority today, however, is the same for both males and females – 18 years. Learners may comment on whether they think it is fair that females may marry at a younger age than males.

Problem 4: Was the marriage or civil union valid? *(Learner's Manual p 353)*

AIM: The object of this exercise is to check whether learners understand when, and why, a marriage or civil union may be annulled (declared invalid).

PROCEDURE		TIME	
1. Divide learners into small groups.		Group discussions:	15 min
2. Each group may consider all seven situations; or give each group two to three questions to consider.		Report back:	15 min
		Discussion:	10 min
3. Report back.		**TOTAL:**	**40 min**
4. General discussion.			

1. The marriage is invalid and may be annulled because Jaggie was under 18 years old and needed the consent of the Minister of Home Affairs.

2. The marriage is invalid because Gladys was under 18 years and needed the consent of her parents to marry Das.

3. The civil union between Pius and Thomas is valid. They are both over 18 and not related to each other too closely through their common ancestor. Cousins are allowed to marry each other.

4. The marriage is invalid because Dawn was forced to marry Cuthbert against her will. In other words, she did not consent of her own free will.

5. The marriage is invalid because Shirley was pregnant by another man before the marriage and did not tell Diana.

6. The marriage is invalid because Theresa is already married to Humphrey. Theresa could be criminally prosecuted for bigamy (see *Learner's Manual* para 2.8.3).

7. The marriage is invalid because Wolfgang is unable to have sexual intercourse with Hilda.

4.1.6   Muslim and Hindu marriages   *(Learner's Manual p 356)*

Problem 5: What should the law say?   *(Learner's Manual p 357)*

AIM: This exercise is designed to enable learners to think about whether the law has been fair in that it now recognises customary marriages that allow people to have more than one spouse, but does not recognise Hindu and Muslim marriages for the same reason. It also makes them realise that other relationships can be regularised, such as civil law marriages.

PROCEDURE
1. Divide learners into small groups.
2. Each group may consider both questions; or if time is short, each group may consider one question.
3. Report back.
4. General discussion.

TIME	
Group discussions:	15 min
Report back:	15 min
General discussion:	15 min
TOTAL:	**45 min**

1. Whether learners think that this law is fair or not may depend on their cultural background. Most Christian or Jewish South Africans would probably argue strongly for a marriage with only one spouse of each sex for any type of marriage, whether it is customary or not.
   On the other hand, traditional African communities, and members of Muslim, Hindu or other religious groups may argue that it is not unfair to allow only men to have more than one wife. One can approach this question from two perspectives: it could be argued that the purpose of the legislation was to recognise customary marriages. Therefore it is not part of customary law for a woman to have more than one husband, but it is for a man to have more than one wife. The law is thus not unfair. From a constitutional point of view, it might be argued that this law constitutes unfair discrimination because it treats men and women differently. Learner responses will vary.

2. Muslim marriages have also not been recognised because they allow a man to have more than one wife. As with customary marriages, Muslim marriages are in the process of being recognised.

This means that Muslim religious law will be incorporated into a new Act of Parliament when it is passed. Once again, learners may argue that such marriages should be recognised because they form part of Muslim religion. In addition, the Constitution gives everyone the right to practise his or her religion. By not recognising such marriages, the law is violating their right to practise their religion. Learners' views will vary.

Hindu marriages are also not recognised in a statute, but will be recognised if conducted by a person who is a registered marriage officer in terms of the Marriages Act of 1961.

Outcomes

After completion of this section learners will be able to:

1. Demonstrate the understanding of the automatic consequences of marriage or civil union.

2. Explain the difference between marriages and civil unions in community of property and marriages and civil unions out of community of property (with and without accrual).

3. Demonstrate an understanding of the roles of spouses and civil union partners in the family.

4. Demonstrate an awareness of the problem of domestic violence.

Assessment criteria

1. The duty of support, including the duty to contribute to household necessaries, is explained.

2. A set of facts is examined and a decision is taken on whether one spouse or civil union partner is legally responsible for certain things bought by the other spouse or union partner without his or her consent.

3. The meaning of a marriage or civil union 'in and out of community of property' and 'ante-nuptial contract' are explained.

4. A description is given of how the 'accrual' system works.

5. An explanation is given on what can be done by married couples or civil union partners who wish to change their type of marriage or union.

6. A set of facts is examined and a decision made on how accrual takes place between spouses or civil union partners.

7. The roles of husbands and wives and civil union partners in the family are identified.

8. An awareness is created that domestic violence is a problem among all sections of South Africa's population.

9. The provisions of the Domestic Violence Act are explained.

10. A set of facts is examined and a decision made on how an instance of domestic violence should be handled.

4.2.1 Things in a marriage or civil union that do not change

(Learner's Manual p 359)

Problem 1: The case of the unpaid bills

(Learner's Manual p 360)

AIM: The object of this exercise is for learners to understand how both parties in a marriage are responsible for the necessary expenses of the joint household.

<table>
<tr><td colspan="2">**PROCEDURE** ☰</td><td colspan="2">**TIME** 🕐</td></tr>
<tr><td colspan="2">
1. Select learners for role-play.
2. Act out role-play.
3. Debrief role-play.
4. Divide learners into small groups and allocate one question from 2–4 to each group.
5. Report back.
6. General discussion.
</td><td>Role-play:
Questions or group discussions:
General discussion:
TOTAL:</td><td>10 min

25 min
10 min
45 min</td></tr>
</table>

1. The learner playing Dino should be angry and tell Betty that he cannot afford to pay for the groceries, clothes and the hi-fi. The learner playing Betty could argue that Dino, as the husband and head of the household, has a duty to support her and the children.

2. Both Dino and Betty should be responsible for the groceries and clothes for their children because they are household necessaries. Dino would probably not be required to pay for the hi-fi because it could be regarded as a luxury rather than a household necessary – but if they had a high standard of living the hi-fi may be regarded as a 'necessary'. Spouses should support each other if they can afford to do so.

3. There is a reciprocal duty of support between the spouses. Although the duty is usually regarded as resting on the husband in favour of the wife, this is only because in practice it is usually the husband who earns more money. Where the circumstances are reversed the duty falls on the wife. However, the claim for support depends on the need for support. If Dino was dependent on Betty for the support of himself and the children she would be liable for necessary expenses like groceries and clothes for the children. But she would not be liable for the hi-fi, as this could be a luxury item. If, however, the family had a high standard of living the hi-fi could be a household necessary and not a luxury.

4. The question gives learners an opportunity to debate this important issue. Learners who support the argument might say that a man is more suited to earning money, while a woman is better able to take care of the house and children. This attitude reflects the reality of many societies where men are usually paid more than women for doing the same work. Learners who oppose the statement may argue that the traditional view of family roles is not supported by the facts. The changing economic and family roles require similar changes in the law. Husbands and wives should share the same burden of responsibility. In civilised societies men and women should be paid equal wages.

4.2.2 Things in a marriage or civil union that may change, depending upon how the parties were married or entered into the civil union *(Learner's Manual p 361)*

Problem 2: What can Jacobus and Edward do? *(Learner's Manual p 363)*

AIM: The object of this exercise is for learners to understand the contractual powers of people married or in a civil union in community of property.

PROCEDURE ▤

1. Divide students into small groups.
2. Each group should answer one question.
3. Report back.
4. General discussion.

TIME	⊙
Group discussions:	10 min
Report back:	20 min
General discussion:	10 min
TOTAL:	**40 min**

1. In terms of the Civil Union Act, 2006, both spouses have equal powers of management over the joint estate. The law says that a partner may now enter into certain acts without the consent of the other partner, except for such acts as are specifically excluded in the Matrimonial Property Act, 1984. Edward does not require Jacobus' consent to enter into an employment contract because this is not mentioned in the Act.

2. For certain transactions, the Matrimonial Property Act says that consent is required but it can be given in any manner. It is not necessary to obtain written consent in such cases; oral or tacit consent is sufficient, eg where furniture or other household property is sold. Edward requires Jacobus' consent but it can be given in any manner.

3. Jacobus may not sell immovable property, such as a flat, belonging to the joint estate without Edward's prior written consent. This means that Edward has to give his written consent beforehand. In addition, his written agreement must be signed by two witnesses.

4. Where Jacobus sells the flat without Edward's consent, the transaction will be null and void. If Martin did not know, and could not reasonably have known that Jacobus should have obtained consent from Edward, then the transaction would have been valid. However, in this case, Martin knows that Jacobus is in a civil union and that Edward had not consented to the sale. The agreement to sell the flat is therefore not valid or enforceable.

Problem 3: Jerry and Ansie decide to divorce   (Learner's Manual p 365)

AIM: This exercise is designed to show learners how the 'accrual system' works.

PROCEDURE ▤

1. Select learners for role-play.
2. Act out role-play.
3. Debrief role-play.
4. Each learner to answer questions 2 and 3 individually.
5. Select learners to report back on answers.
6. Clarify answers.

TIME	⊙
Role-play:	10 min
Prepare answers:	15 min
Individual report backs:	15 min
General discussion:	5 min
TOTAL:	**45 min**

1. The learners playing Jerry and Ansie should discuss what they think would be a fair division of the property. This may or may not be what the law says each is entitled to.

2. The accrual system applies in their case because:
   (a) they were married after 1 November 1984, and
   (b) the ante-nuptial contract did not exclude the accrual system.

3. During the marriage, the value of Jerry's property has increased by R440 000 (R500 000 – R60 000) and that of Ansie by R105 000 (R120 000 – R15 000). The total accrual for their estate is R440 000 + R105 000 = R545 000. This must be shared equally between them. Therefore, Jerry and Ansie each receive R277 500 in addition to the commencement value of their estates. Thus Jerry receives R60 000 + R277 500 = R337 500 and Ansie receives R15 000 + R277 500 = R292 500.

Problem 4: Would you order forfeiture of benefits? *(Learner's Manual p 366)*

AIM: The object of this exercise is to show learners when the court will order forfeiture of benefits.

PROCEDURE		TIME	
1. Explain the case study to the class.		Explanation:	5 min
2. Divide the class into small groups.		Group discussions:	15 min
3. Groups to consider possible arguments on behalf of both parties, and to deliver a judgment.		Report back:	15 min
		General discussion:	10 min
4. Groups report back.		**TOTAL:**	**45 min**
5. General discussion.			

A judge will usually order forfeiture of benefits if the guilty spouse is responsible for breaking up the marriage and the innocent spouse asks for a court order to be made.

If the marriage was in community of property, the guilty spouse will receive only those assets that he brought into the joint estate himself.

Forfeiture of benefits does not mean that a spouse loses his own assets, but merely that he loses the claim that he has to the assets of the other spouse.

Because Ranji and Zoobie were married in community of property, they would each have an undivided half-share in the total value of their joint property, ie R5 500 000 (R5 000 000 + R500 000).

On divorce, the court will usually give them each a half-share, ie R2 250 000. Because Ranji was at fault, the court might not give Ranji any of his share of Zoobie's property.

He will, however, still be entitled to R500 000 which he brought into the joint estate. Learners can decide whether or not they would like to order forfeiture of benefits.

4.2.3 Decisions in marriages and civil unions *(Learner's Manual p 368)*

Problem 5: What do you think should be the roles of husbands and wives and civil union partners? *(Learner's Manual p 368)*

AIM: The object of this exercise is to encourage learners to think about the roles of husbands and wives and civil union partners in the family.

<table>
<tr><td>

PROCEDURE ≔

1. Divide learners into small groups with each group discussing one of the statements; or conduct an opinion poll by giving each learner an opportunity to express an opinion on each item.
2. Report back from small groups or from individual learners.
3. Record responses on blackboard or flip chart.
4. General discussion.

</td><td>

TIME 🕐

Group discussions or opinion poll:	15 min
Report back:	20 min
General discussion:	10 min
TOTAL:	**45 min**

</td></tr>
</table>

The activity can take the form of either small group discussions, with each group discussing one of the statements, or an opinion poll. In the latter case, each learner should be given the opportunity to express an opinion on each item.

The educator could then record the responses on a blackboard or flip chart and discuss the results.

There are no right answers in this activity, but certain points of view are likely to be more common than others. In all cases, learners should be encouraged to give reasons for their answers.

4.2.4 Domestic violence *(Learner's Manual p 369)*

Problem 6: A case of domestic violence *(Learner's Manual p 372)*

AIM: The object of this exercise is to make learners think about ways in which to deal with domestic violence.

<table>
<tr><td>

PROCEDURE ≔

1. Brainstorm meaning of domestic violence.
2. Select learners for role-plays in questions 1 to 4.
3. Conduct role-plays.
4. Debrief role-plays.
5. Divide learners into small groups.
6. Each group to discuss one of questions 5 to 7.
7. Groups report back.
8. General discussion.

</td><td>

TIME 🕐

Brainstorming exercise:	5 min
Role-plays and debriefs:	20 min
Group discussions:	10 min
Report back:	15 min
General discussion:	10 min
TOTAL:	**60 min**

</td></tr>
</table>

1. Learners' answers will differ. Like any other crime, an assault of this nature should be reported. However, many people believe that neighbours should not interfere in each other's family problems. What responsibilities do citizens have when they observe a crime being committed? Does the same apply to domestic violence, or is it different? Learners should be encouraged to say what they think they would do. Would they call the police? What would they tell the police? If they would not call the police, why not?

2. The exercise should show learners the delicate role police officers must play in these situations. Often a wife will be reluctant to lay a complaint against her husband. Do the police need special training to handle this type of situation? If so, what kind of training? Would the police react

differently if the Swarts were unmarried and living together? In terms of the Domestic Violence Act, the police are one of the most important role-players in that most of the provisions in the Act involve the police in one way or another and place many duties on them (see answers to question 3 below).

3. The police need to find out what happened and why. Has Mr Swart beaten his wife in the past? Is there some place Mrs Swart can go to for the night if her husband is not arrested (eg a friend or relative's house or a shelter for abused women)? Does Mrs Swart want her husband arrested? Does Mrs Swart need medical treatment? Are there children, and where can they safely spend the night? Should her wishes be considered? The duty of the police in this case is to assist Mrs Swart by explaining to her what remedies are provided for in the Domestic Violence Act, such as applying for a protection order, laying a criminal charge, or both. If the police suspect that Mrs Swart is in immediate danger, they may arrest Mr Swart on the scene. If Mr Swart is in possession of a dangerous weapon, the police may remove such weapon from his possession.

4. Answers to this problem will vary depending on the learners' individual responses to the situation. Learners should role-play Mr and Mrs Swart and the police officer. Other learners could then be asked how they would have handled the situation differently. Mrs Swart can apply to court for a protection order. Together with the protection order, the court may also issue a suspended warrant of arrest, which means that if Mr Swart abuses her again, he will immediately be arrested. In addition to the remedies provided for in the Act, Mrs Swart may also lay a criminal charge of assault against her husband.

   However, the difference between the protection order and the criminal charge is that the protection order gives her immediate protection while a criminal case sometimes takes a long time to be heard. Mrs Swart might also try to find suitable shelter if she has to move out of the house, and medical care if necessary.

5. A magistrate confronted with the Swart case should grant a protection order if the magistrate thinks that Mrs Swart might be a victim of domestic violence. Factors that will be taken into account are: How badly was Mrs Swart injured? Has the husband abused her in the past? Did Mrs Swart want to lay charges? Is imprisonment of Mr Swart likely to improve the situation? The protection order will tell Mr Swart to stop abusing Mrs Swart. If there is also a criminal charge pending, a magistrate could grant the protection order and issue a warrant of arrest, but suspend the warrant pending the finalisation of the criminal case. Alternatively, if Mr Swart is a real danger to his wife, the magistrate may order that he be held in custody pending his trial for assault.

6. A magistrate dealing with the case may sentence Mr Swart to a term of imprisonment if he or she feels that Mr Swart is a danger to his wife and should be kept away from her for a while. If the magistrate thinks that Mr Swart is not a danger, but needs to be deterred from assaulting his wife again, the magistrate may impose a suspended sentence on Mr Swart. The magistrate may make the suspended sentence conditional on Mr Swart's not assaulting his wife again and on condition that Mr Swart goes for treatment concerning his drinking problem.

7. Educators and learners should ask social welfare departments what programmes are available in their communities to deal with domestic violence.

4.3　Parents and children

Outcomes

After completion of this section learners will be able to:

1. Explain and appreciate the relationship between parents and children.

2. Explain when a child is a 'child in need of care and protection'.

3. Explain the law relating to the termination of pregnancy.

Assessment criteria

1. The legal responsibilities of parents and children are identified and explained.

2. The meanings of 'care' and 'guardianship' are explained.

3. An explanation is given of the position of children born of married parents, children born of unmarried parents, and children of customary marriages.

4. A set of facts is examined to create awareness of the parental duty to support children and the reciprocal obligation owed by children.

5. Sets of facts are examined and decisions made on when parents are responsible for wrongs done by their children.

6. Sets of facts are examined and decisions made on what things children may do without their parents' assistance.

7. Ways in which children become independent of their parents are identified.

8. A description is given of when a child can be regarded as being a 'child in need of care and protection'.

9. Sets of facts are examined and decisions taken on whether the parents are guilty of ill-treatment or abandonment of children.

10. A set of facts is examined and a decision made on whether neighbours should become involved in child abuse and child neglect cases.

11. The conditions under which a pregnancy may be terminated are explained.

12. The conflicting rights involved in the choice to terminate a pregnancy are identified.

4.3.1　Responsibilities between parents and children

(Learner's Manual p 374)

Problem 1: The case of the unworthy father

(Learner's Manual p 375)

AIM:　The object of this exercise is to make learners think about whether people should be forced to marry each other. They should also think about the rights of children born to mothers who are not married.

PROCEDURE		TIME	
1. Divide learners into small groups to discuss the question.		Group discussions:	20 min
2. Report back.		Report back:	15 min
3. Summarise group responses.		General discussion:	10 min
4. General discussion.		**TOTAL:**	**45 min**

Learners are likely to have different views on whether the law should require a man who impregnates a woman to marry her and support the child. They should be asked to give reasons for their answers.

The position, however, is that no one can be forced by law to marry somebody else. If this did occur the marriage could be annulled as it would have been entered into without proper consent (ie under duress).

Eddy could be required to support the child if he is the father. To prove this, Mana might have to make a complaint at the maintenance court so that a paternity action can be brought. The court would then consider the evidence and decide whether Eddy was the father. The prosecutor would bring the action for Mana and it would not be necessary for her to employ an attorney. The action would not cost her anything.

Assuming that Eddy is too young to earn money to support the child, should his parents, as the grandparents of the child, be responsible for supporting it? Should Mana's parents also be responsible for supporting the child? When Eddy begins work, by law he would be responsible for supporting the child. Mana would also be expected to help towards the support of the child. The law provides that both parents must contribute towards the support of their child. And if parents are young and poor, that duty falls onto the grandparents if they are able.

Problem 2: Parental control over children   (Learner's Manual p 377)

AIM: The object of this exercise is to make learners aware of parents' duty of support towards their children.

PROCEDURE		TIME	
1. Divide class into three groups.		Group discussions:	10 min
2. Allocate one question to each group for discussion.		Role-play:	15 min
3. Select learners from each of the groups to role-play the discussions between the parents and the children.		Report back:	15 min
		Summary:	5 min
4. Report back.		**TOTAL:**	**45 min**
5. Summarise group responses.			

1.   Bart could argue that his father has a duty to pay for necessities to support him, such as food and accommodation. Bart's father might argue that Bart is no longer a minor because he is 18 years of age and therefore he must support himself. Bart might argue that he is entitled to a university or other tertiary education if his father can afford it or his brothers and sisters have received it. But if his father is supporting him, his father has the right to decide where the family should

live. If he went to court, the court might order such support conditional on Bart living where his father wants. On the other hand, Mr Khuzwayo's demands should not be unreasonable. If they are unreasonable, it might be necessary for Bart to get somebody to intervene, or even to obtain the assistance of an attorney. Learners playing the roles of Bart and his father should consider the above points of view.

2. If parents unreasonably refuse permission for their children to marry, the children may apply to a judge of the High Court for permission to marry. In this case, as Christina is a mature person of 17 years, and Stoffel is an accountant, presumably with a reasonable job, it is likely that the court would give permission for them to marry. Parents must not unreasonably withhold their consent to a marriage of their minor children. Learners role-playing the conversation between Stoffel, Christina and her parents should use their imagination as to why the parents object and why Christina and Stoffel should be allowed to marry.

3. As Rama is a child, the law gives his parents the right to determine where he lives. The arguments in favour of this include that Rama is supported by his parents and is not able to live on his own. Also, the law should preserve family unity and not interfere in family affairs. The arguments against his having to move with his parents are that the parents might be making a decision that is against Rama's best interests, and the fact that he is nearly 18 years old. Maybe a mediator (eg a friend or relative) should be called in. If the dispute cannot be resolved by a mediator, it might be necessary for Rama to consult an attorney. Learners role-playing the conversation between Rama and his parents should use their imagination as to why the parents wish him to move and why he does not want to go.

Problem 3: Are the parents responsible? *(Learner's Manual p 378)*

AIM: The object of this exercise is for learners to understand when parents are responsible for wrongs done by their children.

PROCEDURE		TIME	
1. Divide the class into three groups.		Group discussions:	15 min
2. Allocate one question to each group for discussion.		Role-play:	10 min
3. Select two learners from each of the groups to role-play the different points of view.		Report back:	15 min
		Summary:	5 min
4. Report back.		**TOTAL:**	**45 min**
5. Summarise group responses.			
6. Clarify the different arguments.			

1. Barend is liable for the damage to Andrew's car. Barend is at fault because he carelessly allowed Engeltjie to run into the street. Engeltjie is only 3 years old and cannot be expected to act responsibly. Even though Andrew crashed into a wall while trying to avoid Engeltjie, he cannot be held liable for causing damage to his own car because he was acting in an emergency. Barend ought to have foreseen that Engeltjie might cause an accident if she ran into the road, and should have taken steps to prevent her doing so. Learners playing the roles of Barend and Andrew should use their imagination when discussing the accident.

2. Gladys will be liable for the injuries caused to Premjee by Goodwill. At the time that Goodwill

collided with Premjee, he was acting as Gladys' 'servant'. Goodwill had the accident while he was carrying out the task that Gladys had asked him to do. He collided with Premjee on his way to the store to buy groceries for the home. Learners can use their imagination when playing the roles of Gladys and Premjee.

3. Lennie's parents will only be liable to replace Sophie's broken window if they allowed Lennie and his friends to play cricket in the backyard and they ought to have foreseen that the cricket ball might be hit out of the yard and break a window. If this were the case, Lennie's parents should have taken steps to prevent harm from happening by stopping the game of cricket. But if Lennie's parents did not know that the children were playing cricket in their backyard, they would not be liable for the broken window. Lennie is under 10 years of age so he cannot be held personally liable for smashing Sophie's window. Learners should use their imagination when role-playing the conversation between Sophie's and Lennie's fathers.

Problem 4: Some questions on the position of children born of unmarried parents or parents not in a civil union
(Learner's Manual p 380)

AIM: The object of this exercise is for learners to think about how children born of unmarried parents or parents not in a civil union are treated by the law.

PROCEDURE
1. Divide the class into small groups.
2. Groups to discuss each question.
3. Report back.
4. Ask learners to explain their answers.
5. Clarify answers.

TIME	
Group discussions:	15 min
Report back:	15 min
Clarification:	10 min
TOTAL:	**40 min**

1. In many countries the law treats children born of married parents or parents in a civil union differently from children born of unmarried parents or parents not in a civil union. This is because, in many societies, children born of unmarried parents or parents not in a civil union are looked down upon and do not have the same rights as children born of married parents or parents in a civil union. The reason for this is probably that society tries to protect children who are born to a married couple or a couple in a civil union. This is done in order to protect the institution of marriage and civil unions and to provide security for the family. There is also a presumption that children born to a married couple or a couple in a civil union are the children of the husband or partner in that marriage or union.

    In the case of children born of unmarried parents or parents not in a civil union, it is sometimes difficult to prove who the father is, although the mother's identity is always clear. It is for this reason that before 1988 children born of unmarried parents could only succeed to their mothers, but not their fathers, if their parents died without making a will. Since 1988, they have been able to inherit from both parents in the same way as children born of married parents. The same now applies to children born out of a civil union.

    An argument in favour of treating children equally irrespective of their parents' marital or union status is that the sins of the parents should not be visited upon their children. If children can prove that certain people are their parents, why should they not inherit in the same way as children born of married parents or parents in a civil union? The main argument, however, is to be found in our Constitution, which says that a person should not be discriminated against on the basis of their birth, status or social origin. Learners can make up their own minds in deciding whether or not it is correct to treat children born of unmarried parents or parents not in a civil union and children born of married parents or parents in a civil union equally.

2. In the past the failure to recognise the rights of a natural father over his child born out of wedlock reflected society's reluctance to recognise children born of unmarried parents as part of the father's family – except in the case of customary law. This was probably done to preserve the institution of marriage. At the same time children were punished by being labelled as 'illegitimate'. Today society still punishes the father by requiring him to maintain the child even though he has no automatic rights of guardianship, care or access to it – he has to apply to court for them. Learners can make up their own minds about whether or not they think that it is fair that mothers get automatic guardianship of children born of unmarried parents.

3. It could be argued that, in a constitutional democracy where discrimination on the grounds of sex and marital status is prohibited, fathers should have the same rights as they have in respect of their children born in wedlock in a civil union, provided they carry out their corresponding duties. They should also have the same rights as the mothers. It might not be fair that a natural father has to pay maintenance for the support of his child born out of wedlock without exercising any rights of guardianship or care. Learners can make up their own minds about whether they think that it is fair that a natural father has to pay maintenance for his child born out of wedlock but may not act as its guardian or care-giver without obtaining a court order.

4.3.2   The duty of support   *(Learner's Manual p 381)*

Problem 5: The case of the rich son   *(Learner's Manual p 382)*

AIM: The object of this exercise is for learners to understand when it is necessary for children to support their parents.

PROCEDURE	TIME	
1. Select two learners to conduct the role-play.	Role-play:	5 min
2. Conduct the role-play.	Group discussions:	20 min
3. Divide the class into small groups and allocate questions 1 or 3 to each group.	Report back:	15 min
	General discussion:	5 min
4. Report back	**TOTAL:**	**45 min**
5. General discussion.		

1. There is a legal obligation on Jan to support his mother if she is poor and cannot afford a place to live. Usually, children are expected to support their parents according to the standards they can comfortably afford.

   The minimum support that Jan must provide should be sufficient for his mother to live in an old-age home. She, however, would prefer to stay on in her own house. It seems that such an arrangement would be well within Jan's means and it could be argued that he should allow her to stay on in her house. The court will consider what is reasonable in the light of Jan's income and his mother's ability to look after herself.

2. The learners playing the roles of Jan and his mother should use their imagination concerning why Jan would like her to move into an old-age home and why his mother would like to continue renting her house.

3. The law says that there is a duty on adult children to support their needy parents. Learners, however, might have differing views on the topic. Some might argue that children do not owe their parents anything once they have grown up, because their grandparents made similar sacrifices for their parents, when they were growing up.

   Others might argue that because there is a duty on parents to support their children, there should be a similar duty on children to support their parents. Most learners, however, will probably agree that the support that must be provided should be what the child or parent can reasonably afford.

Problem 6: Is Martie a major? *(Learner's Manual p 383)*

AIM: The object of this exercise is to show learners how a minor may sometimes be regarded as emancipated by the court.

PROCEDURE	TIME	
1. Divide the class into small groups to discuss the question.	Group discussions:	15 min
2. Report back.	Report back:	15 min
3. General discussion.	General discussion:	10 min
	TOTAL:	**40 min**

When deciding whether or not a minor is emancipated, the court will take into account such factors as the minor's age and, occupation, and how long he or she has been working. The main factor that will influence the court, however, is the extent of the minor's financial independence from his or her parents.

Even though Martie lives with her parents, the fact that she pays them money for board and lodging indicates that she is financially independent. Therefore, Martie could be regarded as emancipated and would not need her father's assistance to bring an action for her wages. She is also 17 years of age and nearly an adult. An emancipated minor, however, does not acquire full legal capacity. Martie would not be able to enter into a marriage without her parents' consent.

Problem 7: Can the child act without assistance? *(Learner's Manual p 384)*

AIM: The object of this exercise is for learners to know what minors may and may not do without their guardians' consent.

PROCEDURE	TIME	
1. Divide the class into small groups.	Group discussions:	10 min
2. Each group discusses one or two questions.	Report back:	20 min
3. Report back.	General discussion:	10 min
4. General discussion.	**TOTAL:**	**40 min**

1. Jody may consent to have her nose straightened by a plastic surgeon because she is over the age of 12 years provided she is assisted by her parent or guardian. However, she cannot force her father to pay for the cost of the operation unless it is a necessary operation and forms part of his duty of support.

2. Salie may not open a building society account because he is under 16 years old. However, because he is over 7 years old, he could open a post office savings account.

3. Khotso may open a post office savings account because he is over the age of 7 years.

4. Vish may not make a will because he is under 16 years old.

5. Paulus may witness a will because he is over 14 years of age.

6. Thandi may consent to an abortion without the assistance (or knowledge) of her parents – provided she understands the nature and effect of the procedure – because the Choice on Termination of Pregnancy Act allows a girl of any age to consent to an abortion. If she does not understand the nature and effect of the procedure, she will need her parent's consent.

7. Shanti may ask a doctor to prescribe a contraceptive pill for her without her parent's consent because she is over 12 years old. However, her parents would not be liable to pay for the cost of her visit to the doctor unless the pill was necessary.

8. Busi may consent to an HIV test because she is over 12 years of age.

4.3.3   Children in need of care and protection *(Learner's Manual p 384)*

Educators should be very sensitive when talking about child abuse and neglect. Some of their learners may have been victims of abuse and neglect. Attorneys, social workers, medical personnel, psychologists and others working in the area of child abuse and neglect could be good guest speakers.

Problem 8: Which are cases of children in need of care and protection?
(Learner's Manual p 386)

AIM: The object of this exercise is to enable learners to recognise whether a child in particular circumstances is a child in need of care and protection.

PROCEDURE	TIME	
1. Divide the class into groups.	Group discussions:	10 min
2. Each group is to discuss one situation.	Report back:	20 min
3. Report back.	Discussion and summary:	10 min
4. General discussion.	**TOTAL:**	**40 min**

1. The definition of a child in need of care and protection in the Children's Act of 2005 includes situations where the child is in a state of physical or mental neglect. Failure to provide adequate care by leaving children aged 7 and 3 years alone for long periods of time could be regarded as child neglect. Kristel could be found to be unable or unfit to have the care of her young children in terms of the Act.

    Kristel could also be found guilty of a criminal offence in terms of the Act.

2. While parents may use reasonable force to discipline their children, beating a child 'black and

blue' is excessive and goes beyond the bounds of reasonableness. It should be pointed out that the courts do not lightly interfere with the parents' rights to discipline their children. The burden of proving that the punishment imposed was unjustified or excessive rests upon the person who brings an action against the parents. If unreasonable punishment occurs on a regular basis, the court may find the parents guilty of ill-treatment of the child under the Children's Act, and the child may be removed to a place of safety. Thus Isaac might be removed to a place of safety if Jason regularly beats him 'black and blue'.

3. Telling a 14-year-old girl that she can do anything she wants, including staying out all night, could be regarded as neglect or failure to provide adequate care. Thus, in terms of the Children's Act, Ray could be deemed to be unable or unfit to have custody of Carla. Most people would agree that children of Carla's age are in need of guidance from their parents. However, in practice, Carla's case would probably not come before the courts unless she was involved in some kind of trouble.

4. Khala would not be regarded as a child in need of care unless Thulani repeatedly uses unreasonable force in spanking Khala. Parents have a right and duty to discipline their children. The fact that Khala cries does not necessarily show that excessive force was used. The class might be interested to know that in Sweden it is a crime to spank your child.

5. Nazeer and Shaida's conduct would probably not be regarded as child abuse but it might not be good parenting. Many people would consider it unreasonable for parents to refuse to allow a teenage son to go out with girls, or to go anywhere without them – unless there are special reasons. A court will seldom interfere in such parental decisions although, under the Children's Act, this might be displaying behaviour that may seriously injure the physical, mental or social well-being of that child. It is unlikely, however, that Ahmed would be regarded as being a child in need of care. To what extent are parents entitled to impose their will upon their children in personal matters? In particular, can parents prevent children from associating with persons whom they might regard as undesirable? It has been said that parents have every right to prescribe with whom their children may be friendly and where they may spend their time. But parents who allow older children to leave home so that they can choose their own friends of both sexes waive their right to object to their children's associating with particular people.

6. The court will definitely find Amos and his sisters to be children in need of care and protection on the basis that they all live in a child-headed household because the great-grandmother can longer do anything for herself or she cannot take care of Amos and his sisters. Rather, she needs someone to take care of her.

7. The court may find Mary to be a child in need of care and protection because her parents cannot afford to pay for her medical treatment. The court may order that the child receive appropriate treatment at state expense if the court finds that the child is in need of medical, psychological or other treatment.

8. The court may find Cindy to be a child in need of care and protection because she is abused by her mother. What do you think the court will do? Do you think the court will provide counselling to Thandeka, put Cindy under the care of her father, or take Cindy to a place of safety?

Problem 9: The case of the beaten boy   (Learner's Manual p 388)

AIM: The object of this exercise is to make learners aware of the difficulties facing neighbours who become involved in child abuse and neglect cases.

PROCEDURE		TIME	
1. Select learners for a role-play.		Role-play:	10 min
2. Conduct a role-play.		Group discussions:	15 min
3. Divide the class into groups and ask each group to discuss one question from 3 and 4.		Report back:	15 min
		General discussion:	5 min
4. Report back.		**TOTAL:**	**45 min**
5. General discussion.			

1. Although people are understandably reluctant to become involved in the affairs of another family, child abuse is a very serious matter that should not go unreported. People who believe that Mr Sadie is using excessive force against Robert would probably agree that the matter should be reported to the police. However, sometimes what appears to be excessive may in fact be reasonable force.

2. This role-play is designed to make learners aware of the difficulty of involving the authorities in private family disputes. Learners should realise the delicate nature of this kind of police work. The police must protect the child against physical abuse, while at the same time respecting the parents' rights to discipline their children.

    Issues that learners should consider in this role-play include: Did the police interview both the parents and the child? Did they conduct the interviews separately? What attitude did the police show towards the parties involved? What action did the police take?

3. If Mr Sadie is taken to court for continually beating and injuring Robert, most people would agree that the court has a responsibility to protect the boy. This might involve placing Robert in a foster home, a children's home or youth centre. Mr Sadie may be found unable or unfit to have custody of Robert in terms of the Children's Act.

    Learners could investigate how child abuse cases are handled in their communities. Are there places to which children can be taken in emergencies?

    Learners should also consider what should be done with abusive parents. Should they be punished or helped? For example, should they be sent to prison or ordered to undergo psychiatric counselling and therapy?

4. Studies show that victims of child abuse often grow up to become child abusers themselves. Learners could be asked to discuss what they think the reasons for this are.

4.3.4   Termination of pregnancy   *(Learner's Manual p 388)*

Problem 10: Termination of pregnancy on demand   *(Learner's Manual p 389)*

AIM: The object of this exercise is for students to understand and appreciate when a legal termination of pregnancy may be done and whether they think that termination of pregnancy should be allowed by the law.

PROCEDURE	TIME	
1. Divide learners into small groups.	Group discussions:	20 min
2. Ask each group to discuss one question.	Report back:	15 min
3. Report back.	Discussion and summary:	10 min
4. General discussion.	**TOTAL:**	**45 min**

1. Learners are likely to have different views on whether it is morally and religiously acceptable to allow termination of pregnancy.

    Some might argue that abortion amounts to murder because it is the killing of a foetus (ie the baby growing inside the mother). They might also raise a constitutional argument that a foetus has a right to life which is violated when a woman terminates her pregnancy. The killing of a foetus is not a criminal offence because a foetus is not a human person. Learners in favour of the Choice on Termination of Pregnancy Act might argue that certain situations may demand that abortions be allowed; for example, (a) when the woman is raped or the victim of incest; (b) when there is a danger to the woman's physical or mental well-being; or (c) there is a danger that the child will be mentally or physically disabled. In addition, learners might argue that it is the woman's right to make decisions regarding her body. Most learners might not agree that a termination of pregnancy on the grounds of social or economic factors should be allowed. This might be the one area where they might suggest change.

2. Learners will probably agree that counselling should be compulsory in the light of the fact that a decision to terminate a pregnancy could have far reaching emotional and psychological effects on the woman. Furthermore, in many cases, women might act on impulse and without appreciating the effects of their decisions in the long term. The counselling must be non-directive, which means that it should give the woman the options but not try to persuade her to make one choice or the other.

3. The question gives learners an opportunity to debate this important issue. Some of the issues that might be raised are that, by not requiring the father's consent, the law is discriminating against him because he is equally a parent to the potential child. His consent should therefore also be required. Conversely, it might be argued that the mother is carrying the child, not the father; therefore he should not be able to make the decision because the Constitution gives her the right to personal security and privacy, which includes reproductive rights.

4. It might be argued that in the case of children, due to their lack of maturity and inability to make sound judgments, the consent of either of their parents, guardian or any adult relative should be obtained. After all, the law protects children in other respects (eg, in contracts, court cases, when getting married) and should thus protect a pregnant minor for the reasons set out in 2 above. The counter-argument might be that parents should not be in a position to force their opinions onto children who are old enough to fall pregnant, as the Constitution gives both children and adults the right to personal security and privacy, which includes reproductive rights.

4.4 Foster care and adoption

Outcomes

After completion of this section learners will be able to:

1. Demonstrate an understanding of the law relating to foster care and adoption.

Assessment criteria

1. An explanation is given of what foster care means.

2. The rights and duties of foster parents are explained.

3. The rights and duties of a child's natural parents when a child has been placed in foster care are identified.

4. The meaning of adoption and how an adoption order is made are explained.

5. A set of facts is examined and a decision is made as to whether an adoption order should be cancelled.

6. A set of facts is examined and a decision is made on whether people of different races or of the same sex should be allowed to adopt children.

7. A simulated hearing of the South African Law Commission is conducted to illustrate the problems that may arise if all adopted children are allowed to know who their natural parents are.

8. The effect of adoption is explained.

4.4.1 Foster care

(Learner's Manual p 391)

Problem 1: Natural parents and foster parents

(Learner's Manual p 394)

AIM: The object of this exercise is to show learners the difference between a child who is voluntarily handed over to foster parents and one who the court orders be removed to a foster home.

PROCEDURE
1. Divide learners into small groups.
2. Ask each group to discuss one question.
3. Report back.
4. General discussion.

TIME	
Group discussions:	10 min
Report back:	15 min
General discussion:	10 min
TOTAL:	**35 min**

1. If Ertjies' uncle and aunt decide to take him into foster care, they will have the right to exercise reasonable discipline over him, and the duty to provide him with food, clothing, accommodation and education. Depending upon the agreement between themselves and his parents, his uncle and aunt might agree to support Ertjies. If Ertjies had been removed by a court order, his uncle and aunt could apply for a maintenance grant from the maintenance court.

   Even though his natural parents have handed Ertjies over to his uncle and aunt, they are entitled to reasonable access to him. Ertjies' father will remain his natural guardian and will have to consent to any of Ertjies' property being sold. They will also have to consent if Ertjies decides to get married while still a minor and to any medical operation that is a serious threat to his life. Ertjies' natural parents also retain the right to remove him from the care of the uncle and aunt at any time.

2. When deciding whether Dolly's mother should have access to her, the court will take into account the mother's background and lifestyle. Usually, the court will lean in favour of giving natural parents access to their children. However, the fact that Dolly has reached the age of puberty and is associating with prostitutes could be a danger to her future development. Therefore, it could be argued that she should not be allowed to see her mother in the company of other prostitutes.

On the other hand, it could be reasonable for Dolly's mother to visit her in the care of her foster parents or in the foster home. The court will make an order that is in the best interests of Dolly.

4.4.2 Adoption
(Learner's Manual p 394)

The question arises whether factors such as religion, cultural background or race should be considered when adoptions are arranged. Unlike in the case of foster care where the children's court has to take into consideration religion, race and culture of the foster parent, the position is different with adoptions. Thus, the adoptive parents may not be refused permission to adopt the child simply because of these considerations – the children's court may consider these factors but is not bound to apply them strictly. However, they may be considered as factors that may influence the court when deciding what is in the child's best interests.

For example, the courts have held it to be in the interests of two female 'coloured' children born out of wedlock that they be adopted by their natural father, who was white.

Problem 2: Would you allow the couple to adopt the child?
(Learner's Manual p 396)

AIM: The object of this exercise is to show learners which factors are taken into account when an adoption order is made. It also illustrates what can be done if the children's court makes an improper decision that goes against the law.

PROCEDURE	TIME	
1. Introduce the exercise.	Group discussions:	10 min
2. Divide the class into small groups.	Report back:	15 min
3. Each group is to consider one question.	General discussion:	5 min
4. Report back.	**TOTAL:**	**30 min**
5. General discussion.		

1. The children's court would have to look closely into Jan's case and not make a decision without referring to the particular facts of the case. The court must be guided by what is in the best interests of the child. Although there may be a cultural and racial difference between Mandla, Zanele and Jan, the court must also look at the home environment and educational opportunities

which would be offered to Jan by his adoptive parents. Will they provide Jan with necessary food, clothing, education, love and care that are expected in a family? If the answer is yes, the court should send the case back to the adoption social worker to reconsider the report.

The importance of religious and cultural background varies with the circumstances, and in particular, the age of the child. Courts have held that any refusal to make an adoption order simply on racial or cultural grounds will be set aside by the High Court on review.

2.   In a similar case, which went to the High Court and thereafter to the Constitutional Court, the court was satisfied that permanent same-sex life partners have the right to establish a family unit and enjoy the same protection as married couples do. The court held that a refusal to allow partners in a same-sex relationship to adopt jointly discriminates against them on the grounds of sexual orientation and marital status, both of which are prohibited in the Constitution.

Each application must be looked at strictly on its own merits and in accordance with the principles set out in the Children's Act. Where indications are that the child is happy and well adjusted to the parents' life partnership, the refusal to allow the adoption might not be in the child's best interests.

Learners can give their opinions as to why raising a child by a couple of the same sex might or might not serve the interests and welfare of the child.

3.   In view of the increasing number of children who need stability in their lives and the fact that there are a few South Africans who are financially well off, it would be unwise not to allow poor people to adopt children. Thus, the Children's Act allows poor people to adopt children and thereafter to apply for a maintenance grant. Consequently, Precious may not be refused permission to adopt Tom on the basis that she is poor. The fact that Precious is a loving and stable mother will give the Tom stability that he needs. In any case, Precious has a decent home, adequate for Tom's wellbeing. What is important is the best interests of Tom.

Problem 3: The case of the mother who changed her mind *(Learner's Manual p 398)*

AIM: The object of this exercise is to illustrate when a mother who gives her child away for adoption may get her child back from the adoptive parents.

PROCEDURE	TIME	
1. Introduce the facts of case.	Introduction:	5 min
2. Divide the class into groups representing Olive's advocate, Basil's advocate, and the judge.	Group presentations:	10 min
3. Groups prepare arguments and judgments.	Presentation of arguments and judgments:	20 min
4. Groups present their arguments for Olive, Elmine and Basil.	General discussion:	10 min
5. Judges give judgment.	**TOTAL:**	**45 min**
6. General discussion.		

1.   Olive's advocate might argue: (a) Olive was emotionally upset at the time she gave her baby away; (b) the adoption is not in the best interests of the baby because Olive is its natural mother; (c) Olive brought her action within the 2-year period; and (d) the baby has only been with Elmine and Basil for three months.

2. Elmine and Basil's advocate might argue: (a) Olive is a single parent and single parents often abuse their children; (b) because she is a single parent, Olive will not be able to look after the child properly; (c) Elmine and Basil, who already have a 3-year-old adopted boy, will be able to give the baby a stable family home; and (d) as Elmine and Basil have looked after the baby for at least three months, the baby regards them as its parents and will suffer emotional distress if taken away from them.
3. As the judge, learners can decide which of the above arguments, and any others that are put forward, they find persuasive. They can then give an appropriate judgment.

Problem 4: Some questions on adoption (Learner's Manual p 399)

AIM: The object of the exercise is to make learners think about the arguments in favour of and against adoptive children's being given access to the identity of their natural parents.

(Note: This exercise can also be used in class as a Law Commission hearing using the jigsaw method – see above para G21 in the *Educator's Manual*. The witnesses should present their evidence in terms of the statements in Problem 4 in the *Learner's Manual*. More witnesses can be introduced if necessary. The Commission should ask the witnesses questions.)

PROCEDURE	TIME	
1. Introduce the lesson by reading the proposed law.	Introduction of lesson:	5 min
2. Ask two students to read the facts.	Group discussions:	10 min
3. Divide the class into small groups.	Report back:	20 min
4. Allocate one question to each group.	General discussion:	10 min
5. Group discussions.	**TOTAL:**	**45 min**
6. Report back.		
7. General discussion.		

After the evidence has been heard, a debate on the proposed law could be held in front of the whole class. The Commission members should try to reach a decision on the law. It might be useful to have two learners argue in favour of the law, two against it, and three neutral. Commission members might wish to introduce amendments to the law such as: (a) lowering the age even further; (b) requiring the consent of one or both natural parents before the information is released; (c) requiring the state to search for the natural parents; and (d) requiring the consent of the adoptive parents.

The debriefing of the hearing could bring out the following factors against opening adoption records in all instances: (a) it would violate the natural parents' rights to privacy; (b) it might prevent adoptions; (c) it might harm the relationship between the adoptive children and their adoptive parents; and (d) it protects the children and their natural parents against the stigma of illegitimate birth.

The factors in favour of doing away with secret adoptions and opening adoption records include: (a) adopted children need roots and the feeling of belonging; (b) denying this information can do psychological damage to adoptees; (c) the adopted child has a right to know; (d) many natural parents would not oppose meeting their natural children again; (e) adopted children might benefit from meeting their natural brothers and sisters; (f) it might re-establish relationships with natural parents; and (g) adopted children need to know their medical and genetic history to the benefit of themselves and their children.

It is important for people to know their genetic history because there have been a few cases where a man and woman have fallen in love, become engaged, and shortly before their wedding, discovered that they are natural brother and sister, adopted by different families.

Answers to the problem

1. This depends upon how the learners balance the above-listed factors. A compromise position would be to require the consent of their natural parents. The issue of who will find them and pay for the search may be a problem.

2. These are arguments against doing away with secret adoptions and in favour of opening up all records. Learners will differ as to whether they think these comments are valid or not.

3. The factors listed above illustrate the possible problems that might be experienced with the proposed law. The amendments listed above might give Commission members some ideas as to how they could rewrite the law.

4. The answer depends largely on the circumstances of the case. In making the decision, Karel's adoptive parents should take into account his maturity, stability, and sense of identity. Most experts recommend that adopted children should be told of their adoption at a fairly young age.

4.5 Family problems: Divorce and maintenance

Outcomes

After completion of this section learners will be able to:

1. Explain the law relating to divorce or separation.

2. Explain the steps to follow in obtaining a divorce and understand the consequences of divorce.

Assessment criteria

1. Some of the factors that commonly lead to a separation or divorce are identified.

2. The difference between a separation and a divorce is explained.

3. An awareness is created of what spouses or civil union partners should do before they decide to separate.

4. The grounds for a divorce are explained.

5. A set of facts is examined to determine when the courts will regard a marriage or civil union as having irretrievably broken down.

6. The steps to be followed in obtaining a divorce are explained.

7. An explanation is given of how family property may be divided and how maintenance is provided for when a couple becomes divorced.

8. The factors which influence the courts when awarding custody to a spouse or civil union partner are identified.

9. A set of facts is examined and a decision is taken on which parent is likely to be awarded care of the children of a marriage or civil union.

10. An explanation is given of how a person applies for maintenance and what happens if maintenance is not paid.

4.5.1   Divorce and separation

(Learner's Manual p 401)

Problem 1: Problems in marriages and civil unions

(Learner's Manual p 403)

AIM: The object of this exercise is to make learners aware of the types of problems that may arise in a marriage or civil union.

PROCEDURE
1. Divide the class into small groups.
2. Have each group discuss one question.
3. Report back.
4. General discussion.

TIME	
Group discussions:	10 min
Report back:	20 min
General discussion:	10 min
TOTAL:	**40 min**

1. Some of the common problems leading to divorce or separation include: (a) incompatibility of lifestyle; (b) career conflicts; (c) disagreements over where and how to live; (d) adultery; (e) boredom;

(f) sexual problems; (g) alcoholism; (h) mental instability; (i) financial problems and (j) problems between children and parents. Learners can choose how they wish to rank the problems.

2. The better people know themselves and their potential spouses or civil union partners, the easier it is to foresee potential problems and to decide whether or not these are likely to occur. However, since people and circumstances are always changing, it is impossible to know exactly what will happen in any particular marriage or civil union.

3. Marriage counsellors say that the most important way of solving marital or civil union problems is to have an open and honest discussion about the problems. When problems arise, it is sometimes useful to obtain assistance from a marriage guidance counsellor. Some people also use mediators; eg a relative or friend (see *Learner's Manual* para 1.3.2.2) to resolve disagreements in their marriages or civil unions. A social worker or marriage guidance counsellor is also a useful mediator in these situations. The kind of help a married or civil union couple needs will depend upon their particular problems.

4. Some of the things that have to be considered when obtaining a divorce are legal fees and, sometimes, fees paid to marriage guidance counsellors. A wealthy couple might also have to consult a tax expert to work out the effect of income tax on a divorce settlement. Divorce may result in a change in life-styles, such as renting or buying a second home, and additional health, life, motorcar or other insurance. There are also other issues like: How will the couple's property be divided? Who will have care of the children? What arrangements will be made for maintenance of and access to the children? Will the wife receive maintenance?

This section tells learners about the options that are available for solving marital or civil union problems. The educator can ask the learners whether they think there should be mediation (see *Learner's Manual* para 1.3.2.2) before a divorce is granted.

The educator might also wish to discuss informal separation agreements and to emphasise that they have no binding effect in court. The main purpose of a separation is that it may serve as a trial period to see if the couple really wants a divorce. It may also be evidence of an irretrievable breakdown of a marriage or civil union in a later divorce action. Whatever the cause of the separation or divorce, matters such as finances, the division of property, care of the children and maintenance must usually be decided. Legal advice is, therefore, important.

Problem 2: The unhappy couple
(Learner's Manual p 404)

AIM: The object of this exercise is to make learners aware of what spouses should do before they decide to separate.

PROCEDURE	TIME	
1. Divide the class into small groups.	Presentation and preparations and group discussions:	15 min
2. Each group is to discuss one question.		
3. Groups with question 3 should prepare role-plays between Ansie and Jan.	Report back on group discussions and role-plays:	20 min
4. Group discussions and role-play presentations.	General discussion:	10 min
5. Report back.	**TOTAL:**	**45 min**
6. General discussion.		

1. The facts do not indicate whether Jan and Ansie have attempted to solve their marital problems by obtaining help from outside their marriage. They should approach a social worker or a marriage-guidance counsellor for assistance. They could also ask family members, friends or a minister of religion for help. Many people think that the divorce rate has increased because couples do not try hard enough to save their marriages and obtain divorces too quickly. The educator might wish to discuss this aspect with learners.

2. If there is going to be a dispute over care of the children or the division of the property, Jan and Ansie should each obtain their own lawyer. Even if they work out an agreement on their own, it would be advisable to ask a lawyer to examine it. It would not be a good idea for them both to have the same lawyer if there is going to be a dispute. In such a case, it would be unethical for an attorney to advise both clients on an equal basis.

3. Jan and Ansie must decide:
   (a) who will have care of their children;
   (b) what responsibilities each parent will have for the care of the children and their maintenance;
   (c) how much money Jan will give Ansie and the children to live on;
   (d) whether Ansie should try to get a job and support herself;
   (e) whether one of them should keep the flat and, if so, what each should pay towards the rent; and
   (f) how they should divide their savings, the car, the furniture and the appliances.

   The role-play may be done in small groups as follows:
   (i) The learners with question 3 should discuss how to role-play Jan and Ansie negotiating an agreement.
   (ii) The learners then act out Jan and Ansie negotiating an agreement.
      The role-play is designed to make learners aware of the traumatic effects of separation – physically, emotionally and financially. The educator might wish to give each group time to work out and write up an agreement.
      The educator might then draw up a table on the blackboard to see how each group dealt with different aspects of the settlement. The table could be drawn up as follows:

Issues decided	Groups					
	1	2	3	4	5	6
Wife's maintenance: does the husband pay?						
Where do the children live?						
Who pays maintenance for the children?						
Will the wife work?						
Who lives in the flat and who moves out?						
Who gets the R3 000 in the savings account?						
Who gets the car, the furniture and the appliances?						

   The role-play can be debriefed by asking the learners who dealt with question 3:
   (a) Did both sides negotiate fairly in each role-play? Were the results fair? How did they differ?

(b) What role did the couple play in each? What role did attorneys and mediators play when they were involved?

(c) What techniques were used by each?

(d) Were the role-plays realistic?

(e) Were the role-plays friendly or aggressive?

4.5.2   Divorce
(Learner's Manual p 404)

Problem 3: Some questions on divorce
(Learner's Manual p 405)

AIM: This exercise is designed to give learners an opportunity to understand the reasons behind the increasing divorce rate and what can be done about it.

PROCEDURE		TIME	
1. Divide the class into small groups.		Group discussions:	15 min
2. Have each group discuss one question.		Report back:	15 min
3. Report back.		General discussion:	5 min
4. General discussion.		**TOTAL:**	**35 min**

1.   Some of the reasons behind the increasing divorce rate might be: (a) the changing economic role of women in marriage – both husbands and wives often work; (b) modern married or civil union couples, unlike previous generations, are less likely to iron out their problems or ignore them and remain married or in a civil union; (c) the role of religion and changing religious views; (d) there is less stigma attached to divorce than in the past; and (e) the increasing number of unmarried people or people not in civil unions who live together.

Questions that arise are: Is society worse or better off as a result of the increasing divorce rate? Are children better or worse off if unhappy, married or civil union parents continue to live together or obtain a divorce?

2.   Arguments in favour of the state making it more difficult to obtain a divorce include: (a) marriage or a civil union is a serious relationship that should not be lightly entered into or ended; and (b) a compulsory 'cooling-off' period and counselling might reduce the divorce rate.

Arguments against making divorce more difficult include: (a) marriage or a civil union is a private relationship between two people and should not be unduly complicated or interfered with by the state; and (b) if a husband and wife or civil union partners decide that their marriage or civil union no longer works, they should not have to go through additional emotional trauma.

Problem 4: Would you grant a divorce?
(Learner's Manual p 407)

AIM: The object of the exercise is for learners to understand when the courts will regard a marriage or civil union as having irretrievably broken down.

PROCEDURE		TIME	
1. Introduce the cases.		Introduction:	5 min
2. Divide the class into small groups.		Group discussions:	15 min
3. Groups discuss one case.		Report back:	15 min
4. Report back.		General discussion:	5 min
5. General discussion.		**TOTAL:**	**40 min**

1. Sonny and Cheryl are both young and have only been married for a year. Although Sonny goes to discos and flirts with other girls, he does not sleep with them. There is no evidence that he fails to support Cheryl, refuses to sleep with her, assaults her, comes home drunk, always sulks and nags her, that they have not lived together as man and wife for the year that they have been married. Cheryl, on the other hand, is entitled to expect that Sonny not upset her by going out to discos alone and flirting with other girls. Sonny's attitude seems immature and maybe he needs counselling concerning his role as a husband. The counsellor might be able to use the fact that Sonny does not wish to be divorced to persuade him to adopt a more responsible attitude. A judge would have to decide whether the marriage has 'irretrievably broken down' or whether, because of their young age, Sonny and Cheryl should be advised to consult a marriage-guidance counsellor before considering divorce.

2. The fact that Gawie comes home drunk nearly every night and often assaults Harold and Stoffie imposes a very heavy emotional burden on his partner and son. Even though he is kind to them when he is sober, it is clear that Harold cannot cope with his continuous drunkenness and violence. Nor should he be expected to – unless Gawie undertakes to be treated for his alcoholism. As things stand at present, Harold would be entitled to argue that their civil union has irretrievably broken down. The learners playing the role of the judge would probably grant the divorce.

Problem 5: Help before and during divorce _(Learner's Manual p 409)_

AIM: The object of this exercise is to make learners think about the usefulness of marriage-guidance counselling before a divorce is instituted. It also makes them consider the role of an attorney in a divorce action.

1. An argument in favour of requiring a couple to see a marriage-guidance counsellor before divorce is that marriage or a civil union is a very serious contractual relationship which the state has an interest in maintaining, and it should not be allowed to be dissolved without some attempt to prevent dissolution. This might also result in fewer cases clogging up the courts.
    The argument against requiring counselling is that marriage or a civil union is a private relationship which the state should not interfere with by requiring counselling before divorce.

2. In a divorce action, spouses or partners might have different interests in deciding child care, maintenance and the division of property. The attorney's role is to act for his or her client. If an attorney has two clients with competing interests, a conflict will exist, so the attorney will not be able to act effectively for both spouses or partners.

3. Poor people who cannot afford a divorce lawyer can apply to Legal Aid South Africa or a legal aid clinic for assistance (see *Learner's Manual* para 1.4.1.4).

Problem 6: If you were the marriage counsellor *(Learner's Manual p 409)*

AIM: The object of this exercise is to show learners how marriage counsellors can help to resolve disputes that might otherwise end in divorce.

PROCEDURE	TIME	
1. Divide the class into small groups of three: the two parties and a marriage counsellor mediator.	Select groups representing Sonny, Cheryl, Gawie, Harold and marriage counsellors:	5 min
2. Each group is to role-play a mediation involving one of the scenarios.	Role-plays:	30 min
3. Report back.	Debrief role-plays:	15 min
4. General discussion.	General discussion:	10 min
	TOTAL:	**60 min**

Mediation: Learners playing the marriage counsellors should use the mediation steps in para 1.3.2.2 of the *Learner's Manual*. The counsellor's role is to help the parties reach an agreement, not to make the decision for them. The counsellor should not take sides and should explain this to the parties.

The steps in the mediation are as follows:
1. The counsellor should relax the parties and explain the procedure to them.
2. The counsellor should ask both parties to tell their sides of the story without interruptions.
3. The counsellor should attempt to identify the facts and issues agreed upon by the parties.
4. Each party should think about possible solutions to the problem and be given an opportunity to say what he or she thinks of each solution.
5. The counsellor should summarise the solutions and attempt to identify those on which the parties agree.
6. The counsellor should help the parties reach an agreement that satisfies both of them.
7. The agreement should be written down and the parties should discuss what will happen if either of them breaks it.

A. Sonny and Cheryl should be placed at their ease and asked to tell their sides of the story. The counsellor should then go through the mediation steps mentioned above until Sonny and Cheryl reach an agreement. If Sonny and Cheryl cannot reach an agreement, the only solution might be divorce.

B. Gawie and Harold should be relaxed and asked to tell their sides of the story. The counsellor should then go through the mediation steps mentioned above. If Gawie and Harold cannot reach an agreement, the only solution might be divorce.

AIM: The object of this exercise is to show learners how a divorce action takes place.

PROCEDURE	TIME	
1. Divide the class into small groups.	Divide into small groups:	5 min
2. Each group to answer one question.	Group discussions – one	
3. Report back.	question each:	15 min
4. General discussion.	Report back:	10 min
	General discussion:	5 min
	TOTAL:	**35 min**

1. As Philamina cannot afford a lawyer, and Adam earns R12 000 a month, her lawyer may claim a contribution from him for the cost of the divorce. He may also claim R3 600 a month from Adam as maintenance for Philamina and the children, as a temporary measure until the court makes a final order concerning the amount of maintenance to be paid.

2. Philamina's lawyer will include the claims in a 'summons' with 'particulars of claim' which will be served on Adam by the sheriff. Adam will have 10 days to defend the action. If he is going to defend the action, Adam should contact an attorney because he will be required to file a 'plea'. This is a legal document setting out his defence. In order to do this, he may require 'further particulars' from Philamina's lawyer. All these steps are complicated and it is usually necessary to employ a lawyer to draw up the necessary pleadings (legal documents). After all the pleadings have been filed, the trial begins and the judge hears the case. Both Philamina and Adam will have to attend court. After the judge has heard all the evidence, he or she will decide whether to grant Philamina a divorce and maintenance.

3. If Adam does not defend the case, only Philamina needs go to court on the day of the hearing. She would have to tell her story to the judge and he or she would have to decide whether her marriage has irretrievably broken down. The judge would also decide how much maintenance should be paid by Adam. If Philamina and Adam have agreed on what should happen to the children and how much maintenance should be paid, they could record their agreement in a consent paper. The judge could then make the consent paper part of the order of divorce.

4. Learners acting as the judge would probably grant the divorce because Adam has deserted Philamina and is living with another woman. It is clear that their marriage has irretrievably broken down. As Adam is earning R12 000 a month, he should be able to pay Philamina and the children R3 600 a month for maintenance, as well as the costs of Philamina's lawyers. In reality, the judge's order would probably be for: (a) divorce; (b) Philamina to have care of the children; (c) Adam to have access to the children; (d) Adam to pay maintenance of R3 600 a month for Philamina and the children, and (e) Adam to pay the costs of Philamina's lawyers (an attorney and an advocate – see *Learner's Manual* para 1.4.1.2).

AIM: The object of this exercise is to show learners how family property is divided and how maintenance is provided for when a couple becomes divorced.

PROCEDURE ☰	TIME ⊘	
1. Divide the class of learners into small groups.	Group discussions:	10 min
2. Ask each group to discuss one question.	Report back:	15 min
3. Report back.	General discussion:	10 min
4. General discussion.	**TOTAL:**	**35 min**

1. Samson and Patricia were married out of community of property before 1 November 1984, so each will keep his or her own property. If they did not change their marital regime to include the accrual system, then Patricia will only be entitled to property in terms of the ante-nuptial contract. In addition, she may request a share of Samson's property on the basis of her contribution to the marriage. The court must take into account the fact that Patricia gave up her career as a nurse to take care of her husband and children.

   On the other hand, if they had changed their marital regime to include the accrual system, they will both have to account for any accrual in the property owned by them. The accrual or increase would then be shared between them. Even if Patricia had not accrued anything during the marriage, Samson would still have to share what he had accrued with her. Patricia may also be entitled to claim maintenance from Samson.

2. It might have been better for Patricia if the couple had been married in community of property. Their property would then have formed a joint estate. On divorce, the property would have been divided into two equal halves. Patricia would have received half of the property and would be entitled to claim maintenance.

   The disadvantage of being married in community of property would have been that Patricia, prior to 1993, could not have entered into any contract without Samson's assistance (see *Learner's Manual* para 4.2.2.1).

3. On divorce, Patricia should claim from Samson a share of the property (to compensate her for giving up her nursing career and her contribution to maintaining the joint household over the years) or accrual (if the marriage was subject to the accrual system) and maintenance for herself and any children still in need of support.

4.5.3 Care and maintenance of children *(Learner's Manual p 414)*

What happens to children in divorce cases is very important. The educator should be sensitive to the fact that some learners might themselves be involved in such a situation.

AIM: The object of this exercise is for learners to realise what factors a court takes into account when awarding care to one or other of the parents.

<table>
<tr><td colspan="2">

PROCEDURE ☰
1. Divide the class of learners into small groups.
2. Ask each group to discuss one question.
3. Report back.
4. General discussion.

</td><td colspan="2">

TIME 🕐

Group discussions:	10 min
Report back:	15 min
General discussion:	10 min
TOTAL:	**35 min**

</td></tr>
</table>

1. The Family Advocate would have placed evidence before the court (eg a social worker's report) concerning who might be the best parent to have care. The Family Advocate would have found out from the children who they would like to go to. This is because they are both old enough to make an informed decision. The judge might also feel that it is necessary to interview the children, but the children's wishes are not the only determining factor taken into account when a judge makes a decision about care. The age of the children will make a difference. The older the children, the more likely it is that the judge will follow the children's wishes. The overriding consideration, however, is the best interests of the children.

   The main factor that the judge should consider is what would be in the best interests of the children. Usually, in the case of very young children, the courts tend to favour giving care of children to the mother, but this is not always so. Here, the children are 7 and 14 years old and have spent most of their time with Mr Samuels. Mrs Samuels has a drinking problem, has deserted the children, and frequently assaulted them without good reason. The fact that she showed no interest in them for a year after she had deserted them indicates that she is not a good mother. It is likely that in these circumstances, a judge would award custody to Mr Samuels.

2. The learners can decide to whom they would award care of the children if the children were (a) 7 and 14 years old and (b) 7 and 4 years old.

Problem 10: Some questions on maintenance   *(Learner's Manual p 417)*

AIM: The object of this exercise is to show learners how one spouse lays a complaint against the other spouse for failure to pay maintenance, and to help learners understand the position of children born of unmarried parents concerning maintenance.

<table>
<tr><td colspan="2">

PROCEDURE ☰
1. Introduce facts of case.
2. Divide into small groups.
3. Each group discuss one question.
4. Report back.
5. General discussion.

</td><td colspan="2">

TIME 🕐

Introduction:	5 min
Group discussions:	10 min
Report back:	15 min
General discussion:	5 min
TOTAL:	**35 min**

</td></tr>
</table>

1. In order to claim the missing maintenance from Vijay, Sheena would have to submit a complaint to the maintenance officer at the maintenance court. The complaint must state that Vijay has failed to maintain her in terms of the divorce order. The maintenance officer will then investigate the case. If the maintenance officer takes the case to court, he or she will summon Vijay to appear in court. The court will then make a decision about the maintenance. Vijay

might argue that conditions have changed and that Sheena is now able to support herself. Sheena might show that conditions have changed so that she needs an increase in maintenance because she can no longer support herself on R1 800. After hearing the evidence, the court will make the final decision.

2. In the case of a child born of unmarried parents, the unmarried mother is usually the legal guardian:

   (a) Although Pauline's mother has a legal duty to support her, Pauline's natural father also has a legal duty to support her.

   (b) If Pauline cannot financially support herself, or if her mother cannot support her, Pauline may ask the maintenance court to order her father to support her. To do this, she would have to prove that the man is her father. Pauline's mother could then apply to the maintenance court for a maintenance order. If, however, her mother does not know who Pauline's father is, and cannot support Pauline, she can apply to the state for a child support grant (see *Learner's Manual* para 5.3.5.2.4).

4.6 Death and the law

Outcomes

After completion of this section learners will be able to:

1. Demonstrate an understanding of the law relating to death, wills and the winding-up of a dead person's estate.

Assessment criteria

1. The meaning of 'death' is explained.

2. The legal and moral problems involved in cases where a doctor is requested to remove a life-support system from an unconscious patient are discussed.

3. The distinction between a funeral, burial, memorial service and cremation is explained.

4.   An understanding is developed of the costs involved in a funeral and why it is necessary to be careful when approached by a funeral business.

5. A set of facts is examined and a decision is taken in whether to order or refuse treatment.

6. A description is given of what happens where a person dies without making a will.

7. Advice is given on what has to be done if a person wants to make a will.

8. How to report a death is explained.

9. An explanation is given on the winding-up of an estate and the duties of an executor.

4.6.1   What is the meaning of 'death'?   *(Learner's Manual p 418)*

Problem 1: What would you do when identifying the body?   *(Learner's Manual p 419)*

AIM: The object of this exercise is for learners to be able to identify when dead bodies that appear to have been mutilated have been operated on for medico-legal purposes; when they may have been mutilated by the event that caused their death; and when they may have been mutilated for illegal purposes.

PROCEDURE	TIME	
1. Divide the class of learners into small groups.	Group discussions:	10 min
2. Ask each group to discuss one question.	Report back:	15 min
3. Report back.	General discussion:	10 min
4. General discussion.	**TOTAL:**	**35 min**

1.   Because death from a stabbing is an 'unnatural death' a post-mortem examination of the body has to be done to decide how the person died and whether anyone was responsible for the death. During a post-mortem the body is cut open all along the front and around the top of the skull so that all the inside body parts can be examined. After the body parts have been

examined by the doctor, the wounds in the body will be sewn up. In this case, the learner could ask whether a post-mortem was done and if so, should be satisfied that the wounds were not caused by illegal activities.

2. If a person is killed in a taxi accident it is regarded as an 'unnatural death' and a post-mortem must be held. During serious motor accidents people's body parts may go missing – especially if the vehicle bursts into flames or explodes. The fact that there are no sewn-up wounds on the body indicates that a post-mortem has not yet been done on the body, so it cannot be removed until the examination has been done. The fact that the person's hands and a foot are missing probably means that they were lost or destroyed at the scene of the accident. However, the learner should check what happened during the accident and whether it is likely that the missing body parts were destroyed. If the learner is suspicious about the missing parts he or she should report the case to the police.

3. The fact that a person's body was found in the bush with his or her private parts missing seems to indicate that this might be a 'muti' murder. The person may have died a natural or unnatural death, but because the body was found in the bush with parts missing, it is likely to be treated as an unnatural death. Therefore a post-mortem would have to be done to find out the cause of death and whether anyone was responsible. The body will not be able to be removed until the post-mortem has been done. The learner could try to find out who the investigating police officer is so that he or she can monitor the progress of the case.

4.6.2   Dying and the law
(Learner's Manual p 419)

Problem 2: Should the life-support machine be switched off?
(Learner's Manual p 420)

AIM: The object of this exercise is to show learners the difficulties involved in deciding whether or not a doctor may engage in 'euthanasia' in cases where a patient has no hope of recovery and is merely being kept alive by a life-support machine.

PROCEDURE	TIME	
1. Divide the class of learners into small groups.	Introduction:	5 min
2. Allocate one question to each group.	Group discussions and	
3. The group allocated question 3 should prepare to conduct a role-play between Karen's parents and her doctors.	role-play preparation:	15 min
	Report back and role-play:	20 min
4. Group discussions.	Debrief and discussion:	5 min
5. Report back by groups dealing with questions 1, 2 and 4.	**TOTAL:**	**45 min**
6. Role-play by group dealing with question 3.		
7. Debriefing of role-play.		
8. General discussion.		

1. This problem is based on the American case of *Karen Quinlan* who, for no apparent reason, went into a coma and was unable to breathe without a mechanical respirator. She was fed through her veins. Her parents asked the doctor to disconnect the respirator because he had said there

was no hope that she would ever come out of the coma and recover. The doctor felt that he had a responsibility to keep her alive and not to end her life. He was also concerned about possible criminal or civil liability for disconnecting the machine.

2. The legal and moral questions involved in this case include whether people have a right to life or a right to die.

People in favour of the right to life might argue that the respirator should not be switched off and that the doctor has a duty to keep Karen alive because (a) legally the Constitution guarantees everyone the right to life and (b) ethically and morally under the Hippocratic Oath doctors are obliged to preserve life.

Those in favour of a right to die with dignity and not to be kept alive artificially on machines might argue that the machine should be withdrawn because (a) legally there is no duty to keep people alive where it would serve no purpose and there is no possibility of the person recovering and (b) morally it is irresponsible to waste resources on hopeless cases.

Other questions that arise are: (a) the costs, both financial and psychological, to the family of the person being kept alive in this condition; and (b) whether either courts or doctors should interfere in a personal decision of the family.

3. Learners are required to place themselves in the position of Karen's parents and the doctors. Opinions might differ on whether Karen's parents should be the people to make the decision. Arguments in favour of parents making such a decision are: (a) they know Karen and what is best for her; (b) she has no chance of recovering; (c) life support is prolonging death – not life and, (d) the court will usually appoint the parents as guardians where a daughter like Karen is unconscious or otherwise incompetent.

Arguments against the parents making the decision are: (a) it should be a medical decision – not a legal decision; (b) no one should make a decision to end someone else's life; and, (c) Karen is not brain dead and is still alive; and, (d) Karen should be kept alive until she dies naturally. The last argument may be based on religious or philosophical beliefs.

[Some facts that may help educators when discussing the *Karen Quinlan* 355 A 2d 647 (NJ 1976) case are the following:

(a) Karen weighed less than 20 kilograms and her position was described as 'foetal-like' and grotesque. Her legs and muscles were rigid and deformed. She had some brain function and other reactions normally associated with being alive, such as moving and reacting to light and sound. She could also smell, blink her eyes, grimace and make cries and sounds. Her blood pressure was normal and she was fed through a tube.

(b) She did not fit neatly into the definition of 'brain death' which is usually used by the medical profession to decide whether or not a person is dead. She was in a 'persistent vegetative state'.

(c) Despite his request, the court recognised that her father had 'a high degree of love for his daughter' and was deeply religious.]

When the learners are asked to place themselves in the role of the doctor, the doctor's possible civil and/or criminal liability for agreeing to withdraw the respirator could be discussed. Some doctors would rather let the court decide than subject themselves to any possible liability. The learners might also discuss the fact that some doctors have said that they frequently switch off life-support systems when they are satisfied that there is no hope of recovery and the families have asked them to do so.

Should doctors be allowed to withhold treatment, including food and water, if a patient is unconscious and has irreversible brain damage? Should there be a further check in case the doctor makes a mistake (eg, a panel of doctors or a court order)?

4.   Arguments by the lawyer on behalf of Karen's parents for ending the use of the support system could include: (a) the doctor's and her parents' belief that there is no hope of recovery; (b) the great expense of keeping her alive; (c) the condition of her body and her poor quality of life (ie, the fact that she is like a 'vegetable'); (d) her right to privacy and not to have her body interfered with; and (e) her parents' right as her guardians to decide for her.

Arguments by the lawyer for the doctor could include: (a) the medical evidence that Karen's body and brain are somewhat 'alive'; (b) the chance that she is able to think; (c) the possibility of future recovery; (d) society's attitude towards mercy killing; and (e) the fact that Karen's parents cannot really speak for her.

The learners playing the role of the judge would have to decide which of the above arguments they find most persuasive.

[Note: In the real case, the American court held that the respirator could be switched off. Karen's father had also asked the hospital to stop feeding her intravenously by means of a drip, but the court held that feeding was a natural and not unusual means of supporting life. In the real case, Karen stayed alive for several years after the respirator had been removed.

Although life-support systems have been removed from brain-dead patients in South Africa with the consent of the relatives and without the court's consent, our courts decided in *Clarke v Hurst NO* 1992 (4) SA 630 (D) that nasogastric feeding of a patient who was in a 'permanent vegetative state' could be stopped at the request of his wife. The court said that although the patient was alive, there was no possibility of his emerging from his vegetative condition and the continual feeding would not serve the purpose of supporting human life as it is commonly known.]

Problem 3: If you were the judge, would you order, or refuse to order, treatment? *(Learner's Manual p 421)*

AIM: The object of this exercise is to give learners a chance to discuss the relationships between the individual, the family, the doctor and the state in deciding who has the right to make life-and-death decisions. Learners should argue the values or ethical conflicts that are present in each case. The following arguments for and against ordering treatment could be considered in each case.

PROCEDURE	TIME	
1. Divide the class of learners into small groups.	Group discussions:	10 min
2. Allocate one case to each group.	Report back:	20 min
3. Group discussions.	General discussion:	15 min
4. Report back.	**TOTAL:**	**45 min**
5. General discussion.		

1.   Arguments in favour of the court's ordering treatment in Ella's case: The state has an obligation to preserve the lives of its citizens and should take positive action to prevent people from killing

themselves or letting themselves die due to lack of medical treatment. Since life is sacred, no one, not even for religious reasons, has the right to decide that a person should be allowed to die. When a person decides to kill himself or herself, or another person, this should be regarded as suicide or murder, which should not be accepted by the state. Ella should not be allowed to kill herself.

Arguments against the court's ordering treatment in Ella's case: People have a constitutional right to practise their religion as they see fit. If Ella believes that she would be spiritually harmed if she had a blood transfusion, the state should not force her to have a blood transfusion. In addition, Ella's constitutional right to privacy gives her the power over her own body to decide what she wishes to do with it.

In real cases, the courts in the United States have ruled in favour of the person who does not wish to have a blood transfusion. It is likely that the courts in South Africa would decide the same way.

2. Arguments in favour of the court's ordering treatments of Manfred are similar to the arguments in Ella's case above. Here, however, they are stronger because allowing Manfred's parents to exercise their religious beliefs would result in the death of Manfred and would be against the Children's Act, which does not allow parents to refuse to consent to medical treatment of their children on religious grounds only.

The arguments against the court's ordering treatment are the same as in Ella's case above. In addition, parents usually have the right to determine what medical treatment their children should receive – but not if it is against the Children's Act.

3. Many physically handicapped people live productive lives even though they are confined to wheelchairs. It could be argued, therefore, that Dube is not acting rationally and that more efforts should be made to convince him that his life is not over. He should be provided with counselling concerning the positive aspects of his future life as a paraplegic.

It could, however, be argued that Dube's quality of life has been so severely changed that he should not be forced to stay on a respirator even if he might not be able to live without it. The court may agree with Dube if it is satisfied that he has made a rational decision. Many people might believe that his reasons are not valid, but generally, the courts will not force people to undergo medical treatment if they do not wish to have it.

4. The issue of who should decide whether a severely handicapped newborn child should undergo serious surgery is difficult. Does the court or the state have the power to force parents to consent to surgery on a newborn child? Who should make the decision?

The argument in favour of Tollie's father having the power to decide is that he is responsible for Tollie and for the costs of his care. He might refuse to allow surgery because he believes Tollie will not be able to live a decent life and because he will be in perpetual pain.

Others might argue that every child has a 'constitutional right to life', even if it is less than full. Not performing the surgery is like killing the child. The child's condition might improve after surgery.

It is likely that the court would appoint a person to look after Tollie's interests. The court, as the upper guardian, might decide to consent to the operation on behalf of Tollie. In emergency cases, the superintendent of a hospital may consent to treatment of a child; otherwise the Minister of Health may do so.

If the court orders treatment for Tollie, do you think that his father should still be held responsible for the financial costs of the treatment?

4.6.3 Funerals (Learner's Manual p 421)

Problem 4: Some questions on funerals (Learner's Manual p 423)

AIM: The object of this exercise is to make learners aware of the problems that might arise if somebody dies in a family. It is also designed to illustrate the costs involved in a funeral and how different religions and cultures have different traditions concerning the disposal of their dead.

PROCEDURE	TIME	
1. Divide the class into small groups.	Group discussions:	10 min
2. Have each group discuss one question.	Report back:	20 min
3. Report back.	General discussion:	5 min
4. General discussion.	**TOTAL:**	**35 min**

1. The answer to this question will depend upon whether or not learners have attended a funeral service. It also depends upon each learner's religious and family background. Learners should understand that it is important to know ahead of time what the wishes of deceased people are. Do they have a will? Have they told their close friends or relatives what they would like to happen should they die? Would they like a burial, cremation, or memorial service, or to donate their bodies to a hospital or research institution? Close relatives usually have the right to decide what should happen during a burial if nothing has been said in the deceased's will. The relatives also have to consider the expenses of the different types of funerals. Once a will has been found, the executor plays an important role in making decisions regarding the property of the dead person. If the deceased leaves sufficient money, the funeral could be paid for out of the estate (see *Learner's Manual* para 4.6.5.2).

2. A *funeral service* usually takes place where the body of the deceased person is present and shortly before it is buried.
   A *burial service* takes place at the graveside or the crematorium when relatives and friends take leave of the deceased person. Generally, at a *memorial service*, the body of the dead person is not present. Sometimes, however, it is present if the memorial service is held before the burial of the deceased person. This often happens where an important political person dies. It may sometimes also take place after the dead person has been cremated or the body has been buried.

3. The main costs involved in a funeral are those concerning: (a) embalming the body; (b) the price of the coffin; (c) the cost of a headstone or tombstone; (d) rent for the use of a funeral parlour; (e) storage costs if the body has to be stored for a period of time; (f) the cost of flowers; and (g) money for the hire of the hearse and motorcars for the mourners. In some communities, the family also has to pay for the hire of buses for, and the cost of feeding, the large numbers of mourners who might attend. Sometimes, these costs can be very high, and some people state in their wills that they do not want an expensive funeral. Some people also insist on being buried in a simple inexpensive pine coffin if they do not want to be cremated. Would learners want to have an expensive or inexpensive funeral? What about funerals for close relatives? Should they be expensive or inexpensive? Why?

4. The learners' answers will depend upon their religious and cultural beliefs. Learners of different

religious and cultural beliefs should be encouraged to share their funeral traditions with the other learners in the class. The educator could introduce the discussion by asking one of the learners to describe his or her community's attitude towards funerals. The educator could then ask the rest of the learners whether any of them belong to communities that have different ceremonies and, if so, what kind of services are performed.

Problem 5: Vuma is approached by a funeral society *(Learner's Manual p 424)*

AIM: The object of this exercise is to make learners aware of the problems that might arise if they are approached by a funeral or benefit society.

PROCEDURE ☰
1. Divide the class into small groups, with some preparing to play Vuma and others, Johannes.
2. Groups prepare role-plays.
3. Select two learners to role-play Vuma and Johannes.
4. Conduct role-play.
5. Debrief role-play and discuss.

TIME	⏱
Introduction:	5 min
Divide into small groups:	5 min
Small groups prepare role-plays:	10 min
Role-plays:	10 min
Debriefing and discussion:	15 min
TOTAL:	**45 min**

Vuma should be on his guard. Sometimes, salespeople from funeral or benefit societies misrepresent the benefits available to members. Vuma should not rely on the words of Johannes. He should ask to see a copy of the contract or membership agreement which lists the benefits of the scheme. Vuma is only 22 years old. He might find that if he pays R100 a month for 40 years he will only be entitled to funeral expenses of R5 000. This means that he would have paid R48 000 (R100 x 12 x 40) to receive a funeral 'benefit' of R5 000.

If Vuma were to die less than four years and two months after taking out the policy, he would benefit, since he would have contributed less than R5 000 assuming that it is possible to obtain a funeral for R5 000 in four years' time. If Vuma were to die after having contributed to the society for more than four years and two months, each additional payment until his date of death will be profit for the society. The longer Vuma lives, the less likely it is that he will obtain a funeral for only R5 000. It might be better for Vuma to put his money into a special savings account. Vuma should also find out whether the contract states that the R100-a-month insurance payment will cover his wife and children if he marries. Vuma would be wise to enquire about the reputation of the funeral society to ensure that it is not a 'fly-by-night' operation.

The above aspects should be canvassed by the learners playing the roles of Vuma and Johannes.

4.6.4 Wills and inheritances *(Learner's Manual p 424)*

Problem 6: People dying without wills: Who will inherit? *(Learner's Manual p 426)*

AIM: The object of this exercise is to show learners how the law of 'intestate succession' is applied.

<table>
<tr><td>

PROCEDURE

1. Divide the class of learners into small groups.
2. Ask each group to discuss one question.
3. Report back.
4. General discussion.

</td><td>

TIME

Group discussions:	10 min
Report back:	15 min
General discussion:	10 min
TOTAL:	**35 min**

</td></tr>
</table>

1. Because Alan died, leaving a wife and two children, rule 2 in the *Learner's Manual* para 4.6.4.2 applies. Maureen would be entitled to R125 000 or the same share as Sally and Alfred, whichever is the larger amount. If Maureen, Sally and Alfred shared the R600 000, they would each receive one third of R600 000; ie, R200 000. Because R200 000 is more than R125 000, Maureen is entitled to R200 000. Sally and Alfred would share the remaining R400 000 between them. Therefore, Sally and Alfred will each receive R200 000.

2. Because Vish dies after his wife, and leaves children and two grandchildren of his deceased daughter, Fariah, rule 3 in the *Learner's Manual* para 4.6.4.2 applies. Narain, Tony, Karthy and Fariah (if she had been alive) would each have received a quarter of the R90 000; ie R22 500. However, because Fariah is dead, Sarah and Shaida will share her R22 500 and each will receive R11 250. Therefore, Narain, Tony and Karthy each receive R22 500, and Sarah and Shaida R11 250 each.

3. In the past, since Thembu and Bongile were married in a customary union, his eldest son, Proteus, would take over as head of the house. Proteus would be responsible for administering the property worth R180 000. However, after the case of *Bhe v The Magistrate* rule 2 in the *Learner's Manual* para 4.6.4.2 applies and Bongile is entitled to R125 000 or a child's share, whichever is more. Therefore she will receive R125 000, and the balance of R55 000 will be shared between the three sons.

4. Because Roelof died without a wife, children or parents, rule 6 in the *Learner's Manual* para 4.6.4.2 applies. Half his property will go to the children and descendants of his father and the other half to those of his mother. Thus, R45 000 will go to his father's side and R45 000 to his mother's side.

    His brothers, Tjaart and Braam, will each receive R22 500 from the father's side (half of R45 000); while Maria, Tjaart and Braam will each receive R15 000 from the mother's side (one-third of R45 000). Therefore Tjaart and Braam will each receive R22 500 + R15 000 = R37 500, and Maria will receive R15 000.

Problem 7: Who inherits from Michael Jack?   *(Learner's Manual p 427)*

AIM: The object of this exercise is to show learners how a will is interpreted.

<table>
<tr><td>

PROCEDURE

1. Introduce the exercise.
2. Divide the learners into small groups.
3. Ask each group to discuss all the questions.
4. Report back.
5. General discussion.

</td><td>

TIME

Introduce exercise:	5 min
Group discussions:	15 min
Report back:	15 min
General discussion:	10 min
TOTAL:	**45 min**

</td></tr>
</table>

1. If Michael dies the day after he makes the will, and his nephew, James Jack, has not completed his BCom degree, James will not inherit the R10 000 (clause 3). The whole of Michael's estate will go to his wife, Jane Jack (clause 4).

2. If Michael and Jane are both killed in a car accident, their son, Paul, will inherit their entire estate (clause 4) – unless Michael's nephew, James, has completed his BCom degree at the University of KwaZulu-Natal by the date of Michael's death. If James has completed his degree by that date, he will inherit R10 000 (clause 3) and Paul will inherit the rest of the estate (clause 4).

3. Michael's nephew, James will only inherit under Michael's will if he completes a BCom degree at the University of Natal (now University of KwaZulu-Natal) in Durban, before Michael dies (clause 3). If he has not completed the degree before Michael dies, the whole of Michael's estate will go to his wife, Jane (clause 4), if she is still alive, or if she is also dead, to his son, Paul (clause 4).

4. If Michael and his wife both die in an accident, Michael's brother, Frederick Jack, becomes guardian of Michael's son, Paul, if he is a minor and will take care of him (clause 5).

5. A will is necessary because the Wills Act of 1953 states that a person cannot make a valid will unless certain formalities are satisfied. The will must be signed by the person making the will and by at least two witnesses, on every page of the will, in each other's presence. They must all sign the last page of the will.

Problem 8: Have you made a will?

(Learner's Manual p 429)

AIM: The object of this exercise is to make learners aware of how important it is for them to make wills.

PROCEDURE		TIME	
1. Divide the class of learners into small groups.		Group discussions:	10 min
2. Each group is to discuss one question.		Report back:	20 min
3. Report back.		Clarification and discussion:	15 min
4. Clarification of answers and discussion.		**TOTAL:**	**45 min**

1. This question is aimed at helping learners understand that, if they die without a will (intestate), the law will decide who will receive their property according to the rules set out in the *Learner's Manual* para 4.6.4.2.

2. It is important to make a will as soon as people have any property they wish to give to certain individuals. The same applies if people have property they do not wish to give to certain people. If people are not mentioned in a will they will not inherit. A person who is 16 years of age or more is entitled to make a will.

3. Most people would probably agree that it is beneficial to make a will because: (a) people will know what the dead person wishes to do with his or her property; and (b) the dead person's estate will be wound up sooner if a particular person is nominated as an executor.
   If no will is made, there are two disadvantages: (a) it takes much longer to wind up the estate; and (b) people who the deceased might not want to inherit from the estate may be able to do so in terms of the laws affecting people who die without a will (see the *Learner's Manual* para 4.6.4.2).

4. It is usually useful to consult an attorney when making a will – especially if the will is likely to be complicated. Attorneys are able to foresee the types of problems that may arise and provide safeguards against them. Attorneys also try to work out exactly what their clients want (eg, who benefits if one of the heirs dies before the person making the will). Attorneys can also be appointed as executors to wind up the estate. Attorneys will also make sure that all the formalities in the Wills Act have been complied with. In the case of very simple wills (eg, a husband leaving everything to his wife or children), it is possible to buy a 'will form' from a stationery shop. If this is done, however, the person making the will must ensure that the proper formalities in the Wills Act are followed and that the will says exactly what he or she wants. It is generally safer to obtain legal advice when making a will.

4.6.5   Winding up a dead person's estate   *(Learner's Manual p 429)*

Problem 9: If you were named executor   *(Learner's Manual p 431)*

AIM: The object of this exercise is to make learners aware of what an executor or executrix (a female executor) is required to do.

PROCEDURE
1. Divide the class of learners into small groups.
2. Ask each group to discuss the question.
3. Report back.
4. General discussion.

TIME	
Group discussions:	15 min
Report back:	15 min
General discussion:	10 min
TOTAL:	**40 min**

Learners can decide for themselves if they think that they could carry out the duties of an executor. They can also discuss whether or not they think that they would need a lawyer to assist them.

It is important for learners to realise what the duties of an executor are (see the *Learner's Manual* para 4.6.5.2) because they might one day be called upon to perform such duties or to assist relatives in performing them. They should discuss situations where a lawyer will be needed; for example, if there are complicated court procedures, or income tax questions, intricate property to be distributed, or a complex will. Another issue that the educator might wish to discuss with the class is the cost of funeral and burial services.

Further reading

4.1 The family and marriage

Cronje DSP & Heaton J *South African Family Law* 3 ed (2010)

Cronje DSP & Heaton J *Casebook on South African Family Law* 3ed (2010)

Skelton A & Carnelley M (eds) *Family Law in South Africa* (2010)

Van Heerden B (ed) *Schafer's Family Law Service* (loose-leaf)

Civil Union Act 17 of 2006

Marriage Act 25 of 1961

Recognition of Customary Marriages Act 120 of 1998

Daniels v Campbell NO 2004 (5) SA 331 (CC) – limited recognition of Muslim marriages: Maintenance of Surviving Spouses Act and Intestate Succession Act also apply to monogamous Muslim marriages.

Du Plessis v Road Accident Fund 2004 (1) SA 359 (SCA) 12 – common-law right of claim for loss of support extended to same-sex couples in a permanent life partnership.

Fourie v Minister of Home Affairs 2005 (3) SA 429 (SCA) and *Minister of Home Affairs v Fourie* 2006 (1) SA 524 (CC) – common-law definition of marriage as limited to heterosexual persons declared unconstitutional – same-sex partners allowed to marry.

Govender v Ragavayah 2009 (3) SA 178 (D) – limited recognition of Hindu monogamous marriages: Intestate Succession Act was extended to monogamous Hindu marriage.

Hassam v Jacobs NO 2009 (5) SA 572 (CC) – limited recognition of Muslim marriages: inheritance rights of wives in terms of Intestate Succession Act extended to include polygamous wives.

Khan v Khan 2005 (2) SA 272 (T) – limited recognition of Muslim polygamous marriages: enforcement mechanisms of the Maintenance Act extended to wives in polygamous Muslim marriage.

Moola v Aulsebrook NO 1983 (1) SA 687 (N) – a marriage that has not been solemnised by a competent marriage officer may be putative.

Ryland v Edros 1997 (2) SA 690 (C) – limited recognition of Muslim marriage – courts may recognise and enforce between the parties the contractual obligations that flowed from monogamous Muslim marriage.

Singh v Ramparsad 2007 (3) SA 445 (D) – non-recognition of Hindu marriages: courts cannot pronounce parties divorced if they elected to practice a faith that did not allow divorce.

Smith v Smith 1948(4) SA 61 (N) – voidable marriages: marriage set aside after the wife indicated that she had been forced into marriage.

4.2 Husbands and wives and civil union partners

Cronje DSP & Heaton J *South African Family Law* 3 ed (2010)

Hahlo HR *The South African Law of Husband and Wife* 5 ed (1985)

Skelton A & Carnelley M (eds) *Family Law in South Africa* (2010)

Van Zyl L *Handbook of the South African Law of Maintenance* 3 ed (2010)

Constitution of the Republic of South Africa, 1996

Domestic Violence Act 116 of 1998

Maintenance Act 99 of 1998

Marriage Act 25 of 1961

Marriage and Matrimonial Property Law Amendment Act 3 of 1988

Matrimonial Property Act 88 of 1984

Wills Act 7 of 1953

Daniels v Campbell NO 2004 (5) SA 331 (CC) – limited recognition of Muslim marriages: Maintenance of Surviving Spouses Act and Intestate Succession Act also apply to monogamous Muslim marriages.

Du Plessis v Road Accident Fund 2004 (SA 359 (SCA) 12 – common-law right of claim for loss of support extended to same-sex couples in a permanent life partnership.

Govender v Ragavayah 2009 (3) SA 178 (D) – limited recognition of Hindu monogamous marriages: Intestate Succession Act extended to monogamous Hindu marriage.

Gumede v President of the Republic of South Africa 2009 (3) SA 152 (CC) – monogamous customary marriage is regarded as marriage in community of property.

Reloomel v Ramsey 1920 TPD 371 – necessaries of a household depend on the financial position, means and social status of the spouses or the family.

Ryland v Edros 1997 (2) SA 690 (C) – limited recognition of Muslim marriage – courts may recognise and enforce between the parties the contractual obligations that flowed from monogamous Muslim marriage.

Van der Merwe v Road Accident Fund 2006 (4) SA 230 (CC) – a spouse may recover from his or her spouse damages in respect of bodily injuries that are attributable to the negligence of the spouse).

4.3 Parents and children

Boezaart T (ed) *Child Law in South Africa* (2009)

Bosman-Sadie H & Corrie L A *Practical Approach to the Children's Act* (2010)

Cronje DSP & Heaton J *The South African Law of Persons* 3 ed (2008)

Skelton A & Carnelley M (eds) *Family Law in South Africa* (2010)

Spiro E Law *of Parent and Child* 4 ed (1985)

Children's Act 38 of 2005

Choice on Termination of Pregnancy Act 92 of 1996

Constitution of the Republic of South Africa, 1996

Domestic Violence Act 116 of 1998

Christian Lawyers Association of South Africa v The Minister of Health 2005 (1) SA 509 (T); 2004 (4) All SA 31 (T) – minors' ability to consent to termination of pregnancy independently.

F v F 2006 (3) SA 42 (SCA) – children's rights are paramount: relocation of one parent against the best interests of the child.

Fish Hoek Primary School v WG 2010 (2) SA 141 (SCA) – both biological parents of a child are liable for payment of school fees of a child even if the parents were never married, and even if the non-custodial parent did not enrol the child at the school.

HG v CG 2010 (3) SA 352 (ECP) – children have a right to participate in all decisions made about them, taking into account their age and maturity.

J v Director General, Department of Home Affairs 2003 (5) SA 621 (CC) – a child born to a married couple as a result of artificial fertilisation must be regarded as the child of those spouses.

J v J 2008 (6) SA 30 (C) – co-holders of parental rights and responsibilities can make decisions independently of each other.

McCall v McCall 1994 (3) SA 201 (C) – the court prescribed a list of factors that must be taken into account when determining the best interests of the child.

Petersen v Maintenance Officer, Simon's Town Maintenance Court 2004 (2) SA 56 (C) – the court developed the common law to allow extramarital child's claim against paternal grandparents.

S v M (Centre for Child Law as Amicus Curiae) 2008 (3) SA 232 (CC) – best interests of the child can be limited and cannot assume dominance over other constitutional rights.

4.4 Foster care and adoption

Bosman-Sadie H & Corrie L A *Practical Approach to the Children's Act* (2010)

Cronje DSP & Heaton J *South African Family Law* 3 ed 2010

Children's Act 38 of 2005

Wills Act 7 of 1953

AS v Vorster NO and Others 2009 (4) SA 108 (SE) – rescission of adoption order after the mother withdrew consent for the adoption of her baby.

Bester en 'n Ander v Die Meester 1985 (4) SA 70 (T) – adoptive parents included in the term 'natural parents' for the purposes of Administration of Estates Act.

Board of Executors v Vitt and Others 1989 (4) SA 480 (C) – adopted child should be included in the term 'lawful issue' in his adoptive father's will.

C and Another v Commissioner of Child Welfare, Wynberg 1970 (2) SA 76 (C) – matching language, culture and religion are requirements in foster care orders as against adoption orders.

4.5 Family problems: Divorce and maintenance

Bosman-Sadie H & Corrie L A *Practical Approach to the Children's Act* (2010)

Van Zyl L A *Handbook on South African Law of Maintenance* 3 ed (2005)

Cronje DSP & Heaton J South *African Family Law* 3 ed (2010)

Cronje DSP & Heaton J *Casebook on South African Family Law* 3 ed (2010)

Skelton A & Carnelley M *Family Law in South Africa* (2010)

Van Heerden B (ed) *Schafer's Family Law Service* (loose-leaf)

Children's Act 38 of 2005

Divorce Act 70 of 1979

Maintenance Act 99 of 1998

Marriage and Matrimonial Property Law Amendment Act 3 of 1988

Matrimonial Property Act 88 of 1984

Frankel's Estate v The Master 1950 (1) SA 220 (A) – the law of the place where the husband was domiciled at the time of marriage determines the matrimonial property system.

Mngadi v Beacon Sweets & Chocolate Provident Fund 2003 (2) All SA 279 (D) – failure to pay maintenance: court ordered provident fund to retain lump sum withdrawal benefit to secure future children's maintenance.

Reyneke v Reyneke 1990 (3) SA 927 (E) – courts can only make maintenance order if the person against whom it is made is able to pay it.

Schneider-Waterberg v Schneider-Waterberg (2009) JOL 24515 (WCC) – divorce action must be instituted in a court in whose jurisdiction one or both of the parties are domiciled on the date on which the action was lodged.

Schwartz v Schwartz 1984 (4) SA 467 (A) – courts have no discretion not to grant divorce once it has been proved that marriage has broken down irretrievably.

Singh v Ramparsad 2007 (3) SA 445 (D) – non-recognition of Hindu marriages: it is not for the courts to pronounce parties divorced if they elected to practice a faith that did not allow divorce.

Wijker v Wijker 1993 (4) SA 720 (A) – fault principle remains one of the elements that plays a role in determining the patrimonial consequences of divorce.

4.6 Death and the law

Jamneck J & Rautenbach C (eds) *The Law of Succession in South Africa* (2009)

Skelton A & Carnelley M (eds) *Family Law in South Africa* (2010)

Administration of Estates Act 66 of 1965

Constitution of the Republic of South Africa, 1996

Intestate Succession Act 81 of 1987

Maintenance of Surviving Spouses Act 27 of 1990

Wills Act 7 of 1953

Karen Quinlan 355 A 2d 647 (NJ 1976)

Clarke v Hurst NO 1992 (4) SA 630 (D)

Bhe v Magistrate, Khayelitsha 2005 (1) SA 580 (CC) – females' capacity to inherit: Black Administration Act and the customary rule of male primogeniture were declared unconstitutional and the Intestate Succession Act was extended to customary law of intestate succession.

Daniels v Campbell 2004 (5) SA 331 (CC) – the court extended application of the Intestate Succession Act to spouses in Muslim and Hindu marriages.

Gumede v President of the Republic of South Africa 2009 (3) SA 152 (CC); 2009 (3) BCLR 24 (CC) – customary law of succession: the KwaZulu Act on the Code of Zulu law and the Natal Code of Zulu Law were declared unconstitutional insofar as they afford full ownership of property during the marriage to the head of the family only.

Harris v Assumed Administrator, Estate MacGregor 1987 (3) SA 563 (A) – intestate succession: where a deceased dies without having made a will or without leaving a valid will, his or her intestate estate vests on the date of his or her death.

In re Leedham 1901 (18) SC 450 – the deceased's intention to provide for the devolution of his estate was sufficient regardless of whether he intended that the particular document should be his will.

Kidwell v The Master 1983 (1) SA 509 (E) – formalities: a nine centimetre gap between the end of the writing and the testator's signature was held not to be as close as reasonably possible to the concluding words of the will and therefore made the will invalid.

Sim v The Master 1913 CPD 187 – formalities: an unsigned document left by the testator which provided for several charitable bequests was not a valid charitable will.

Spies NO v Smith 1957 (1) SA 539 (A) – where it can be proved that the testator made a will as a result of coercion, fraud, or undue influence, such a will is invalid because it expresses someone else's will.

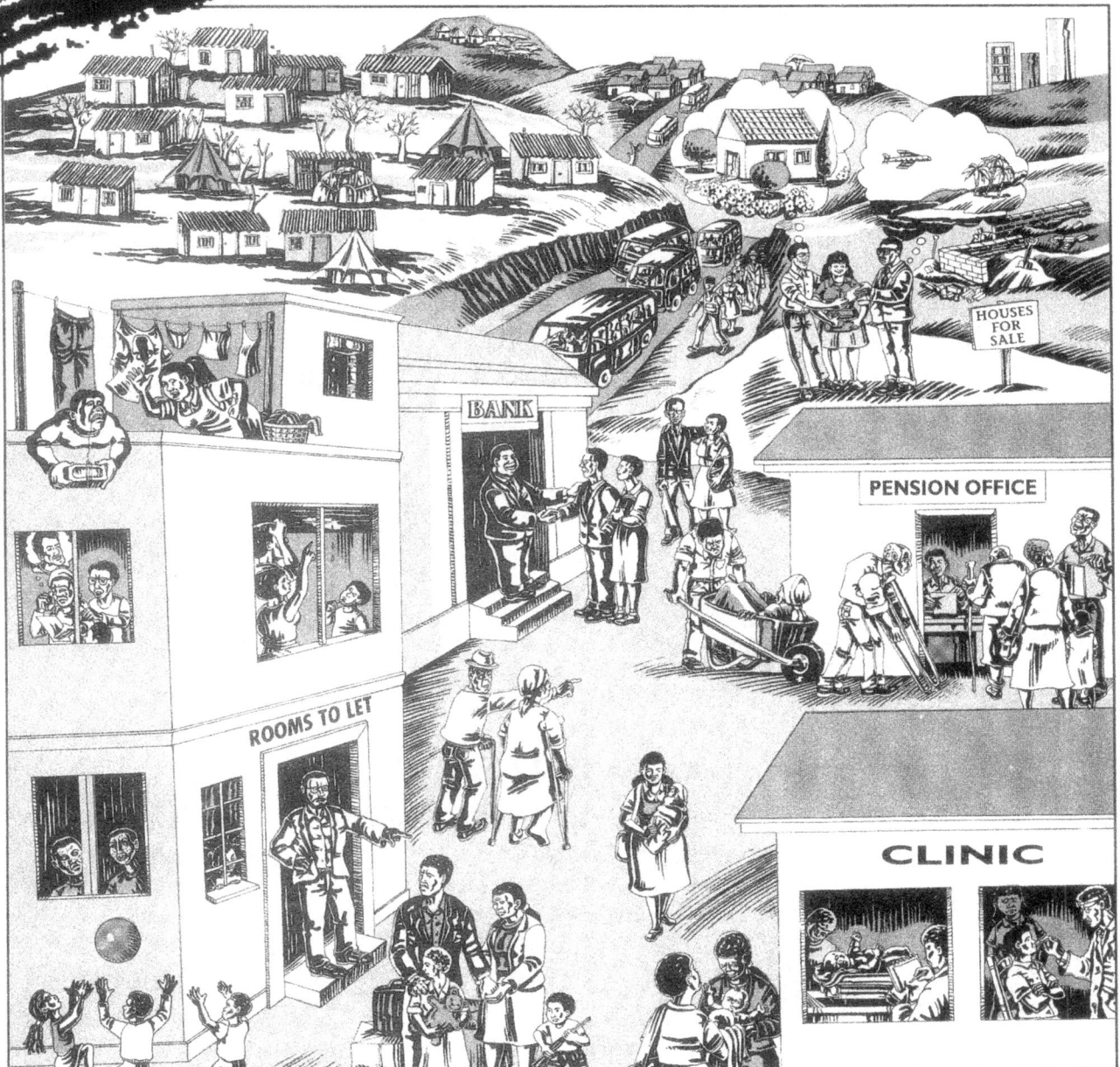

Street law

5. Socio-economic Rights

CONTENTS

PART FIVE

Socio-economic rights

5.1 Socio-economic rights

Outcomes

After completion of this section learners will be able to:

1. Explain the importance of socio-economic rights.

Assessment criteria

1. The meaning of socio-economic rights and their relationship to the Constitution is explained.
2. A distinction is made between socio-economic rights and civil and political rights.
3. A decision is taken on whether socio-economic rights should be enforceable by the courts.
4. A set of facts is examined and a decision is made on the duties of the state towards certain people regarding socio-economic rights.
5. Agencies are identified where people whose socio-economic rights have been violated can seek help.
6. A set of facts is examined and a decision is made on whether the government is entitled to close a school.

5.1.2 Which socio-economic rights are included in the Constitution? *(Learner's Manual p 445)*

Problem 1: Some questions on socio-economic rights *(Learner's Manual p 445)*

AIM: The aim of this exercise is for learners to think about and discuss the issues that often arise concerning the enforcement of socio-economic rights as opposed to those that arise in respect of civil and political rights.

PROCEDURE
1. Introduction.
2. Divide learners into small groups and allocate one question to each group.
3. Report back.
4. Discussion and summary

TIME	
Introduction:	5 min
Group discussions:	10 min
Report back:	10 min
Summary and discussion:	10 min
TOTAL:	**35 min**

1. Learners in favour of the enforceability of socio-economic rights could argue that:
   (a) No one category of rights is more important than any other. Social and economic rights are as important as civil and political rights. Both categories of rights are interdependent, indivisible and mutually reinforcing. To say that socio-economic rights should not be enforceable by the courts would suggest that these rights are less important than civil and political rights.

(b) Socio-economic rights play an important role in improving the lives of people. They address the real-life socio-economic experiences of people, especially the poor. They offer resources and opportunities to assist people to lead a dignified life – social benefits that no other category of rights can address.

(c) The enforceability of socio-economic rights raises as many difficult budgetary issues as civil and political rights. For example, to realise the right to vote (a political right), the state must set up and finance an electoral commission. Similarly, in order to ensure access to a fair trial, the state must provide legal representation to an accused who cannot afford to pay for a lawyer.

Learners against the enforceability of socio-economic rights could argue that:

(a) Civil and political rights are more important than socio-economic rights because they deal with issues that are inherently important for human beings. Socio-economic rights reflect the ideals of society and are not human rights worthy of enforcement in the courts.

(b) Socio-economic rights pose problems regarding the principle of separation of powers because judges then deal with matters of budgetary allocation and resource prioritisation. These matters are usually reserved for the executive (which is politically elected) and not judges (who are appointed).

(c) Socio-economic rights are dependent on huge financial and other resources being realised. They cannot be realised immediately like civil and political rights. Not all states have the necessary resources to give effect to these rights. Therefore, the courts may impose an unreasonable burden on the state to realise these rights when it does have the capacity to do so.

2. Examples of the interdependence of human rights are:

(a) the right to human dignity is violated if people suffer from starvation or hunger, or have no shelter or clothing; and

(b) a person's right to life is threatened if he or she does not have food or access to health care services.

Learners can suggest others.

Problem 2: Should there be a right to clothing? *(Learner's Manual p 445)*

AIM: The purpose of this exercise is to get the learners thinking about whether there should be a right to clothing at state expense.

PROCEDURE	TIME	
1. Introduction.	Introduction:	5 min
2. Get learners to take a stand 'In favour', 'Against' or 'Undecided'.	Take a stand:	20 min
	General discussion:	5 min
3. Learners present their arguments.	**TOTAL:**	**30 min**
4. General discussion.		

1. Learners in favour of the inclusion of a right to clothing in the Constitution could say that the right to clothing would enable people who have no clothes or blankets to protect themselves

from cold to claim such protection from the state. The inclusion of this right would ensure that poor people were not exposed to health risks. Also, the right to clothing cannot be separated from human dignity. Clothing one's body is part of leading a dignified life. If people cannot afford to clothe themselves, the state should assist them through its welfare system.

2. Learners against the violation of a right to clothing could argue that it would be unreasonable to expect the state to clothe or provide blankets to everyone who needs them. It cannot be obliged to do so. People have the responsibility to clothe themselves and their families. Parents and guardians have a legal duty to clothe their children. If they are unable to do so, they may get help from the state or other stakeholders under humanitarian law, not human rights. Many organisations provide blankets and clothes to street communities. Individuals have a moral obligation to help others. The state should, at the very least, encourage people to do so.

3. Learners who are undecided should give their reasons for being so.
   See above paras G16 and 17 for how to use 'Take a stand' and the PRES formula for this exercise.

5.1.3 What are the government's duties in respect of socio-economic rights? *(Learner's Manual p 445)*

Problem 3: Testimony of Emily Mphanya at the Poverty Hearings in the North West Province *(Learner's Manual p 447)*

AIM: This exercise is aimed at providing an opportunity for learners to analyse a set of facts and decide whether the government is obliged to provide a widow with social assistance.

PROCEDURE		TIME	
1. Introduction.		Introduction:	5 min
2. Divide the class of learners into small groups.		Group discussions:	10 min
3. Get each group to discuss one question.		Report back:	10 min
4. Report back.		General discussion:	10 min
5. General discussion.		**TOTAL:**	**35 min**

1. Socio-economic rights involved in this case study are: (a) the right of access to social security, including social assistance; (b) the right of access to sufficient food and water; (c) the right to life and human dignity; and (d) the right of access to health care services.

2. The state has a duty to look after vulnerable people by protecting and fulfilling their rights such as providing housing, health care, food, water and social security within its available resources. Vulnerable people include widows, orphans, the elderly, the unemployed, etc.

5.1.6 Can socio-economic rights be limited? *(Learner's Manual p 448)*

Problem 4: Socio-economic rights and limited resources *(Learner's Manual p 449)*

AIM: The aim of this exercise is to make learners think critically about how the government ought to prioritise expenditure within its limited resources.

1. Introduction.
2. Divide the class of learners into two large groups – each group to discuss one question.
3. Subdivide large groups into smaller groups to argue for or against the proposition in their question.
4. Groups preparing for question 1 give arguments for and against.
5. Groups preparing for question 2 give arguments for and against.
6. Judges for question 2 give their judgments.
7. General discussion.

TIME ⊙

Introduction:	5 min
Preparation of arguments:	15 min
Presentation of arguments:	20 min
Judges give judgements:	10 min
General discussion:	10 min
TOTAL:	**60 min**

1. Social assistance for non-nationals:

   Arguments that the group representing non-nationals could make:

   (a) Non-nationals (not permanent residents) are human beings like anyone else. Our Constitution says that everyone has the right to social security, including social assistance. This right, as stated in the Constitution, does not exclude anyone, therefore the state is obliged to ensure access to social assistance for all people within its territory.

   (b) Non-nationals are a vulnerable group of people. Most of them do not have the means to buy food and other basic necessities. They might end up begging for these or committing crimes in order to survive. They do not get employed for various reasons, or if they are employed, they are often exploited and given very low wages. They often do not even have the legal documents that will enable them to get social welfare assistance.

   (c) The state is obliged by international law to provide material and financial assistance to everyone within its borders who needs such help, especially refugees and asylum seekers. The state has an obligation to develop policies or programmes that cater for the needs of this group. If it fails because of limited resources, it should demonstrate that it has exhausted all available avenues to help them.

   Arguments that the group representing the Department of Social Development could make:

   (a) The Constitution protects the rights of citizens of South Africa, not non-nationals. Therefore, the state is not constitutionally obliged to provide social assistance to this group of people.

   (b) Even if they are obliged to do so by international law or the Constitution, the state maintains that the rights of South African citizens should be protected first, taking into account the country's limited resources. Thereafter, they could consider whether resources were available to cover the needs of non-nationals.

   (c) The socio-economic difficulties facing most non-nationals are no worse than those facing South African citizens, for whom the department is primarily responsible.

2. The effects of the arms deal on the education system:

   Arguments by lawyers for the parents against the government choosing to strengthen the defence system at the expense of children's right to education could include:

   (a) The country is not threatened by war. Therefore, arms are not needed as a matter of urgency.

   (b) The country needs to invest in the education of its children for the future of the nation. To postpone or deny children their right to education would be to deny them a future.

(c)   Not all children will have the option of going to another school. Some children, whose parents cannot afford transport fees, might be forced to drop out of school.

Arguments by lawyers for the government justifying the government choosing to strengthen its defence system at the expense of children's rights to education could include:

(a)   The strengthening of the defence system is a matter of national concern. Wars against a country can never be predicted. In case it happens, the Department of Defence must be prepared to protect the nation. The country must also provide peace-keeping forces for Africa in terms of its international obligations.

(b)   While education is also important for children, the effect of cutting school budgets is not as harmful as the risks of having a defenceless nation. Affected children have the option of going to other schools, whereas the nation has no other way of protecting itself against the enemy.

The judges must listen to the arguments and might decide which they find most persuasive. They should then give their judgments with reasons.

5.2 Education rights

Outcomes

After completion of this section learners will be able to:

1.   Explain the meaning of education rights and the duties of the state in respect of them.

Assessment criteria

1.   Different elements of education rights are identified.

2.   A set of facts is examined and a decision made on whether the government is fulfilling its duty regarding school facilities.

3.   A decision is taken on the impact a failure by the government to deliver textbooks and workbooks is likely to have on learners.

4.   A decision is taken on whether inequalities in the educational system can be addressed by abolishing 'feeder zones' for schools.

5.   A set of facts is given and a decision taken on whether certain learners may be turned away from school.

6.   The procedure for applying for exemption from paying school fees is explained.

7.   A set of facts is examined and a decision made on whether learners may be taught in the language of their choice.

5.2.1   What are education rights?   *(Learner's Manual p 450)*

Problem 1: Case study: The primary school where learners bring their own chairs   *(Learner's Manual p 450)*

AIM: The aim of this exercise is to provide learners with a set of facts which require them to think about a situation in a rural school and to relate it to their own schools.

PROCEDURE	TIME	
1. Introduction.	Introduction	5 min
2. Divide learners into small groups.	Group discussions:	10 min
3. Each group to discuss one question.	Reports back:	10 min
4. Report back.	Discussion and summary:	10 min
5. General discussion.	**TOTAL:**	**35 min**

1.   Learners who think that the Eastern Cape Department of Education is not providing the children of Qunu with their right to basic education could argue that the Department has (a) not built enough classrooms; (b) not provided enough desks and chairs; (c) allowed two grades to be taught at the same time; (d) not given the principal an office; and (d) not provided a staffroom

or store room. They could further argue that it should not be necessary for people from foreign countries to provide school facilities which the government should pay for from taxpayers' money.

Learners who think that the Department is providing basic education could argue that the Department has (a) paid for the teachers; (b) built classrooms; and (c) continues to maintain the school building. Because Qunu is in a remote rural area and the government has a shortage of resources rural schools cannot expect to have the same facilities as those in the big towns.

2. Learners will decide for themselves whether they think that their school experiences similar problems to those at the primary school.

3. Most learners would probably argue that it is the duty of the government, not foreign funders, to fix the problems at schools like the primary school. However, some learners may argue that South Africa is a developing country with limited resources and that it is reasonable for foreign donors to assist.

4. Learners can decide for themselves whether they think that South Africa needs more schools and better facilities. They can be referred to the information in the box in para 5.2.2.2 to give them some background.

5. Learners can decide for themselves whether they think that their school has enough resources and facilities to enable them to learn.

6. Learners can report whether their community protects their school against vandalism and theft.

Problem 2: How does the failure to deliver textbooks and workbooks affect learners? *(Learner's Manual p 451)*

AIM: The object of this exercise is to get the learners to think about how the failure to deliver text books and work books would affect them.

PROCEDURE ⬛		TIME 🕐	
1. Introduction.		Introduction	5 min
2. Divide learners into small groups.		Group discussions:	10 min
3. Each group to discuss the question.		Reports back:	10 min
4. Report back.		Discussion and summary:	5 min
5. General discussion.		**TOTAL:**	**30 min**

Learners will have their own ideas about how the failure to deliver textbooks and workbooks will affect them, depending on when the books are delivered.

5.2.2 What does it mean to have a right to education? *(Learner's Manual p 451)*

Problem 3: Should 'feeder zones' be abolished or kept? *(Learner's Manual p 452)*

AIM: The object of this exercise is to get the learners to think about what might happen if 'feeder zones' are abolished or kept.

PROCEDURE		TIME	
1. Introduction.		Introduction	5 min
2. Divide learners into small groups.		Group discussions:	10 min
3. Each group to discuss one question.		Reports back:	10 min
4. Report back.		Discussion and summary:	5 min
5. General discussion.		**TOTAL:**	**30 min**

1. Arguments in favour of 'feeder zones' are that (a) they preserve the character of local communities; (b) they accommodate learners who live close to the schools; (c) they allow the school to reflect the racial make-up of the community; and (d) they make it easy to arrange after-hours activities (eg sport for learners who live far away from the school).

2. Arguments against 'feeder zones' are that they (a) prevent learners from poor schools from attending better schools; (b) prevent diversity in schools as learners only come from the local community; (c) are used to keep out students from different cultures; and (d) prevent learners from disadvantaged communities from getting better job opportunities once they leave school.

3. Learners can decide for themselves, if they were the MEC for Education, whether they would try to end the inequalities in schools by abolishing 'feeder zones'.

Problem 4: How does your school measure up? *(Learner's Manual p 453)*

AIM: The object of this exercise is to get the learners to think about how their school measures up to the findings in the Race Relations Survey in the box in para 5.2.2.2.

PROCEDURE		TIME	
1. Introduction.		Introduction:	5 min
2. Questions and answers to encourage learners to share their experiences.		Question and answer:	35 min
		General discussion:	5 min
3. General discussion.		**TOTAL:**	**45 min**

Learners can decide for themselves how they think that their school measures up to the conditions mentioned in the box in para 5.2.2.2.

Problem 5: Can the learners be turned away from school? *(Learner's Manual p 453)*

AIM: The object of this exercise is to get the learners to analyse a set of facts and decide whether the learners should have been turned away from school.

PROCEDURE		TIME	
1. Introduction.		Introduction:	5 min
2. Divide the class of learners into small groups.		Group discussions:	10 min
3. Give each group two questions to discuss.		Report back:	10 min
4. Report back.		Debriefing:	5 min
5. Summarise responses.		**TOTAL:**	**30 min**
6. General discussion.			

The Constitution provides a right to basic education and says that no one can be unfairly discriminated against on any grounds including race, sex, gender, sexual orientation, etc. In addition, the Promotion of Equality and Prohibition of Unfair Discrimination Act (Equality Act) says that no one can be discriminated against on the basis of his or her socio-economic status (eg indigent or HIV/AIDS-positive). The state has a duty to protect people against unfair discrimination. The Department of Education cannot develop policies that violate this right.

Learners can consider each scenario and decide whether or not they think that the exclusion of the learners from school was fair or unfair.

The instructor should be aware that everyone on the list should be protected by the state against discrimination, as they fall under the categories of persons who are protected by the legislation referred to below in brackets:

1. HIV/AIDS (Equality Act);
2. gender or sex (Constitution);
3. poor socio-economic status (Equality Act);
4. poor socio-economic status (Equality Act);
5. race (Constitution);
6. sexual orientation (Constitution);
7. poor socio-economic status (Equality Act);
8. poor socio-economic status (Equality Act);
9. poor socio-economic status (Equality Act); and
10. poor socio-economic status (Equality Act).

Problem 6: Appealing against a decision not to grant an exemption from school fees
(Learner's Manual p 455)

AIM: The aim of the exercise is to allow learners an opportunity to write a letter of appeal to a provincial Head of Department concerning a refusal to grant exemption from school fees by a school governing body.

PROCEDURE	TIME	
1. Introduction.	Introduction:	5 min
2. Divide the class of learners into small groups (preferably no more than three persons per group).	Group discussions:	15 min
3. Give clear instructions on what should be included in the letter.	Reading letters:	10 min
4. Read some of the letters.	Open discussion:	5 min
5. General discussion.	**TOTAL:**	**35 min**

The letter should:
1. set out the facts of what happened (eg where the application was made and the economic status of the family);
2. state the decision of the school governing body that is being appealed against;
3. state whether other steps were taken to resolve the issue before it was brought to the attention of the Head of Department;
4. set out the reasons for appealing against the decision; and
5. propose what you would like to see happening in this case.

Problem 7: Was the learner entitled to be taught in the language of her choice?

(Learner's Manual p 457)

AIM: The object of the exercise is for learners to think about when school children should be entitled to be taught in the language of their choice.

PROCEDURE	TIME	
1. Introduction.	Introduction:	5 min
2. Divide learners into three groups:	Preparations for arguments:	10 min
For Question 1: (a) Lebo's parents; (b) parents of Afrikaans-speaking learners; and (c) the school governing body.	Presentation of arguments:	15 min
For Question 2: (a) Tumi's parents; (b) parents of Zulu-speaking learners; and (c) the school governing body.	Decision by school governing body:	5 min
3. Each group (except group (c)) prepares arguments on the given set of facts. Group (c) thinks about the issues.	Debrief:	10 min
4. Give group (c) some simple procedures for conducting a hearing (eg 5 minutes each to present arguments; 5 minutes for questions and clarifying issues; 5 minutes for giving the decision).	**TOTAL:**	**45 min**
5. Groups (a) and (b) present arguments to group (c), the school governing body.		
6. Group (c), after considering all the arguments, delivers its ruling (with reasons).		
7. Debrief.		

1. Lebo's parents could argue that (a) Sotho-speaking learners have the right to be taught in the language of their choice, either Sotho or English; (b) the use of Afrikaans as the medium of instruction when they cannot understand it denies them the right to education and this is shown by their poor results; (c) English is a middle-ground language for everyone in the school – eg just as it would be unfair to teach in Sotho to Afrikaans-speaking learners, it is similarly unfair to teach in Afrikaans to Sotho-speaking learners.

   The parents of Afrikaans-speaking learners could argue that (a) the school is dominated by Afrikaans-speaking learners, many of whom do not necessarily understand English, which has been proposed by the Sotho-speaking learners; (b) Afrikaans-speaking learners also have the right to education in the language of their choice – given that the dominant group of learners in the school is Afrikaans-speaking, it makes sense that Afrikaans was the chosen language.

   The school governing body could decide that after considering all the circumstances, it is practically possible and fair to adopt a policy that promotes the use of Afrikaans as a medium of instruction over other languages for more or less the same reasons as those advanced by the Afrikaans-speaking learners. It could further argue that the policy was also in response to the high failure rate among the dominant group of Afrikaans-speaking learners, largely caused by the previous use of English, which learners did not understand as a medium of instruction.

2. The same arguments could be made in the case of Tumi except that she is Tswana-speaking and the majority of learners are Zulu speakers.

5.3 Social welfare rights

Outcomes

After completion of this section learners will be able to:

1. Explain the law concerning social security and assistance.

Assessment criteria

1. The law and regulations governing social assistance are identified.
2. The requirements for applying and qualifying for different social grants are identified.
3. A set of facts is examined and a decision is made on whether certain people qualify for social grants.
4. A set of facts is examined and a decision is made on how certain people can access their social grants.
5. A set of facts is examined and a decision made on how to solve certain problems concerning social grants.

5.3.6 What happens if the application is unsuccessful or the grant is suspended or cancelled? *(Learner's Manual p 464)*

Problem 1: Does the person qualify for a social grant? *(Learner's Manual p 465)*

AIM: The aim of the exercise is for learners to examine a set of facts and decide which social grant a person may access.

PROCEDURE	TIME	
1. Introduction.	Introduction:	5 min
2. Divide the class of learners into small groups.	Group discussion:	10 min
3. Give each group one question to answer.	Report back:	20 min
4. Report back.	General discussion:	5 min
5. General discussion.	**TOTAL:**	**40 min**

1. War veterans' pensions are paid to people who fought in a war for South Africa and are over 60 years of age. As Radebe fought for South Africa in the Namibian war and is older than 60 years, he is entitled to a war veteran's pension.
2. Joe is entitled to receive a disability grant because of his bad medical condition.
3. Mary is entitled to a social relief of distress grant because her condition is temporary. When the child is born, she must apply for a child support grant
4. The child is entitled to receive a disability grant because she was born blind.
5. Derrick is likely to have his pension cancelled on the basis of his improved financial status.

6. Because Betty is already receiving money from the Compensation Commissioner, she is not entitled to a disability grant.
7. Gawie and Jill are entitled to a child support grant for their children under 14 years of age. They may also be entitled to a social relief of distress grant until the child grant comes through.

Problem 2: How can the people get their social grants? *(Learner's Manual p 466)*

AIM: The aim of this exercise is for learners to examine a set of facts and decide how the people concerned could get their social grants.

PROCEDURE	TIME	
1. Introduction.	Introduction:	5 min
2. Divide learners in small groups.	Group discussions:	10 min
3. Give each group one question to answer.	Report back:	10 min
4. Report back.	General discussion:	10 min
5. General discussion.	**TOTAL:**	**35 min**

1. Jama can get a family member or a friend to apply on her behalf. This family member must have all Jama's necessary documents, including her own identity document and a letter written by Jama confirming that he or she is an authorised person.
2. Fanyana must go to the office of the Department of Social Development which he has been using to inform them of the change of address and where he will be staying.
3. If Stoffel has not received his pension for two months he should visit the pensions office in Pretoria and complain. If the pensions office does not help him, he could consult a Justice Centre of Legal Aid South Africa, an advice office, a legal aid clinic or the Legal Resources Centre.
4. As Jomo Ntuli lives in a flood-stricken area of the country, and he and his family are destitute, they could be entitled to social relief. Sometimes a special fund is set up for the victims of floods, in which case an application could also be made to the flood relief fund. Jomo should apply to the Director-General of the Department of Social Development for a social relief grant.
5. Charlene should go to the nearest office of the Department of Home Affairs to make an application. She must emphasise the urgency of the application to the Department. She will be given a temporary certificate and identity document which she can use to apply for the child support grant.
8. Dejewo will not qualify to benefit from social grants or social relief of distress grants unless he is legally resident in the country. If he appeals against the refusal of his asylum status and succeeds he will qualify, even though he will not be a South African citizen.

5.3.7   How to collect a social grant *(Learner's Manual p 466)*

Problem 3: How would you solve these problems relating to the payment of social grants? *(Learner's Manual p 466)*

AIM: The aim of this exercise is for learners to think about how problems regarding social grants can be solved.

<table>
<tr><td>

PROCEDURE ≔

1. Introduction.
2. Divide learners into small groups.
3. Allocate one question to each group.
4. Report back.
5. General discussion.

</td><td>

TIME 🕐

Introduction:	5 min
Group discussions:	10 min
Report back:	20 min
General discussion:	5 min
TOTAL:	**40 min**

</td></tr>
</table>

Learners may suggest the following:

1. Pay-out points should be at convenient places. Where beneficiaries have bank accounts or post office accounts their pension money will be transferred directly into their accounts by the South African Social Services Agency. A mechanism should be put in place to enable elderly people to have easier access to pay-out points.

2. This is because pay-out points run out of money. Pay clerks should be given sufficient money to distribute to make sure that no pensioners are turned away. In many cases direct payments are now made into bank or post office accounts by the South African Social Services Agency.

3. Pay-out points should have proper facilities such as toilets, chairs, first-aid kits, water, wheelchairs, portable beds and electricity. In rural areas, this should be a requirement before a trading store is chosen as a pay-out point. The stores benefit financially because the pensioners spend their money there.

4. Proper arrangements (eg ramps) should be made for disabled people who require access to pay-out points.

5. Beneficiaries should be told well in advance – preferably when they are collecting their pensions – when the next pension day pay-out will be.

6. This is unlawful and unconstitutional. The pay clerks concerned should be reported to the social welfare authorities as well as a paralegal office or university law clinic.

7. All beneficiaries are entitled to a receipt that shows what is paid to them. If this is refused, they should contact a paralegal advice office or a law clinic.

8. This is unlawful and unconstitutional. It should be reported to the social welfare authorities as well as a paralegal advice office or legal aid clinic.

9. This is unlawful and unconstitutional. It should be reported to the social welfare authorities as well as the police, a paralegal advice office or a legal aid clinic.

10. Pay clerks should be given sufficient money to pay all the pensioners. This should be reported to a paralegal advice office or a legal aid clinic. Wherever possible direct payments should be made into bank or post office accounts by the South African Social Services Agency.

5.3.8   Private welfare and assistance   *(Learner's Manual p 467)*

Problem 4: Private welfare and assistance in your town   *(Learner's Manual p 468)*

<table>
<tr><td>

PROCEDURE ≔

1. Introduction.
2. Questions and answers to encourage learners to share their experiences.
3. General discussion.

</td><td>

TIME 🕐

Introduction:	5 min
Question and answer:	35 min
General discussion:	5 min
TOTAL:	**45 min**

</td></tr>
</table>

Learners can be asked to investigate which private welfare and assistance organisations exist in their town and report back to the class.

5.4 Health rights

Outcomes

After completion of this section learners will be able to:

1. Explain the law concerning the right of access to health care.

Assessment criteria

1. An explanation is given of what people are entitled to in terms of health rights.

2. A set of facts is examined and a decision made on whether certain people are entitled to emergency medical treatment.

3. An explanation is given of when pregnant mothers and prisoners living with HIV are entitled to access anti-retroviral treatment.

4. An explanation is given of the meaning of 'informed consent' by patients.

5. A set of facts is examined and a decision made on whether certain children are entitled to consent to medical treatment.

6. A set of facts is examined and a decision made on whether certain people are entitled to a termination of pregnancy

7. The law governing medical aid schemes is explained.

8. Some questions regarding medical aid schemes are raised and answered.

9. An explanation is given of how to lay a complaint against health workers.

10. A set of facts is examined and a decision made whether certain people qualify for free medical treatment.

5.4.2   What do health rights mean?   *(Learner's Manual p 470)*

Problem 1: The case of the kidney patient who is refused dialysis   *(Learner's Manual p 471)*

AIM: The aim of the exercise is to enable learners to prepare arguments that could have been made in a case of a patient who was refused dialysis treatment, and to give a judgment on the case.

PROCEDURE
1. Read the case study.
2. Divide learners into three groups: (a) lawyers for Soobramoney; (b) lawyers for the hospital, and (c) the judges.
3. Learners prepare their arguments and think about likely judgments.
4. Learners present their arguments.
5. Judges give their judgments.
6. General discussion.
7. Inform learners what the Constitutional Court decided in the case.

TIME	
Introduction:	5 min
Group preparations:	10 min
Group presentations:	15 min
General discussion:	10 min
TOTAL:	**40 min**

1. Lawyers for Soobramoney could argue that the right of access to health care services is a crucial to the lives of the people. It cannot be subjected to cost when the life of a person is at stake. Had Soobramoney been given the dialysis treatment as he requested, he would probably have been alive today. By ruling against Soobramoney, the court would be saying that the right could not help him, did not apply to his case, and therefore, he should be left to die. This approach makes money the paramount determinant of people's lives, yet the right to life is one of the most fundamental rights in the Constitution.

2. Lawyers for the hospital could argue that the right of access to health care services is limited by the availability of resources. The hospital cannot afford to give dialysis treatment to everyone equally. They have limited machines for this purpose and had to design rational and fair criteria for putting patients on these machines. To put Soobramoney on a machine would have probably cost the hospital more than R250 000. Soobramoney did not meet the requirements set in the criteria. This was a rational decision based on limited resources.

3. The judges in favour of the hospital succeeding could decide that Soobramoney does not have an unlimited right to claim a service from the state. The hospital's policy on the dialysis treatment is rational and fair. Soobramoney's condition is not curable and he needs dialysis treatment indefinitely. He suffers from chronic illnesses that cannot be cured. Emergency medical treatment does not apply to chronic illnesses but rather to 'acute' situations where a person has been severely injured or has an illness that can be cured. Given the limited resources, not everyone in need of a service can get it. By giving preference to organ-transplant patients, the hospital will be able to make the dialysis machines available to more people and not just a select few.

   Judges in favour of Soobramoney succeeding could decide that the right to life is more important than any other right and that even if the hospital has limited resources it must give preference to people who are in immediate danger of dying if they are not treated. Whether their death will be caused by a chronic illness or an acute incident should make no difference.

Note: In *Soobramoney's* case, the Constitutional Court held that the selection criteria used for kidney dialysis patients was reasonable and justifiable because it allowed people access to a limited number of machines on a rational basis. The court also held that 'emergency medical treatment' did not mean treatment when a person was facing death at the end of a chronic illness, but rather where his or her life was in danger because of some 'dramatic, sudden situation or event which is of a passing nature in terms of time' (eg a motor accident). Mr Soobramoney lost his appeal and subsequently died.

Problem 2: Do the patients require 'emergency medical treatment'?

(Learner's Manual p 472)

AIM: The aim of this exercise is for learners to decide whether the patients require 'emergency medical treatment'.

<table>
<tr><td>

PROCEDURE

1. Read the case studies.
2. Divide learners into small groups
2. Allocate one question to each group.
3. Groups prepare their answers.
4. Groups present their answers.
5. General discussion.

</td><td>

TIME

Introduction:	5 min
Groups prepare to answer separate questions:	10 min
Group presentations:	15 min
General discussion:	10 min
TOTAL:	**40 min**

</td></tr>
</table>

1. Sipho's situation could be considered an emergency situation within the meaning of the right. This is an accident situation that requires urgent medical treatment. Sipho needed urgent treatment to stop the bleeding and save his life. The nurses should have tried to treat him not turn him away.

2. Bonga's situation does not fall within the right to emergency medical treatment but under the right of access to health care services. The state is obliged to provide access to ant-retroviral drugs to an extent that it has the resources to do so.

Note: The teacher may wish to consider using the decision of the Constitutional Court in *Minister of Health and Others v Treatment Action Campaign* (2002) (see *Learner's Manual* under Problem 2).

5.4.6 Full knowledge and consent ('informed consent')
(Learner's Manual p 475)

Problem 3: Was an 'informed consent' obtained? *(Learner's Manual p 476)*

AIM: The aim of the exercise is to enable learners to identify whether an informed consent was obtained for the patients in the case study.

<table>
<tr><td>

PROCEDURE

1. Read the case study.
2. Divide learners into small groups
3. Ask learners to discuss the case in their small groups. Allocate the question to each group.
4. Groups prepare their answers.
5. Groups present their answers.
6. General discussion.

</td><td>

TIME

Introduction:	5 min
Groups prepare to answer the question:	10 min
Groups present their answers:	15 min
General discussion:	10 min
TOTAL:	**40 min**

</td></tr>
</table>

Learners who decide that the doctor did get an informed consent could argue that the patient knew that there something wrong with his leg and that the doctor would try to cure it once he found out what was wrong with it. As the patient's leg was cancerous and he would only live for six months if his leg was not cut off, it was reasonable for the doctor to cut it off immediately rather than waiting for the patient to wake up and go through the shock of having to be put to sleep again so that he could have another operation.

Learners who decide that the patient did not give an informed consent could argue that cutting off a person's leg is a very serious operation and the patient should have been consulted before this was done. Maybe he would rather have lived for only six months with two legs than later have only one leg. The doctor should have woken him up and got his consent before doing such a radical operation.

Problem 4: Are the children able to consent to or refuse the blood transfusions?

(Learner's Manual p 478)

AIM: The aim of the exercise is to enable learners to identify whether the children in the case studies have the legal capacity to give an informed consent to accept or refuse treatment.

PROCEDURE	TIME	
1. Read the case studies.	Introduction:	5 min
2. Divide learners into small groups	Groups prepare to answer	
2. Allocate one question to each group.	separate questions:	10 min
3. Groups prepare their answers.	Group presentations:	15 min
4. Groups present their answers.	General discussion:	10 min
5. General discussion.	**TOTAL:**	**40 min**

1. Patients who are old enough to consent to a medical procedure are also old enough to refuse treatment. A 15-year-old is able to consent to a medical treatment without his parent's consent – provided he is sufficiently mature – because he is over 12 years old. Medical treatment means a medical procedure to cure a person without being 'invasive' like an operation where a patient is cut open. If a blood transfusion is medical treatment, the 15-year-old is old enough to refuse it as well, even if it will result in his death. If learners decide that a blood transfusion is too serious a procedure to be regarded as treatment but should be regarded as an operation, the boy would need his parent's consent. In this case his parents support him so in both cases he will be able to refuse treatment.

2. The same principles mentioned in question 1 above apply to the 13-year-old. Parents, however, may not refuse medical treatment for their child on religious grounds. The doctor would have to follow the wishes of the 13-year-old.

3. A girl of any age can consent to a termination of pregnancy provided she is mentally capable of giving an informed consent. People who are legally able to give consent for medical procedures are also able to decide who has information about their medical procedures. The Termination of Pregnancy Act states that a young person's parents do not have to be consulted or informed if the girl is able to give consent.

4. The same principles as those in question 1 above apply in this case. A 16-year-old is old enough to give consent to medical treatment and to refuse such treatment. If a blood transfusion is regarded as an operation the boy's parents would have to agree with his decision. However, in emergencies patients may be treated without consent provided it is not against their known wishes.

5.4.8 Termination of pregnancy

(Learner's Manual p 479)

Problem 5: Does the person qualify for a legal termination of pregnancy?

(Learner's Manual p 480)

AIM: The aim of the exercise is to enable learners to identify whether patients in the case studies qualify for a legal termination of pregnancy.

PROCEDURE	TIME	
1. Read the case studies.	Introduction:	5 min
2. Divide learners into small groups	Groups prepare to answer	
2. Allocate one question to each group.	separate questions:	10 min
3. Groups prepare their answers.	Group presentations:	15 min
4. Groups present their answers.	General discussion:	10 min
5. General discussion.	**TOTAL:**	**40 min**

1. A 12-year-old girl may terminate her pregnancy without her parent's consent if she is mature enough to give an informed consent. During the first 12 weeks she may terminate the pregnancy for any reason she likes. She merely has to consult a midwife or doctor.

2. From the 13th up to the 20th week of the pregnancy a woman may terminate her pregnancy provided the doctor she consults thinks that she satisfies one of the lawful grounds for an abortion. One of these grounds is where the continued pregnancy would seriously affect the woman's social or economic position. It could be argued that this would apply to a professional model.

3. As previously mentioned, from the 13th up to the 20th week of the pregnancy, a 13-year-old school girl could terminate her pregnancy on the grounds that it affects her social position (as a school girl) or that it is a danger to her health.

4. After the 20th week a pregnancy may only be terminated on very limited grounds. One of these grounds is if the unborn baby would be defective.

5. Rape is only a ground for terminating a pregnancy if the woman or girl is in her 13th up to 20th week of pregnancy. After the 20th week the grounds are very restrictive and rape is not one of them.

5.4.11 Medical schemes

(Learner's Manual p 481)

Problem 6: Some questions on medical aid schemes *(Learner's Manual p 483)*

AIM: The aim of this exercise is to allow learners an opportunity to reflect on how medical aid schemes work.

PROCEDURE	TIME	
1. Introduction.	Introduction:	5 min
2. Divide learners into small groups.	Group discussions:	10 min
3. Each group to discuss one question.	Report back:	10 min
4. Report back.	General discussion:	5 min
5. General discussion.	**TOTAL:**	**30 min**

1. This question enables learners to share their family experiences concerning medical aid schemes. Depending on the community and neighbourhood, many learners may come from families who cannot afford to join a medical aid scheme or who are unemployed. If so, they might have to rely on the state's assistance for medical aid.

   Other learners may not know whether or not their families belong to medical aid schemes. Those whose parents work for the public service are likely to know whether their parents belong to a medical aid scheme.

2. Some learners might say that all employers should provide medical aid to their employees. Such aid enables workers and their families to be guaranteed medical assistance when they require it. However, other learners may say that employees should be given an opportunity to choose their own medical aid scheme. Furthermore, others may argue that it is unfair that all workers have to join a medical aid scheme, especially those who are healthy, or who do not have families. It might be argued that joining a medical aid scheme should be voluntary and not compulsory for workers.

3. If a patient, who is a member of a medical aid scheme, chooses to consult a doctor who has 'contracted out', the medical aid scheme will usually pay the doctor's fees at the medical aid scheme rate. The patient would then have to pay the difference between what the medical aid scheme pays and the actual amount charged by the doctor. A patient who wishes to stay in a private hospital might only be compensated by the medical aid scheme for the cost of staying in a government hospital. The patient would then have to pay the difference between the cost of staying in a private hospital and the cost of staying in a government or provincial hospital. Before checking into a private hospital, a patient should find out how he or she will be charged (eg for a day or a half-day at a time). If they are to be charged by half-days, they should find out when the hospital's half-day begins. For example, some hospitals charge from 12 noon. This means that a patient who checks in at 11 am will be charged half a day for the period 11 to 12 noon (even though they are only there for an hour on the day).

4. There are two main ways of claiming under a medical aid scheme: one is to send the account direct to the medical aid society if the doctor, dentist or eye doctor's accounts are in accordance with the normal rates. In this case, it may sometimes be necessary also to send a claim form together with the account. The other is to pay the doctor directly and then claim back the money from the medical aid scheme.

   If, however, the doctor has 'contracted out' of medical aid, the account cannot be sent direct to the medical aid scheme. The patient must first pay the doctor and then recover the amount to be paid (at the normal rate by the medical aid scheme), by sending a receipt. Alternatively, the patient may send a full account to the medical aid scheme before paying the doctor. If this is done, the patient will receive a cheque from the medical aid scheme for its share, and the patient will have to send payment to cover the full amount to the doctor or hospital. Accounts should always be sent to the medical aid scheme as soon as possible, otherwise the full amount might not be paid by them.

   Usually the doctor's account will state whether the full amount should be paid by the patient first, or whether the account should be sent directly to the medical aid scheme.

5. Medical aid schemes sometimes limit the maximum amount of treatment for certain illnesses that patients may claim in any one year. They might limit the amount that can be claimed for new false teeth, spectacles or even the number of times spent in a hospital or nursing home or visiting a doctor in any one year. Medical aid schemes also do not usually cover cosmetic surgery (eg for

face lifts), nor do they cover services from people who are not registered medical practitioners; for example, chiropractors might not be covered by some schemes. Medical aid schemes also do not pay for patent medicines or for things such as bandages, contraceptives, tonics, etc. They might also limit the amount each year that may be spent on medicines and drugs.

6. This is similar to the second question. If the state provided free medical aid for everybody, it would not be necessary for people to join private medical aid schemes. Some people might argue, however, that people who can afford to pay for medical treatment should be made to do so. They might also say that if people wish to employ expensive doctors and stay in expensive hospitals they should be allowed to do so. Others might argue that free medical aid for everyone is fair, because rich people pay towards state medical services through their taxes, and should not have to pay again. The government has begun to introduce the first phase of a 14-year phasing-in programme for a National Health Insurance scheme.

5.4.13 People who cannot afford to pay for medical treatment
(Learner's Manual p 484)

Problem 7: Do they qualify for free medical treatment? *(Learner's Manual p 484)*

AIM: The object of the exercise is for learners to examine a set of facts and decide whether the people concerned qualify for free medical treatment.

PROCEDURE	TIME	
1. Introduction.	Introduction:	5 min
2. Divide learners into small groups.	Group discussions:	10 min
3. Allocate one question to each group.	Report back:	10 min
4. Groups discuss their questions.	General discussion:	5 min
5. Report back.	**TOTAL:**	**30 min**
6. General discussion.		

1. An 80-year-old pensioner is entitled to free medical treatment. The fact that she receives a pension suggests that she cannot afford to meet basic needs.

2. Shaida cannot get free medical treatment from a private doctor paid for by the state. However, she can get free medical treatment from a public hospital or clinic.

3. Tembu is entitled to be transported to the hospital or clinic by an ambulance. He could get someone to call the hospital for an ambulance.

4. Petrus is entitled to get free medical treatment from a state hospital because he cannot afford a doctor and has contracted a lung disease from mining.

5. Thandi is entitled to get free medical treatment from a state hospital because she is only 6 years old and her grandmother, with whom she lives, is a pensioner.

6. If Daniel is poor and cannot afford going to a private dentist he is entitled to get free dental care and false teeth.

5.5 Food rights

Outcomes

After completion of this section learners will be able to:

1. Explain the law concerning the right to food.

Assessment criteria

1. The meaning of the right of access to sufficient food is given.

2. Barriers to access to food are identified.

3. Different departments that are responsible for realising the right to food are identified.

4. A set of facts is examined and decision made on whether certain groups of people and their families qualify for free food from the state.

5.5.1 Why is it important to understand food rights?

(Learner's Manual p 485)

Problem 1: 'I am nothing – I am just a person of God' (Learner's Manual p 486)

AIM: The object of the exercise is for learners to examine a set of facts and decide what the government and others should do to address hunger and malnutrition.

PROCEDURE	TIME	
1. Introduction.	Introduction:	5 min
2. Divide learners into small groups.	Group discussions:	15 min
3. Give each group one question to discuss.	Report back:	10 min
4. Report back.	General discussion:	10 min
5. General discussion.	**TOTAL:**	**40 min**

1. Learners could say that Joyce and her family should get help from the government. She should be entitled to a social relief or distress grant, and to be assisted through emergency food schemes and agricultural starter packs so that she can develop a garden from which she can feed herself and her family.

2. According to the Constitutional Court in *Grootboom*, parents with children are no different from those without. However, children and their poor parents should be attended to as people in desperate situations in terms of food and other basic needs. If Joyce's children are under the age of 9 years, she should apply for a child support grant (see *Learner's Manual* para 5.3.5.2.4). The fact that she has children puts her household in a more difficult position.

3. Learners could say people do not have access to food because of unemployment, high prices of food, lack of access to productive land, poor implementation of food programmes (eg emergency food schemes) or poor uptake of social grants.

4. The right to food is linked to many rights. These include the right to life, human dignity, access to health care services, water, land, property and social security, as well as the right to practise a trade and occupation, etc.

5. Learners could say that the government must ensure that households are food secure by facilitating access to resources such as land and water so that people can feed themselves. Also, learners may say that the government must create more jobs so that parents can have money to buy food for their children. Some learners may say that the government health institutions (hospitals and clinics) must be well-equipped and resourced to provide treatment and supplements to children affected by malnutrition. There should be educational programmes on nutrition.

5.5.2 What does the right of access to sufficient food mean?

(Learner's Manual p 486)

Problem 2: A debate on food security in South Africa *(Learner's Manual p 487)*

AIM: The aim of the exercise is to allow learners an opportunity to debate the issues concerning food security in South Africa.

PROCEDURE
1. Introduction.
2. Divide learners into two large groups: one to argue in favour of the government's point of view and the other against.
3. Subdivide large groups into three small groups to prepare arguments for their large group.
4. Conduct a debate by the spokespersons of each smaller group within the large group for both sides.
5. Vote on the result of the debate.
6. General discussion.

TIME	
Introduction:	5 min
Prepare for the debate in groups:	15 min
Conduct the debate:	20 min
General discussion:	5 min
TOTAL:	**45 min**

1. The group in support of the governments' statement could argue that:
   (a) The level of hunger and malnutrition is so high that it would be impossible to expect the government to feed its poor people.
   (b) Food is a commodity that is owned by private companies. The government does not manufacture or sell food and has limited control over food supplies.
   (c) The right to food is not a right to be fed but a right to feed oneself. The state can only help people feed themselves through laws, policies and programmes.
   (d) The right to food depends on many other rights, such as whether people have access to land, water, money, etc – things that states have limited control over.

2. The group against the government's statement could argue that the right to food is not impossible to realise because:
   (a) The state should not only have the political commitment to implement the right but should act in line with that commitment.

(b) The fact that there is widespread hunger means that the right to food is important.

(c) The state should develop programmes and policies that provide and assist people with food parcels and access to land for production of food. It should strengthen its social welfare system and the public works programme so that people have the financial power to buy food.

3. After the debate, learners should indicate by a show of hands which view they support. For how to conduct a debate see *Educator's Manual* para G8 above.

5.5.3 What are the common barriers to access to adequate food?
(Learner's Manual p 487)

Problem 3: Some questions on barriers to sufficient food *(Learner's Manual p 488)*

AIM: The object of the exercise is to allow learners an opportunity to think about some of the barriers to having access to sufficient food, using real-life examples.

PROCEDURE		TIME	
1. Introduction.		Introduction:	5 min
2. Divide leaners into small groups.		Group discussions:	10 min
3. Allocate one question to each group.		Report back:	10 min
4. Report back.		General discussion:	10 min
5. General discussion.		**TOTAL:**	**35 min**

Instructors can ask learners for their answers to questions 1 and 2. Their answers should include factors in addition to those listed in the *Learner's Manual* para 5.5.3.

5.5.4 What food programmes have been implemented?
(Learner's Manual p 488)

Problem 4: What food programmes exist in your area? *(Learner's Manual p 490)*

AIM: The object of the exercise is to allow learners to reflect on their own experiences and observations relating to food programmes in their areas.

PROCEDURE		TIME	
1. Introduction.		Introduction:	5 min
2. Individual reflections by learners on food programmes in their areas.		Individual reflections:	10 min
		Sharing of reflections:	15 min
3. Sharing of reflections.		General discussion:	5 min
4. General discussion.		**TOTAL:**	**35 min**

This is an open-ended exercise. Depending on learners' experience, answers to this question will vary significantly.

5.6   Housing rights

Outcomes

After completion of this section learners will be able to:

1.   Explain the law regarding access to adequate housing.

Assessment criteria

1.   The meaning of the right of access to adequate housing is explained.

2.   A set of facts is examined and a decision is made on whether or not the people concerned are entitled to be provided with housing by the state.

3.   The laws governing evictions are identified and explained.

4.   A set of facts is examined and a decision is made on whether the landlord may evict the occupiers.

5.   An explanation is given on how to access housing subsidies and housing loans.

6.   A set of facts is given and a decision made on which persons qualify for a housing subsidy.

7.   A set of facts is given and a decision made on whether the persons concerned qualify for a housing loan.

8.   Dishonest ways of buying and selling houses are identified.

9.   Sets of facts are given and decisions are made on how people exposed to dishonest ways of buying and selling houses should react.

10.   An explanation of the nature, context and effect of a deed of sale is given.

11.   An explanation is given on what a mortgage bond is and how to apply for one.

12.   The law governing the renting of houses is explained.

13.   A decision is made on what people should look for when renting houses.

14.   An explanation is given on how to lodge a complaint concerning rental agreements.

15.   A set of facts is given and a decision made on the rights and duties of landlords and tenants.

16.   A set of facts is given and a decision made on whether to rent or buy a house.

5.6.2   What does the right of 'access to adequate housing' mean?   *(Learner's Manual p 492)*

Problem 1: The case of the sports field squatters   *(Learner's Manual p 493)*

AIM: The aim of this exercise is for learners to think about the arguments that could have been presented in the Constitutional Court, and to discuss what constitutes 'adequate housing'.

1. Introduction.
2. Divide class into small groups.
3. Give each group one question to discuss.
4. Divide the groups discussing question 1 into two categories: one half preparing arguments for Grootboom, the other for the state.
5. Report back.
6. General discussion.

TIME

Introduction:	5 min
Group discussions:	15 min
Report back:	15 min
General discussion:	10 min
TOTAL:	**45 min**

1. Legal representatives for Mrs Grootboom and her community could argue that the community is entitled to have access to adequate housing at state expense and that children have the right to shelter. Because children are involved, the state is obliged to provide them with shelter immediately as well as other necessary services such as sanitation, sufficient water and electricity. They could also argue that the right of children to shelter does not depend on available resources and therefore it should be given to them immediately.

   Legal representatives for the state could argue that there are a lot of people who are as desperate for houses as Mrs Grootboom and her community. The state has developed policies and programmes that will enable people to get adequate houses over a period of time. The members of the Grootboom community are also entitled to benefit from these measures. However, they should apply for these like everyone else in the same conditions. If the Grootboom community received shelter or adequate housing on demand, it would make the government's measures useless, as it would allow for 'queue jumping'. They could also argue that parents with children should not have an advantage regarding 'adequate housing' over others who are also in need of a house.

2. The Constitutional Court said that the government should devise a comprehensive and co-ordinated plan that will ensure that everyone has access to adequate housing and, in particular, that children and those in a desperate situation are specially catered for in the programme. If the programme does not contain the above features, it will be declared unreasonable and will not be in compliance with the Constitution.

3. Learners who discuss this question should come up with their own ideas concerning what they regard as 'an adequate house'. They should answer the questions asked in items (a) to (f).

5.6.3 What does the right to protection against arbitrary eviction mean?

(Learner's Manual p 494)

Problem 2: The case of the farmland squatters

(Learner's Manual p 497)

AIM: The aim of this exercise is to allow learners to argue as lawyers and decide as judges whether the farmland squatters in the *Modderklip* case should have been evicted.

<table>
<tr><td>

PROCEDURE

1. Introduction.
2. Divide learners into three groups: (a) lawyers for the government; (b) lawyers for Modderklip; and (c) judges.
3. Each group (except group (c)) prepares arguments on the given set of facts. Group (c) thinks about the issues.
4. Give group (c) some simple procedures for conducting a hearing (eg 5 minutes each to present arguments; 5 minutes for questions and clarifying issues; 5 minutes for giving the decision).
5. Groups (a) and (b) present arguments to group (c) the judges.
6. Group (c), after considering all the arguments, delivers its judgment (with reasons).
7. Debrief.

</td><td>

TIME

Introduction:	5 min
Preparations for arguments:	10 min
Presentation of arguments:	15 min
Decision by judges:	5 min
Debrief:	10 min
TOTAL:	**45 min**

</td></tr>
</table>

1. Learners acting as lawyers for the government can argue that the government does not have suitable land and resources to rehouse the squatters.

2. Learners acting as lawyers for Modderklip Boerdery could argue that the duty is on the government to find land and it was not the duty of private landowners to do so. If the government cannot evict the squatters it must at least pay compensation to the landowners.

3. The judges can decide which arguments appeal to them after they have heard each side's arguments.

5.6.4 How is the right of access to adequate housing being implemented?

(Learner's Manual p 498)

Problem 3: Do the people qualify for a housing subsidy scheme?

(Learner's Manual p 498)

AIM: The object of the exercise is to examine a set of facts and decide whether the people involved qualify for a housing subsidy scheme.

<table>
<tr><td>

PROCEDURE

1. Introduction.
2. Divide the class of learners into small groups.
3. Give each group a question to discuss.
4. Report back.
5. General discussion.

</td><td>

TIME

Introduction:	5 min
Group discussions:	10 min
Report back:	10 min
General discussion:	5 min
TOTAL:	**30 min**

</td></tr>
</table>

1. Gerald does not qualify for a housing subsidy because he owns the house he has been paying off for the past seven years.

2. The Motene family do not qualify for a housing subsidy because they already own a house. They might qualify for some form of disability grant for their daughter, Rose.

Problem 4: Edward wants to buy a house

(Learner's Manual p 500)

AIM: The aim of the exercise is for learners to analyse a set of facts and decide whether or not a person can afford to buy a house.

PROCEDURE ≔
1. Introduction.
2. Divide the class of learners into small groups.
3. Ask each group to discuss Edward's case.
4. Report back.
5. General discussion.

TIME 🕐	
Introduction:	5 min
Group discussions:	10 min
Report back:	10 min
General discussion:	5 min
TOTAL:	**30 min**

Edward should also take into account the transfer duty, insurance premiums, inspection fees, stamp duty, rates and taxes, and conveyancing fees.

Problem 5: Should a home loan be granted?

(Learner's Manual p 501)

AIM: The object of the exercise is for learners to determine whether a home loan should be granted to the people concerned.

PROCEDURE ≔
1. Introduction.
2. Divide the class of learners into small groups.
3. Small groups each discuss one question.
4. Reports back.
5. Summary.

TIME 🕐	
Introduction:	5 min
Discussions in small groups:	10 min
Reports back:	10 min
Summary:	5 min
TOTAL:	**30 min**

1. Joyce and Boland Company: ('Redlining' – refusing loans because of where people live)
   (a) Learners arguing on behalf of Boland Company could argue that Joyce lives in an area which has enormous risk factors for their business.
   (b) Learners arguing on behalf of Joyce could say that they need a loan to build a house in an area of their choice. They could say that the Bank should not discriminate against them on the basis of where they stay and would like to stay. The area they have chosen does not mean that they cannot pay back the loan.

2. Kobus and Siyathuthuka Bank: (Refusing loans because it is not in the interests of the business making the loans)
   (a) Learners for the Siyathuthuka Bank could argue that they cannot give loans to Kobus because he earns far less than what they require as a minimum salary package. It would be dangerous to the business of the bank if they were to give loans to people who are not likely to be able to afford the repayments.
   (b) Learners for Kobus could argue that the decision of the bank is discriminatory. He believes that he can pay back the loan and that his financial status is likely to improve over a period of time.

Problem 6: How can employers help workers to buy homes?

(Learner's Manual p 503)

AIM: The object of the exercise is for learners to discuss how employers can help workers to buy homes.

PROCEDURE	TIME	
1. Introduction.	Introduction:	5 min
2. Divide the class of learners into two large groups of Mr Hope, the employer, and Mr Thami, the worker.	Role-play preparations:	10 min
3. Subdivide large groups into small groups of Mr Hope and Mr Thami and ask them to prepare for the role-play.	Role-play presentations:	10 min
	Debrief and discussion:	10 min
4. Choose one learner from each group to role-play the discussion between Mr Hope and Mr Thami.	**TOTAL:**	**35 min**
5. Debrief and discussion.		

Mr Thami should ask Mr Hope whether he could obtain a loan to buy a house. Mr Hope should tell Mr Thami that there are a number of ways in which he could help. For example by: (a) lending money to pay for a deposit on the house; (b) giving a small amount each month to Mr Thami as a housing allowance to help him pay off the loan; (c) paying part of the interest each month; (d) guaranteeing the amount of the deposit for the house; (e) lending money to pay for the 'transfer costs'; and (f) approaching a bank on Mr Thami's behalf to help him obtain a loan.

The learner playing Mr Thami should decide which form of assistance he would like from Mr Hope.

Problem 7: Mr Nyathi is asked to pay a deposit

(Learner's Manual p 506)

AIM: The object of the exercise if for learners to analyse a set of facts and decide what Mr Nyathi should do.

PROCEDURE	TIME	
1. Introduction.	Introduction:	5 min
2. Divide the class of learners into small groups representing Mr Nyathi and Mrs Kani.	Role-play preparations:	10 min
	Role-play presentations:	10 min
3. Group preparations for role-play.	Debrief and discussion:	10 min
4. Role-play discussion between Mr Nyathi and Mrs Kani.	**TOTAL:**	**35 min**
5. Debrief and discussion.		

Mr Nyathi should ask to see a copy of an agreement before he considers paying a deposit. The offer of a receipt by the agent is not sufficient. Mr Nyathi should go further and contact Fast Homes to check whether Mrs Kani is indeed acting for them. He should ask Mrs Kani for a breakdown of the building programme over the three-month period, and check with the township manager to find out if it is possible. Mr Nyathi should only pay a deposit if he is satisfied that: (a) Mrs Kani is acting for Fast

Homes; (b) the township manager confirms that the house can be built within three months; (c) there is a proper written agreement reflecting the full purchase price of the house, how it is to be paid off, and the date by which the house will be completed; (d) he receives a receipt for any money paid; and (e) he can make the necessary arrangements to pay off the house.

The role-play should include the statements made by Mrs Kani in Problem 7 in the *Learner's Manual* and the enquiries by Mr Nyathi.

Problem 8: Mrs Mphahlele is asked to sign an agreement *(Learner's Manual p 507)*

AIM: The object of the exercise is for learners to examine a set of facts and decide if the borrower should sign an agreement or not.

PROCEDURE	TIME	
1. Introduction.	Introduction:	5 min
2. Divide the class of learners into small groups representing Mrs Mphahlele and Mr Fingo.	Role-play preparations:	10 min
	Role-play presentations:	10 min
3. Group preparations for role-play.	Debrief and discussion:	10 min
4. Role-play discussion between Mrs Mphahlele and Mr Fingo.	**TOTAL:**	**35 min**
5. Debrief and discussion.		

As Mrs Mphahlele cannot read and will not know what is in the agreement, she should ask somebody to read it and explain it to her. The person who reads and explains the contract to her should not be Mr Fingo or anybody connected with him. The best thing for Mrs Mphahlele to do is to ask Mr Fingo if she may keep the agreement for a couple of days so that she can get an independent person to explain it to her. It will also give her a chance to see if she can afford to buy the house for R300 000. If Mr Fingo refuses to allow Mrs Mphahlele to keep the agreement for a couple of days, she should refuse to do business with him. The role-play should bring out these considerations.

Problem 9: Mrs Luthuli is approached by Ms Batha, an estate agent *(Learner's Manual p 509)*

AIM: The object of the exercise is for learners to examine a set of facts and decide if a home owner will be prejudiced by an estate agent's offer to buy the house.

PROCEDURE	TIME	
1. Introduction.	Introduction:	5 min
2. Divide the class of learners into small groups representing Mrs Luthuli and Ms Batha.	Role-play preparations:	10 min
	Role-play presentations:	10 min
3. Group preparations for role-play.	Debrief and discussion:	10 min
4. Role-play discussion between Mrs Luthuli and Ms Batha.	**TOTAL:**	**35 min**
5. Debrief and discussion.		

Mrs Luthuli should not consider Ms Batha's offer. The chances are that after a few months Ms Batha will sell the house to somebody else at a large profit and Mrs Luthuli will be ejected from her home. Even if she were not ejected Mrs Luthuli would no longer own the house and would have to pay rent to Ms Batha. There is no guarantee that Ms Batha will not increase the rent, so that eventually Mrs Luthuli might have to pay in rent what she used to pay in bond repayments.

The above considerations should be brought out in the role-play. What Mrs Luthuli should do is approach her bank and ask them to increase the period of her loan, so that she has to pay less each month.

Problem 10: Mr Marivati is offered help in paying off his bond
(Learner's Manual p 509)

AIM: The aim of the exercise is for learners to examine a set of facts and decide whether the owner should accept the offer of assistance to pay off the bond from a stranger.

PROCEDURE
1. Introduction.
2. Divide the class of learners into small groups representing Mr Marivati and Miss Suni.
3. Group preparations for role-play.
4. Role-play discussion between Mr Marivati and Miss Suni.
5. Debrief and discussion.

TIME	
Introduction:	5 min
Role-play preparations:	10 min
Role-play presentations:	10 min
Debrief and discussion:	10 min
TOTAL:	**35 min**

Mr Marivati should first check that he is not paying too much for the house. He should ask his bank to value the house for him. He can also compare the prices of similar houses in his neighbourhood by reading newspaper or estate agents' advertisements, and asking the sellers.

Mr Marivati should not enter into an agreement in which his repayments, including water, electricity, insurance and rates exceed R1 500 (25% of his monthly income of R6 000).

If Miss Suni's offer is genuine, Mr Marivati should insist that it is included in the deed of sale and will continue for as long as he is paying off the house. Then, even if the bond rates go up, R1 000 a month might not be enough to offset the difference between what he can afford and the monthly repayments.

Mr Marivati should rather ask Miss Suni to sell him a cheaper house, so that bond repayments, water, electricity, insurance and rates do not exceed R1 500 a month.

The role-play should include the above considerations.

Problem 11: What to look out for when buying houses
(Learner's Manual p 511)

AIM: The aim of the exercise is to give learners an opportunity to think about things that buyers of houses should look out for when deciding to buy a house.

PROCEDURE		TIME	
1. Introduction.		Introduction:	5 min
2. Divide the class of learners into two large groups: one in pairs to prepare the role-play in question 1; the other to report back on question 2.		Pair preparations:	15 min
		Presentation of role-play:	10 min
		Debrief of role-play:	5 min
3. Subdivide the second large group into small groups to report back on question 2.		Report back on question 2:	10 min
		General discussion:	5 min
4. Conduct the role-play using two of the pairs.		**TOTAL:**	**50 min**
5. Debrief role-play.			
6. Report back on question 2.			
7. General discussion.			

1. This may depend upon where learners live or have lived and their feelings about the advantages and disadvantages listed below.

    The possible advantages and disadvantages of different areas are as follows:

    (a) *City*:

    Advantages: more jobs, cultural activities, sporting events, movies, restaurants, higher wages, greater variety and mix of different types of people.

    Disadvantages: higher prices, less available housing, more crime, more crowded, more pollution, less parking, more noise and less access to the natural environment.

    (b) *Suburbs*:

    Advantages: more space, less crime, better recreation, better schools and bigger properties.

    Disadvantages: less access to cultural and sporting events, must travel some distance to work, higher priced homes (but some may have lower-priced housing), less variety and mix of different types of people.

    (c) *Small town*:

    Advantages: less crowded, everybody knows everybody else, greater sense of community, less crime, quieter and greater variety of different people than in the suburbs.

    Disadvantages: less access to cultural and sporting events, possible lower quality schools, and fewer job opportunities.

    (d) *Rural*:

    Advantages: less crowded, more open space, more access to quiet country life, less crime, lower prices of housing and cheaper to live.

    Disadvantages: low wages, fewer job opportunities, less access to cultural and sporting events, and fewer government services.

    The students preparing for and conducting the role-play can use their imaginations concerning the types of questions they will ask and the answers they will give.

2. The things that a buyer should look out for when inspecting a house they wish to buy are set out in the *Learner's Manual* para 5.6.4.10.8.2.

Problem 12: Some questions on buying and selling a house
(Learner's Manual p 514)

AIM: The aim of the exercise is to give learners an opportunity to think about certain important issues when buying or selling a house.

PROCEDURE
1. Introduction.
2. Divide the class of learners into small groups.
3. Give each group one question to discuss.
4. Report back.
5. General discussion.

TIME	
Introduction:	5 min
Group discussions:	10 min
Report back:	20 min
General discussion:	10 min
TOTAL:	**45 min**

1. The main difference between a deed of sale for buying a house or land, and most other agreements, is that it must be in writing and signed by the buyer and seller or their agents. It will not be legally binding until they sign it.

2. Buyers of land or houses only become owners of the property when the deed of transfer shows that the property has been transferred into their names. Transfer takes place when the deed of transfer (or title deed) of the property, including the buyer's name, are registered with the Registrar of Deeds at the deeds office.

3. The kinds of clauses in deeds of sale that protect the seller usually state that: (a) 'occupational interest' will be paid by the buyer if the property is occupied by him or her before it is transferred; (b) the rates and taxes on the property have to be paid from the date of occupation by the buyer; (c) the property is sold 'voetstoots', with all its faults, and the seller will not be liable if there are any hidden defects in it; and (d) the seller may claim certain damages if the buyer does not carry out the conditions of the agreement.

4. At common law, the risk of damage to the property passes to the buyer after the contract of sale has been entered into, before delivery has taken place. This means that, as soon as the buyer and seller have signed the deed of sale, the risk will pass to the buyer. Usually, however, the deed of sale states that the risk will only pass to the buyer after he or she takes possession of the property.

5. The buyer usually pays the transfer costs in a deed of sale. This is often specifically mentioned in the agreement.

6. Conditions that might make the land less valuable are, for example, those that allow other people to build a road on the property, or allow them to use the driveway. These are called 'servitudes'. Buyers can find out about these types of conditions by asking the seller to show them a copy of the title deed or deed of transfer. Title deeds and deeds of sale should be carefully read by buyers before any agreements of sale are signed.

Problem 13: Mr Truro wishes to buy a house
(Learner's Manual p 515)

AIM: The object of the exercise is for learners to examine a set of facts and decide whether the person in question can afford to buy a house.

5.6   Housing rights   •   305

PROCEDURE		TIME	
1. Introduction.		Introduction:	5 min
2. Divide the class of learners into pairs.		Discussions in pairs:	10 min
3. Learners discuss the set of facts.		Report back:	15 min
4. Report back.		General discussion:	5 min
5. General discussion.		**TOTAL:**	**35 min**

Mr Truro will have to pay R100 000 as a deposit because he can only get a bond for R900 000, and the house costs R1 000 000. He will also have to pay another R30 000 in transfer costs. Thus, his R200 000 savings could be used to pay the deposit and transfer costs. Mr Truro earns R50 000 a month: 25% of this is R10 250. Therefore, Mr Truro could afford to pay the R10 000 a month from 25% of his monthly income. In addition to his bond repayments, Mr Truro will have to pay for water, electricity, insurance and rates. Thus, he might spend more than 25% of his monthly income on his house if he takes out a 20-year loan. Maybe if he asked for a 30-year loan he would be in a better position to meet all his payments.

Problem 14: Some questions on second bonds   (Learner's Manual p 516)

AIM: The aim of the exercise is to give learners an opportunity to discuss their understanding of second bonds.

PROCEDURE		TIME	
1. Introduction.		Introduction:	5 min
2. Divide the class of learners into small groups.		Group discussions:	10 min
3. Give each group one question to discuss.		Report back:	10 min
4. Report back.		General discussion:	5 min
5. General discussion.		**TOTAL:**	**30 min**

1. A second bond is a bond granted over a property in addition to the first bond already granted to banks. A second bond may be granted to a person like the seller or an estate agent if the bank does not lend the buyer enough money to pay the full purchase price. If the property is sold, the first bond-holder will be paid before the second.
2. When deciding whether or not to take out a second bond, the buyer should make sure that he or she can afford it. The buyer should not spend more than 25% of his or her salary to pay back both bonds each month.

5.6.5   Promoting and protecting access to adequate housing   (Learner's Manual p 516)

Problem 15: The Chitris look for a house to rent   (Learner's Manual p 518)

AIM: The object of this exercise is to enable learners to think about what things to look for, and what questions to ask the landlord when looking for a house to rent.

<table>
<tr><td>

PROCEDURE ⣿

1. Introduction.
2. Divide learners into two large groups: one to prepare a list of things to look for when renting, the other to prepare to role-play the Chitris and the landlord.
3. Subdivide the first large group into pairs to prepare a list of things to look for when renting.
4. Subdivide the second large group into small groups of Chitris and landlords to prepare for the role-play.
5. Report back from the pairs in the first large group.
6. Conduct and debrief the role-play between the Chitris and the landlord from volunteers from the small groups in the second large group.
7. General discussion.

</td><td>

TIME 🕐

Introduction:	5 min
Group preparations:	10 min
Report back from first large group:	
	10 min
Role-play and feedback by second	
large group:	10 min
General discussion:	5 min
TOTAL:	**40 min**

</td></tr>
</table>

1. A list of things that the Chitris should look for might include: nearby parks and recreation facilities; the general condition of the building; good working spaces in the kitchen; enough bedrooms (size and number); sufficient storage space; adequate lighting; functioning windows and toilets; reasonable rent; a landlord who will make repairs; good public transport; good parking and good lease provisions. They should also include the things mentioned above in para 5.6.5.1.2 of the *Learner's Manual*.

2. Some of the questions the Chitris might ask the landlord are: What is the rent to be paid? What is the due date for rent? What is the size of the 'key deposit' and conditions of its return? What is the length of the lease? What conveniences exist in the neighbourhood (shopping, transport, schools, playgrounds, nurseries, etc)? What needs repairing before moving in? Will the landlord do any repairs that are necessary from time to time? Could they discuss the flat with the previous tenant?

Problem 16: What are the rights and duties of landlords and tenants?

(Learner's Manual p 520)

AIM: The object of the exercise is for learners to examine a set of facts and decide whether the landlord or the tenant has the duty to fix what has happened.

<table>
<tr><td>

PROCEDURE ⣿

1. Introduction.
2. Divide the class of learners into small groups.
3. Give each group one question to discuss.
4. Report back.
5. General discussion.

</td><td>

TIME 🕐

Introduction:	5 min
Group discussion:	10 min
Report back:	10 min
General discussion:	5 min
TOTAL:	**30 min**

</td></tr>
</table>

1. There is a duty on the tenant to look after the premises and hand them back to the landlord at the end of the lease in the same condition as when the lease began. As the tenant's child has smashed the windows and dirtied the walls, there would be a duty on the tenant to see that the

windows are repaired and the walls cleaned or repainted. This applies even though there is a duty on the landlord to maintain the property so that it is fit for the purposes for which it was rented. It was the fault of the tenant's child that the property was damaged, and there is a duty on the tenant to make sure that the damage is repaired. In the discussion, the landlord's argument should be that the tenant is responsible for the repairs, and the tenant should insist that the landlord has a common-law duty to maintain the property

2. At common law, there is a duty on the landlord to repair the leaks in the roof of the house and the damage to the paintwork and the wooden floors. Sometimes, however, a lease might contain a condition which places the duty of repairs on the tenant. Such a condition may be imposed if the tenant is being given a reduced rental. (A tenant, however, should not sign a lease with such a clause in it unless he or she receives some special benefits under the lease.) The landlord's argument could be that the leaks are due to an act of God, and she should not be held responsible for the repairs. The tenant should argue that the landlord has a common-law duty to repair the premises.

3. If the peeling paint on the walls of the flat is due to reasonable wear and tear, there would be no duty on the tenant to repaint them. The landlord would have to arrange for the walls to be repainted. This should be brought out in the discussion. The same applies to the carpets.

4. If Duma's brother, Paulus, throws Joseph out of the room that he has rented from Duma, there would be a duty on Duma either to regain possession of the room for Joseph, or to pay Joseph for the increased costs of renting another room as a result of being ejected. If a landlord does not protect a tenant from being dispossessed, he or she may be liable for any damages suffered by the tenant. This should be brought out in the discussion.

Problem 17: The Phalas are evicted

(Learner's Manual p 522)

AIM: The object of the exercise is to give learners an opportunity to think about possible ways to solve the Phalas' eviction problem.

PROCEDURE	TIME	
1. Introduction.	Introduction:	5 min
2. Divide the class of learners into groups.	Group discussions:	15 min
3. Groups must write a short opinion advising the Phalas of their rights and duties as well as possible ways of resolving the problem.	Reading opinions:	15 min
	General discussion:	5 min
4. Reading of opinions by group spokespersons.	**TOTAL:**	**40 min**
5. General discussion.		

Mr Phala may obtain a court order to put the family back in the house. The landlord would then be forced to go through the proper procedures to obtain an eviction order to eject Mr and Mrs Phala. Therefore, as they have been unlawfully ejected, the Phalas should consult a lawyer, or, if they cannot afford a lawyer, they should approach a legal aid clinic, Legal Resources Centre, or the Legal Aid Board for help.

Mrs Phala should not break the lock to get back into the house because she is not allowed to take the law into her own hands. If she did break the lock, she could be charged with the crime of malicious injury to property (see *Learner's Manual* para 2.6.2).

Mr Phala may also lodge a complaint against the landlord with the Rental Housing Tribunal about an unfair practice. The Tribunal will investigate the matter. In the meantime, the landlord may be forced to allow the Phalas to stay in the house until the Tribunal makes its decision on the matter.

Problem 18: Should Dawie and Koekie buy or rent the house?
(Learner's Manual p 524)

AIM: The aim of the exercise is to enable learners to analyse a set of facts and advise on the advantages and disadvantages of buying or renting a house, and on the best option for Dawie and Koekie, given their situation.

PROCEDURE
1. Introduction.
2. Divide learners into small groups.
3. Allocate questions 1, 2 and 4 to separate groups.
4. Allocate role-play to group 3.
5. Reports back from groups 1, 2 and 4.
6. Conduct role-play by group 3.
7. General discussion.

TIME	
Introduction:	5 min
Group discussions:	10 min
Reports back by three groups:	10 min
Role-play by one group:	10 min
General discussion:	5 min
TOTAL:	**40 min**

1. Reasons why Dawie and Koekie should buy the house include: (a) their monthly mortgage repayments of R2 400 a month will help to pay off the balance of the purchase price, some of which will be recovered if the house goes up in value and they sell it; (b) they will own the property; and (c) their mortgage repayments will probably not change much, while rents might increase dramatically.

2. The reasons why Dawie and Koekie should not buy (and rather rent the house) include; (a) the R15 000 deposit might use up all their savings; (b) there is no guarantee that the house's value will increase; (c) it might make them nervous to have such a large portion of their assets tied up in a single investment; (d) they will have to pay for maintenance and repairs to the house; and (e) monthly costs might be more if they buy than if they rent.

3. The role-play is an effective method of getting learners to discuss the advantages and disadvantages of buying a house. To do this effectively, learners will need to spend some time preparing beforehand, and should discuss the arguments in 1 and 2 above.

4. Dawie and Koekie could obtain help to buy the house from a bank or finance house.

5.7   Water rights

Outcomes

After completion of this section learners will be able to:

1.   Explain the law concerning water and water rights.

Assessment criteria

1.   The laws that protect the right to water are discussed.

2.   The rules relating to licensing for the use of river water are identified.

3.   A decision is made on whether people in the townships should pay different rates for water than people in other residential areas.

4.   An explanation is given on what can be done if access to a basic water supply is limited.

5.7.1   Introduction
(Learner's Manual p 527)

Problem 1: Some questions on the lack of access to water
(Learner's Manual p 528)

AIM: The aim of the exercise is to allow learners to discuss their own experiences with regard to access to water services in their areas.

PROCEDURE		TIME	
1. Introduction.		Introduction:	5 min
2. Divide learners into small groups.		Group discussions:	10 min
3. Allocate one question to each group.		Reports back:	10 min
4. Reports back from groups.		General discussion:	5 min
5. General discussion.		**TOTAL:**	**30 min**

1.   Learners would probably say that they find it difficult to go through the school day without water and sanitation. Water is needed in school for human consumption, for certain courses like home economics and agriculture, etc. Sanitation is also crucial for human nature and dignity.

2.   Learners would probably say that many people living in rural areas lack a supply of clean water. People rely on running water from rivers, dams and lakes for domestic use. For those who live in urban informal settlements, there would normally be inadequate infrastructure or none at all. Some learners would probably say that the process of redressing the apartheid system, where white landowners had ownership of water resources, is slow. Some learners would say that the minimum of six kilolitres of water is not sufficient for all domestic household needs. The cutting-off of water is also a barrier to sufficient water.

3.   Some learners would say that the government is not moving speedily enough. There are a lot of people who have to rely on traditional ways of getting water, like fetching it from a river. This has

put the health of many people at risk because of pollution of water or the generally unhealthy state of the water. A number of cholera and diarrhoea outbreaks have occurred as a result. Some learners would probably say that the government is moving speedily enough. They might argue that they see progress in increasing access to water in their areas, and may have statistics to support this.

5.7.2 What is the right of access to sufficient water? (Learner's Manual p 528)

Problem 2: Should different rates be charged in different areas for water and electricity? (Learner's Manual p 529)

AIM: The aim of this exercise is to get learners thinking critically about whether different rates should be charged for different areas.

PROCEDURE	TIME	
1. Introduction.	Introduction:	5 min
2. Divide learners into small groups.	Group discussions:	10 min
3. Ask each group to discuss the question.	Reports back:	10 min
4. Reports back from groups.	General discussion:	5 min
5. General discussion.	**TOTAL:**	**30 min**

The *City of Pretoria v Walker* case allows for differential treatment of people in the townships and in the suburbs. This basically means that people who are well off and choose to stay in exclusive areas should pay more than those in townships.

Some learners would agree that, because of the inequalities in our society, many people, especially those in townships, might not be able to afford to pay the high rates that those in the former white residential areas pay. Also, it would be difficult to operate water meters in the townships because the people are used to paying less or nothing at all.

Some learners might not agree, and say that it is unfair for those who are paying more. People should be treated equally. This judgment finds otherwise. It perpetuates unequal treatment in society. Also, everyone should uphold the culture of payment for services delivery. The judgment encourages people to dodge payments instead of encouraging the '*Masekhane*' principle.

5.7.4 Can access to the water supply be limited or cut off? (Learner's Manual p 530)

Problem 3: Some questions on access to water (Learner's Manual p 531)

AIM: The object of the exercise is to give learners an opportunity to think about some of the crucial policy issues concerning access to water services.

PROCEDURE	TIME	
1. Introduction.	Introduction:	5 min
2. Divide the class of learners into small groups.	Group discussion:	5 min
3. Give each group one question to discuss.	Report back:	15 min
4. Group discussions.	General discussion:	5 min
5. Report back.	**TOTAL:**	**30 min**
6. General discussion.		

1. **Free water or not?**

   Learners might say that people should not pay for water. They could argue that water is a natural resource that flows in rivers and into lakes. It should not be commercialised, and people should not be denied access to this resource because the free market system has limited its access. Other learners might say that people should pay for water. They could argue that to provide access to adequate and clean water is expensive. For instance, water providers have to install pipes that will deliver clean water to households. This is what people should pay for, not water *per se*.

2. **Is six kilolitres of free water enough?**

   Learners might say that a free water supply of six kilolitres is not adequate, especially if there are many people in the households and there are many other domestic needs for water, such as gardening, etc. It is therefore necessary to determine the size and type of household to determine whether six kilolitres of free water is enough.

3. **Cutting off the water supply?**

   The local authority may not cut off the water supply if people cannot pay for it. Poor people are protected against unreasonable actions by local authorities. Everyone is entitled to a basic water service and cannot be deprived of this because they cannot pay. People will have to prove that they cannot afford to pay for their water bills. If it is found that they can pay, the local authority may, after following certain procedures, cut off the water supply.

4. **Where can people go for help when their water supply is cut off unreasonably?**

   People whose water supply has been cut off unreasonably may approach the South African Human Rights Commission, the Legal Resources Centre, or a university legal aid clinic for legal help.

5.8 Land rights

Outcomes

After completion of this section learners will be able to:

1. Explain the law concerning land and property rights.

Assessment criteria

1. The meaning of the right of access to land and property is explained.

2. The components of the land programme in South Africa are identified and explained.

3. People who qualify for the Land Redistribution for Agricultural Development (LRAD) grant are identified.

4. Different ways in which people can access land (ie land restitution, land redistribution, and land reform) are explained.

5. A set of facts is given and a decision made on how the people concerned can access land.

6. Guidelines are drawn up for inclusion in the constitution of a communal property association.

7. A set of facts is given and a decision made on whether a person living on a farm can be protected from eviction

5.8.1 Introduction

(Learner's Manual p 532)

Problem 1: Is South Africa dealing with the problem of landlessness effectively?

(Learner's Manual p 533)

AIM: The aim of the exercise is to give learners an opportunity to express their opinions on whether South Africa is dealing with the problem of landlessness effectively and efficiently.

PROCEDURE
1. Introduction.
2. Divide the class of learners into small groups.
3. Get each group to discuss the question.
4. Report back.
5. General discussion.

TIME	
Introduction:	5 min
Group discussions:	10 min
Report back:	10 min
General discussion:	5 min
TOTAL:	**30 min**

Some learners would probably argue that the government programmes on land, especially land restitution, are very slow in tackling the problem of landlessness in the country. The statistics show that the problem is still huge and that the government should increase the pace of giving land back to the people, and make other land programmes such as land reform and redistribution more accessible to the poor. There is also a need for proactive public education and awareness programmes about these measures.

5.8.2 What are land rights?

(Learner's Manual p 533)

Problem 2: Is the right to property a limitation on land reform?

(Learner's Manual p 533)

AIM: The aim of the exercise is to make learners aware of how the right to property might restrict land reform.

PROCEDURE	TIME	
1. Introduction.	Introduction:	5 min
2. Divide the class of learners into small groups.	Group discussions:	10 min
3. Get each group to discuss the question.	Report back:	10 min
4. Report back.	General discussion:	5 min
5. General discussion.	**TOTAL:**	**30 min**

Learners would probably say that the property clause slows down progress in land reform and restitution because it gives a right to property to those who may have to give it back later. For example, some white people, who acquired land during and as a result of apartheid laws and policies, do not want to give up the land and might use the courts to oppose attempts to restore it to dispossessed communities.

5.8.4 How can people access land?

(Learner's Manual p 534)

Problem 3: How can they access land?

(Learner's Manual p 536)

AIM: The object of the exercise is for learners to analyse a set of facts and decide from which specific programme the people can benefit.

PROCEDURE	TIME	
1. Introduction.	Introduction:	5 min
2. Divide the class of learners into small groups.	Group discussions:	10 min
3. Each group to discuss one question.	Report back:	15 min
4. Report back.	General discussion:	5 min
5. General discussion.	**TOTAL:**	**35 min**

1. Settlement programme: She must apply to the Provincial Committee.
2. Land Redistribution and Agricultural Development sub-programme: He must be prepared to undergo a training programme in farming and to make a contribution in cash, kind or labour.
3. Land Redistribution and Agricultural Development sub-programme: They must be willing to live on or near the land, to undergo a training programme in farming, and to make a contribution in cash, kind or labour.
4. Settlement/Land Acquisition Grant: They must be prepared to undergo a training programme in farming and to make a contribution in cash, kind or labour.

Problem 4: Forming a communal property association   *(Learner's Manual p 537)*

AIM: The aim of the exercise is to provide learners with information on how to form a communal property association.

PROCEDURE	TIME	
1. Introduction.	Introduction:	5 min
2. Divide the class of learners into small groups to prepare rules to guide and bind CPA members.	Group discussions:	20 min
	Report back:	20 min
3. Group discussions on rules to be included in CPA constitution.	Debriefing:	10 min
4. Report back.	**TOTAL:**	**55 min**
5. Debriefing.		

Rules to be included in the Constitution might include:

1. Everyone should participate equally in the use of the land and in the decision-making.
2. Everything should be done in a transparent manner.
3. The composition of the leadership structure must take gender equality into account.
4. There must be proper consultation of members in decision-making.

5.8.5   Mobilising people to enforce the right of access to land
(Learner's Manual p 540)

Problem 5: What are Mvuso's rights?   *(Learner's Manual p 541)*

AIM: The object of the exercise is for learners to examine a set of facts and to determine whether the person involved is protected against eviction.

PROCEDURE	TIME	
1. Introduction.	Introduction:	5 min
2. Divide the class of learners into small groups.	Group discussions:	10 min
	Report back:	15 min
3. Each group to discuss one question.	General discussion:	5 min
4. Report back.	**TOTAL:**	**35 min**
5. General discussion.		

1. The Land Reform (Labour Tenants) Act, because she was a domestic worker, not a farm worker, and had the right to reside on the farm and graze her livestock there.
2. No. The correct procedures were not followed. Only the Land Claims Court can order an eviction, not the new owner.
3. Mr Mvuso has the right not to be evicted from the property under the Constitution and Land Reform (Labour Tenants) Act.

5.9 Environmental rights

Outcomes

After completion of this section learners will be able to:

1. Explain the law relating to environmental rights.

Assessment criteria

1. The law governing environment rights is discussed.

2. The principles of the National Environmental Management Act (NEMA) are applied to a case of pollution.

3. Methods of protecting the environment against new developments are identified.

4. A set of facts is examined and a decision is made on how to protect the community against dust pollution using the NEMA principles.

5.9.1 Introduction
(Learner's Manual p 542)

Problem 1: Some questions on environmental pollution *(Learner's Manual p 543)*

AIM: The aim of the exercise is to provide an opportunity for learners to reflect on their personal experiences of pollution of the environment in their areas, or cases they have learnt about.

PROCEDURE		TIME	
1. Introduction.		Introduction:	5 min
2. Divide the class of learners into small groups.		Group discussions:	10 min
3. Each group to discuss one question.		Report back:	15 min
4. Report back.		General discussion:	5 min
5. General discussion.		**TOTAL:**	**35 min**

1. If people are exposed to a polluted environment, they might end up suffering from a number of diseases such as cholera, tuberculosis or diarrhoea. These diseases might also result in the deaths of some people.

2. This is an open-ended question. Educators should allow learners to come up with as many of their personal experiences as possible. The educator should encourage learners to use newspaper clippings to identify cases of environmental pollution in their regions or elsewhere.

5.9.2 What do environmental laws say?
(Learner's Manual p 543)

Problem 2: Applying the NEMA principles to a case of environmental pollution
(Learner's Manual p 544)

AIM: The object of the exercise is for learners to determine how to resolve, using NEMA principles, the problems identified by the groups in Problem 1 above.

PROCEDURE		TIME	
1. Introduction.		Introduction:	5 min
2. Divide learners into small groups (same groups as in Problem 1).		Group discussions:	10 min
3. Each group to use NEMA principles to solve the problem identified by it.		Report back:	15 min
		General discussion:	5 min
4. Report back.		**TOTAL:**	**35 min**
5. General discussion.			

(**Note:** This exercise is linked to Problem 1 above. Each group must choose one example of environmental pollution and apply the NEMA principles to it.)

5.9.4 How to stop actions that harm the environment and health

(Learner's Manual p 547)

Problem 3: Taking action against the mining companies *(Learner's Manual p 548)*

AIM: The aim of this exercise is for learners to analyse a set of facts and to decide how to resolve the problem using the Constitution and the NEMA principles.

PROCEDURE		TIME	
1. Introduction.		Introduction:	5 min
2. Divide learners into small groups (different to those in Problems 1 and 2 above).		Group discussions:	15 min
		Report back:	15 min
3. Give each group one question to discuss.		General discussion:	10 min
4. Report back.		**TOTAL:**	**45 min**
5. General discussion.			

1. The constitutional rights of the community include: the right to a healthy environment free from pollution; the right of access to health care services; the right to life; and the right to human dignity.
2. When taking action against the company, the community may decide to go for one of the following options:
   (a) laying a complaint against the company with the local or provincial authority or with the director-general of the relevant department;
   (b) asking for conciliation, mediation or arbitration – to be paid for by the state; or
   (c) going to court against the company and/or the state. The company would be sued for violating the community's right to a pollution-free environment. The state would be sued for not protecting the community against the company – for not fulfilling the duty to protect (see above para 5.1.3).

(**Note:** See guidelines in *Learner's Manual* paras 5.9.4.1 and 5.9.4.2 for taking action under the NEMA principles.)

Further reading

5.1 The Constitution and socio-economic rights

Constitution of the Republic of South Africa, 1996

Khoza S (ed) *Socio-Economic Rights in South Africa: A Resource Book* 2 ed (2007) 13–86

Liebenberg S & Pillay K (eds) *Socio-Economic Rights in South Africa: A Resource Book* (2000)

Soobramoney v Minister of Health, KwaZulu-Natal 1998 (1) SA 765 (CC); 1997 (12) BCLR 1696 (CC)

Government of the Republic of South Africa v Grootboom 2001 (1) SA 46 (CC); 2000 (11) BCLR 1169 (CC)

Minister of Health v Treatment Action Campaign (No 1) 2002 (5) SA 703 (CC); 2002 (10) BCLR 1075 (CC)

Khosa v Minister of Social Development 2004 (6) SA 505 (CC); 2004 (6) BCLR 569 (CC)

President of the Republic of South Africa and Another v Modderklip Boerdery (Pty) Ltd 2005 (5) SA 3 (CC); 2005 (8) BCLR 786 (CC)

Mazibuko v City of Johannesburg 2010 (4) SA 1 (CC)

5.2 Education rights

Khoza S (ed) *Socio-Economic Rights in South Africa: A Resource Book* 2 ed (2007) 407–439

Liebenberg S & Pillay K (eds) *Socio-Economic Rights in South Africa: A Resource Book* (2000)

Motala v University of Natal 1995 (3) BCLR 374 (D)

Christian Education South Africa v Minister of Education 2000 (4) SA 757 (CC); 2000 (10) BCLR 1051

5.3 Social welfare rights

Khoza S (ed) *Socio-Economic Rights in South Africa: A Resource Book* 2 ed (2007) 375–406

Liebenberg S & Pillay K (eds) *Socio-Economic Rights in South Africa: A Resource Book* (2000)

Social Assistance Act 13 of 2004

Khosa v Minister of Social Development 2004 (6) SA 505 (CC); 2004 (6) BCLR 569 (CC)

5.4 Health rights

Dhai A & McQuoid-Mason D *Bioethics, Human Rights and Health Law* (2011)

Khoza S (ed) *Socio-Economic Rights in South Africa: A Resource Book* 2 ed (2007) 371–310

Liebenberg S & Pillay K (eds) *Socio-Economic Rights in South Africa: A Resource Book* (2000)

Children's Act 38 of 2005

Choice on Termination of Pregnancy Act 92 of 1996

Criminal Law (Sexual Offences and Related Matters) Amendment Act 32 of 2007

Medical Schemes Act 131 of 1998

National Health Act 61 of 2003

Tobacco Products Control Act 83 of 1993

Jansen van Vuuren v Kruger 1993 (4) SA 842 (A)

Castell v De Greef 1994 (4) SA 408 (C)

Soobramoney v Minister of Health, KwaZulu-Natal 1998 (1) SA 765 (CC); 1997 (12) BCLR 1696 (CC)

B v Minister of Correctional Services 1997 (4) SA 441 (C); 1997 (6) BCLR 789 (C)

Minister of Health v Treatment Action Campaign (No 1) 2002 (5) SA 703 (CC); 2002 (10) BCLR 1075 (CC)

N v Government of the Republic of South Africa (No 1) 2006 (6) SA 543 (D); 2007 (1) BCLR 84 (D)

5.5 Food rights

Khoza S (ed) *Socio-Economic Rights in South Africa: A Resource Book* 2 ed (2007) 311–342

Brand D 'Right to food' in Brand D & Heyns C *Socio-Economic Rights in South Africa* (2005) 153

5.6 Housing rights

Khoza S (ed) *Socio-Economic Rights in South Africa: A Resource Book* 2 ed (2007) 229–270

De Vos P 'Right to housing' in Brand D & Heyns C *Socio-Economic Rights in South Africa* (2005) 85

Extension of Security of Tenure Act 62 of 1997

Home Loan and Mortgage Disclosure Act 63 of 2000

Housing Act 107 of 1997

Prevention of Illegal Eviction from and the Unlawful Occupation of Land Act 19 of 1998

Rental Housing Act 50 of 1999

Government of the Republic of South Africa v Grootboom 2001 (1) SA 46 (CC); 2000 (11) BCLR 1169 (CC)

President of the Republic of South Africa and Another v Modderklip Boerdery (Pty) Ltd 2005 (5) SA 3 (CC); 2005 (8) BCLR 786 (CC)

5.7 Water rights

Khoza S (ed) *Socio-Economic Rights in South Africa: A Resource Book* 2 ed (2007) 343–374

National Water Act 36 of 1998

Water Services Act 108 of 1997

City Council of Pretoria v Walker 1998 (2) SA 363 (CC)

Federation for a Sustainable Environment v Minister of Water Affairs case no 35672/12 [2012] ZAGPPHC 128, 10 July 2012, North Gauteng High Court (unreported)

5.8 Land rights

Khoza S (ed) *Socio-Economic Rights in South Africa: A Resource Book* 2 ed (2007) 193–228

Communal Property Associations Act 28 of 1996

Extension of Security of Tenure Act 62 of 1997

Interim Protection of Informal Land Rights Act 31 of 1996

Land Reform (Labour Tenants) Act 3 of 1996

Prevention of Illegal Eviction from and the Unlawful Occupation of Land Act 19 of 1998

Restitution of Land Rights Act 22 of 1994

Zulu v Van Rensburg 1996 (4) SA 1236 (LCC)

Nkuzi Development Association v Government of the Republic of South Africa 2002 (2) SA 733 (LCC)

President of the Republic of South Africa and Another v Modderklip Boerdery (Pty) Ltd 2005 (5) SA 3 (CC); 2005 (8) BCLR 786 (CC)

5.9 Environmental rights

Khoza S (ed) *Socio-Economic Rights in South Africa: A Resource Book* 2 ed (2007) 163–192

Legal Resources Centre *Environmental Justice Project Report* (2002)

Environment Conservation Act 73 of 1989

National Environmental Management Act 107 of 1998

Promotion of Access to Information Act 2 of 2000

Promotion of Administrative Justice Act 3 of 2000

Street law

6. Employment law

CONTENTS

PART SIX

Employment law

6.1 Employment and applying for a job

Outcomes

After completion of this section learners will be able to:

1. Explain the laws affecting workers or employees who apply for a job.

Assessment criteria

1. A set of facts is examined and a decision is made on whether a job advertisement is discriminatory.

2. A set of facts is examined and a decision is made on whether certain questions during a job interview were discriminatory.

3. Sets of facts are examined and decisions are made on whether the testing of job applicants should be allowed.

4. A set of facts is examined and a decision is made on whether affirmative action should be allowed.

6.1.1 Applying for a job *(Learner's Manual p 558)*

Problem 1: Are these advertisements discriminatory? *(Learner's Manual p 559)*

AIM: The object of this exercise is to teach learners about the concept of an unlawful, discriminatory advertisement and how the Employment Equity Act protects job applicants from discriminatory practices.

PROCEDURE		TIME	
1. Introduce task.		Introduce task:	5 min
2. Divide the class of learners into small groups.		Group discussions:	10 min
3. Each group to discuss one question.		Report back:	25 min
4. Group discussion.		General discussion:	5 min
5. Report back.		**TOTAL:**	**45 min**
6. General discussion.			

1. By specifying that the applicant should be a male, this is clearly discrimination on the grounds of gender. In fact, the Advertising Standards Act prohibits such advertisements from even being placed in the newspaper. By asking for a 'young' man, this would also be discrimination on the grounds of age. The only time that discrimination on the grounds of age is allowed is if people are dismissed on reaching their normal or agreed retirement age or if their being young is an 'inherent requirement of the job' (that is, it is essential for them to be able to perform their job), which is not the case in this example.

2. By asking specifically for 'Zulu-speaking employees' to work at a busy butchery in KwaZulu-Natal, this would appear to be discrimination on the grounds of language or even ethnic origin or culture. However, if all the customers at the butchery speak only Zulu, it would be an inherent requirement of the job. Unless this is the case, the requirement seems to be unjustified.

3. By requiring 'women' to apply for the position, this would be discrimination on the grounds of gender. It might be argued that it is an 'inherent requirement of the job' because of the nature of the business being an 'exotic dance club', but it may also be possible to have male exotic dancers.

4. It is acceptable to require an applicant to have a university qualification, such as a BCom degree, for the position of accounts manager. However, the requirement must be necessary and not merely a way of keeping applicants out of a job that does not require a university degree. (For example, more white applicants might have university degrees than black applicants, and this could then result in indirect discrimination.)

5. This is discrimination on the grounds of age. Some jobs, such as air-hostesses, have an age limitation. Learners should be encouraged to discuss whether this is reasonable and essential for the performance of the job.

6. This seems to be acceptable as job experience is a usual requirement. However, the Employment Equity Act states (with regard to affirmative action appointments – discussed in *Learner's Manual* para 6.1.1.4.1) that where a person is otherwise suitable for a position and is lacking relevant job experience, this should not be held against him or her.

7. This is discrimination on the basis of 'family responsibility' and 'marital status'. It could perhaps be argued that night work is not suitable for married people or those with families – but this is not necessarily the case.

8. This would seem at first glance to be discrimination on the basis of HIV/AIDS, but it is not. In fact, the advertisement specifically requires HIV-positive persons to work at a HIV Learner Counselling Centre. It is not discriminating against them because the Centre requires people who are HIV-positive. Does it discriminate against people who are not HIV-positive?

Problem 2: The job interview
(Learner's Manual p 560)

AIM: The aim of this exercise is to give learners an opportunity to learn job application and interviewing skills.

PROCEDURE	TIME	
1. Divide the class of learners into small groups of four each.	Explain task:	5 min
2. Each group should consider the questions asked and decide whether they are appropriate or not.	Group discussion:	10 min
	Report back on questions:	10 min
3. Report back on questions.	Role-play:	5 min
4. Each group should select one person to act as the employer, Mr Naidoo, and another as the applicant, Joan Smith. They should then role-play the interview and Joan Smith should respond to the questions in an appropriate manner.	Report back on role-play:	10 min
	General discussion:	5 min
	TOTAL:	**45 min**
5. The other two members of the group should critique the answers given, decide whether any of her answers were incorrect or improper, and should suggest alternative responses.		
6. Report back on role-plays.		
7. General discussion.		

Question 1

1. This is acceptable.
2. It is not acceptable to ask an applicant's age unless age is an 'inherent requirement of the job'. The question might be justified to find out how long a person had been working, but it would have been better to ask for years of experience.
3. It is not acceptable to discriminate against non-South African citizens if they have relevant work permits. It will be acceptable to ask the applicants whether they are South African citizens, and if not, whether they have work permits.
4. This is discrimination on the grounds of 'marital status'. If Joan answered in the affirmative, and then was not employed, this would clearly be discrimination on the grounds of marital status.
5. This is discrimination on the grounds of 'family responsibility', 'birth' or 'pregnancy'.
6. You have to establish why this question was asked, but it would appear to be an acceptable question.
7. It would have to be relevant to the job to establish whether an applicant has a criminal conviction. To simply ask whether he or she has ever been arrested is unfair, as it might have even been a wrongful arrest. It might be a requirement of some jobs that a person does not have a criminal conviction; for example, a lawyer cannot have a criminal conviction and an educator may not be convicted of being a paedophile.
8. This might be discriminatory, as height requirements often have a disparate impact on women (ie, it might seem to be a neutral requirement, but few women may be able to comply, and this would lead to indirect discrimination). The same might apply to weight requirements as men are generally heavier.
9. This is unfair on the grounds of 'religious discrimination'.
10. This would be unfair on the basis of 'language' or 'culture' discrimination – unless speaking Xhosa is an inherent requirement of the job.
11. This is discrimination on the basis of HIV/AIDS status and an invasion of privacy.
12. This would seem to be sexual harassment (see *Learner's Manual* para 6.8.2.), where a person will only be offered a job in exchange for a sexual favour.
13. This seems to be an irrelevant and unnecessary question.

Question 2

Learners in groups of four should then be required to role-play the interview. One person should be the employer, Mr Naidoo, and the other the applicant, Joan Smith. Joan Smith should respond to the questions in an appropriate manner. The other two members of the group should critique the answers given, decide whether any of her answers were incorrect or improper and should suggest alternative responses. They should also indicate which answers were particularly good and why.

Question 3

In the report back, the groups should indicate how well they think Joan Smith did in the interview, and whether she asserted her rights and maintained a proper demeanour in the interview.

Problem 3: When should aptitude and medical tests be allowed?
(Learner's Manual p 562)

AIM: The aim of this exercise is for learners to become familiar with the provisions of the Employment Equity Act with regard to medical, HIV/AIDS, and psychometric testing.

PROCEDURE	TIME	
1. Introduce the exercise.	Introduction:	5 min
2. Each learner should consider the questions individually.	Individual work on questions:	15 min
3. Report back by individual learners.	Report back:	15 min
4. General discussion.	General discussion:	5 min
	TOTAL:	**40 min**

Learners should understand that medical testing is not allowed unless it is necessary in the light of the medical facts, employment conditions, social policy, distribution of employee benefits and the inherent requirements of the job. Similarly, psychometric testing should not be allowed unless the test is shown to be scientifically valid and reasonable, can be fairly applied to employees, and is not biased against an employee or group of employees.

1. An eyesight test would be justifiable in light of the requirements of the job.
2. This might be seen as an invasion of privacy, but it could be argued that it is an inherent requirement of the job that all employees be drug- and alcohol-free.
3. The HIV/AIDS test would only be allowed if the employer applies to the Labour Court for permission. The Labour Court will give permission if it thinks that the test is necessary and reasonable in order to prevent a threat or danger to patients. The Hepatitis C test will only be allowed if the employment conditions necessitate it – where, for instance, the nurses are involved in surgery or the patients are exposed to their blood.
4. This would seem to be acceptable.
5. Although an IQ test is scientifically valid, it does not seem to be necessary for the position of an accountant.

Problem 4: Is affirmative action necessary?
(Learner's Manual p 564)

AIM: The aim of this exercise is to allow learners to understand the concept of affirmative action and to understand its purpose.

Question 1

PROCEDURE	TIME	
1. Introduce exercise.	Introduction:	5 min
2. Each learner should consider the questions individually.	Consider the questions individually:	10 min
3. Report back by individual learners.	Report back:	10 min
4. General discussion.	General discussion:	10 min
	TOTAL:	**35 min**

Question and answer

As both Mandla and Sarie fall into designated groups, both are entitled to benefit in terms of the company's affirmative action policy. However, it is important to assess the needs of the company and to establish which designated group is under-represented at Fast Sales Co. Although it would appear that Sarie is better qualified for the job, it is important to establish whether a tertiary qualification is needed to perform the job.

Question 2

PROCEDURE ⋮☰		TIME 🕓
1. Divide class into two groups: one to argue in favour of affirmative action, and the other against it. 2. Subdivide the two groups into small groups to prepare arguments. 3. Each small group should elect a spokesperson. 4. Small groups prepare arguments. 5. Spokespersons meet to coordinate arguments for large group teams. 6. The educator or a learner could act as a chairperson. 7. Conduct the debate. 8. Have the team in favour of affirmative action make its argument before the team opposed to it. 9. At the end, all learners vote for one of the arguments.		Introduce debate: 5 min Divide the class into large and small groups: 5 min Groups prepare arguments: 10 min Spokespersons meet to coordinate arguments for large group teams: 5 min Conduct debate: 15 min Vote: 5 min **TOTAL: 45 min**

DEBATE

Possible arguments:

Advantages of affirmative action:

1. Even though apartheid has been abolished, we need more proactive steps to be taken to make our workplaces more representative.
2. Some employers will be more resistant to change and have to be forced to make affirmative action appointments.
3. Employees who have come from disadvantaged backgrounds need to be given an opportunity, as they will not be in an equal position to get jobs due to lack of experience and other qualifications.
4. It is a short-term concept (only meant to be in place for approximately five years) to correct the problems of the past.
5. There are already positive results in the workplace.

Disadvantages of affirmative action:

1. It makes affirmative action employees feel that they are token appointments and not really deserving of the job.
2. Affirmative action appointments are often given the job, and then left to struggle with the work without adequate training and assistance.
3. It causes antagonism between affirmative action appointments and old employees.
4. It requires employers to do a race-classification exercise.
5. It ends up being a long-term concept.

For how to conduct a debate where there are large number of learners see *Educator's Manual* para G8.

6.2 Contracts of employment

Outcomes

After completion of this section learners will be able to:

1. Explain the law relating to contracts of employment.

Assessment criteria

1. The laws regarding employment contracts are identified.

2. A set of facts is examined and a decision is made on whether a person is an employee or an independent contractor.

3. The duties of employees and employers are identified.

Problem 1: Drawing up an employment contract (Learner's Manual p 565)

AIM: The aim of this exercise is to allow learners to think about all the information that should be included in an employment contract.

PROCEDURE
1. Introduce exercise.
2. Learners to be divided into pairs.
3. Learners to brainstorm all the information they think should be included in an employment contract, giving reasons.
4. Report back by pairs.
5. General discussion.

TIME	
Introduction:	5 min
Brainstorming:	10 min
Report back:	10 min
General discussion:	5 min
TOTAL:	**30 min**

The following information should be included:
1. the employer's name and address;
2. the employee's name and address;
3. the employee's occupation or a brief description of the work to be done;
4. the place of work;
5. the date of commencement of work;
6. the employee's ordinary work hours and work days;
7. the employee's salary;
8. the overtime rate;
9. other payments to be made to employee;
10. the date when the salary will be paid;
11. details of any deductions from salary;
12. amount of leave that can be taken; and
13. the period of notice.

6.2.1 Who is an employee?

(Learner's Manual p 565)

Problem 2: Identifying a person as an employee or an independent contractor

(Learner's Manual p 568)

AIM: The purpose of this exercise is to get learners to realise that the distinction between employees and independent contractors is not always clear. They need to understand that the classification will affect the protection afforded to them in terms of the Labour Relations Act and the Employment Equity Act, which do not extend to independent contractors. Learners also need to be made aware that often employers will attempt to make an employee look like an independent contractor in order to escape responsibilities. A legal presumption has been introduced to assist employees in this situation.

PROCEDURE	TIME	
1. Introduce exercise.	Introduction:	5 min
2. Divide class into small groups.	Group discussions:	10 min
3. Allocate one question to each group.	Report back:	20 min
4. Report back.	General discussion:	10 min
5. General discussion.	**TOTAL:**	**45 min**

1. Using the presumption, it appears that Barry is an employee on a 6-month fixed-term contract. He is part of the organisation as he has an office at the company. He has probably also worked more than 40 hours a week for the company for more than three months (but we do not know this for sure). The onus then shifts to the employer to rebut this presumption. Using the dominant-impression test, he does not seem to be under the control of the employer as he is not supervised, he works his own hours, he is only paid on completion of the job of work (which is very significant), and he only files monthly reports. This would seem to indicate that he is an independent contractor.

2. Joe would definitely be an independent contractor, both in terms of the presumption and the dominant-impression test. In terms of the presumption, he is not economically dependent upon, nor under the control of, Sam. He uses his own tools of the trade. On the dominant-impression test, he is paid on completion of the job, he does not even do the work himself, and he is not controlled or supervised in any way.

3. It would seem that Peter is an employee. Learners must realise that it is not always necessary for employees to be supervised at all times, as long as they are ultimately under the control of their employer. Peter is allocated work to do, is provided with tools and equipment, and is paid monthly and not on completion of the job.

6.3 Labour laws and social benefits

Outcomes

After completion of this section learners will be able to:

1. Explain the laws that apply to skills, health and safety and benefits of the workplace.

Assessment criteria

1. The purpose and application of the Basic Conditions of Employment Act is explained.

2. The concept of paternity leave is discussed.

3. The purpose and application of the Occupational Health and Safety Act is explained.

4. The principle of minimum wages is discussed.

5. The purpose and application of the Skills Development Act is explained.

6. A set of facts is examined and a decision is made on the most appropriate benefits for an employee.

7. The purpose and application of the Compensation for Occupational Injuries and Diseases Act is explained.

6.3.1. Basic conditions of employment *(Learner's Manual p 570)*

Problem 1: Understanding the Basic Conditions of Employment Act *(Learner's Manual p 571)*

AIM: The aim of this exercise is to make learners aware that, in the absence of the Basic Conditions of Employment Act, employees are likely to be exploited, as they are invariably in a more vulnerable position.

PROCEDURE	TIME	
1. Divide class into small groups.	Introduce exercise:	5 min
2. Each group to discuss one question.	Group discussions:	10 min
3. Report back.	Report back:	10 min
4. General discussion.	General discussion:	5 min
	TOTAL:	**30 min**

1. The Basic Conditions of Employment Act is necessary to protect vulnerable workers from exploitation. It is very common for the employer to be in a much stronger bargaining position than employees and employees are often vulnerable. They are also often desperate for a job and will agree to any condition imposed upon them, no matter how unfair. The Act ensures that employee's basic rights are protected. Even if employees want to work more than the maximum hours permitted by the Act, they are prevented from doing so. While some people think that this is unfair, as it should be up to the individual to decide on his or her working hours, it is necessary to prevent exploitation by imposing these minimum conditions. Learners should be asked to think about the

sweatshops in China where child labour is used and employees work 18-hour days for $1 per day. This would not happen if there was an Act like the Basic Conditions of Employment Act.

2. Paternity leave is not recognised in South African law and the only leave a father is allowed when a child is born is three days family responsibility leave. In some companies this has increased to five days. Learners should debate the merits of allowing paternity leave. It is recognised in some overseas countries. Is it a violation of the constitutional right to equality to allow employees maternity leave, but not paternity leave?

6.3.3   Minimum wages

(Learner's Manual p 572)

Problem 2: Do you agree with minimum wages? (Learner's Manual p 572)

AIM: The aim of this exercise is to encourage learners to debate the advantages and disadvantages of having a minimum wage. They need to be made aware that, without a minimum wage, some employees will be exploited. For example, there have been many reported cases of domestic workers being paid only R400 a month.

PROCEDURE

1. Divide class into two large groups: one should argue in favour of minimum wages, and the other should argue against it.
2. Subdivide the large groups into small groups to prepare arguments for the large groups' point of view.
3. Each small group should elect a spokesperson to represent their large group team.
4. Small groups prepare arguments.
5. Spokespersons meet to coordinate for large group teams.
6. The educator or a learner could act as a chairperson of the debate.
7. Conduct the debate.
8. Have the team in favour of minimum wages make its argument before the team opposed to it.
9. At the end of the debate, all the learners should vote in favour of one of the arguments.

TIME

Introduce the debate:	5 min
Divide class into large and small groups:	5 min
Small groups prepare arguments:	10 min
Spokespersons to coordinate arguments for large group teams:	5 min
Conduct debate:	15 min
Vote:	5 min
TOTAL:	**45 min**

Possible arguments:

Advantages:

1. Employees will not be exploited by employers.
2. There will not be huge discrepancies in salaries.
3. Employees can earn a living wage.

Disadvantages:

1. Loss of jobs for employees.
2. Discourages employers from employing new employees.
3. No freedom of choice for employees who would rather earn a lower wage than none at all.

6.3.6 Social benefits

(Learner's Manual p 574)

Problem 3: What benefits are appropriate?

(Learner's Manual p 574)

AIM: The aim of this exercise is to make learners aware that benefits do not form part of the employee's salary and are additional perks that can be negotiated in the employment contract. The employer is under no obligation to provide additional benefits to employees.

PROCEDURE
1. Introduce exercise.
2. Divide into small groups.
3. Groups consider the question.
4. Report back.
5. General discussion.

TIME	
Introduction:	5 min
Groups consider the question:	10 min
Report back:	10 min
General discussion:	5 min
TOTAL:	**30 min**

Learners should understand that different benefits are more appropriate for some employees than others.

Kim would benefit from medical aid, pension benefits, study allowance, free parking, entertainment allowance and a travel allowance.

Benefits that would not be appropriate unless she is going to get married soon or move out of her parent's home are maternity benefits, childcare benefits (like a crèche facility) and a housing allowance.

6.4 Collective bargaining and trade unions

Outcomes

After completion of this section learners will be able to:

1. Explain the meaning of collective bargaining and how trade unions work.

Assessment criteria

1. The concept of collective bargaining is explained.
2. The advantages and disadvantages of belonging to a trade union are discussed.
3. The rules that apply to strikes are identified.
4. A set of facts is examined and a decision is made on whether the conduct during a strike was lawful or unlawful.
5. A negotiation exercise is undertaken and an agreement reached.

6.4.4 Negotiating wages and working conditions *(Learner's Manual p 576)*

Problem 1: The annual wage negotiation *(Learner's Manual p 577)*

AIM: The aim of this exercise is to make learners aware of the increased power wielded by employees collectively. They should also be made aware of the consequences of failed negotiations between employers and unions and that strike action is costly and damaging for all parties and for the economy.

PROCEDURE	TIME	
1. Learners should be divided into groups of six.	Introduction to exercise:	10 min
2. Each group should be further divided into two groups of three, with one group representing the employer and the other group representing the employees/union.	Negotiations:	20 min
	Report back:	10 min
	General discussion:	5 minn
3. The groups should try to negotiate a settlement between the employer's offers and the employees' demands using persuasion (and any other tactics). If a settlement is not reached the employees will go on strike, which will be damaging to both the employer's business (unable to operate) and the employees (will not be paid).	**TOTAL:**	**45 min**
4. Once a settlement has been reached the groups should draw up a collective agreement that reflects the compromise.		
5. Learners should then give feedback to the class on their negotiations, particularly about how they managed to get the other side to concede on issues and what tactics they used to convince the other party (eg whether they traded positions, used forceful arguments, lied to the other side, etc).		

For how to conduct a negotiation refer learners to the *Learner's Manual* para 1.3.2.1.

6.4.5   Strikes
(Learner's Manual p 578)

Problem 2: The role of unions
(Learner's Manual p 580)

AIM: The aim of this exercise is for students to engage in a debate in favour of and against having unions in the workplace, as well as to understand what is meant by essential services and lawful conduct.

Question 1:

PROCEDURE	TIME	
1. Divide class into two teams: one should argue in favour of having unions at the workplace and the other against it.	Introduce the lesson:	5 min
2. Subdivide the teams into small groups to consider arguments in favour of their team's position.	Divide into small groups:	5 min
3. Each small group should elect a spokesperson to represent their team.	Prepare arguments:	10 min
4. The spokespersons should meet and refine the arguments for their team.	Refine team arguments:	5 min
5. The instructor or a learner could act as a chairperson.	Conduct debate:	10 min
6. Conduct the debate.	Vote:	5 min
7. Have the learners in favour of unions at the workplace make their arguments before the learners opposed to it.	General discussion:	5 min
8. Learners should vote in favour of one of the arguments.	**TOTAL:**	**45 min**
9. General discussion.		

For how to conduct a debate involving large number of learners see *Educator's Manual* para G8.

Advantages:
1. Unions negotiate better working conditions and wage increases for union members, as employers are likely to take unions more seriously than non-unionised employees.
2. Unions can represent employees in disciplinary hearings, retrenchment consultations and other grievances.
3. Unions are skilled negotiators and very well acquainted with labour laws.
4. Collective action is more powerful than individual action; for example, the threat of a strike is more serious than the threat of one employee refusing to work.

Disadvantages:
1. Unions cause animosity between employer and employees.
2. Unions sometimes have their own political agenda.
3. There is a higher incidence of strikes.
4. They hinder communication between employer and employees.

Question 2:

<table>
<tr><td>

PROCEDURE

1. Class to discuss the question in pairs.
2. Report back
3. General discussion.

</td><td>

TIME

Discussions in pairs:	5 min
Report back:	10 min
General discussion:	5 min
TOTAL:	**20 min**

</td></tr>
</table>

Learners should understand the purpose of classifying employees as 'essential services'. They should be encouraged to debate which services should be seen as posing a 'danger to the life and safety of others' if not provided.

Examples of essential services are: police force, ambulance drivers, fire department, air traffic control, nurses in high care wards, electricity department and the sewerage department. What about municipal workers such as refuse collectors? (If rubbish is not collected after a few weeks this could endanger the health of people.)

Question 3:

<table>
<tr><td>

PROCEDURE

1. Divide class into pairs.
2. Allocate one example to each pair.
3. Each pair to consider whether their example constitutes lawful conduct.
4. Report back.
5. General discussion

</td><td>

TIME

Introduction:	5 min
Discussions in pairs:	10 min
Report back:	15 min
General discussion:	10 min
TOTAL:	**40 min**

</td></tr>
</table>

(a) This is a go-slow, which is only lawful if the proper strike procedure is first followed.

(b) This is unlawful behaviour as it is misconduct.

(c) This is an unlawful dismissal as lawfully striking employees (who have followed the proper strike procedure) are protected against dismissal.

(d) This is lawful because the principle of 'no work, no pay' applies.

(e) If they are classified as an 'essential service' then this will be an unlawful strike.

(f) There is no issue of mutual dispute between the employer and employees and this would not be a lawful strike. However the employees are committing misconduct by absenting themselves without the employer's permission and can be dismissed or disciplined.

6.5 Disciplinary codes

Outcomes

After completion of this section learners will be able to:

1. Explain the purpose and application of disciplinary codes.

Assessment criteria

1. The purpose of a disciplinary code is explained.
2. The concept of progressive and corrective discipline is explained.
3. An example of a disciplinary code is given.
4. A disciplinary code is drafted.

6.5.3 Corrective and progressive discipline *(Learner's Manual p 582)*

Problem 1: Drafting a disciplinary code *(Learner's Manual p 583)*

AIM: The object of this exercise is to make learners aware that disciplinary codes will vary according to the particular workplace and will have been negotiated and agreed to by the employer and union/employees. Their purpose is to codify the rules at the workplace and to give the employer a mechanism with which to deal with breaches of these rules.

PROCEDURE
1. Introduce exercise.
2. Divide class into pairs.
3. Pairs brainstorm disciplinary code for a manufacturing plant.
4. Report back.
5. Class to consider if answers would change in a retail store situation.
6. General discussion.

TIME	
Introduction:	5 min
Divide class into pairs:	2 min
Pairs brainstorm disciplinary code for a manufacturing plant:	13 min
Report back:	10 min
Pairs consider retail store situation:	10 min
General discussion:	5 min
TOTAL:	**45 min**

As the factory uses very expensive and dangerous machinery, safety is an important issue and drinking alcohol on duty would be regarded as very serious, as would leaving a workstation unattended. As the machines are switched on at 8 am daily and switched off every day at 5 pm, punctuality is also important.

In a retail store situation the most serious offences would be: theft, smoking and drinking on duty, insubordination, not wearing proper uniform and lateness.

Insubordination, assault, sexual harassment and absenteeism are always treated as serious offences, irrespective of the type of business.

Less serious offences would include leaving the workstation unattended or untidy, and negligent work.

Suggested offences and disciplinary actions

OFFENCE	1ST	2ND	3RD	4TH
DRINKING ON DUTY	Dismissal			
INSUBORDINATION	Final written warning	Dismissal		
LATENESS	Final written warning	Dismissal		
ABSENTEEISM	Written warning	Final written warning	Dismissal	
THEFT	Dismissal			
ASSAULT	Final written warning/ dismissal			
SMOKING ON DUTY	First written warning	Final written warning	Dismissal	
FAILURE TO WEAR PROTECTIVE CLOTHING AND EQUIPMENT	Written warning	Final written warning	Dismissal	
LEAVING WORKSTATION UNTIDY	Verbal warning	Written warning	Final written warning	Dismissal
LEAVING WORKSTATION UNATTENDED	Final written warning/ dismissal			
SEXUAL HARASSMENT	Final written warning/ dismissal			
NEGLIGENT WORK	Written warning	Final written warning	Dismissal	

Outcomes

After completion of this section learners will be able to:

1. Explain the meaning of privacy and its application in the workplace.
2. Explain the law regarding 'whistle blowing'.

Assessment criteria

1. The meaning of privacy and its limits at the workplace are discussed.
2. The employer's right to perform drug tests and searches at the workplace is discussed.
3. The employer's right to perform polygraph tests on employees is discussed.
4. The employer's right to regulate an employee's use of e-mail and the Internet at work is discussed.
5. A set of facts is examined and a decision is taken on whether the employee's rights to privacy were infringed.
6. A set of facts is examined and a decision is made on whether the disclosures by the 'whistle-blower' are protected by the Protected Disclosures Act.

6.6.6 Polygraph tests

(Learner's Manual p 586)

Problem 1: Were the employees' rights to privacy infringed?

(Learner's Manual p 586)

AIM: The object of this exercise is to make learners realise that the right to privacy is not totally protected at the workplace, and that employers are entitled to infringe upon this right where it is necessary and reasonable to do so.

PROCEDURE		TIME	
1. Introduce exercise.		Introduce exercise:	5 min
2. Divide class into small groups.		Divide class into groups:	2 min
3. Allocate two questions to each group.		Allocate questions to groups:	3 min
4. Groups to consider questions.		Groups consider questions:	10 min
5. Report back.		Report back:	20 min
6. General discussion.		General discussion:	5 min
		TOTAL:	**45 min**

1. The manager of the construction company is entitled to give an honest reference to the manager of the cement company and this might necessitate him disclosing negative comments about her working abilities. He should not, however, disclose private personal information.
2. It is acceptable for employees' bags to be searched provided that this is done in a correct manner and all employees are treated equally.

3. It is acceptable to install security cameras provided that the employees are aware of them and provided that they are not put in the toilets etc.

4. It is acceptable for the company to have an e-mail policy which prohibits employees from using e-mail for their private use. If this policy is in place, Pat is entitled to monitor the electronic mail between her employees. Whether she can fire Jim will depend upon the disciplinary code and how seriously it treats the private use of e-mail. If it has not been treated very seriously in the past then it is unlikely that dismissal will be an appropriate punishment.

5. It is acceptable for an employer to have a dress code or requirements regarding appearance, including hairstyles. These requirements must however be reasonable and necessary, and not discriminatory. For example, Rastafarians who have dreadlocks can claim that it is religious discrimination to require them to cut off their dreadlocks. The courts would then have to assess whether the requirements of the workplace justify this. Maybe Lionel could cover his hair while at work?

6. Employees cannot be forced to take a polygraph test, but if they refuse to do so, it will appear to be very suspicious and may result in a negative inference being drawn about them. An employee cannot be dismissed for refusing to take a polygraph test.

6.6.7 'Whistle blowing' *(Learner's Manual p 587)*

Problem 2: Were the disclosures protected? *(Learner's Manual p 588)*

AIM: The object of this exercise is to make learners realise that it is an employee's right to report his or her employer for non-compliance with legislation and that employees should be protected from any negative consequences of their doing so.

PROCEDURE
1. Introduce exercise.
2. Divide class into small groups.
3. Each group to discuss one question.
4. Groups to discuss the questions.
5. Report back
6. General discussion.

TIME	
Introduction of exercise:	5 min
Group discussions:	10 min
Report back:	20 min
General discussion:	5 min
TOTAL:	**40 min**

1. Stephen is entitled to report his employer for breaking a law, provided that this allegation is correct and it is not merely a suspicion.

2. If Temba feels that he has been discriminated against he needs to follow proper procedures. These involve lodging a grievance with the CCMA for conciliation and then taking the matter to the Labour Court. He cannot simply report his employer to the CCMA for alleged racist behaviour.

3. This would not be protected and in fact would be a breach of the common-law duty to remain loyal to an employer.

4. This would be a protected disclosure because the employer has failed to comply with health and safety legislation.

5. This would not be a protected disclosure and Sue and Premilla could be defaming their employer and could be held legally liable. They also would be in breach of their common-law duty to be loyal to their employer.

6.7 Employment equity

Outcomes

After completion of this section learners will be able to:

1. Explain the purpose and application of the Employment Equity Act.

Assessment criteria

1. The Employment Equity Act is explained.

2. Different forms of discrimination are identified.

3. The purpose and nature of employment equity plans are discussed.

4. An arbitration exercise involving discrimination is undertaken.

6.7.2 Forms of discrimination

(Learner's Manual p 589)

Problem 1: Examples of discrimination

(Learner's Manual p 590)

AIM: The object of this exercise is to make learners realise that many of the grounds of discrimination overlap.

PROCEDURE	TIME	
1. Introduce exercise.	Introduction:	5 min
2. Class to brainstorm different examples of grounds of discrimination.	Brainstorm examples:	20 min
3. Examples written on blackboard or flipchart.	General discussion:	10 min
4. General discussion.	**TOTAL:**	**35 min**

The designated groups of discrimination are: race, gender, sex, pregnancy, marital status, family responsibility, ethnic or social origin, colour, sexual orientation, age, disability, religion, HIV status, conscience, belief, political opinion, culture, language or birth.

Problem 2: Examples of indirect discrimination

(Learner's Manual p 590)

AIM: The object of this exercise is to make learners understand what is meant by indirect discrimination.

PROCEDURE	TIME	
1. Introduce exercise.	Introduce exercise:	5 min
2. Class to brainstorm different examples of indirect discrimination.	Brainstorm examples:	20 min
3. Examples written on blackboard or flipchart.	General discussion:	10 min
4. General discussion.	**TOTAL:**	**35 min**

The different examples should be based on the listed grounds of 'race, gender, sex, pregnancy, marital status, family responsibility, ethnic or social origin, colour, sexual orientation, age, disability, religion, HIV status, conscience, belief, political opinion, culture, language or birth'.

There are infinite examples of indirect discrimination but it is important that the neutral criteria used have a discriminatory effect. Examples would include requiring all employees to satisfy height requirements that might exclude women; requiring all employees to be able to perform manual labour that could exclude women; requiring short hair that could exclude Rastafarians, etc.

Problem 3: An arbitration between mineworkers and their employer

(Learner's Manual p 592)

AIM: The object of this exercise is for learners to experience an arbitration involving issues of employment equity.

PROCEDURE	TIME	
1. Introduce exercise.	Introduce exercise:	5 min
2. Number off participants in groups of three as numbers one, two and three. The number ones are to act as the workers' organisation; the number twos are to act as arbitrators; and the number threes are to act as the owners of the mine.	Groups of representatives of mineworkers, mine owners and arbitrators prepare for arbitration:	10 min
3. Place all the number one, two and three participants in separate groups: the number ones should prepare arguments for the workers' organisation and the questions they would like to ask the mine owners; the number twos should prepare to conduct the arbitration and should prepare the questions they would like to ask the number ones and threes; the number threes should prepare arguments for the mine owners and the questions they would like to ask the workers' organisation.	Groups of three each conduct arbitrations:	15 min
	Arbitrators in each group give decisions:	5 min
	Report back:	10 min
	General discussion:	5 min
4. The participants should return to their original groups of three and the number twos should conduct the arbitrations between the representatives of the workers and owners in their small groups.	**TOTAL:**	**50 min**
5. Reports back from arbitrators.		
6. General discussion.		

This exercise requires learners to role-play an arbitration in groups of three following the guidelines for the conducting of an arbitration (see the *Learner's Manual* para 6.7.2.5).

The arbitrators should make each side tell their version, asking questions where necessary. He or she should allow the parties to cross-examine each other. Each arbitrator should then give a final and binding decision with reasons.

Questions

1. Number off participants in groups of three as numbers one, two and three. The number ones are to act as the worker's organisation; the number twos are to act as arbitrators; and the number threes are to act as the owners of the mine.

2. Place all the number one, two and three participants in separate groups: The number ones should prepare arguments for the worker's organisation and the questions they would like to ask the mine owners; the number twos should prepare to conduct the arbitration and should prepare the questions they would like to ask the number ones and threes; the number threes should prepare arguments for the mine owners and the questions they would like to ask the workers' organisation.

3. The participants should return to their original groups of three and the number twos should conduct the arbitrations between the representatives of the workers and owners in their small groups.

[Adapted from McQuoid-Mason D, O' Brien E & Green E *Human Rights for All* (1991)]

6.8 Unfair labour practices and sexual harassment

Outcomes

After completion of this section learners will be able to:

1. Understand what is meant by unfair labour practices and sexual harassment.

Assessment criteria

1. The concept of an unfair labour practice and the different forms of sexual harassment are identified.

2. An employer's obligations in respect of sexual harassment at the workplace are discussed.

3. A set of facts is examined and a decision is taken on whether or not the conduct was sexual harassment.

6.8.2 Sexual harassment

(Learner's Manual p 594)

Problem 1: Was it a case of sexual harassment?

(Learner's Manual p 596)

AIM: The object of the exercise is to make learners aware that sexual harassment is very subjective and will depend upon how 'threatened' the particular employee feels. They should be aware that sexual harassment takes many different forms and that even an act of putting up a poster in an employee's office which makes a co-employee feel uncomfortable will be construed as sexual harassment.

PROCEDURE		TIME	
1. Introduce exercise.		Introduce exercise:	5 min
2. Divide class into small groups.		Groups to consider questions:	10 min
3. Each groups to consider one question.		Report back:	25 min
4. Group discussions.		General discussion:	5 min
5. Report back.		**TOTAL:**	**45 min**
6. General discussion.			

1. If the male workers have created a 'hostile working environment' for Sally, even if unintended, this would constitute sexual harassment.

2. If this makes an employee feel uncomfortable it will be regarded as sexual harassment.

3. This would not be sexual harassment if there is no sexual undertone or innuendo to the swearing.

4. Sexual harassment applies to both male and female employees alike. If the male employee feels offended by having his bottom pinched he would be able to allege sexual harassment.

5. This is sexual harassment if it makes a woman employee feel uncomfortable and offended.

6. This is clearly sexual harassment as it involves a sexual favour scenario.

7. If this creates a 'hostile work environment' it would constitute sexual harassment, even if the harasser is a woman.

Outcomes

After completion of this section learners will be able to:

1. Explain the law regarding the termination of employment through dismissal.

Assessment criteria

1. The different types and meanings of dismissal are identified.

2. A set of facts is examined and a decision made on whether the termination of employment was a constructive dismissal.

3. A set of facts is examined and a decision made on whether the dismissals were automatically unfair.

4. A set of facts is examined and a decision made on whether the dismissals were substantially unfair.

5. A set of facts is examined and a decision made on whether the dismissals were procedurally fair.

6. A set of facts is examined and a decision made on what would be a suitable punishment for different acts of misconduct.

7. A set of facts is examined and a decision made on whether the dismissals for incapacity were fair.

8. The rules that apply to retrenchments are identified.

9. A set of facts is given and a decision taken on what types of dismissals have occurred.

6.9.1 The meaning of dismissal
(Learner's Manual p 597)

Problem 1: Was it constructive dismissal?
(Learner's Manual p 598)

AIM: The object of this exercise is to make learners aware that constructive dismissal can only be claimed where the working relationship becomes intolerable, and not simply where the employee resigns due to dissatisfaction or anger.

PROCEDURE	TIME	
1. Introduce exercise.	Introduction to exercise:	5 min
2. Divide class into small groups.	Groups to consider questions:	10 min
3. Allocate one question to each group.	Report back to class:	20 min
4. Groups to consider questions.	General discussion:	5 min
5. Report back.	**TOTAL:**	**40 min**
6. General discussion.		

1. Unless the working relationship has broken down and become intolerable, and Sandy cannot be expected to put up with it any longer, this would seem to be constructive dismissal. Employers are entitled to chastise their employees as long as it is not a personal vendetta to get the employee to resign.

2. If Sandile's employer's conduct has caused the working environment to become intolerable this could be constructive dismissal. The CCMA will test to see whether Sandile had options other than resigning (which he might have had, as he could have referred a grievance to the CCMA/Labour Court for a determination of racial discrimination).

3. This would not be constructive dismissal as Mandy's employer is entitled to search her bag if he suspects her of theft. Her working relationship was not rendered intolerable as a result.

4. This would be sexual harassment and the resignation would constitute a constructive dismissal.

6.9.2   Types of dismissals
(Learner's Manual p 599)

Once employees prove that their dismissal falls within one of the categories of automatically unfair dismissal in the Labour Relations Act, the onus immediately shifts to the employer to prove that it was fair. If the employer is unable to do this, then the dismissal will be regarded as unfair.

Problem 2: Were the dismissals automatically unfair? (Learner's Manual p 600)

AIM: The object of the exercise is to make learners aware that the categories of automatically unfair dismissals are given special protection by the Labour Relations Act (victimisation, discrimination, etc).

PROCEDURE	TIME	
1. Introduce exercise.	Introduce exercise:	5 min
2. Divide class into small groups.	Groups consider questions:	10 min
3. Each group to consider one question.	Report back:	25 min
4. Groups to consider questions.	General discussion:	5 min
5. Report back to class.	**TOTAL:**	**45 min**
6. General discussion.		

1. Mary is dismissed for reasons related to her pregnancy and her dismissal will be automatically unfair. As she missed only 20 days of work, which is within her sick leave entitlement, her dismissal cannot be justified on this basis.

2. Sipho is dismissed for leaving work without the permission of his employer and not for union membership. This will not be automatically unfair. It may be unfair if it is found that his misconduct was not sufficiently serious to justify dismissal.

3. It is acceptable to dismiss unlawfully striking workers. Only if lawfully striking workers were dismissed would it be an automatically unfair dismissal.

4. This is automatically unfair as Anand is dismissed for making a protected disclosure and exercising his rights in terms of an Act.

5. This is discrimination on the grounds of sexual orientation and is an automatically unfair dismissal.

6. While this would appear to be discrimination on the grounds of age, it is not unfair if Sarah has reached the normal or agreed retirement age. It would appear that 65 would be normal retirement age unless a later retirement age was agreed upon in her employment contract.

Problem 3: Were the dismissals substantively fair? *(Learner's Manual p 603)*

AIM: The object of this exercise is to enable learners to apply the test for assessing substantive fairness to practical examples. They need to understand that not every offence of misconduct will justify dismissal.

PROCEDURE	TIME	
1. Introduce exercise.	Introduce exercise:	5 min
2. Divide class into small groups.	Groups to consider questions:	10 min
3. Allocate one question to each group.	Report back:	15 min
4. Groups to consider questions.	General discussion:	5 min
5. Report back.	**TOTAL:**	**35 min**
6. General discussion.		

1. As Jim's misconduct (assault) is not at the workplace, it is not a disciplinary offence and he may not be fairly dismissed.
2. Some rules at a workplace are so important that an employee ought to know about them. Bheki should have known about this rule because it is very important. He cannot claim that the dismissal was unfair.
3. Zama is guilty of theft, which is a dismissible offence and very serious. However, the small value of the item stolen and her personal history (eg that she is the sole breadwinner and supports her husband and three children) should be considered in deciding whether the dismissal is fair.
4. Theft is very serious and a dismissible offence. Her long service record may be a mitigating factor, but if the relationship of trust between her and her employer is damaged, dismissal will be appropriate.
5. It is important that all employees are treated the same (consistently). As Doris already has a final written warning for lateness and she repeats the misconduct, the dismissal is appropriate.

Procedural requirements differ according to the size of the business. As long as the employee has a chance to have a say (called *audi alterem partem*), it is acceptable for smaller businesses to have much more informal disciplinary hearings.

Problem 4: Were the dismissals procedurally fair? *(Learner's Manual p 604)*

AIM: The object of this exercise is for learners to understand that the basic right to procedural fairness applies even if the employee is quite obviously guilty of the misconduct (eg caught red-handed).

<table>
<tr><td colspan="2">

PROCEDURE

1. Introduce exercise.
2. Divide class into small groups.
3. Allocate one question to each group.
4. Groups to consider questions.
5. Report back.
6. General discussion.

</td><td>

TIME

Introduce exercise:	5 min
Groups to consider questions:	10 min
Report back:	15 min
General discussion:	5 min
TOTAL:	**35 min**

</td></tr>
</table>

1. Even though there is clearly a good reason to dismiss Riaan, he is still entitled to a disciplinary hearing. He might have a good reason for being in possession of the company property and is entitled to be heard.

2. It is important that the presiding officer is independent and neutral. If he is the person who caught Mandla assaulting a co-worker this will not be the case.

3. Talia is entitled to be present at the disciplinary hearing. It cannot be held in her absence unless the employer makes a reasonable effort to contact her and is unable to.

4. Neil is entitled to be represented by a co-worker or a shop steward, but not his cousin.

5. Mary must be given a notice to attend a disciplinary hearing that specifies the offence with which she is being charged.

Problem 5: What is a suitable punishment?   *(Learner's Manual p 605)*

AIM: The object of this exercise is to enable learners to apply the concept of progressive and corrective discipline to the imposition of punishment.

<table>
<tr><td colspan="2">

PROCEDURE

1. Introduce exercise.
2. Divide class into small groups.
3. Allocate one question to each group.
4. Groups to consider questions.
5. Report back.
6. General discussion.

</td><td>

TIME

Introduce exercise:	5 min
Groups to consider questions:	10 min
Report back:	15 min
General discussion:	5 min
TOTAL:	**35 min**

</td></tr>
</table>

1. This is not so serious. A verbal or first written warning would be appropriate.

2. This is a serious offence. Dismissal or a final written warning is appropriate.

3. This is not serious – maybe just a verbal warning.

4. As this is a repeated offence it must be treated more seriously. Dismissal is appropriate.

5. This is not misconduct, so no punishment is appropriate.

6. This is insubordination and is a serious offence, but it would depend upon how rude the employee was. A final written warning or a suspension may be appropriate.

7. This might have been a mistake and not misconduct at all. The employee has had a clean track record for the last seven years and should be treated more leniently. A warning would be appropriate.

Problem 6: Some questions on dismissals for incapacity (Learner's Manual p 609)

AIM: The object of this exercise is to enable learners to understand that incapacity for poor work performance is very different from ill health or injury; therefore different considerations and procedures apply.

PROCEDURE	TIME	
1. Introduce exercise.	Introduce lesson:	5 min
2. Divide class into small groups.	Groups to consider questions:	10 min
3. Allocate one question to each group.	Report back:	20 min
4. Groups to consider questions.	General discussion:	5 min
5. Report back.	**TOTAL:**	**40 min**
6. General discussion.		

1. Misconduct is intentional wrongdoing and the employee should be disciplined for this. Incapacity is not due to fault but rather an inability by the employee to do the job, either as a result of ill health or poor work performance. Probation is a testing period to assess an employee's suitability for the job, without committing to employing the employee on a permanent basis. It also gives the employee an opportunity to prove himself or herself within the probationary period.

2. Employees have to be given a chance to improve their performance before being dismissed for incapacity. As Sue has only been employed for three weeks it is unlikely that this has happened. If the managing director is unhappy with her work he must call her to a meeting and tell her his concerns. He should ask her whether there are any problems, and whether she needs any training or assistance, and then give her a reasonable opportunity to improve her work. If she does not improve after this she can be dismissed for incapacity after a final hearing.

3. This is a work-related injury. The employer must take all reasonable steps to accommodate Jabu (eg by hiring a temporary replacement until he recovers). As this is a temporary injury and he will recover in six months, it is not unreasonable to expect the employer to make a temporary arrangement until his return. It would be very unfair to dismiss Jabu.

4. This is a permanent injury. The only question is whether the employer can adapt Mira's duties or find her a new job at the clothing factory. If this cannot be done she can be dismissed.

Problem 7: Testing the fairness of retrenchments (Learner's Manual p 611)

AIM: The object of this exercise is for learners to understand that as retrenchments are no-fault dismissals, extensive procedures exist to ensure that retrenchments are avoided wherever possible, and that the effects are alleviated.

PROCEDURE	TIME	
1. Introduce exercise.	Introduce exercise:	5 min
2. Divide class into small groups.	Brainstorming in groups:	10 min
3. Groups to brainstorm answers to questions.	Report back:	15 min
4. Report back.	General discussion:	5 min
5. General discussion.	**TOTAL:**	**35 min**

1. Learners in small groups should brainstorm these examples:
    (a) Economic reasons – downturn in economy, less of a demand for the product manufactured, etc.
    (b) Technological reasons – introduction of automation.
    (c) Structural reasons – restructuring departments to make them more efficient causing job losses, closing down branches of a company, etc.
2. Employers can try to cut down other expenses at the company. Examples could be: having no wage increases for a period of time; not allowing overtime; taking away a benefit (for example, no free parking); not replacing employees who resign; encouraging voluntary retrenchment (where older employees resign), etc.
3. LIFO (last in, first out – the employees that were hired last are fired first); skills (employees with particular skills can be retained); and productivity (if a proper productivity test is used, productive employees can be retained).

Problem 8: What is the reason for the dismissal?   *(Learner's Manual p 611)*

AIM: The object of this exercise is for learners to identify the different grounds for dismissal.

PROCEDURE	TIME	
1. Introduce exercise.	Introduce exercise:	5 min
2. Divide class into small groups.	Each group to consider two	
3. Each group to consider two questions.	questions:	10 min
4. Groups to consider questions.	Report back:	20 min
5. Report back.	General discussion:	5 min
6. General discussion.	**TOTAL:**	**40 min**

1. Incapacity for poor work performance.
2. Retrenchment.
3. This is either misconduct or incompatibility, which is a type of incapacity.
4. Automatically unfair dismissal as discrimination.
5. Alcoholism is an illness, so the answer would be incapacity due to ill health.
6. Retrenchment, but it seems that unfair selection criteria were used. It could however be argued that LIFO applies.
7. Automatically unfair dismissal.
8. Misconduct.
9. Automatically unfair dismissal.
10. Misconduct.

6.10 Resolving labour disputes

Outcomes

After completion of this section learners will be able to:

1. Explain how to resolve a labour dispute and the dispute resolution mechanism available to unfairly dismissed employees.

Assessment criteria

1. An explanation is given about the CCMA and its functions.

2. Methods of dispute resolution such as mediation, conciliation and arbitration are explained.

3. A negotiation and mediation exercise is undertaken.

6.10.4 Arbitration
(Learner's Manual p 615)

Problem 1: Negotiation and mediation exercise
(Learner's Manual p 615)

PROCEDURE		TIME	
1. Introduce exercise.		Introduce exercise:	5 min
2. Divide learners into pairs.		Divide class into pairs:	5 min
3. Learners individually read scenarios.		Allocate roles:	5 min
4. Learners negotiate in pairs.		Conduct negotiations:	15 min
5. Report back.		Report back:	10 min
6. Mediators assist pairs to negotiate.		Conduct mediation:	15 min
7. Report back.		Report back:	10 min
8. General discussion.		**TOTAL:**	**65 min**

1. Negotiation exercise

Learners should be divided into pairs. It is often more interesting to get the pairs to be of mixed genders.

Learner must read the scenario (on their own) and rank the five people from least favourite (1) to most favourite (5), without showing their rankings to anyone else.

Once this is done, each pair must try to negotiate a compromised ranking. They can use any tactics they wish – they can use powerful and forceful arguments to try to convince the other party; they can try and trade positions on certain rankings; they can call the other parties' bluff and not disclose their positions; they can refuse to budge from their position. After approximately 15 minutes try to establish whether there are still pairs who cannot reach a compromise.

2. Mediation exercise

A third learner should then be appointed as a mediator to try and help the learners to reach a compromise. The mediator must help the parties either together or by discussing it separately with each side. The mediator is not allowed to force an agreement on the parties but must just try to help them negotiate. The mediator can try and trade off positions so that there is give and take from both sides. The mediator should be given about 15 minutes to intervene.

After this is complete the educator should have a feedback session with the class to discuss their experiences, finding out what were the most successful negotiation tactics used. Remind learners that while this exercise is fun, in the workplace it deals with much more serious issues, and the parties are much more emotionally involved. In the workplace if an issue is not resolved it could lead to a strike, which is very serious.

6.11 Remedies for unfair dismissals

Outcomes

After completion of this section learners will be able to:

1.   Explain the remedies that are available to unfairly dismissed employees.

Assessment criteria

1.   The remedies that are appropriate for unfairly dismissed employees are discussed.
2.   A set of facts is examined and a decision is made on the appropriate remedies for dismissal.

6.11.1 Appropriate remedies

(Learner's Manual p 616)

Problem 1: What remedy is suitable?

(Learner's Manual p 616)

AIM: The object of this exercise is to make learners understand that reinstatement, although a primary remedy (first choice), is not always the most appropriate remedy.

PROCEDURE	TIME	
1. Introduce exercise.	Introduce exercise:	5 min
2. Divide class into small groups.	Groups to consider questions:	10 min
3. Allocate one question to each group.	Report back:	20 min
4. Groups to consider questions.	General discussion:	5 min
5. Report back.	**TOTAL:**	**40 min**
6. General discussion.		

1.   This will be substantively fair, but procedurally unfair, as Jason was not given any form of disciplinary hearing. He will not be entitled to reinstatement but only compensation.
2.   He will not want reinstatement as he has found a new job. Compensation will be appropriate.
3.   If the relationship between the employer and Pretty has not broken down reinstatement will be appropriate.
4.   Reinstatement will be appropriate.

Further reading

6.1 Employment and applying for a job

Code of Good Practice on Key Aspects of HIV/AIDS, Item 7.1.5

Constitution of the Republic of South Africa Act, 1996, section 9

Employment Equity Act 55 of 1998, sections 6 and 7

6.2 Contracts of employment

Du Toit D et al *Labour Relations Law* 3 ed (2000)

Grogan J *Dismissal* (2010)

Grogan J *Workplace Law* 7 ed (2003)

Van Niekerk A, Christianson MA, McGregor M, Smit N & Van Eck BPS *Law@work* (2008)

Code of Good Practice: Who is an employee?

Labour Relations Act 66 of 1995, section 213

Labour Relations Amendment Act 42 of 2002, section 200A

Denel (Pty) Ltd v Gerber (2005) 26 *ILJ* 1256 (LAC); [2005] 9 BLLR 849 (LAC)

SA Broadcasting Corporation v McKenzie (1999) 20 *ILJ* 585 (LAC)

6.3 Labour laws and social benefits

Basic Conditions of Employment Act 75 of 1997, sections 9, 16, 18, 20, 21, 22, 23, 25, 26, 27, 32, 33, 34, 35 and 42

Compensation for Occupational Injuries and Diseases Act 130 of 1993, section 47 and Schedule 4

Occupational Health and Safety Act 85 of 1993, section 8

Skills Development Act 97 of 1998

6.4 Collective bargaining and trade unions

Cohen T, Rycroft AJ & Whitcher B *Trade Unions and the Law in South Africa* (2009)

Du Toit D et al *Labour Relations Law* 3 ed (2000)

Grogan J *Collective Labour Law* (2010)

Grogan J *Dismissal* (2010)

Van Niekerk A, Christianson MA, McGregor M, Smit N & Van Eck BPS *Law@work* (2008)

Labour Relations Act 66 of 1995, sections 4, 5, 6, 21, 23, 64(2), 64(3), 65, 66, 68, 71, 75, 95–106 and 213

NUM v East Rand Gold & Uranium Co Ltd 1992 (1) SA 700 (A); 1991 *ILJ* 1221 (A)

East Rand Gold & Uranium Co Ltd v National Union of Mineworkers (1989) 10 *ILJ* 683 (LAC)

SACTWU v Sheraton Textiles (1997) 18 *ILJ* 1412 (CCMA); (1997) 5 BLLR 662 (CCMA)

SACTWU v Marley Flooring (SA) (Pty) Ltd t/a Marley Flooring (Mobeni) (2000) 21 *ILJ* 425 (CCMA)

Gobile v BP Southern Africa (Pty) Ltd & others (1999) 20 *ILJ* 2027 (LAC)

Picardi Hotels Ltd v FGWU & others (1999) 20 *ILJ* 1915 (LC); [1999] 6 BLLR 601 (LC)

FAWU & others v Rainbow Chicken Farms (2000) 21 *ILJ* 615 (LC); [2000] 1 BLLR 70 (LC)

Ceramic Industries Ltd t/a Betta Sanitary Ware v National Construction Building & Allied Workers Union (2) (1997) 18 *ILJ* 671 (LAC)

Public Servants Association of South Africa v Minister of Justice and Constitutional Development & others [2001] 11 BLLR 1250 (LC)

Tiger Wheels Babelegi (Pty) Ltd t/a TSW International v National Union of Metalworkers of SA & others (1999) 20 *ILJ* 677 (LC)

SACWU & others v Afrox Ltd (1999) 20 *ILJ* 1718 (LAC); [1999] 10 BLLR 1005 (LAC)

Modise & others v Steve's Spar Blackheath 2001 (2) SA 406 (LAC); (2000) 21 *ILJ* 519 (LAC); [2000] 5 BLLR 496 (LAC)

Mzeku & others v Volkswagen SA (Pty) Ltd & others 2001 (4) SA 1009 (LAC); (2001) 22 *ILJ* 1575 (LAC); [2001] 8 BLLR 857 (LAC)

6.6 Privacy at work and protected disclosures

Constitution of South Africa, 1996, section 14

Protected Disclosures Act 26 of 2000

6.7 Employment equity

Dupper O, Garbers C, Landman A, Christianson M & Basson A *Essential Employment Discrimination Law* (2004)

Grogan J *Dismissal, Discrimination and Unfair Labour Practices* (2005)

Van Niekerk A, Christianson MA, McGregor M, Smit N & Van Eck BPS *Law@work* (2008)

Constitution of the Republic of South Africa Act, 1996, section 9

Employment Equity Act 55 of 1998, sections 6(1), 6(2), 13 and 15

Association of Professional Teachers & another v Minister of Education & others (1995) 16 *ILJ* 1048 (IC)

Swart v Mr Video (Pty) Ltd (1998) 19 *ILJ* 1315 (CCMA)

Leonard Dingler Employee Representative Council & others v Leonard Dingler (Pty) Ltd & others (1998) 19 *ILJ* 285 (LC)

Louw v Golden Arrow Bus Services (Pty) Ltd 2001 (1) SA 218 (LC); (2000) 21 *ILJ* 188 (LC)

Louw v Golden Arrow Bus Services (Pty) Ltd (2001) 22 *ILJ* 2628 (LAC)

Stojce v UKZN & another (2006) 27 *ILJ* 2696 (LC); 2007 (3) BLLR 246 (LC)

6.8 Unfair labour practices and sexual harassment

6.8.1 Unfair labour practices

Du Toit D et al *Labour Relations Law* 3 ed (2000)

Grogan J *Dismissal* (2010)

Grogan J *Workplace Law* 7 ed (2003)

Van Niekerk A, Christianson MA, McGregor M, Smit N & Van Eck BPS *Law@work* (2008)

Labour Relations Act 66 of 1995, section 186(2)

Department of Justice v CCMA & others (2004) 25 *ILJ* 248 (LAC); [2004] 4 BLLR 297 (LAC)

Dlamini v Toyota SA Manufacturing [2004] 25 *ILJ* 1513 (CCMA)

6.8.2 Sexual harassment

Dupper O, Garbers C, Landman A, Christianson M & Basson A *Essential Employment Discrimination Law* (2004)

Grogan J *Dismissal* (2010)

Code of Good Practice on the Handling of Sexual Harassment Cases in the Workplace Employment Equity Act 55 of 1998, section 6(1) and 6(3)

Grobler v Naspers Bpk & 'n ander 2004 (4) SA 220 (C); (2004) 25 *ILJ* 439 (C)

Ntsabo v Real Security CC (2003) 24 *ILJ* 2341 (LC)

6.9 Termination of employment through dismissal
6.9.1 The meaning of dismissal

Du Toit D et al *Labour Relations Law* 3 ed (2000)

Grogan J *Dismissal* (2010)

Grogan J *Dismissal, Discrimination and Unfair Labour Practices* (2005)

Grogan J *Workplace Law* 7 ed (2003)

Van Niekerk A, Christianson MA, McGregor M, Smit N & Van Eck BPS *Law@work* (2008)

Labour Relations Act 66 of 1995, section 186(1)

National Automobile and Allied Workers Union v Borg Warner SA (Pty) Ltd 1994 (3) SA 15 (A); (1994) 15 *ILJ* 509 (A)

Pretoria Society for the Care of the Retarded v Loots (1997) 18 *ILJ* 981 (LAC)

Ouwehand v Hout Bay Fishing Industries (2004) 25 *ILJ* 731 (LC)

Owen & others v Department of Health, KwaZulu-Natal (2009) 30 *ILJ* 2461 (LC)

Solid Doors (Pty) Ltd v Commission Theron & others (2004) 25 *ILJ* 2337 (LAC)

6.9.2 Types of dismissals
6.9.2.1 Automatically unfair dismissals

Du Toit D et al *Labour Relations Law* 3 ed (2000)

Grogan J *Dismissal* (2010)

Grogan J *Dismissal, Discrimination and Unfair Labour Practices* (2005)

Grogan J *Workplace Law* 7 ed (2003)

Van Niekerk A, Christianson MA, McGregor M, Smit N & Van Eck BPS *Law@work* (2008)

Labour Relations Act 66 of 1995, sections 185 and 187

Protected Disclosures Act 26 of 2000

Adcock Ingram Critical Care v CCMA & others (2001) 22 *ILJ* 1799 (LAC)

CWIU v Algorax (Pty) Ltd (2003) 24 *ILJ* 1917 (LAC)

Fry's Metals (Pty) Ltd v NUMSA (2003) 24 *ILJ* 133 (LAC)

Mashava v Cuzen & Woods Attorneys (2000) 21 *ILJ* 402 (LC)

SA Rugby (Pty) Ltd v CCMA & others (2006) 27 *ILJ* 1041 (LC); [2006] 1 BLLR 27 (LC) 30

6.9.2.2 Dismissal for misconduct

Cohen T, Rycroft AJ & Whitcher B *Trade Unions and the Law in South Africa* (2009)

Du Toit D et al *Labour Relations Law* 3 ed (2000)

Grogan J *Collective Labour Law* (2010)

Grogan J *Dismissal* (2010)

Grogan J *Dismissal, Discrimination and Unfair Labour Practices* (2005)

Grogan J *Workplace Law* 7 ed (2003)

Van Niekerk A, Christianson MA, McGregor M, Smit N & Van Eck BPS *Law@work* (2008)

Labour Relations Act 66 of 1995, section 188

Code of Good Practice: Dismissal, items 3, 4 and 7

Engen Petroleum Ltd v Commission for Conciliation, Mediation & Arbitration (2007) 28 *ILJ* 1507 (LAC); (2007) 8 BLLR 707 (LAC)

Sidumo & another v Rustenburg Platinum Mines Ltd & others 2008 (2) SA 24 (CC); (2007) 28 *ILJ* 2405 (CC)

Toyota SA Motors (Pty) Ltd v Radebe & others (2000) 21 *ILJ* 340 (LAC); [2000] 3 BLLR 243 (LAC)

6.9.2.2.5 Types of misconduct

Grogan J *Dismissal* (2010)

Van Niekerk A, Christianson MA, McGregor M, Smit N & Van Eck BPS *Law@work* (2008)

Adcock Ingram Critical Care v CCMA & others [2001] 22 *ILJ* 1799 (LAC)

Anglo American Farms t/a Boschendal Restaurant v Komjwayo (1992) 13 *ILJ* 573 (LAC)

Dauth and Brown & Weir's Cash & Carry (2002) 23 *ILJ* 1472 (CCMA)

Hoch v Mustek Electronics (Pty) Ltd [2000] 21 *ILJ* 365 (LC)

Lebowa Platinum Mines Ltd v CCMA [2002] 5 BLLR 429 (LC)

6.9.2.3 Dismissal for incapacity

Du Toit D et al *Labour Relations Law* 3 ed (2000)

Grogan J *Dismissal* (2010)

Grogan J *Workplace Law* 7 ed (2003)

Van Niekerk A, Christianson MA, McGregor M, Smit N & Van Eck BPS *Law@work* (2008)

Labour Relations Act 66 of 1995, section 188

Lebowa Platinum Mines Ltd v CCMA [2002] 5 BLLR 429 (LC)

6.9.2.4 Dismissal for operational requirements

Cohen T, Rycroft AJ & Whitcher B *Trade Unions and the Law in South Africa* (2009)

Du Toit D et al *Labour Relations Law* 3 ed (2000)

Grogan J *Collective Labour Law* (2010)

Grogan J *Dismissal* (2010)

Grogan J *Dismissal, Discrimination and Unfair Labour Practices* (2005)

Grogan J *Labour Litigation and Dispute Resolution* (2010)

Grogan J *Workplace Law* 7 ed (2003)

Van Niekerk A, Christianson MA, McGregor M, Smit N & Van Eck BPS *Law@work* (2008)

Labour Relations Act 66 of 1995, sections 189 and 189A

BMD Knitting Mills (Pty) Ltd v SACTWU (2001) 22 *ILJ* 2264 (LAC); [2001] 7 BLLR 705 (LAC)

CWIU v Algorax (Pty) Ltd [2003] 24 *ILJ* 1917 (LAC)

Decision Surveys International (Pty) Ltd v Dlamini [1999] 5 BLLR 413 (LAC)

Fry's Metals (Pty) Ltd v NUMSA (2003) 24 *ILJ* 133 (LAC)

Mazista Tiles (Pty) Ltd v NUM & others (2004) 25 *ILJ* 2156 (LAC); [2005] 3 BLLR 219 (LAC)

National Union of Metalworkers of SA v Atlantis Diesel Engines (Pty) Ltd (1993) 14 *ILJ* 642 (LAC)

Rustenburg Platinum Mines Ltd (Rustenburg Section) v Commission for Conciliation, Mediation & Arbitration & others 2007 (1) SA 576 (SCA); (2006) 27 *ILJ* 2076 (SCA)

SATAWU v Old Mutual Life Assurance Company South Africa Ltd (2005) 26 *ILJ* 293 (LC); [2005] 4 BLLR 378 (LC)

SACCAWU & others v Gallo Africa (2005) 26 *ILJ* 2397 (LC)

SACTWU & others v Discreto (A Division of Trump & Springbok Holdings) (1998) 19 *ILJ* 1451 (LAC); [1998] 12 BLLR 1228 (LAC)

SACWU & others v Afrox Ltd (1999) 20 *ILJ* 1718 (LAC); [1999] 10 BLLR 1005 (LAC)

6.11 Remedies for unfair dismissals

Grogan J *Labour Litigation and Dispute Resolution* (2010)

Van Niekerk A, Christianson MA, McGregor M, Smit N & Van Eck BPS *Law@work* (2008)

Labour Relations Act 66 of 1995

CWIU & others v Latex Surgical Products (Pty) Ltd (2006) 27 *ILJ* 292 (LAC); [2006] 2 BLLR 142 (LAC)

www.ingramcontent.com/pod-product-compliance
Lightning Source LLC
Chambersburg PA
CBHW072059220326
41599CB00030BA/5753